5/18/81

FOR <u>ALL</u> MY CUZ'S.

Edgar Gordon, my
Tried to win birds w
But one Bronka Lewin
Knew what was doing,
So now they're both cuzzens o'mine.

My next cuz was young Michael Dick
Whose shtick was to stick with his prick
His cute sister Paula
May have let someone maul 'er
But none of us know 'bout that trick.

Pete

THE NEW LIMERICK

THE NEW LIMERICK

2750 UNPUBLISHED EXAMPLES
AMERICAN AND BRITISH

EDITED BY

G. LEGMAN

Ferndale Editions
London

This edition published 1980 by Ferndale Editions,
London, under licence from the proprietor.
ISBN: 0-905746-22-8

CONTENTS

AN . EVER . WRITER .
TO . A . NEVER . READER .
NEWS .

UNGENTLE Reader (for I know you well), you have here a new Book, never staled with the plaudits of the press, never clapper-clawed with the palms of the vulgar ; not sullied with the smoky breath of the multitude. These two thousand seven hundred new Limericks, now first published here, have — three quarters of them or more — never before been printed anywhere or at all. As for the rest, a few hundred poor foundlings have indeed come furtively to light in private issues, murky mimeographed or hektographed editions of some dozen run-off sheets, unreadable in smeary purple ink. Wherein Readers have been abused with divers stolen and surreptitious copies, maimed and deformed by the frauds and stealths of injurious impostors that exposed them. Even these are offered now to your view, cured and perfect of their limbs, and all the rest absolute in their numbers as the Unknown Poets conceived them. And believe me this, that when they are gone, and this book out of sale one day, you will scramble for it, and set up a new Inquisition to find you out copies. Take this for a warning, and at the peril of your pleasure's loss ; but thank fortune for the scrape it has made to be now amongst you.

Nor is it to be thought that this has been the work of a single hand ; of a single month or year. Decades have been spent — two decades and a half — tracking the unknown and often over-modest limerick Poets and collectors to their study chambers, and the brewhouses that seem somehow best to excite their ticklish Muse. Libations have been poured out lavishly there, paid for (you may be sure) from the compiler's slender pocketbook over the silent years. To garner here a new sheaf, there a new sequence, sometimes just one new but exhilarating gem. Here indeed are many gems of Anglo-American bawdy wit, but you will have to dig for them, as I did, to turn up those that just suit the special peculiarities of your humour.

Meanwhile, in America and elsewhere, pawky pirates rushed to bring out their shabby selections of the original work: hopeless imitations, and plain, piratical thefts. Until, at last, proper printings could be legally undertaken of *The Limerick* under the New Freedom in London and New York since 1970. A sad story, and long, of which the cold details — minus a few that the moment has not yet come to tell — are there to be read by those who can decipher them, in the annotated Bibliography at the end of this volume. Along with full details of every printed work or other placed under debt here, and certain published collections of similar materials which have been used only comparatively or not at all. A *chronological list* of the sources and collections actually drawn from will be found following this Foreword, and each & every limerick in the text is thus identified to its original source by the *date* following it. And occasionally too by an added initial, for example *A,* representing special limerick poets or collectors — in this case myself — whose originals or collections have spread over many years or decades. To accentuate the folklore element in these limericks, now newly published, many of which are still at the stage of recent personal poetry, folk-transmitted versions have in all cases been preferred to versions already in print or supplied by their authors, and oral variants have thus been incorporated in numerous limericks throughout. The date serves in these cases to indicate the original source.

Where two dates follow any limerick, the second is the actual source of the text: the first date is that of the earliest known variant printing or collecting. The letters *ff.* before or after a date indicate the rare limericks known to have been composed by women. Others should perhaps also be so marked, but the information is lacking. Women do not often like bawdy limericks, in which they generally figure as both villain and victim. A few disorganized females have been found in recent years, however, willing to match the standard cruel and castratory anti-woman limericks with equally cruel and castratory anti-man limericks of their own concocting.

One further depressing note. Despite the presumed New Freedom since the late 1960's, at least as to sex (the hatches are down tight on political freedom these years, which *may be* why they are easing up a little on the sex?) almost all the collectors and all but three of the original limerick poets have urgently insisted that their true names not be published. Sometimes with a panicky insistence that rather surprises one in this "postlapsarian world (as Dr. Rayna Green has called it) deluged with X-rated films, bottomless bars, and leather shops." Meanwhile, perfectly lunatic fantasy sadism is shamelessly unleashed on an international scale in all the "media arts," as mass brainwashing for the genocides to come — when the food runs short.

One wonders sometimes why certain limerick fanciers so enthusiastically write, recite, and circulate the rhymes of which, in the end, they are so ashamed. One part of the explanation is doubtless the fact that a surprisingly large percentage of limerick specialists — at least those I have met or heard of — are of the homosexual persuasion. Norman Douglas, for one, the Grand (Dirty) Old Man of the limerick art, expressed neither shame nor shyness about his psychosexual peculiarity, as his courageously signed volume *Some Limericks* (1928) tranquilly displays on many a page. Not every limerick poet, even today, dares to parade such studied forthrightness. Yet one of the problems of editing the present volume has been keeping the new "Gay Liberation" limericks of the 1960's and since down to a reasonable proportion of the text, while diminishing somewhat the gossipy bitchiness to which they are prone, especially the Oedipal tendency to fantasy humorously about the sexual lives and presumed perversions of notables of the moment.

This is much in the line of the obscene and insulting "apotropaic" or evil-averting songs made against victorious generals by their own soldiers and people, in both ancient and modern times, to give vent to and thus drive off the "evil spirits" of hatred and jealousy in the vanquished — and in their own lowly troops and civilians. For example, at the return of the victorious hero David from the slaughter of Goliath and the Philistines (in *1 Samuel,* xviii. 6–8), a usage I have discussed much further in *The Horn Book,* pages 387–90. This tradition was nobly carried on, at the Renaissance and since, by the Goliard poets at the Feast of Fools, and in the Italian and later the French and British burlesque "academies" and drinking-clubs.

It is still very much alive, as can be seen in the transactions of the "Chestnut Club" (probably really the Papyrus Club of Boston) presented in the very rare miscellany volume, *The Stag Party* (1888), starring the bawdy poems written for and read before the club by Eugene Field. Also and especially in Mark Twain's "Some Remarks on the Science of Onanism," an address to the Stomach Club of Paris in 1879, and his later similar stag-address and poem, *The Mammoth Cod,* which was delivered before a convivial Boston club of that name at the sailing-party for a cruise by the whole club on a millionaire member's yacht in 1902, as I have attempted to show in the long-posthumous first edition of this bagatelle of Twain's (Milwaukee : Maledicta Press, 1976).

With the exception of the Minutes and Proceedings of the Society of the Fifth Line, in Chicago, specifically devoted to the limerick, most of the printed materials emanating from American private clubs of this type in the present century, such as the Dutch Treat Club, the Philadelphia Sketch Club, and various other commercial artists', journalists', and businessmen's clubs are pitifully expurgated, though privately printed and all that. (See further, my *No Laughing Matter,* pages 749–58, under "Mocking Authority-Figures.") The gossip columnist Earl Wilson's extraordinary conspectus, *Show Business Laid Bare* (New York, 1974), pages 22–25, gives for the first time publicly a few samples of this type of aggressive banter, as delivered at luncheons given by the Friars Club in New York for various theatre celebrities.

The "roastmaster" may announce, for example, in crude terms paraphrased by Wilson, that the guest of honor "of course has had and still may have gonorrhea, and once gave his little sister that disease. He is no stranger to syphilis, and in a pinch he will do it to a nanny goat." This is precisely in the style of Twain's *Mammoth Cod* address, though much cruder ; nor does it forget the age-old sideswipes at the food served : "The chicken tasted like it was fucked to death." To avoid libelling anyone but myself, I will observe only that I have received my share of similarly unflattering limerick tributes over the years, all cheerfully accusing me of perversions Krafft-Ebing seldom heard of, while struggling doughtily with my unrhymable names (both). See the Index here, plus the further *gentillesses* of Limericks 2:2129 and 2340, by two different friends aching with jealousy of my purported perversions, who rhyme on "France" rather than mentioning me by name, but get there just the same.

Since the publication of *The Limerick : First Series* now a quarter of a century ago, there has been a good deal of junk activity in connection with the publishing of bawdy limericks in both America and England. With the exception of the new science-fiction limericks, and the outstanding originals by the late John Coulthard and the equally witty and productive Albin Chaplin more recently, along with the Transactions of the Society of the Fifth Line in Chicago — see the Bibliography — almost all the newly printed collections, both American and British, and whether published as books or as random pages in "men's" magazines and other gynecological gazettes, have been slavishly taken at first or second hand (and generally pusillanimously expurgated) from *The Limerick*. Plus, of course, some small additions of Weak Sisters and topical items of the compilers' own brew, in particular against Women's Liberation ; though simultaneously the liberation of Blacks, Yellows, Reds, and other unfashionable colors still seems highly desirable — as long as they are not women.

Though listed in the Bibliography, most of these recent printed collections have scrupulously *not* been made use of here, except for purposes of comparative annotation, which has in any case been held to a strict minimum. I feel I have thus done my research duty, and have left a trail ; and I leave all this dreary printed matter to whoever has the courage and the patience to wade through it. There is already quite an enormous collection of the even drearier "clean" limericks (the Hall Collection) filed on index cards in the Indiana University Folklore Archive, though it is questionable whether most of these are really authentically transmitted folklore in any sense.

In fact, so much weak, would-be sexual material, and so many obvious cleanups of authentically circulating erotic limericks have appeared since the 1950's, especially in the "men's magazine" industry and in purportedly naughty gifte bookes — a tiresome brew — that the former chapter division, "Weak Sisters," used in *The Limerick,* has had to be dropped here for lack of space to print them all. I trust that the replacement by an entirely new chapter, on the one really new theme in modern limericks, "Science Fiction," will be welcome instead. To which have been added the newly-discovered "Martian Chronicles," with translations from the Flemish.

An excellent insight into the manner of operation of the expurgatory compilers above-noted is artlessly offered in a letter I received, dated December 1st, 1969, from one of them, the late John A. Yates, anonymous compiler of *Rugby Jokes* and *Son of Rugby Jokes, &c.* (London : Sphere Books, 1968–70), who hacked together the latter volumelets by writing up in the British dialect a number of jokes also to be found in my large volume, *Rationale of the Dirty Joke : First Series* (1968), jokes seldom or never otherwise found in England.

As the publisher also wanted some pages of limericks, to ventilate the text as it were, Mr. Yates cannily invested 25 shillings in a copy of Norman Douglas's classic collection, *Some Limericks,* which had just been published openly for the first time in England, but found it "all mucky, with long comments," and therefore not much use for his purpose. Far more valuable to him was a current 5-shilling pocket item, *There Was A Young Lady,* signed 'Hugh De Witt,' again largely duplicating unexpurgated materials in *The Limerick.* Here is how Mr. Yates then describes himself as going to work :

> I need upwards of 60 fresh limericks for the book, and this I have been getting down to, with more success than I would have dared to hope. (*a*) I found I had a knack for writing them, and improve with practice ; this has given me about 30. (*b*) I got another 30 from de Witt, by altering, improving, and in some cases entirely re-writing out of recognition almost, some from there. Often only the theme is left.

Shakespeare couldn't have said it better.

II

MEANWHILE, valuable and authentic collections of folk originals have been preserved in private mimeographica, mostly stemming from college fraternities and drinking clubs, and in the unofficial and sometimes secret publications of favorite bawdy songs by officers in the armed services — especially the Air Force — among whom limericks are often *sung,* with a chorus : in Britain "Sing Us Another One, Do," and in America "Waltz Me Around Again, Willie" (In China They Never Eat Chili). As noted, there has also been a particularly significant flowering of science-fiction satires in limerick form, the only new theme in over a century. These were first seen in a mimeographed pamphlet *Salacious Science Limericks,* issued privately for science-fiction fans in 1952, but the historian should observe in the First Series here the earlier science-fiction limericks 1:358–59 and 1:1204 (on the Lorentz contraction), all three attributed to the murder-mystery writer, the late Anthony Boucher, and dated about 1945. The new science-fiction limericks have been made the subject of a special chapter here.

To avoid misunderstanding I would add that all further limericks collected by myself, "in the field" or by correspondence with poets and collectors over the years, are given immodestly with the initial *A* (for Addenda) following their dates. But — and I consider this important to insist upon — *I am in general not their author.* Certainly I have written a few limericks myself: mostly topical and anti-literary pieces, such as Limerick 2:2502, "Recipe for a Bestseller." These will not be difficult to identify. But the limerick has always been an anonymous art-form, and out of respect for this tradition no real attempt has been made, as one compiler remarked many years ago, "pitilessly to track down the authors of all this dirty doggerel." In point of fact, the *A*-initialled limericks include originals by over twenty different poets that I know of. I do not wish to be credited with their work.

The caption-titles ornamenting certain limericks and the limerick-sequences (see the list of these, page 560) are in many cases as supplied by their authors or derived from their letters of transmission. Not terribly witty, I admit, these are intended simply to aerate the otherwise unrelenting typography of the text. Special sources are indicated by dates starred with an asterisk (*) and are elucidated in the rather circumspect Notes at the end of the volume. Here brief necessary explanations, over a hundred further variants, and a few folklore parallels are given; but humorous and didactic excursi on the style of Norman Douglas's

Some Limericks have not been attempted. The Minutes and Proceedings of the society of the Fifth Line continue to keep this ancient tradition alive.

A technical point. Though I have said almost all I care to say on the subject of the limerick, its history and art, in the long Introduction added to *The Limerick : First Series* (1970), there are two mysterious matters on which something more might usefully be added here. First : *Why are limericks written, and why are they so popular among English-speaking people?* (We will come back to this question below.) And second : *How are limericks written?* Often in company, and with plenty of alcohol and exhibitionism loosening up one's repressions — that is understood. But beyond that, what is the actual technique?

Dr. Clifford Crist, himself one of the great limerick collectors in American universities during the 1930's and '40's, has insisted at some length in his *Playboy's Book of Limericks* (Chicago, 1972) pages xvii and following, that the composition of a limerick does or should proceed crabwise, from bottom to top, beginning "with the Fifth Line." He accordingly dedicates his book to the Society of that name, adding : "This line is the crux of the good limerick." That has not altogether been my experience.

As opposed to Dr. Crist's theory that limericks are or should be based on *a good last line,* created first (as a known example see Limerick 2:90, "A Real Lover"), I believe that most limerick poets consciously begin with some personal or place name or topical theme, on which they see an obvious sexual rhyme *or which they wish to celebrate or satirize,* or of which the exoticism strikes them as a challenge to find any rhyme at all. Consider for example the classic, usually attributed to Swinburne, on Aberystwyth (Limerick 1:1), and the wholly improbable example (2:1266) on Kzyltu in Kazakhstan! Another common beginning is with the two-stress anapestic couplet, forming the third and fourth lines as limericks are usually printed. This is essentially where most of the *action* of any limerick resides, though a good fifth-line resolution-of-the-action is obviously important too. In fact, almost any bouncey couplet, such as :

> In the midst of a feel
> She emitted a squeal . . .

or :

> Whilst he was discursin'
> He was feeling her person . . .

can be developed into a limerick, with the choice of the rhyming name in the first line then being made on the basis of the fifth-line "snapper" or punchline decided upon. Or the reverse! Technically, the most important line in a limerick is often the stalwart and inobtrusive second (usually beginning with "Who . . . ") which is responsible for setting the scene in spare and economical detail. The hardest line is admittedly the fifth and last, where most unsuccessful limericks limp tritely to an inconclusive halt, or fall totally flat in unintended bathos.

Another peculiarity, fortunately uncommon, is that of limerick poets who become enamored of a given set of silly rhymes such as *tits/fits,* or *niece/piece,* or *whore/more* (all authentic examples), and then proceed compulsively to construct half a dozen or a score of bad limericks all on the subject and rhymes, hopelessly ringing all possible changes in the hope of stumbling on one good limerick at last. To my knowledge, they never succeed. That is not the way to write limericks, or any other kind of poetry. Some limerick poets also dutifully produce both bawdy and polite versions of the same limericks for different audiences. I have often received such matched sets, composed of the real limericks *and* their polite fake-ups, sometimes helpfully distinguished as "Mixed Company" versus "Stag," or similar. As one astonishing example in many ways, see the anti-patriotic Limerick 2:1311 and its Note. In the line of simple limerick plagiarism, which by the way is exceedingly common, there are probably just as many "dirty-ups" of clean originals, as there are "clean-ups" of dirty ones.

Now as to the harder question : *Why are limericks written at all, and in such large numbers, and why are they so popular,* especially among the more-or-less educated classes in the English-speaking world? Obviously, limericks are a form of erotic folklore and folk-poetry, and as such they are proliferated and exchanged specifically for their bawdry, on a shock basis. The educated class that so loves limericks is much less given to any other form of erotic folklore except jokes (and graffiti, privately), and a rather small repertory of the bawdy songs and ballads left over from college or army days, which are mostly the prerogative of the "uneducated" classes that ignore limericks.

But the wit and even the bawdry of limericks are really only the sauce or spice, like the concentration on the *youth* of the protagonists in nearly half of all limericks : "There was a young man of, *&c.*" There are even a few aberrant souls — not many — who actually enjoy clean limericks nearly as much as bawdy ones, or so they say. At bottom, I believe it is the limerick form itself which carries the secret of its enormous popularity, now for nearly two centuries. Not the rhythm and not the rhyme, clever and unexpected as these may be ; but simply the formal insistence upon a personal or geographical NAME featured in the opening line, and then rhymed as amusingly or outrageously as possible, and never used again.

After many decades of openly collecting bawdy limericks, and of covertly studying limerick poets and reciters, I have come to the unshakable conviction that the bawdy subject-matter and violently aggressive content of limericks would not be acceptable to either the limerick poets or to their cultivated audiences without *the screen-concentration on the personal or geographical name ending the first line of the limerick,* and of course the rhymes developing from this. Perhaps this also explains why limericks can often allow themselves to be so much more gruellingly detailed about their obscenity than any other form of erotic folklore, humor, or balladry. A masochistic friend of mine was the author of Limerick 1:1136, of the horrible-castration variety, and ending "The size of my phallus, Was just right for Alice, Till the night that she bit off the knob!" When I asked him why he wrote it, he said : "For the *rhyme.*" The most total statement of castration by a woman is Limerick 1:1371, on the Queen of Baroda, a tremendous favorite among limerick fanciers, and endlessly collected, ending : "The walls of her halls, Were festooned with the balls, And the tools of the fools that bestrode her." Though I do not know who wrote that limerick, I am sure that if I met him and asked him why, he too would tell me : "For the *rhyme,*" of which, obviously, a great deal is being made. But that cannot be the psychological truth, which is really that under the mask of humor (and rhyme), anything goes — *Jokers wild!*

As to the concentration on names, and its ego-assuaging vindication of private personal worth and position (even if only for having the longest cock in the county), suffice it to say here that limericks bravely avoiding any personal or geographical names in their opening line may occasionally achieve a certain popularity for their wit : for example Limerick 1:1269, on the "cinematic emporium." But they are crushingly in the minority by comparison with the mass of favorite limericks concentrating maniacally on names — *names!* — *NAMES!!* — your name and mine — and the names of the towns we hail from, and are glad we left. *A masque of names,* in which we blurt out our deepest-hidden secrets and unveil our most private fears, fancies, and imagined deficiencies in doggerel rhyme, under the satirical mask of each other's names. *You write one about me, and I'll write one about you!*

The darkest secret of the bawdy limerick will therefore be found only in another simple question, which is never asked at all : *Who are limericks about?* Who, really, are the impossible idiots and unavowable perverts whose anatomical anomalies and erotic peculiarities are the inexhaustible subject of all this doggerel humor? What are their real names, and the names of the real towns in which they live, which are surely not — or not only — Aberystwyth, Wales, and Intercourse, Pa.?

The question obviously answers itself. Limericks are the tragi-comic autobiographies of the Pagliacci's who write and recite them. They are the erotic fantasies and the lightly glozed sexual secrets of their authors and of those who enjoy reading or hearing them : the college professors, lawyers, actors, advertising-men, army officers, journalists, computer salesmen, topographers, engineers, science-fiction fans, fraternity brothers, and Mensa members who so carefully *do not appear* in these self-mocking little thumbnail autobiographies, stripping some pitiful little human tragedy naked in five lines, under the paper-thin disguise of exaggerated verbal humor and rhyme. Autobiographies all carefully pegged instead to the other fellow's name! Only the rare limerick poet is ever so frank as to call *himself* a pervert (Limerick 2:2561), or even a pussyhound. It is more fun to use the listener's name instead.

The ithyphallic but impotent young man of Devizes (Limerick 2:311), the arch-castratory Queen of Baroda (1:1371), and the endless monstrous offspring of zoöphilous intercourse with every animal from aardvark to yak and zebra, are thus simply you — and me — and the wives & children we have luckily got rid of, or wish we could. Evidently, the more exaggerated our mutual disguise in this *masque of names,* this carnival frolic of sexual self-unveiling and unambivalent verbal aggression, the better. You write one about me, and I'll write one about you! . . . That way, no one will ever really be sure. Decoded, what this offer palpably means is the same thing that jokes mean under their cosmetic layer of laughter — the whistling-in-the-dark anguish of Figaro's "*I laugh, so that I may not cry.*" That is our epigraph: You hold the mask of laughter over my name and my unavowably shameful face, and I will hold the mask over yours.

III

A CURIOUS question often asked is: *Why are there no limericks in any other language than English?* Actually, this is not quite so. To begin with, bawdy and semi-bawdy limericks imitated from the English-language forms are today fairly common in both Germany and especially in Holland and Dutch-speaking Belgium, where the milder kind have often been printed in the newspapers there, at least since the 1940's. No further proof is necessary than the erotic limerick-sequence or set here first published, "The Martian Chronicles" (2:2654 and following). However, this does not answer the real question. I would therefore like to note briefly here a few of the authentic national poetic forms, similar in inspiration if not in form to the limerick, in other modern Western languages. The German-speaking cultures, for example, have their own perfectly enormous float of short, bawdy folk-rhymes, but these are almost always in the quatrain ("*Vierzeiler*") form, or as the five-line "Frau Wirtin" verses or Tales of My Landlady, on which see Note 1:1730 and F. L. Wells, in the Bibliography to the First Series, for further details.

These invariably concern the landlady, "Frau Wirtin," and her horny crew of boarders; and the inspiration is indeed very close to that of English-language limericks, though the rhyming scheme is not the same. Large collections of bawdy German "fourliners," which are often in dialect, have been published in *Kryptádia* (1888) vol. IV: pp. 79–133, anonymously collected in the Austrian Alps by the German philologist Gustav Meyer; and especially by Emil Karl Blümml, in *Anthropophytéia* (1905–6) vols. II–III, and in his *Erotische Volkslieder aus Deutsch-Österreich* (Vienna: Dr. R. Ludwig? 1907), pp. 103–159; as well as in Blümml's series with 'Josef Polsterer,' *Futilitates* (Vienna, 1908), vol. I: pp. 117–156, and finally his *Der Spittelberg und seine Lieder* (Vienna, 1924) with Gustav Gugitz, under the pseudonyms of 'K. Giglleithner & B. Litschauer,' collected in the brothel quarter of old Vienna. The erotic folk-rhymes of German-speaking children have more recently been collected in Ernest Borneman's monumental *Unsere Kinder, im Spiegel ihrer Lieder* and *Die Umwelt des Kindes* (Olten, Switzerland : Walter-Verlag, 1973–74).

The excessively verbose French language, though it has a very large fund of bawdy students' and soldiers' songs, does not now favor brief folk-rhymes of any kind, except those of schoolchildren ("*comptines*"), on which see J. Baucomont's collection, *Les Comptines de langue française* (Paris : Seghers, 1961) and Claude Gaignebet's masterly *Le Folklore obscène des enfants* (Paris : Maisonneuve & Larose, 1974). The great wealth of Italian erotic folklore and folk-rhyme is most fully presented in Dr. Rafael Corso's *Das Geschlechtsleben . . . des Italienischen Volkes* (Nicotera, 1914 ; *Anthropophytéia* : Beiwerke, vol. VII) with texts in Italian and German translations. Of extreme value also is the first "underground" collection of the Italian students' bawdy songs and farces, *Il Libretto Rosso dell'Universitario : Raccolta di commedie, drammi, ballate, cazzate, sproloqui e Canti Goliardici,* anonymously issued in Ferrara in 1968 (reprinted 1972?) with a second series issued by 1976 as *I Canti Goliardici, No. 2* (Milan: Williams-Inteuropa) edited by Alfredo Castelli; and another similar collection by Roberto Brivio, *Canzoni sporche all' osteria.* All three, remarkable volumes.

As neither Dr. Corso nor the *Libretto Rosso dell'Universitario* gives any text of the following quatrain song, quite similar in "name" inspiration to our limericks, entitled "The Joyous Sacred Mysteries," I give this here as recollected in 1976 by the Venetian poet and folklore collector Sgr. Giuliano Averna, from the singing of schoolboys aged about sixteen, at Abano Terme near Padua in 1957. The fifteen numbered quatrains — actually tailed couplets — were sung to a religious tune, and there were many variants. In his excellent *Canti Goliardici, No. 2,* pages 72–76, Castelli gives a much longer pantheon, extending to forty-six devastatingly anatomical saints.

I SACRI MISTERI GAUDIOSI

Nel *primo* mistero gaudioso
Si contempla San Cirillo
Che con il cazzo fatto a spillo
Inculava i microbi. — *Amen!*

Nel *secondo* mistero gaudioso
Si contempla Santa Agnese
Che con le pezze del marchese
Lucidava i calici. — *Amen!*

Nel *terzo* mistero gaudioso
Si contempla San Teodoro
Che con una secchia di sboro
Benediva il popolo. — *Amen!*

Nel *quarto* mistero gaudioso
Si contempla Santa Veronica
Che con la mona a fisarmonica
Suonava i valzer. — *Amen!*

Nel *quinto* mistero gaudioso
Si contempla San Giosué
Che con il cazzo rosso e blé
Correggeva i compiti. — *Amen!*

Nel *sesto* mistero gaudioso
Si contempla San Vittore
Che con il cazzo a trimotore
Rimpatriava i reduci. — *Amen!*

Nel *settimo* mistero gaudioso
Si contempla San Liborio
Che con il cazzo a littorio
Inculava il Duce. — *Amen!*

Nell'*ottavo* mistero gaudioso
Si contempla Santa Marta

Che con la fica fatta a barca
Faceva le crociere. – *Amen!*

Nel *nono* mistero gaudioso
Si contempla San Giuliano
Che giocando al calcio con l'ano
Parava i gol. – *Amen!*

Nel *decimo* mistero gaudioso
Si contempla Sant'Ilario
Che con il cazzo sul binario
Deragliava i rapidi. – *Amen!*

Nell'*undicesimo* mistero gaudioso
Si contempla Santa Cunegonda
Che con la mona fatta a fionda
Tirava ai passeri. – *Amen!*

Nel *dodicesimo* mistero gaudioso
Si contempla San Raffaele
Che con lo sboro dolce come miele
Faceva pasticcini. – *Amen!*

Nel *tredicesimo* mistero gaudioso
Si contempla Santa Elisabetta
Che con la mona a valigetta
Faceva il contrabbando. – *Amen!*

Nel *quattordicesimo* mistero gaudioso
Si contempla San Gaudenzio
Che con il cazzo a lambicco
Distillava l'assenzio. – *Amen!*

Nel *quindicesimo* mistero gaudioso
Si contempla Santa Ildegarda
Che con la mona a spingarda
Abbordava le fregate. – *Amen!*

It would be wrong not to mention, at least, the erotic folklore and folk-poetry of the Spanish-speaking world, which has one of the most lushly flowering and remarkable funds of such lore in existence, though it does not seem to lend itself (since the time of Martial) to short or formulary poetic bawdy satire in limerick style. Owing to a particularly brutal religio-political censorship in Spain itself, for centuries, the erotic lore of the peninsula has apparently never been published, except for the currently appearing and elegant volumes of Dr. Camilo José Cela's *Diccionario Secreto* (Madrid : Ediciones Alfaguara, 1968–71). But there are splendidly full and unexpurgated compilations from Argentina : *El Plata Folklore* by 'Victor Borde' [Lehmann-Nitsche], published in 1923 as a supplementary volume to the *Anthropophytéia* series (Beiwerke, vol. VIII) ; and more recently from Mexico, in the riotous typographical splurge of *Picardía Mexicana* and *Nueva Picardía Mexicana* (México : Costa-Amic, 1960–71) by A. Jiménez-Farias, plus the one-word dictionary, *El Chingolés,* by P. M. de Usandizaga y Mendoza (1972), and the matching folk poetry in *Versos Picarescos Mexicanos,* by José Michel.

Probably closest of all to the bawdy English-language limericks are the remarkable Russian *chastushki* (quatrains). Numerous pre-Revolutionary examples are given in Prof. Friedrich S. Krauss's anonymous "Folklore de l'Ukraine, et de la Grande Russie," in *Kryptádia* (Paris, 1898), vol. V : pages 1–214, at pages 44–127, among the bawdy "Wedding Songs." See further, on Russian erotic folklore, folksong, and speech, Dr. Bernhard Stern-Szana, *Geschichte der öffentlichen Sittlichkeit in Russland* (Berlin, 1907–19), end of vol. II ; and my own introduction to Aleksandr N. Afanasyev's *Russian Secret Tales* (New York: Brussel & Brussel, 1966), pages vii–xii and xx. The erotic *chastushki* have much increased in underground circulation in post-Revolutionary times during our century ; these have fortunately been very fully collected by Prof. Victor Raskin, now of the Hebrew University in Jerusalem, who plans to publish them with

English equivalents in the forthcoming *Maledicta: The Journal of Verbal Aggression*. One example, and this far from the bawdiest (in translation):

Oh, how boring it is in Kazan
Dancing this old-fashioned quadrille.
Go get circumcized, Ivan,
And let's emigrate to Israel!

IV

ONE CAN hardly pass over without notice the visible attempt by the better twentieth-century limerick poets, both bawdy and polite, to get away from the tiresome and wasted opening line (also falsely accented) beginning with "There *was*. . . ." The late Carlyle Ferren MacIntyre, who wrote hundreds of original limericks, among them the exceedingly popular "While Titian was mixing rose-madder" (Limerick 1:1473), wrote almost none beginning with "There was," and told me he hated them. Similarly, John Coulthard's thousands of originals also totally avoid this. Thus, as he phrased it in a letter written just before his death in 1966 (having been born with the century), "adding 20% more space for the action," in the brief five lines of what is after all a very limited verse-form.

The innovation of the "active" first line is not recent. It will be found briefly exploited in the earliest surviving erotic limerick collection, *Cythera's Hymnal, or Flakes from the Foreskin* (1870, see Limerick 1:1122) and in others. By the early 1900's, which were in fact the heyday of the limerick and of all other kinds of folk-poetry in English, limerick openings avoiding "There was . . . " came to be widely developed in the polite forms especially. For example, Carolyn Wells's "Two tutors who tooted the flute" and "A flea and a fly in a flue." Also in the then-new mock autobiographical examples, such as Anthony Euwer's "For beauty

I am not a star," and Gelett Burgess's never-to-be-forgotten castration symbolic "I'd rather have fingers than toes." But only MacIntyre and Coulthard among the bawdy limerick poets, and the redoubtable Albin Chaplin more recently, have resolutely transcended the formulary "There was" in much of their output.

One hopes their example will be followed, and that such openings will one day be as outmoded as are "Learic" last lines today, helplessly repeating the first-line rhyme : this is something seen almost not at all in modern limericks. (Exception, Limerick 2:1022.) Complex and multisyllabic rhyme-sets are of course always *de rigueur,* as are purposely daft and improbable rhymes such as *governor/shovenor* and *Kubrick/sub-pubric,* in the burlesque rhyming tradition of Samuel Butler's *Hudibras* and *Dildoïdes* in the 1660's. Thus arrogating to the limerick the sort of freedom Milton must have been dreaming of in *Paradise Lost,* as to "things unattempted yet in prose or rhyme."

Several enthusiasts, seduced by statistics, have suggested that it might be interesting to count and compare the active and inactive openings in the limericks presented here, and other formal and linguistic elements, such as "inevitable" and oft-used rhymes of the *France/pants* variety, as well as the erotic vocabulary employed. I feel that work of this kind should be left for the computers — on which see Limerick 2:2195, "Technological Fall-out." For the statistically minded, it may be noted here that the percentages of the chapter-subject concentrations in the present 2,750 examples have proved strikingly similar to those in the 1,739 of *The Limerick,* omitting from the calculation in both the admitted miscellaneous or catch-all chapters, "Strange Intercourse," "Assorted Eccentricities," and "Chamber of Horrors." Of course, such percentages have very little socio-historical meaning on so small a scale as this, yet it is certainly significant that the largest chapter is again "Organs" (8.9% of the total in *The Limerick,* to 9.6% here). While the shortest chapters are again the purposefully narsty-narsties of "Abuses of the Clergy," "Diseases," and "Gourmands": now respectively 3.4%, 2.7%, and 1.4% of the total.

As to the far more difficult question – *Which limericks are the funniest?* – numerous connoisseurs to whom I have posed this question over the years have almost all assured me that, though *wit* sometimes seasons the presentation of even the most outlandish perversions in limerick form, the truly funniest examples will generally be found in the two chapters "Zoöphily" and "Excrement." Why this should be so – meaning, why such limericks should raise the greatest laugh in many people – I do not know. The zoöphilous limerick is certainly trying to *tell us something,* or "laugh off" something very sad, and really about human beings under its pretended belief in the ancient superstition that such miscegenational couplings can be fertile. Zoöphilous limericks are not really about animals at all, anymore than are *Aesop's Fables.* As to the excrementitious, this is essentially the basic anal-aggressive level of all "dirty jokes," and of humor and vituperation generally, whether rhymed or not, as I have tried to demonstrate at some length in the Introduction to *No Laughing Matter* (1975).

Let me end with a confession. If I have made myself a specialist in bawdy limericks and their history, it is not because I particularly like limericks or think them strikingly witty and hilariously funny in all cases, though obviously their authors think so. Some are funny: some are not. And some are perfectly repulsive. I do not think it an accident that the broad folk-audience much prefers the larger sweep of the bawdy song or ballad, which not only has infinitely larger developmental possibilities (note the pressing in this direction by the limerick-sequences or sets), but also usually can avoid the limerick's temptation to petty linguistic humor, and is also seldom so excruciatingly abnormal about its self-confessed sexual goals and nightmares. I hope one day soon to publish a very large collection – actually an archive – of unexpurgated folksongs and ballads in

English, both American and British, historical and modern. These represent an important folk art in practically all languages, but the published collections in English so far are hardly more than a sampling. Falstaff says it very well, and forever: *"Come, sing me a bawdy song — Make me merry."* (*1 Henry IV,* III.iii.14.)

Essentially, I have dedicated myself to collecting the raw materials of English-language erotic folklore in prose and verse, on a very broad scale and without consulting my own tastes, for over forty years now, since I was a schoolboy of seventeen. At least partly because no one else would do so. This specialization has led to few accolades and more than a few public insults, such as my being referred to disdainfully in the honest Dutch bookseller Nicholas Schors's *Memoirs of an Erotic Bookseller* (by 'Armand Coppens', London: Skilton, 1969), page 171, as "that vain genius . . . with the thing about dirty limericks and four-letter words." True — too true. But, odd as it may seem, though I tell many jokes and have collected thousands of them, I seldom write and never recite limericks. Perhaps I have heard too many.

I have simply taken down on paper over the years, without prejudice or literary criticism, whatever erotic folklore and folksong came into my net, which I admit has been flung very wide. My patent has been Robert Burns' lines on an earlier folklore collector, Captain Francis Grose: *"A chiel's amang you, taking notes, And faith, he'll prent it!"* It was not possible, nor would it have been in keeping with my proposed research, to pick & choose only those items which I myself enjoyed or might want to add to my repertory, or with whose prejudices I agreed. It is not possible now. My intention has not been to create erotic art anthologies — a project well worth undertaking, but which would be premature at the present time, since the materials are not yet all on record. Instead, I have preferred to try to create a definitive series of folkloristic, psychological, and socio-historical documents, of which the intrinsic erotic materials cast a very powerful light on us and on our times.

A better critic than myself, and certainly a better limerick poet, Professor Morris Bishop, has expressed in a letter to me written from Athens (May 27th, 1952) an even more sweeping disenchantment with the limerick than my own. He says :

> It all seems long ago and far away to me. The limerick is a curious phenomenon both for the *littérateur* and the psychologist, but on the whole it bores me. Its formula has been so well established that it is almost capable of mass production. Perhaps I don't get around as much as I used to ; it has certainly been years since I sat in a session wherein the newer limericks were exchanged, and I shall willingly go to my grave without sitting in another such session. Yet such is the proper environment for the dirty limerick. Remove the highballs, the hyena-laughter, the gleaming eyes revealing the inner titillation, and the limerick – a trigger mechanism – loses its magic. A series of them in cold print are depressing ; they are the corpses of limericks. At least, so I felt when I read Norman Douglas' book. Indeed, so I felt when I met Norman Douglas a couple of times in London. He did his best to be racy, shocking, the smiter of bourgeois morality. But bourgeois morality had already out-distanced him ; he seemed merely senile and pitiful. And lest I too appear senile and pitiful, I make my peace with the unalterable verities.

In a further article, one of the most penetrating ever written "On the Limerick" (in the *New York Times Book Review,* January 3rd, 1965), Professor Bishop spells out slashingly what he only hints at here in "the hyena-laughter, the gleaming eyes." Reviewing the late Conrad Aiken's verbigerous *A Seizure of Limericks,* Bishop comments icily on the title : "*Seizure* is good ; a mild taste for limericks can lead to seizures, addiction, septic logorrhea and compulsive recitation neuroses." *Septic logorrhea* is good too.

Nothing else in the socio-cultural activity of the educated class which, alone, really fancies and creates limericks, tells half so much about its unconscious psychological makeup, its sexual bogeys and peculiarities, its inadequacies, impotencies, and frustrations, and *what you can expect of it in an emergency, if push comes to shove.* If one's "favorite joke," as I have made the underlying theme of *Rationale of the Dirty Joke,* is a helpless unveiling of the joketeller's scaredest guts, and a psychological S.O.S. sent out to whoever will listen ; the limerick-reciter's limerick is surely nothing less than his blitz-psychoanalysis or diagnostic, performed by and on himself. Sometimes *her*self too, but this is still uncommon.

A man who makes up a Negro-hating or woman-hating chauvinist sex-piggery joke or limerick, and tells it compulsively to all comers with a shit-eating grin, *is* a chauvinist pig — and not only about sex — and you can bet your bottom dollar on that! And so is the fortunately still rather rare female chauvinist, who telegraphs her castratory punch over the cocktail glass (the Queen of Baroda without her little Indira Gandhi knives : see Note 2:1642), by screaming out delightedly the same sort of female sexist sowishness. It will not wash, to try to convince us that the reciter's real pleasure in such subject-matter resides strictly in the prosodo-æsthetic exhilaration of the *rhyme.*

One last word. *Are the limericks presented here true folklore?* Some are, and some not yet. Some will never be. Of the 4,600 or more limericks included in the two series of the present collection (and their Notes), only perhaps a tenth can be considered already to have entered the authentic stream of orally transmitted folklore. These are the ones that appear repetitively in all the collections, and that "everyone knows," and imagines himself to be tired of. The limericks that gain folk acceptance in this way will live, and will be endlessly repeated. They are the most significant. As to the rest, what does it matter? Call them folk-art if you like. For good or for bad, they are poetry. And they are the only kind of rhymed poetry being written today in English that has the slightest chance of survival in oral circulation —

something available now to even the most popular of "popular songs" for only a few brief months or weeks.

In the impossibility of making an editorial choice that would please everyone, it has seemed preferable to err on the side of fulness. Like other anthologists before me, I have tried to range over the whole field and to choose the best. Many hundreds — actually thousands — of the new limericks made available to me over the last twenty-five years have in fact been rejected out of hand as impossibly dull, flat, *non-situational,* merely dirty, or unbearably kitschy-camp. Without some leaven of wit, or at least some unbuttoned and hilarious nonsense, bawdy limericks are seldom endurable at all in large numbers. The worst (prosodically, not morally) have been separated here, as in the First Series, in a brief final chapter entitled "Chamber of Horrors," which some contrary souls insist on finding the funniest of all. Again, the prejudices, the cruelty, and the humorless quality of many of the limericks included here are deeply regretted. However, no falsification of the material has been made.

G. LEGMAN

La Clé des Champs
Valbonne (*Alpes-Maritimes*)
FRANCE

SOURCES

1888. *The Stag Party* (Boston?)
1904C to 1945C. Aleister CROWLEY.
1919E to 1954E. E. E. CUMMINGS.
1930. *Lyra Ebriosa* (Norfolk, Va.).
1933. *The "Wrecks"* (Reno).
1942A to 1977A. Limerick Addenda.
1944. FIFE : South Pacific MS.
1945. *To Solace the Blind* (Frankfurt-am-Main).
1945R to 1959R. 'Gregory-Boomer-Fouff' (mimeo).
1948. Crist College Collection.
1948U to 1957U. *Union Jack* (MS.).
1949. [LAVENDER] *Lost Limericks* (mimeo).
1950. [Clement WOOD] *Around the Horn.*
1952. *Salacious Science Limericks* (mimeo).
1952L. LARSON : *Barnyard Folklore.*
1953. Fifth Line Society : *Transactions.*
1954. 'LeDernier CRI & D. Letzte SCHREY'.
1954J to 1959J. JOHNSON MSS.
1955. 'Count Palmiro VICARRION'.
1955M to 1966M. Carlyle Ferren MacINTYRE.
1956. 'Dick HARDE': *Lusty Limericks* (mimeo).
1958. *The Tenth Muse Lately Hung Up* (MS.).
1958P. STARR : *Fighter Pilots Hymn Book.*
1960. 'Dr. Spurl S. VERSENKT' : *IBM Limericks.*
1962. *Snatches & Lays* (Australia).
1963. *Be Pure!* (Perth, Australia).
1963B to 1971B. 'Roger HERWELL' (mimeos).

1964. *The Martian Chronicles* (Flemish MS.).
1965 to 1966. *The Cathouse of Time* (MS.).
1967. 'Charles L. DODGSON'.
1967K. Mark ACHESON.
1968. *Close Harmony & Barbershop Chords.*
1968G. 'G. BARR': *Science Fiction Limericks.*
1969. 'HARLEY-DAVIDSON'.
1970. Poul ANDERSON : *Night of the Dinosaur.*
1971. 'SEDLEY' : *Piety & Playfulness.*
1971*ff. Corn on the Cob* (MS.).
1972. 'Lee DOTSON'.
1973. *Klimericks : An Orgy* (London MS.).
1974. Brian ALDISS : *Solar System's Survey.*
1975. Albin CHAPLIN.
1976A to 1977A. Limerick Addenda.

INITIALS	E : 1919-54	L : 1952
see date	*ff* : 1971	M : 1955-66
A : 1942-77	G : 1968	P : 1958
B : 1963-71	J : 1954-59	R : 1945-59
C : 1904-45	K : 1967	U : 1948-57

THE NEW LIMERICK

I

LITTLE ROMANCES

1

Here are neatly turned odes of small span,
Much concerned with our bodily plan,
    And the intercorporeal
    Highly sensorial
Love-life of woman and man.

1973.

2

There was a young girl of Aberystwyth
Who screwed every man that she kissed with.
    She tickled the balls
    Of the men in the halls,
And pulled on the prongs that they pissed with.

1948.

3

Back in the days of old Adam
The grass served as mattress for madam,
    And they spent the whole day
    On the sex that today
They would bounce on box springs, if they had 'em.

1966.

4

A doctor said sadly, " Alas!
From the data that I can amass,
    What causes male droop—
    And I have all the poop—
Is the feminine excess of ass."

1975.

5

A lush little lady of Amble
Went out for a casual ramble.
On a side road this maid
Was tipped up and laid—
But then, of course, *all* life's a gamble.

1965.

6

There was a young girl from Annista
Who dated a lecherous mister.
He fondled her titty,
Got one finger shitty,
Then screwed up his courage and kissed 'er.

1948.

7

Said Eve as she reached for the apple,
And prepared that primordial grapple :
" With the proper sales talk
Adam surely won't balk,
For if anyone falls, why, that sap'll! "

1966.

8. AUTOEROTIC

You'll never know *how* good you are
Till you try to make love in a car.
Many a man meets defeat
On a darkened back seat ;
It's only the experts break par.

1965.

9

Said a hipshot young bride of Atlantic :
" This fucking is driving me frantic.
I hate to disparage
The sex side of marriage,
But a whole night of cock's unromantic! "

1965.

10

A young bride and groom of Australia
Remarked as they joined genitalia:
  " Though the system seems odd,
  We are thankful that God
Developed the genus *Mammalia.* "

1965.

11

Connoisseurs of coition aver
That young British ladies don't stir.
  This condition in Persia
  Is known as inertia,
And it's *not* the response I prefer.

1974A.

12

There was a young lady from Baylor
Who fell madly in love with a sailor.
  Since they met at a dance
  He was forced to wear pants,
And he had to turn sideways to nail her.

1957A.

13

That glamorous blonde, young Miss Bell,
Forgot to reserve a hotel;
  But a kind man from Fife
  Tucked her in with his wife,
And gave her some crumpet as well.

1973.

14

There was an old codger named Ben
Who had a most terrible yen.
  The problem was not
  The how, why, or what,
But the who and the where and the when.

1957R.

15

There was an old lady of Bingly
Who wailed, " I do hate to sleep singly.
    I thought I had got
    A bloke for my twat,
But he seems rather queenly than kingly. "

1939C.

16

On a date with a charming young bird,
His erotical feelings were stirred.
    So with bold virile pluck
    He inquired, " Do you fuck? "
She said, " Yes, but please don't use that word. "

1975.

17

Joe the milkman has quit our block,
Leaving seventeen housewives in shock.
    He milked 'em, he worked 'em,
    He jerked 'em, and ferked 'em—
Now *I'll* have to take care of his flock.

1965.

18

An irate young lady named Booker
Told her husband, " You beast, I'm no hooker!
    If you want it queer ways,
    Go to whores for your lays! "
So he packed up his tool and forsook 'er.

1966.

19

A rapist who reeked of cheap booze
Attempted to ravish Miss Hughes.
    She cried, " I suppose
    There's no time for my clothes,
But PLEASE let me take off my shoes! "

1965.

20

There was a young lady named Bower
Who dwelt in an Ivory Tower.
    But a poet from Perth
    Laid her flat on the earth,
And proceeded with penis to plough her.

1975.

21

There was a young lady of Brabant
Who slept with an impotent savant.
    She admitted, " We shouldn't,
    But it turned out he couldn't—
So you can't say we have when we haven't. "

1974A.

22. MAUD FITZGERALD

A delighted, incredulous bride
Remarked to her groom at her side :
    " I never could quite
    Believe till tonight
Our anatomies *would* coincide. "

1966A.

23

There was a young lady named Brigid
Who everyone thought was quite frigid.
    But a passionate Celt
    Made her reticence melt,
And with passion our Brigid grew rigid!

1974A.

24

There was a young lady named Brook
Who never could learn how to cook.
    But on a divan
    She could please any man—
She knew every darn trick in the book!

1967A-1975.

25

A highly bored damsel named Brown
Remarked as she laid herself down :
  " I hate to be doing
  This promiscruous screwing,
But what else can you *do* in this town? "

1965.

26

An insatiable satyr named Bruce
Likes his women delightfully loose.
  He finds 'em out dancing,
  And twisting and prancing,
And puts 'em to very good use.

1966.

27

A German composer named Bruckner
Remarked to a lady while fuckener :
  " Less *lento,* my dear,
  With your cute little rear ;
I like a hot *presto* when muckener! "

1976A.

28

A seducer of housewives named Brutus
Said, " Though the narrow denounce us and hoot us,
  What we can't abide
  Ain't the jealous and snide ;
It's the small-minded husbands who shoot us. "

1965.

29

I would like to say, Mister Bunce,
I'm a great connoisseur of hot cunts.
  And in all my lewd life
  I've met none like your wife,
So why leave her to me, you big dunce?

1966.

30. LIFE

Handsome woman. — Lovely bust.
Fine young fellow. — Stirred-up lust. —
Babies' diapers. —
Bottom wipers. —
Years of struggle. — Coffin. — Dust.

1976A.

31

Though his plan, when he gave her a buzz,
Was to do what man normally does,
She declared, " I'm a Soul—
Not a sexual goal! "
So he shrugged and called someone who was.

1971*

32

There was an old man of Calcutta
Who spied through a chink in the shutter.
But all he could see
Was his wife's bare knee,
And the back of the bloke who was up her.

1948U.

33

There was a young lady of Carmia
Whose housekeeping ways would alarm ya.
At every cold snap
She would climb in your lap,
So her little base burner could warm ya.

1945-1970A.

34

'Tis a custom in Castellamare
To fuck in the back of a lorry.
The chassis and springs
Are like woodwinds and strings
In the midst of a musical soirée.

1951R.

35

There is a young girl in Cheyenne
Who has an attraction for man,
For her body is svelte
And she loves to be felt,
And she helps with her hips all she can.

1948.

36

There was a young lady of Chiswick
Who consulted a Doctor of Physic.
He tested her hormones
And sexual performones,
Then prescribed her a strong aphrodisic.

1974A.

37

There was a young lady called Ciss
Who went to the river to piss.
A young man in a punt
Put his hand on her cunt ;
No wonder she thought it was bliss.

1944*

38

To his bride said a numskull named Clarence :
" I trust you will show some forbearance.
My sexual habits
I picked up from rabbits,
And occasionally watching my parents."

1966.

39

She stood there and peeled off her clothes,
And begged for a bang : goodness knows
I am surely impure
And I sizzled to scrure,
But the push had gone out of my hose.

1965.

40. THE HIGHER LEARNING

A lass at the foot of her class
Asked a brainier chick how to pass.
She replied, " With no fuss
You can get a B-plus,
By letting the prof pat your ass. "

[41]

" In my studies I'm very sincere,
I fuck for the skinny old dear.
Cum laude I'll blaze
In arrays of straight-A's
If he lasts till the end of the year. "

[42]

The other girl tittered with glee :
" I can see that's the system for me.
I'll go through like a dream,
Though I'm sure it will seem
I've been screwed—to a certain degree. "

1953A.

43

Mrs. Kelly is partial to cocks ;
Mr. Kelly likes rye on the rocks.
When he's under the weather
They can't get together,
So others get into her box.

1972.

44

There was a young woman of Condover
Whose husband had ceased to be fond of 'er.
Her pussy was juicy,
Her arse soft and goosey,
But peroxide had now made a blonde of 'er.

1966A.

45

There was a young girl of Coxsaxie
Whose skirt was more mini than maxi.
  She was fucked at the show
  In the twenty-third row,
And once more going home in the taxi.

1967A-1975.

46

His shy bride admitted to Crandall
That for years she'd worked off with a candle,
  But a cock like his dick
  Gave her ten times the kick,
Though it strained her wee peehole to handle!

1965.

47

The bedsprings next door jounce and creak :
They have kept me awake for a week.
  Why *do* newlyweds
  Select squeaky beds
To develop their fucking technique?

1965.

48. A TOAST

We dedicate this to the cunt,
The kind the broad-minded guys hunt :
  All hail to the twat,
  Willing, thrilling, and hot,
That wears peckers down, limp and blunt!

1966.

49

Two lovers went out for a stunt
On the Thames in a flat-bottomed punt.
  She said, " Nobody's near ;
  With my free-traders here,
All's clear, dear, from back or from front. "

1973.

50

He played smooch and stinkfinger with Daisy
Till this virgin was gotch-eyed and hazy.
    Then his gargantuan pole in
    Her pink, tight, and swollen
Young cunt just about drove her crazy.

1966A.

51. A FOLKTALE RETOLD

Cinderella slipped off to the dance,
Where she dropped off a slipper, by chance.
    She was followed and wed,
    Then rushed off to bed,
Where Prince Charming got into her pants.

1972.

52

To his wife said the jealous Lord Dawes:
"Slip this chastity belt in your drawers!"
    But her lover, a Celt,
    Found the key to her belt
While Lord Dawes was away at the wars.

1974A.

53

"I *do* love a lay every day,
So whenever you're coming this way
    Just phone in advance
    And I'll jerk off my pants,
And we're set for a sexy soirée!"

1965.

54

The heroine of my little ditty
Was had by a lad from the city.
    She exclaimed: "What a sin!"
    When he put his thing in,
But when he pulled it out: "What a pity!"

1956J.

55

A house dick there once was called Doroughty,
Employed by a Vassar sorority.
  It was not for the pay
  But the chance of a lay,
For propinquity gives high priority.

1957R.

56

" If newlyweds come, " said Miss Dove,
" I give them the room just above.
  When they do their lovemaking
  I can hear the bed shaking,
Like it used to when *I* was in love. "

1973.

57

There was a young lady from Dumfries
Who said to her boyfriend, " It's *some* freeze!
  My navel's all bare,
  So stick it in there,
Before both my legs and my bum freeze. "

1950.

58

There was a young monarch named Ed
Who took Mrs. Simpson to bed.
  As they bounced up and down
  He said, " Bugger the crown!
We'll give it to Albert instead. "

1936A.

59

There was a young woman named Ellie
Who, when fellows lay down on her belly,
  Would spur them along
  With shouts of " I'm gone! "
Or " Darling, come shoot me your jelly! "

1959*

60. MOMENT OF TRUTH

With his penis in turgid erection,
And aimed at woman's mid-section,
Man looks most uncouth
In that Moment of Truth,
But she sheathes it with loving affection.

1965.

61

That would-be sophisticate, Etta,
Claimed nothing could shock or upsetta.
But her neighbors, named Rucking,
She one day spied fucking,
And her panties grew wetta and wetta.

1966.

62. DON JUAN SPEAKS

I remember, as autumn nights fall,
My springtime of cock and of ball.
My ruddy John Thomas
Made plenty of mamas;
My motto: FUCK ONE AND FUCK ALL!

1976A.

63

A girl who came east from the farm
Exclaimed, "City life has its charm.
Take the pleasures of orgasm—
Every girl in New York has 'em,
But in Kansas they're viewed with alarm."

1953.

64

A passionate lady named Fay
Told friend Joe as he staggered away:
"On the Passamaquoddy
We consider it shoddy
To stop after one little lay."

1965.

65. STAND TO YOUR GLASSES, MEN !

All hail to the naked fe-male,
Big of bust, round of rear, pretty tail!
  Her lack of resistance
  Keeps the race in existence ;
May our yen for her tail never fail!

1965.

66

Little Jane and her brother had fiddled,
And she wept that by God she'd been diddled,
  For she found he'd a cock
  Where she, 'neath her frock,
Had only the hole where she tiddled.

1973.

67

There was a young lady from Fife
So gorgeous she started much strife :
  Her tight ass and proud bubby
  So inflamed one poor hubby,
He began to throw rocks at his wife.

1967A-1975.

68. GRASSHOPPER JACK

At the picnic we missed Jack and Flo,
And no one had seen the pair go.
  After what seemed like hours
  They returned bearing flowers,
But we know where they went—ho, ho, ho!

[69]

Jack's grasshopper pants appeared green,
And on the back of Flo's dress could be seen
  More green spots and grasses—
  Perhaps, as time passes,
They both may decide to come clean.

1965.

70

With his pecker stretched limp on the floor
And the bitch still imploring for more,
    He said, " Ten hours screwing
    Have been my undoing—
I simply can't fuck anymore! "

1966.

71

A weary bride—poor little fluff—
Said, " My pussy's all tender and rough.
    I realize, Cyril,
    You're terribly virile,
But seventeen times is ENOUGH ! "

1965.

72

A young girl of exquisite form
Was quite choosy with whom she'd perform.
    But when out in a gale
    She'd fuck every male,
Saying, " Any old por*k* in a storm. "

1971 *ff.*

73

A frantic young bridegroom named Fowle
Scrutinized his bride's cunt with a scowl.
    And he growled, " Wait a minnit!
    Now, how can I plug *in* it,
Unless you first pull out that towel? "

1965.

74

We met at the airport in France,
And it seemed such a perfect romance.
    But now I'm Pierre's bride,
    He just snores by my side,
And won't even take off his pants!

1973.

75

There was a young lady named Frances
Who often went into deep trances.
 During these her best beau
 Was not at all slow
To deftly slip into her pantses.

1959*

76

There was a young fellow named French
Who was screwing a girl on a bench.
 His prick was so small
 It did no good at all:
His shortcomings disgusted the wench.

1948.

77

According to old Sigmund Freud
Life seldom is so well enjoyed
 As in human coition
 (In any position)
With the usual organs employed.

1974A.

78

A frustrated nympho named Frome
Told her boyfriend one midnight in Nome:
 "If your penis stays dead
 You can hop out of bed,
Put your clothes all back on, and GO HOME!"

1965.

79

"Can it be," cried a thrice-diddled Gertie,
"That the minds of all men are so dirty?
 For there on the bed
 With a hardon lies Ed,
And yelling *Let's fuck!* since 8:30."

1966.

80

There was a fine dandy, Beau Geste,
Who approached a young girl with great zest.
    But when she had stripped,
    And he was unzipped,
The dead bird just stayed in its nest.

1953.

81

The birdwatcher focused his glasses,
And spied in the brush two bare asses.
    He'd been looking for crows
    But forgot about those,
And his gonads became swollen masses.

1965.

82. NIGHTPIECE

It's time to make love. Douse the glim.
The fireflies twinkle and dim.
    The stars lean together
    Like birds of a feather,
And the loin lies down with the limb.

1957*

83

There was a young fellow named Goring
Who used his own wife for his whoring.
    When they said, "Thrice-a-nighting
    Must be quite exciting?"
She replied: "It's excessively *boring*."

1968A.

84

The enjoyment of sex, although great,
Is in later years said to abate.
    This well may be so,
    But how would I know?—
I'm now only seventy-eight.

1974A.

85

riverrun where can you guess?
Finnegans Wake is a mess.
    Will you help me get even?
    Said leftover Stephen.
yes I said yes I will Yes.

1966A.

86

Said a fussy old bachelor named Harridge:
"Connubial life I disparage.
    Every time I get hot
    And poke some girl's spot,
She thinks it's an offer of marriage."

1965.

87

A naïve young fellow named Harry
Met dozens of loose girls in Gary.
    But he kept on ducking
    His chances for fucking,
Unaware he was a latent young fairy.

1949.

88

There was a young fellow named Hatch
Who thought he had made a great catch.
    His inducement to flirt
    Was a wee mini-skirt,
But beneath was a great maxi-snatch!

1970A.

89

The bedsprings bang Bernie's bald head,
While above him Mae moans on the bed.
    Her husband is using her,
    Poor Bernie's abusing her—
In a whisper—one squeak and he's dead!

1966.

90. A REAL LOVER

Touching all chords of her woman's heart,
He plead his suit with highest art.
Perplexed, confused,
With love suffused,
She slowly sighed her legs apart.

1922*

91

There was an old fellow named Hewing
Whose heart stopped while he was a-screwing.
He gasped, "Really, Miss,
Don't feel bad about this—
There's *nothing* I'd rather die doing."

1975A.

92

Yes, living is all uphill hoeing:
Whenever I get a girl going,
Stick my finger a notch
Or two up her crotch,
I find the dumb bunny is flowing!

1950.

93

There is a young miss named Honorée,
When a man says to her, "I adore 'ee,"
She opens her twat
To give him a shot,
And then gets extremely encore-y.

1950.

94

Two romantic young lovers, quite horny,
Found fucking in bed much too corny.
So they wooed in a wood,
Which would have been good
Had the mossy banks not been so thorny.

1973.

95

A young mountain lad name of Horton
Once called on his gal for some courtin'.
  She had doused with perfume
  Labeled " Hill-Billy's Doom, "
And he stood there just pantin' and snortin'.

1967A-1975.

96. HISSES FROM THE MRS.

My sex life is pretty humdrum :
When I'm ready, and want George to plumb,
  He says, " Wait a minute—
  I've hardly got in it— "
Then before I begin it, he's come.

1973.

97

Said the wife of the great intellectual :
" My problem is quite frankly sexual.
  When for hubby I pant
  He just quotes Will Durant,
And remains, in the sack, ineffectual. "

1972.

98

There was a young boy named Jed
Whose dong was big and blood-red.
  Said his girlfriend, " Your prick
  Is too rough and too thick—
Let's go to the movies instead. "

1968.

99

A dumb t.v. addict named Joe
Never mastered the dial, and so
  The poor sonofabitch
  Just sang 'long with Mitch,
Though he wanted the Steve Allen show.

1967*

100

There was a young student named Jones
Who'd reduce any maiden to moans
By his wonderful knowledge,
Acquired in college,
Of the nineteen erogenous zones.

1956.

101

There was a young lady named Kate
Who asked for a drink from her date:
"Just two fingers for me."
But he gave her full three—
She was Fucked by the Finger of Fate!

[102]

But observe this young girl in a pickle,
The finger of Fate must be fickle:
His love, the man swore,
In great torrents would pour,
But the best he could do was a trickle.

1967A-1975.

103

There was a young fellow of Keating
Whose pride took a terrible beating.
That happens to males
When they learn the details
Of their wives' extramarital cheating.

1945.

104

There was a young lady named Kent
Who gave up her husband for Lent.
The night before Easter
When Jesus released her,
It didn't make a damned bit of difference
because in the meantime he'd been running
around with a lot of other women.

1953.

105

Said the newlyweds staying at Kitely :
" We turn off the electric light nightly.
It's best to cmbark
Upon sex in the dark—
The *look* of the thing's so unsightly! "

1973.

106

" Well, I took your advice, Doc, " said Knopp ;
" Told my wife that she'd like it on top.
She bounced for an hour,
Till she ran out of power,
And the kids, who got bored, made us stop. "

1965A.

107

There was a young man reading Lawrence
To his inamorata in Florence.
When they came to the page
Where he fucks her with rage,
He flooded her guts with his torrents.

1948.

108

To a diffident fellow named Legman
A broad whinnied, " Please, must I beg, Man,
Like *this* for a lay?
I'm willing to pay,
Just to sample the joys of your peg, Man! "

1965.

109

There was a young lady from Leicester
Who allowed the young men to molest her.
For a kiss and a squeeze
She would spread both her knees,
And she'd strip to the buff if they pressed her.

1974A.

110. CLASSIFIED ADVERTS.

ARE YOU elderly, sex-starved or lonely?
We can help you. Just write " Matey Me. "
 At Gateshead-on-Tyne
 We stock every line
Of sex aid—best quality only.

[111]

COME AND SEE our French goods—you can try 'em,
Fit them on for right size when you buy 'em :
 Strong, smooth, and reversible,
 The thinnest dispersible—
Any *odd* shape you need, we supply 'em.

[112]

TRY OUR Rubber Girl-Friend (air-inflatable)
Perennially young (quite insatiable).
 Our satisfied clients,
 From mere midgets to giants,
Say she's incredibly sexy and mateable.

[113]

NONE COULD BETTER our sex limousine,
With its neat, built-in Fucking Machine :
 Engine-powered, this connects
 To suit either sex,
And adjusts to the fat and the lean.

[114]

FOR WIDOWER—wanted, housekeeper.
Not too bloody refined, a light sleeper.
 When employer's inclined
 Must be game for a grind—
Pay generous, mind, but can't keep her.

1973.

[115]

COME TO NOAH'S for wine and strong waters,
And for diddling in clean, classy quarters.
I assure every guest
I've made personal test
Of my booze, and my beds, and my daughters.

1972A.

116

At midnight he turned out the lights,
While she quickly slipped out of her tights.
Then noisy bed-squeaking,
Low moans, breathless speaking—
Thus man celebrates his sex rites!

1965.

117

To her gardener a lady named Liliom
Said, " Billy, plant roses and trillium. "
Then she started to fool
With the gardener's tool,
And wound up in the bed of sweet William.

1945.

118

That sweet little lady named Lou
Has got me all worried and blue.
She's one of those gals
That fucks all your pals,
Then makes all your girlie friends too!

1961A.

119

A ticklish young titter named Lucy
Cried, " I'm not only ticklish, I'm goosey.
A thumb in my bum
Makes me peepee and come,
And *does* my cunt ever get juicy! "

1965.

120

To her father cried hot Miss McCutcheon :
"To hell with our family escutcheon!
At the very first chance
Off come these stretch-pants,
So my pussy can start right in *smutchin'!*"

1965.

121

"When a lady feels low," says McGee,
"Make your help both effective and free.
Steer clear of analysis
And suggest, instead, phalluses :
I have found that she'll always agree."

1970.

122

Shed a tear for the WREN named McGinnis
Who brought her career to a finis.
She did not understand
The sudden command
To break out the Admiral's pinnace.

1945.

123

There was a young fellow, McNair,
Took a girl on a date on a dare.
When he showed his virility
She displayed her agility—
The result was a bang-up affair.

1957J.

124. COCKTALE HOUR

"Why, yes, I know Lulu McScrew.
But I didn't know Lulu knew *you*.
She's sure quite a gal,
But tell me this, pal,
Is that *X* on her ass your tattoo?"

1965.

125

There was a young bride named McWing
Who thought sex a delirious fling.
When her bridegroom grew ill
From too much (as they will)
She found other men do the same thing.

1966.

126

There was a young man from Madrid
Who yelled at the queen, " Oh, you kid! "
The scandalized queen
Said, " What do you mean?
You just kiss my ass! " And he did.

1950.

127

A willing young girl in Marin
Viewed her drunken friend's cock with chagrin.
Said she, " That much booze
Cancels out any screws.
Would you please poke your forefinger in? "

1965.

128

Said a busty young bunny named Maugham :
" I *do* wish the guys would keep calm.
They twiddle my tits
With their hot, sticky mitts,
And it drives me half daft when they paw 'em! "

1965.

129

There was a young fellow named Mavern,
Longed to probe in a young lady's cavern.
By guile and strong drink
He did just what you think,
In the grass out behind the town tavern.

1966.

130

Said Edna St.Vincent Millay,
As she lay in the hay all asplay :
  " If you can make wine
  From these grapes, I opine
We'll stay in this barn until May. "

1955.

131

A happy young whore from Milpitas
Said : " Man has found nothing to beat us.
  Golf, fishing, and fights
  All have their delights,
But *nothing* beats good old coeetus! "

1965.

132

There was a young girl named Miranda
Who said to her beau in all candor :
  " This antique *chaise longue*
  Is not very strong—
Er, why don't we try the veranda? "

1974A.

133

An innocent bride from the Mission
Remarked, on her first night's coition :
  " What an intimate section
  To use for connection,
And, lord! what a silly position! "

1966.

134. CONVERSATION AT MIDNIGHT

A nervous young bridegroom named Moore
Told his bride, " Dear, I know that it's sore.
  But don't *scream* when we do it—
  Please put your mind to it—
The neighbors are all keeping score. "

1965.

135

There was a young girl of Moravia
Whose beauty would surely enslave ya.
    While her double knee-action
    Lent further attraction
To her wholly amoral behavia.

1945.

136

The young lover always wants more,
Till the tip of his penis is sore.
    Then most men like a go
    Twice a week, say, or so ;
But at ninety the whole thing's a bore.

1973.

137

A dolly from Morningside Heights
Says sex provides all her delights.
    When she hasn't the rag on
    She gets half a jag on,
And spends her time fucking of nights.

1965.

138

Dejected and limp was young Morse,
And his girl was left full of remorse.
    They confined their maneuvers
    For so long to *hors d'œuvres*
That he failed when they tried the main course.

1975.

139

A base basso buffo in Napoli
When deprived of his tail acts so scrappily
    That a dumb kettle-drummer
    Loaned his wife one whole summer,
Though admittedly rather unhappily.

1965.

140. HISTORY WITHOUT MYSTERY

Consider the Emperor Nero—
Of many lewd tales he's the hero—
Though he scraped on the fiddle
He just couldn't diddle,
And his *real* batting average was zero.

1945.

[141]

Cleopatra, the queen of the Nile,
Fooled Caesar with overmuch guile.
Her titties were stunning,
Her pussy was cunning,
Which diverted his interests a while.

1971A.

[142]

Messalina, the queen of King Zeep,
Would wait till the king was asleep,
Then sneak out on all fours
And work out with the whores,
And then back into bed she would creep.

1975A.

[143]

A bandit was bold Robin Hood,
His motives were misunderstood.
He stole all the riches
From rich sons of bitches—
Well, it's better than pulling your pud!

1970A.

[144]

Joan of Arc was a frigid young bitch,
Her pussy gave never a twitch.
Refusing to whore,
She strode off to war,
And they burnt the poor girl as a witch.

1976A.

[145]

King Henry the Eighth was a man
Whose libido got far out of hand.
    With bollocks of brass
    And a velvet-cased ass,
He raped all the maids in the land.
(Just horsin' around . . .) 1971A.

[146]

Marie-Antoinette used to cash in
On her faded old charms, much in fashion.
    From lovers and sweeties
    She got favorable treaties
In the throes of testicular passion.

1972.

[147]

Napoleon was a quaint little runt :
He always was chasing some cunt.
    But when he gained fame
    Things weren't the same—
The cunt now came chasing the runt.

1971.

[148]

Then last came Victoria Regina
Whose reign was the best—never finer!
    But alas, all the women
    With frustrations were brimmin',
Until Freud delved the frigid vagina.

1974A.

[149]

Now who in American history
Belongs in this long list so blistery?
    Our presidents are shit,
    The rich roll in it ;
So let's leave the question a mystery.

1975A.

150

After one hot naked night in New Britain
With a wholly immoral sex kitten,
    A fellow from Bode
    Shot off his last load,
And sighed, "Back to your knittin'—I'm quittin'!"

1965.

151

Today's bit of local hot news
Concerns the schoolteacher, Miss Hughes:
    In a burst of imprudence
    She laid horny male students—
She's now kept for the Dean's private use.

1965.

152. MOMENT OF TRUTH

Ruth peeked through the keyhole last night
And saw by the dawn's early light
    The parlormaid, Kitty,
    With husband Joe at her clitty,
And she wet her pink pants at the sight.

1965.

153

These hot newlyweds of North Hyde
Flip a coin every night to decide
    Who will be the rid*ee,*
    And tonight we see Bee
Mounting Clyde to begin the night's ride.

1966.

154

A thoughtful young bride of North Lyme
Said, "Although sex is simply divine,
    As I told Aloysius,
    Between douches and dishes
I'm in hot water most of the time!"

1965.

155. CONFIDENTIALLY . . .

I dislike all this crude notoriety
I am getting for my impropriety.
All that *I* ever do
Is what girls ask me to—
I admit I get lots of variety.

1965A.

156

A twitchy young bitch named O'Brien
Sighed, " Joe, you just keep right on tryin'.
I'll leave you my card,
And when it gets hard
You *wire* me, or drop me a lian. "

1966.

157

Dear Charlotte's bedsprings need oiling,
For when sexual action is boiling
Her audible labors
Inform prudish neighbors
She's back in the sack, hotly toiling!

1965.

158

Everyone but that dumbbell, O'Neal,
Knows his wife has an afternoon deal.
For at two every day
A guy stops for a lay—
Depending on how I may feel!

1966.

159

To his nurse said the famous physician,
In the throes of illicit coition :
" Though it's getting quite late,
Let the damn patients wait!
Please assume the post-partum position. "

1965.

160

There was a young lady of Pinner
Whose hubby came home to his dinner.
And guess what he saw
As he opened the door:
The arse of the man who was in her.

1948U.

161

When Daddy and Mom got quite plastered,
And their shame had been thoroughly mastered,
They told their boy, Harry:
"Son, we never *did* marry,
But don't tell the neighbors, you bastard!"

1965.

162

A bashful young girl from Podunk
Her very first dance she did flunk.
With her *soul full of hope*
She had used the wrong soap,
And so simply sat there and stunk.

1967A-1975.

163. THE BUNNY SPEAKS:

I've found if you act pornographic
You'll discover men aren't seraphic.
If you play it like bitchy
Their pants become itchy,
And your prat's pounded flat by the traffic.

1965.

164

During opening hours at our pub
There is plenty of drink and good grub.
If you want just a nibble,
The youngest Miss Tibble
Runs our ball games and Cockfighting Club.

1973.

165. PAGING LYDIA PINKHAM!

There was once a coed from Purdue
Who decided her loves were too few.
  She took Vitamin E,
  Which discolored her pee,
And she's now an insane three-way screw.

1976A.

166

So pleased was a lady named Pyle
When a Boy Scout assisted in style,
  She inquired, "In what way
  Can I brighten *your* day?"
He said, "Flash me that vertical smile!"

1975.

167

The last time I slept with the Queen
She said, as I whistled *Ich dien*:
  "It's royalty's night out
  But please put the light out—
The Queen may be had, but not seen."

1953*

168. HINC ILLÆ LACRIMÆ

There was a young fellow named Randitt
Who decided to be a love bandit.
  But when he rolled in girls' arms
  And they unleashed their charms,
He found that his heart couldn't stand it.

1967A-1975.

169

A housewife from Rehoboth Acres
Got fed up with door-to-door fakers.
  "Each one, I find,
  Has *one* thing on his mind!"
Such was her lament to her makers.

ff. 1961A.

170

An old maid whom one fondly remembers
Said, "My days are now clearly September's.
All my fires have burned low—
I'll admit that it's so—
But your poker feels great in my embers!"

1972.

171

There was a young girl of renown
Who'd been made by each male in her town.
Her morals were loose
As the bowels of a goose,
And her eyes were a sad rectum brown.

1948.

172

A horny young major named Riggle
Took a 31st nurse for a jiggle.
She said, "Christ, what a screw!
All the bastard could do
Was three little jerks and a wiggle."

1944.

173

Said a young bridegroom boarding at Rye,
To his bride who was dreadfully shy:
"Now we're properly wed
And together in bed,
If you *can't,* you can bloody well try!"

1973.

174

"It's a young wife I need," said the sage,
"Who'll react to my sexual rage.
My old girl's got no spring,
And I do the whole thing—
Damn hard work for a man of my age!"

1973.

175

The cute little schoolteacher said,
As she gleefully hopped into bed :
  " If the lads and the lasses
  In my hygiene classes
Could see me right now, they'd drop DEAD! "

1965.

176. RIGHT ON !

I was never thought clever at school,
And by some was considered a fool.
  But at all Cupid's stunts
  Where they prove stupid cunts,
It's the duds like me last out the spool.

1973.

177

A lewd polo player named Schwartz
Spied a blonde wearing flesh-colored shorts.
  He skipped the next chukker
  Expressly to fukker—
That's what's nice about out-of-door sports!

1965.

178. HISSES FROM THE MRS. (II)

You can't blame me, dear husband, for scorning
A cock that just shrinks without warning.
  If *you* had a tiddly
  As game as my widdly,
I'd keep you plugged in until morning!

1973.

179

He was known as a wonderful screw,
With his dink in the pink all day through.
  But those great days of plenty
  Were through after twenty :
Now the ink in his dink has turned blue.

1970A.

180

Said an unhappy female named Sears :
" The world is just full of those queers!
Every party I go to
There's no one to say *no* to ;
The men swish about waggling their rears. "

1965.

181

The thoughts of the Playboy on sex
Are seldom if ever complex.
He comes in a trice
Which is not very nice,
And *not* what his Bunny expects.

1965A.

182

" As the curtains get shabbier and shabbier,
His Lordship gets crabbier and crabbier.
I must really admit
I'm the reason for it,
For my figure gets flabbier and flabbier! "

1973.

183

Give a thought to the Empress of Sheba,
Who thought Solomon called her *Mein Liebe.*
She brought him wild asses,
And grapes from Parnassus,
Whilst he gave her—what?—heeba-jeeba.

1959*

184

There's nothing like living in sin
If you've got a nice place to live *in,*
Not to mention a gal
Who is more than a pal,
With a hole that just fits your pin.

1967K.

185

There was once a professor named Snife
Who grew tired of foxhole life.
He longed for the class-room,
Where he had more ass-room,
And nights in bed with his wife.

1944.

186

When you lay a young girl on the sod,
It isn't the size of your prod,
It's the way that you diddle
Your ladyfriend's middle
That improves her relations with God.

1975.

187

There was a young lady of Spain
Who took off her clothes on the train.
A brave matador
Fucked her twice on the floor,
And once on the plain in the rain.

1975.

188

It seems a young damsel named Spencer,
Than whom few young damsels are denser,
Was beguiled by the flattery
Of a satyr named Slattery . . .
What later occurred we must censor!

1966.

189

A buxom young beauty of Spitz
Bared lovely, voluptuous tits,
Provoking a Pole
Till his spunk filled her hole
While his hands had her squirming in fits.

1953U.

[190]

" Listen, bud, " cried the maiden from Spitz,
" You'll find all gals' crotches have splits.
I've the rag on today,
So there'll be no bed play—
And take your big mitts off my tits! "

1966.

191

Said a hot-holed young siren in Stead :
" For weeks Peter's pecker's been dead.
If I don't get laid soon
By that impotent goon,
I'll be found in some other guy's bed. "

1965.

192. FOOTPRINTS ON THE DASHBOARD

Junior sex in my auto must stop,
Or my son must locate a new prop.
What's so disconcertible
In my poor old convertible
Are those high-heel holes punched through the top.

1970A.

193

" We feel, " said the Lady of Strand,
" That the park on the beach is just grand.
There are plenty of benches
For young lads and their wenches,
And their fannies are out of the sand. "

1975.

194

Said Napoleon, Emperor Supreme,
While scouting around for a queen :
" I'd much rather squeeza
Maria Louisa,
Than sleep with that bitch Josephine. "

1945.

195

Some girls get unduly suspicious
When you paw at their *corpus delicious.*
    They claim it's just rudeness,
    When really it's lewdness,
And your intentions are wholly lubricious.

1965.

196

A distinguished professor from Swarthmore
Had a date with a sexy young sophomore.
    As quick as a wink
    He stripped to his dink,
But he found that the sophomore'd got off more.

1966A.

197

A promiscuous housewife named Tabors
Is serviced by all her male neighbors.
    Said she, "Though it's boring
    To do all this whoring,
It *does* sort of lighten my labors."

1966.

198. COLLEGE DAZE

Those youngsters not out of their teens
Are impatient of lectures by Deans,
    On restraining desires
    And banking the fires
That burn in their skirts and their jeans.

[199]

They go on exerting their wills,
They use neither condoms nor Pills,
    They dooes what they pleases,
    Catch *ghastly* diseases,
And their poor parents pick up the bills.

1970A.

200

The bride, pinioned down in Room Ten,
Sent out for a meal, now and then.
    Said she, " Sex is sweet,
    But I still hafta eat ;
Willya slide off a minute, please, Ben? "

1965.

201

Said a bright young teenager from Texas :
" I'm certainly glad there's two sexes.
    For fucking's a pleasure
    That boys and girls treasure—
It prevents all those Freudian complexes. "

1965.

202

At the sight of my neighbor's glad thighs,
Old Faithful makes efforts to rise.
    But after ten nights
    Of her bedroom delights,
The tail-light burns low in my eyes.

1966.

203. FAMOUS LAST WORDS

If intercourse causes thrombosis,
While continence gives you neurosis,
    I'd prefer to expire
    In the flames of desire
Than live on in the mess of psychosis.

1966A.

204

A dizzy young dancer named Tillie
Said, " Willy, you're perfectly silly.
    What's wrong with your noodle?
    I said diddle, not doodle—
You're going to lay me today, willy-nilly! "

1965.

205

Said an old English gent, a real toff :
“ Fill up your glasses! Let’s quaff
To mini-skirt joys
Which enable the boys
To begin where their fathers left off! ”

1968A.

206

There once lived two elves in the trees,
Who made love ’ midst the rustle of leaves.
With a prick like a pimple,
And a cunt like a dimple,
They screwed with the greatest of ease.

1945R.

207

For those two little birds in the tree,
Or for rabbits and cats, you’ll agree,
To mate female with male
Is the point of life’s tale,
So why this reluctance with me?

1973.

208. DOLL TEARSHEET’S SONG

I’ll dance upon tables and trip upon trenchers,
And lie with the lads—all the best of your wenchers :
So spend all your shillings,
Your pounds and your pence ;
’ Twill all be worth nothing a hundred years hence!

[209]

Come, spend all your substance on wenching and wine,
The grave or the poorhouse will have all in time :
Why struggle for honours,
Why cudgel for pence?—
’ Twill all be forgotten a hundred years hence!

1976A.

210. ALL THE HORSEMEN KNEW 'ER

A whorish horsewoman named Trott
Just loved to give samples of twat.
    Every day without fail
    There were males on her tail:
All the horsemen knew 'er as hot!

1966.

211

Said an unhappy cocksman named Tuck:
"Some nights a guy's shit out of luck.
    For there seldom is heard
    A discouraging word
To match Millie's '*No, I won't fuck!*'"

1965.

212

There was a young lady whose twat
Her lover could never make hot.
    Said she, as his javelin
    Ripped into her ravelin':
"I hope *you're* having fun, 'cause I'm not."

1959J.

213

So here's to the lady named Twenn,
Who loves lying under the men!
    That way, when she's screwing,
    She knows what she's doing,
Though she gets a flat arse now and then.

1966.

214

Though the Boers on South Africa's veldt
Perhaps don't appear very svelte,
    Those sexy Boer dollies
    They sure get their jollies
When the Boers poke their pricks in their pelt.

1965.

215

There's a story they tell about Venus
Who, while taking Adonis's penis,
    Exclaimed, " Whoa! my love,
    Draw it back and then shove
Till there's nothing but gism between us. "

1948.

216

Girls polish the *membrum virile*
Of that lustful old satyr, O'Reilly.
    He lures them indoors
    And slips down their drawers,
Gets their little cracks quivering highly!

1976A.

217

Our favorite lay-date, Miss Visser,
We could poke 'er and stroke 'er and kiss 'er,
    And fuck 'er at will—
    We'd be doing it still,
But she up and left town : God! we miss 'er!

1965.

218

The wife of the raider Von Luckner
Admitted her husband was stuckner.
    She oft went to sea with him
    In order to be with him,
And to give him the pleasure of fuckner.

1948.

219

There once was an amorous WAC
Who wanted a prick in her crack.
    She met up with a jerk
    Who made *her* do the work—
The result was a crick in her back.

1948.

220

A sad old ex-satyr named Weir
Remarked as he wept in his beer :
“ As a sexual hero
My status is zero—
I ain't had it up for a year. ”

1965.

221

The love life of many hot wenches
Occurs in parked cars and park benches,
Porch rockers and bed,
Where they're happy to spread ;
But *do* avoid wet-bottomed trenches!

1965.

222. MAYBE BETTER?

An observant young man of the West
Said : “ I've found out by personal test,
That men who make passes
At girls who wear glasses
Get just as good ass as the rest. ”

1966.

223

There was an old man from Westphalia
Who was always prepared to regalia
With lewd exposés
Of his numerous lays,
And descriptions of their genitalia.

1953.

224

Sighed a newlywed damsel of Wheeling :
“ A honeymoon seems so appealing.
But for nearly two weeks
I've heard only bed squeaks,
And seen nothing but cracks in the ceiling! ”

1965.

225. BEDIQUETTE FOR BEGINNERS

As a dentist he'll say, " Open wide! "
And you as his hot, willing bride
Will spread your plump thighs
Like you did for us guys,
And guide hubby's pecker inside.

[226]

As a plumber, the poor silly fool
Will do as he does as a rule :
Your show of affection
Should cause an erection,
But you'll find he's forgotten his tool!

[227]

As an ad man, your bridegroom will say,
Just before your first church-sanctioned lay,
On beholding your hole :
" Let's run it up a pole,
And see if a breeze flaps it today. "

[228]

As a golfer, he'll harden his bun
When you're stripped for coitional fun,
And with a stiff stroke
Spread your hips for the poke,
And make his first real hole-in-one!

[229]

As an electrician, young Burkitt
Will say with a bit of a smirk, " It
Now isn't a sin,
So I'm going to plug in,
And I hope we don't run a short circuit! "

1966.

230

A rapscallion stallion of Witter
Said : " I am the local pinch-hitter.
The sex-deprived wives
Let me lighten their lives—
I leave many a twatter a-twitter! "

1966.

231

There was an old woman from Wooster
Who wanted the farmer's young rooster.
" Do give me that cock
That's as hard as a rock. "
" Not me! " said the farmer, and goosed her.

1970A.

232. COITO ERGO SUM

Till explained by that wise Dr. X,
What did grandmama know about sex?
And poor grandfather too,
Did he know what to do?
Or, when at it, foresee its effects?

1973.

233

A sex-starved professor at Yale
Planned for weeks how to get him some tail :
He would wink, now and then,
At both women and men,
But with all that he managed to fail.

1965.

234

You may not believe me, and yet,
Old gals are the very best bet.
They don't yell, tell, or swell,
And they fuck hard as hell,
For it may be the last one they'll get!

1967A-1975.

II

ORGANS

235

There's a very hot babe at the Aggies
Who's to men what to bulls a red rag is.
The seniors go round
Hanging down to the ground,
And one extra-large Soph has to drag his.

1948.

236

You Women's Lib gals won't agree,
But dependent on men you must be :
You'll still need a him
With a rod firm and trim,
To puggle your water-drains free!

1973.

237

The genital area of Ann
Will accommodate any size man,
From the wee that cause titters
To the mighty twat-splitters
That cause screams peasants hear in Japan.

1965.

238

Getting Cheryl to shed her apparel
Is like shooting goldfish in a barrel.
But her genital area
Is so vast it'll scareya,
And you venture inside at your peril.

1965.

239

A half-Spanish Moor named Arribia
Engaged in some whoring in Libya,
And developed his joint
To the interesting point
Where it hung all the way to his tibia.

1953.

240

There was a young lass of Ashtabula
Who spent a night in the village cooler
For betting the Judge
A half pound of fudge
Twice his length wouldn't cover a ruler.

1948.

241

There once was a judge of Assize
Whose bollocks were not the same size.
He'd look at the right
With a gasp of delight,
But the left one brought tears to his eyes.

1956U.

242

Cried Miss Pratt : " What are *you* staring at?
I know—you don't have to say that!
All you guys want of me
Is a poke where I pee,
And it's pounding my ass mighty flat! "

1966.

243. EVERY TIME !

Said a snooty young thing from Australia :
" Now concerning the male genitalia,
Men brag of their size
Till you're sure you've a prize,
Then exhibit *wee* paraphernalia. "

1965.

244

A buxom young steno named Baines
At her work took particular pains.
  But the principal feature
  Of this charming young creature
Was she ran more to bosom than brains.

1966A.

245

There were two brothers named Baird
Who thought all things should be shared.
  With tits, which are two,
  Their arrangement would do,
But with cunt, which is one, 'twas absurd.

1953.

246

In Rome, well preserved behind bars,
They found in a cache of old jars,
  The cunnus of Venus,
  Great Jupiter's penis,
And, they *think*, the left knocker of Mars.

1970A.

247

The penis of long-peckered Baste
He keeps neatly coiled 'round his waist.
  When a girl shows affection
  He uncoils in erection,
And she's knocked galley-west by his haste!

1966.

248

A yogi from far-off Beirut
For women did not care a hoot.
  But his organ would stand
  In a manner quite grand
When a snake charmer played on his flute.

1967A-1975.

249

Lady Reginald Humphries (belie
-ve it or don't) had a vulva so wee,
    she disposed of the sexual
    needs of Lord Rex through a l-
audably disciplined flea.

1944E.

250

A great big fat cop of Belle Isle
Had a pecker that made the whores smile.
    It was teeny and skewed,
    He could only get screwed
When the girl kept on twisting meanwhile.

1975A.

251

A Red politician named Beria
Had a limb of such length that nary a
    Girl that he tailed
    But woefully wailed :
" You're up in the whooping-cough area. "

1954J.

252. NIL DESPERANDUM

There was a poor freak from Berlin
Whose balls hung from under his chin.
    Despite Nature's joke
    His morale never broke,
Though shaving did cause him chagrin.

1960.

253

Another young man from Berlin
Had a prick most exceedingly thin.
    With this long, slender peter
    He could screw a ureter
If he only knew how to get in.

1948.

254

Said a fat old whore of Big Rise:
"I can hardly believe me own eyes!
But there waves a pecker
That's a certain cunt-wrecker,
An' I ain't fuckin' none o' that size!"

1966.

255

A mechanical marvel was Bill,
He'd a tool that was shaped like a quill.
With this fabulous dink
He could squirt purple ink,
And decorate lampshades at will.

1970A.

256. FRINGE BENEFITS

Whenever you go on a binge
With a girl somewhat plump, do not cringe
At the layers of fat
Where her pussy is at,
You'll find benefits all 'round the fringe.

1975.

257

An astonished young lady named Bissell
Let out a lascivious whistle,
When her boyfriend stripped nude.
He remarked, "Though it's crude,
Please observe that ain't muscle—it's missile!"

1966.

258

A sad-eyed old satyr named Blaine
Finds his dangler a cause to complain.
In its youth a real terror,
Now it's failed its old wearer—
The mere thought of it gives him great pain.

1965.

259

There once was a fellow named Blatt
Whose girlfriend was built rather flat.
    But I've heard that he'll say
    To his friends any day :
"I'm glad to exchange tit for twat."

ff. 1968A.

260

Arrived late, 'twas the doctor's mild boast
That he'd severed a penis, almost.
    From the hostess a groan :
  "You cut clear to the bone?"
And the men drank a toast to their host.

1945A.

261

There was a topographer bold
Who fucked a fat lady, I'm told.
    He mapped every cranny
    She had in her fanny,
And fucked every wrinkle and fold.

1975.

262

Said a brilliant young surgeon named Booling :
"Till now, we have only been fooling.
    Soon it hardly will vex us
    To interchange sexes ;
It's simply a case of retooling."

1970A.

263

There was a seductive Brazilian
Who tinted her twat bright vermilion.
    Admiring her work,
    She said with a smirk :
"That cunt, she is one in a million!"

1965.

264

A joyful young lady named Brenda
Was born with a double pudenda.
    This made her so rigorous
    You had to be vigorous,
Or you couldn't get on her agenda.

1975.

265

Another young lady, named Brickley,
The hair on her crotch sprouted thickly.
    She made dates in advance
    To give suitors a chance,
For they never could find it too quickly.

1975.

266. THE HIGHER LEARNING (II)

There was a young coed named Bridget,
Wore skirts far too short for a midget.
    Every lad in the class
    Knew the map of her ass,
And each crease and crevasse of her twidget.

[267]

Another young girl, from Arabia,
You wouldn't believe her behavia.
    She sat in each class
    With her skirt 'round her ass,
And winked at the prof with her labia!

1948-1970A.

268

The busty display of Miss Bristol
Gets the fellows as hot as a pistol.
    Her plastic bikini
    Is terribly weeny,
And her *reason's* transparent as crystal.

1966.

269

A long-peckered lecher named Brock
Used a barrow to carry his cock.
    He has such massive balls
    He can't go through halls,
And must leave them at home under lock.

[270]

So here's this lewd fellow named Brock,
Who loves to play golf with his cock.
    Its ungodly size
    Horrifies other guys,
And gals shit their pants from sheer shock!

1966.

271

There was a young lady named Brown
Who taught her vagina to clown.
    It could nibble a plum
    And chew JuicyFruit gum,
So her cunt was the freshest in town.

1975.

272

A leprous old bastard named Bryce
Had balls that were spotted like dice.
    They were worthless as could be
    In the way that balls should be,
But a fabulous gambling device!

1953.

273

Queen Mary found Scotsmen are built
With a truly remarkable tilt.
    To her royal surprise
    Every member would rise
Every time she reached under a kilt.

1958.

274

A lewd-minded dolly named Bunce,
By nature endowed with two cunts,
At night dreams & drools
Of a man with two tools
Who could fuck both vaginas at once!

1966.

275

An old Ozark farmer with bunions
Supported his sore feet on trunnions.
This let his dong dangle
At just the right angle
To use it for plowing the onions!

1965.

276

There was a young flapper named Bunny
Who asked, " What is wrong with my cunny?
I've tried fornication
With men of each nation,
But my twitchet's still itchy—it's funny. "

1950.

277

There was a young fellow named Buster
Who had pricks in a multiple cluster.
He could have an erection
In every direction,
And afterwards serve as a duster.

1948.

278

There was a young lady from Byer
Whose hemlines got higher and higher.
But the size of her thighs
Provoked merely surprise,
And extinguished the flames of desire.

1974A.

279

A beautiful Lydy named Butts
Was God, gas, grease, gamboge, and guts.
The dairies of Dorset
That bulged from her corset
Were highly esteemed by the Knuts.

[280]

I wanted that sensitive slut's
Young soul to bed out in my hut's
Back garden.—A rose
To bewitch both my nose
And my eyes, but—Oh, too many but's!

1924C.

281

There was a shorthorn from Calatt
Whose pecker was flabby and flat.
He dosed it with yeast—
It's a footrule, at least,
And what could be stiffer than that?

1950.

282. OLD CLASSIC

An Aesthetic young miss of Calcutta
Set all the men's hearts in a flutter.
Her bubs were immense,
Her arse was intense,
And her cunt was too utterly utter!

1881*

283

A sexy young girl from Cape Cod
Had to carry her breasts in a hod.
Her shape was perfection
And caused many an erection,
But when she bent over, MY GOD!

1968.

284

There was a young man of Cape Hatteras
Who kept poking holes in the matteras.
Alas and alack,
'Twas his wife's narrow back-
side : he'll have to get one with a fatter ass.

1970A.

285

There's a luscious young charmer named Carmen
Who fucks for bums, boxers, and barmen.
Says she, " The effete
Have more brains, but less meat—
I prefer hairy fellows who *are* men! "

1965.

286

There was a young chippy named Carol
Had a twat like a crack in a barrel.
You could huff and could puff,
And could busily stuff,
But your pecker was never in peril. (Or Carol.)

1953.

287. THE STRENUOUS LIFE

So hairy a cunt had Miss Carrier
That no man could get past the barrier.
That is, no man but Brungle,
Who had lived in the jungle,
And crashed his way through with a terrier.

1975.

288

Then there was that man of Cathay
Who said to a lady one day :
" I've got nothing in mind
Except your behind,
And that in a *very* big way! "

1967K.

289

There was a young Chinaman, Chang,
Who had a gargantuan whang.
    Said he, " You just wait
    Till I reel it out straight,
And I'll give you the world's biggest bang! "

1968.

290

There was a young lady named Chard
Whose cunt was exceedingly hard.
    Even Buster McGuckin,
    Who was used to rough fuckin',
Could not get inside without lard.

1948.

291

Said a Guardsman observing his charger :
" I *do* wish my tassel were larger.
    Could I change with my horse,
    I would do so, of course,
And put in for high stud-fees like Rajah. "

1973.

292

There was a young lady of Chester
Who fell in love with a jester.
    Her breath came out hotly
    At the sight of his motley,
But the head of his wand most impressed her.

1945.

293

A lascivious young lecher named Chew
Had balls that were crooked and blue.
    But he used them with ease
    On the heathen Chinese,
For their coozies were also askew.

1948.

294. JUST THIS ONCE . . .

There was a young girl named Cholmondeley,
Witty, warm-hearted, and colmondeley.
No girl could be finer
But she lacked a vaginar,
A sad and arresting anolmondeley.

1944A.

295

With his Chinese singsong girl young Christopher
Soon found why all men were quite pissed off her.
Her cunt, if you please,
Was off ninety degrees,
And not one man in ten got the gist of her.

1975.

296

The curly cunt-hair on cute Claire
Makes the men in the nudist camp stare.
And like tigers they fight
To see *who* spends the night
Splitting open Claire's pubical hair.

1966.

297

An inquisitive bridegroom named Clyde
Tried hard to look up in his bride.
He cried, " Dammit! cunts
Get small all at once,
But they certainly start plenty wide. "

1965.

298

An impotent fellow named Condrey
Sent his flabby old cock to the laundry.
They returned it in March,
Straight and stiffened with starch :
How to wear his pants now is his quandary.

1965.

299

There was a young Commonwealth copper
Whose pride was a really fine whopper :
Twice 'round the bed,
Then over his head,
And then up his arse for a stopper.

1945R.

300

The joyprong on Ichabod Creep
Makes trollops he trafficks with weep.
His twenty-inch tool
Gets small use, as a rule,
For you find damn few whores half that deep!

1966.

301

There was a young lady of Crewe
Whose cunt was so straight and so true
That the navy, when fighting,
Could use it for sighting,
And at full range could sink a canoe.

1975.

302

That beautiful lady, Culard,
Said : " Niggers earn all our regard.
My dinge has a cock
As hard as a rock,
And in length it is almost a yard! "

1950.

303

There was a young lady whose cunt
Was not placed exactly in front.
If you wanted to ride
You approached from the side,
Which, it must be allowed, is a stunt.

1948.

304

The toe of a postman from Dallas
Developed a sizable callus.
His wife wistfully said
How she wished that instead
It had been on the head of his phallus.

1967A.

305

Mighty proud of her snatch was Miss Datchett.
For hours she would just sit and scratch it,
And say with a smile:
" It has tone, it has style—
There ain't many snatches to match it! "

1965.

306

The passionate ass on Miss Day
Is a great place for sexing and play.
Voicing animal sounds
As her comely bum bounds,
She insists you repeat right away.

1965.

307

The sex kitten gasped when friend Decker
Brought forth his long, red-headed pecker.
After one frightened glance
She pissed her pink pants,
And cried, " Not for *me,* that cuntwrecker! "

1966.

308

Once a young British army deserter
Asked his girlfriend if intercourse hurt her.
She replied, " Sometimes, Tommy,
If it's big, like salami,
But not when it's like your frank*furt*er. "

1955J.

309. PECUNIA OLET

There was a young girl from Des Moines,
A whiz at rotating her loins.
  What's even more strange,
  Her cunt could make change,
With nickels and dimes and such coins.

1948A.

[310]

Another young lady named Hunt
Could pick up loose coins with her cunt.
  But it couldn't make change,
  Which narrowed her range,
And kept her from playing the Paramount.

1970A.

311

No wonder that man of Devizes
Is the winner of so many prizes.
  His staff, when at ease,
  Goes twice 'round his knees,
And it tickles his chin when it rises!

1969A.

312

A young sex professor named Dingle
Made all the girls' nerve-endings tingle.
  And his groovy red cock
  Caused a grave mental block
In those who preferred to stay single.

1974A.

313

The *derrière* Carrie displays
Never fails to delight and amaze.
  She puts every ounce
  Into use with a bounce!
And her boyfriend's ecstatic for days.

1966.

314

Said a diffident lady named Drood,
The first time she saw a man nude:
“I'm glad I'm the sex
That's concave, not convex,
For I *don't* fancy things that protrude.”

1965.

315. GRAFFOOTTI

There was a young man from Dundalk
Whose penis was made out of chalk.
He would futter his spouse
Out in front of their house,
And mark up his score on the walk.

1963B.

316

There was an odd man of Dundee
Whose pecker was shaped like a key!
Said he: “If gals' peeholes
Were all shaped like keyholes,
What a helluva world this'd be!!”

1966.

317

There was a young lady from Durbar
Who swore that no cock could perturb her,
Till a Turk from Khartoum
Knocked the shit from her womb
With his fifteen-inch cunny-disturber.

1950.

318

There was a young fellow named Dutton
Whose balls were the size of a button.
But he had a great dong,
Over ten inches long—
And what could he do with it? Nuttin'.

1953.

319

An athlete there was of East Anglia
Whose sinews were masses of ganglia.
    But his racing he ceased
    When his penis decreased,
While his balls grew progressively danglier.

1945.

320

Cried a long-peckered person named Ed:
'I *hate* fucking flat on a bed.
    With my twenty-inch tool
    I look like a fool,
For I'm up near the ceiling, instead!"

1966.

321

A daring young doctor named Edison
Decided old standards to jettison.
    He measured men's tools
    By linguistical rules,
And established new canons of medicine.

1954J.

322

Two circus girls, richly endowed
For bosoms won applause long and loud.
    But on tour in Berlin
    They just couldn't win—
Two bare-assed baboons held the crowd.

1973.

323. YOU BETTER BELIEVE IT!

She knew all about men, thought Eulalia,
And all about their genitalia.
    When along came a Negro—
    They grow larger than we grow—
And distorted her paraphernalia.

1945R.

324

Said a passionate lady of Ewell :
" The fellows of course want my jewel.
But I make my selection
By length-in-erection—
Twelve inches is fine, as a rewell. "

1965.

325

A mulatto with cream-colored eyes
Is of note for the shape of her thighs :
Ellipsoid in contour,
You just can't get on to 'er ;
Every movement occasions surprise.

1953.

326

There was a young man of Fall River
Whose tool was as thin as a sliver.
It would dart in and out
Like a speckled brook trout,
But the scales always made the girls shiver.

1972A.

327

The figure of lovely Miss Farrow
Resembles not willow but yarrow.
'Twould be rather a fraud
If you called her a *broad,*
For she goes with her beaux like a *narrow.*

1970.

328. MAN, THE ANIMAL

Of all the mammalian features
On our lovable feminine creatures,
I go blindly at once
For their tits and their cunts,
And I suck and I fuck without teachers!

1965.

329

There was once a young lady of Fez
(She went by the name of Chavez)
    And her tits, we are told,
    If completely unrolled
Would stretch from Madrid to Juarez.

1969.

330

Yiddle, the orchestra fiddler,
Has such a magnificent diddler
    That girls, on first viewing,
    Scream in shock : " Nothing doing! "
Though now and then one lets him twiddler.

1965.

331

There was an old fellow named Fife
Who had lived a lascivious life.
    When his organ was limp
    As an overboiled shrimp,
He brought what was left to his wife.

1967A-1975.

332

There was a young man from the Fort
Whose prick was uncommonly short.
    But the dome of St. Paul's
    Wouldn't cover his balls,
And he never spent less than a quart.

1953.

333

A talented *frotteur* from France
Had singular nerves in his glans.
    With one casual trail
    He would learn each detail
Of the size, shape, and taste in gals' pants.

1971 *ff*.

334

A curious fellow named Frank
Had a penis shaped just like a crank.
  To achieve an insertion
  Was quite an exertion,
But a friendly whore gave it a yank.

1955A.

335. VARIATIONS ON A THEME

The cock of a fellow named Fred
Was adorned with a corkscrew head.
  When at last he laid eyes
  On a cunt the right size,
He was foiled by a left-handed thread!

[336]

His cock like a corkscrew expanded,
A spiral vagina demanded.
  His search lasted years
  And ended in tears—
The thread of her cunt was left-handed.

1969A.

337

Odette, nationality French,
Would open her cunt with a wrench.
  When once she forgot
  To bolt up her slot,
She killed twenty men with the stench.

1957A.

338

An old fornicator of Friant
Whose cock, year by year, became pliant,
  Remarked, " As to screwing,
  It's been my undoing,
And the whores now have lost a good client. "

1966.

339

A silly young bride had the gall
To laugh at her husband's left ball.
    She had him so flustered
    He finally blustered:
"Well, dear, your clitor-is too small."

1971 *ff.*

340

Have you heard when Mahatma Gandhi
Stepped up to the bar for a brandy?
    He lifted his sheet
    To wipe off his cheek,
And the barkeep said, "Christ! it's a dandy."

1945R.

341

Big tits on the stripper, Miss Gill,
At the topless joint give us a thrill.
    Their soft, swaying motions
    Give all the boys notions,
As she shakes them with infinite skill.

1965.

342

Said a girl who bought Kotex at Gimbels:
"Men all think of sex and sex symbols.
    And they just feel disgust
    For my tiny, wee bust—
For brassieres all I use are two thimbles!"

1965.

343

There was a young man of Glengarry
Whose cock was too heavy to carry.
    So he put it on wheels
    And hired trained seals
For his opening night in Wilkes-Barre.

1945-1970A.

344

There was a young lady named Glubb
Whose cunt was as big as a tub.
  There was room for her groom
  With a mop and a broom,
And some space for an evergreen shrub.

1975.

345. FEMALE CHAUVINIST

Henrietta was peevish and glum:
Women's Lib said, "You're under man's thumb."
  So they doctored her widdly
  And made her a tiddly—
Now she's Henry, and at her by gum!

1973.

346

A busty young girl of Grand Prairie
Has tits hardly seen in a dairy.
  But in matters of sex
  These have splendid effects
On all but the senile and fairy.

1965.

347

The round, rosy rear of Miss Greer
Has been voted the "Arse of the Year"
  By the nudists who know her,
  And it's hailed, furthermo-er,
By the pratwatcher, cocksman, and queer.

1966.

348

There was a young lady named Grimes
Who spent all her nickels and dimes
  On satin and lace
  To hold her in place
And keep her abreast of the times.

1945.

349

Oh the truth makes us titwatchers groan,
For that lush-breasted gal in Athlone
Whose bust looked unmatchable
Proved to have both detachable :
The poor thing has *no* tits of her own!

1965.

350. THE UNSCREWTABLE ORIENT

There was a young sailor named Guest
Who was struggling to get on the nest.
Said his young Chinese wanton :
" Don't forget you're in Canton,
The tramlines all run East to West! "

1968A.

351. RIDDLE

What's reddish and roundish and hairy,
And hangs from a bush light and airy ;
Often hidden away
From the broad light of day
Beneath a stiff prick?—A gooseberry.

1973.

352

The bosom on lovely Miss Hamill
No bra will, I'm sure, ever trammel.
I forget woe and care
When I leer at her pair—
Thank God that I am a mammal!

1965.

353

Under Harry, cried heated-up Harriet,
As her loverboy started to bury it :
" I love your doohickey,
But it must be quite sticky,
And an awful darn nuisance to carry it."

1966.

354

There was a young man named Hasdrubabel
Who had only one real and one rubber ball.
    Not to be out-witted,
    His wife was two-teated :
She had one rubber bub, and one rubbable.

1948.

[355]

Another young fellow, named Hatch,
His wife had a cubical snatch.
    In no way out-witted
    (She was also three-titted)
He possessed a square root to match.

1953-1970A.

356. SONATA APPASSIONATA

Said the famous conductor, John Hatchett,
To a young lady cellist named Datchet :
  "You have, 'twixt your thighs,
    My dear, a great prize,
An instrument noted for beauty and size—
So please don't just sit there and scratch it!"

1974A.

357

There was a young lady whose heinie
Was round, pretty, pink, soft and shiny.
    But she took all her joys
    With immature boys,
As her twat was so terribly tiny.

1948.

358

The breasts of a lady named Helen
Were the size of a young watermelon.
    When bared to the breeze
    Men's passion would freeze,
And they'd run away, screamin' and yellin'.

1945-1970A.

359

I know a young medico, Hodges,
Whose penis, I've found, often lodges
In nurses and patients
Who like its dilations,
Its curves, twists, and manifold dodges.

1948.

360

There was a young man from Hong Kong
Whose pride was his elegant dong.
When girls asked, " Do you use it? "
He replied, " Just amuse it,
And you'll get it too much and too long. "

1948.

361

There was a young maiden named Hoople
Whose bosom was triple, not duple.
She had one tit removed,
But it grew back improved :
At present Miss Hoople's quadruple.

1953.

362

An Eskimo maiden named Horner
Was inspecting her puss-in-a-corner.
She said, "Jesus, what hair!
It looks like a bear.
If papa goes by, I'm a goner! "

1950.

363

Kay wants a man hung like a horse,
So I'm picked as a matter of course.
When all other dates fail
I can count on her tail,
Which is *twice* as hot since her divorce.

1965.

364

A stalwart young Klansman named Hugh
Once dreamed he turned into a Jew.
He awoke with a shock
And examined his cock,
And found the poor thing had turned blue.

1971B-1974A.

365

Oh! Mrs. Humby, Mrs. Humby
(Oh, how can your kisses so numb be?)
If your face is so fair
That's exposed to the air,
How beautifully white must your bum be.

1882*

366

A peculiar young lady named Hunt
Has cunts both behind and in front.
She's hot for coition
In any position
That the hard-peckered try for a stunt.

1965.

367

To a young virgin friend said Miss James:
"Sex is The Most in fun games.
What's pointed *at* you
Ain't like on a statue,
For where marble dangles, meat aims!"

1966.

368

A busy young fellow named Jasper,
The size of whose cock was a gasper,
Met hardly a maid
He hadn't waylaid:
He'd exhibit his tool, and enclasp 'er.

1971 *ff.*

369

There was a young fellow named Jerry
Whose prick was the longest in Kerry.
When he came to a stream
He would lower his beam,
And skim folks across like a ferry.

1948.

370

Remarked a hot dolly named Jewel :
" What I want is a real fuckin' fool!
A big-muscle boy
Is a visual joy,
But *I* want the fool with the tool! "

1966.

371

There was a young fellow named Jones
Whose girlfriend had prominent bones,
And more than her share
Of superfluous hair
Around all her erogenous zones.

1974A.

372. FREAK PLAY

Said the two-peckered goon to Miss Kelly :
" I'm sorry my fucking's so smelly.
But to put it quite blunt,
With you with one cunt,
My other cock blows on your belly. "

1965.

373

I have fun when I peek through her keyhole
And watch my girl play with her peehole.
I would willingly screw her,
But I can't get in*to* her,
She has such an incredibly wee hole!

1966.

374

The wild fighting pasha Khalil
Had muscles much harder than steel.
Just the clink of his balls,
As he stormed through the halls,
Made his concubines titter and squeal.

1967K.

375

A daughter of joy from Khartoum
Had a vagina noted for room:
Enormously clitoris'd,
Her cunny would fit a wrist
Pushed all the way up to her womb!

1950.

376

The one-balled new spouse of our Kitty
We feel is deserving of pity.
Except that the catch is
His one-balledness matches
Our Kitty, who has but one titty.

1966.

377

For his concert a flutist named Kress
Was in such a hurry to dress
That, on a high run,
His fly came undone—
His organ got raves from the press.

1970A.

378

A lusty old guy from Lahore
Had a penis of six feet or more.
You'd think he'd be glad
But instead he was sad—
He could use but the first three or four.

1948.

379

There's a buxom young wench in Lamar
Who has mammæ too copious by far.
    One luscious bazoom
    Fills up half the room,
And you can't go around her in par.

1948-1970A.

380. THE TITMAN SPEAKS

You can have all your super-assed lasses ;
A babe with Big Tits gets my passes.
    For a big, bouncey bust
    Stirs man's animal lust—
Big asses are just for the masses!

1965.

381

A concert musician named Liszt
Had a strange anatomical twist :
    It hung to his knees,
    And swung in the breeze,
But it only would work when he pissed.

1975A.

382

There was a young girl from Llandudno
Who married a batsman from Tudno.
    His midstump was small,
    He had no balls at all :
What he'd called the match for she did nud know.

1973.

383

A palæontologist, Locke,
Found a fossilized Jurassic cock.
  " Is it Tyrannosaurus?
    It's long, black, and porous—
And Christ, it's still hard as a rock! "

1974.

384. DAIRY MAID

A loathsome young lady named Lou
Had titties that hung to her shoe.
And her cunt was a wow,
For it sagged like a cow,
And when fucked from behind she would moo.

1975.

385

Said the bawdyhouse madam to Lyle,
As she viewed his sad prong with a smile:
"That poor little pimple
Looks more like a dimple—
Are you trying to start a new style?"

1966.

386

The penis of Grandfather Lynch
As a clothesline is used, in a pinch.
On the days his wife washes
He dons pipe and galoshes,
And reels the thing out with a winch!

1965.

387

There once was a well-hung machinist
Who danced with a cute little Venus.
"Please be careful," he said,
"When you step, where you tread.
That's twice now you've tromped on my penis."

1954A.

388

The boobies on young Miss McBean
Are the two cutest mammæ I've seen.
Which is why I propose
To follow my nose
To the valley that lies in between.

1965.

389

That super-cocked fellow, McDecker,
Is mighty damn proud of his pecker.
 In sexual clinches
 His turgid twelve inches
A girl finds will nigh onto wreck 'er!

1966.

390

There was a young man named MacDougal
Whose cock was bell-shaped like a bugle.
 Well adapted for pissing,
 'Twas delightful for kissing,
And for blissing that's known as con*ju*gal.

1945R.

391. PORCUPRIX

The dong of the Dean of McGill
Is adorned with a porcupine quill.
 "It looks odd," he agreed,
 "But the thing's guaranteed
To give the most frigid a thrill."

1945-1970A.

392

The cunt hair of young Miss McLees
She carefully parts when she pees.
 She resorts to this measure
 Not so much for the pleasure,
But she *must*—the hair hangs to her knees!

1965.

393

The left tit of sweet Miss McNair
I consider the best of her pair.
 When I sit at her right
 And squeeze it each night,
It sure makes her old parents stare.

1966.

394

The peach fuzz of young Miss McSweeney
Curls out from her teeny bikini.
  It's a glorious sight,
  To be viewed with delight,
And it stirs even grandpappy's weenie.

1965.

395. HANDS OFF!

The titties on Kitty McTwitty
Are the two biggest bubs in the city.
  Every titman that sees 'em
  Has this wild urge to squeeze 'em,
But it's "Just look; don't touch!"—more's the pity.

1965.

396

Cried whorish young Mrs. McWhorter:
"If that cock of yours was much shorter,
  You could never fuck *me*!
  Somewhere there must be
A man with a goddam ripsnorter!!"

1966.

397

A German composer named Mahler
Had his testes insured for a dollar.
  One ball was so small
  It was nothing at all;
The other, considerably smaller.

1970A.

398

A lass named Veronica Mapes
Sported mammæ the size of small grapes.
  She started to scratch 'em,
  In an effort to hatch 'em,
Till all that remained were the scrapes.

1953.

399

There was an Italian named Marc
Who pissed one night in the park.
  But the cops caught the peasant:
  His dong was fluorescent,
And glowed like a torch in the dark.

1945.

400

There was a young maiden named Marge.
Who dived in the nude from a barge.
  A man in a punt
  Disappeared up her cunt—
An organ admittedly large.

1948.

401

Said a modest young thing, Marguerite,
Whose charms were both neat and petite:
  "Though quite long, your prick is
  Not nearly as thick as
The tool of my *other* friend, Pete."

1968.

402

To his girl said the Cornish marine:
"You've the knobbiest coastline I've seen.
  To put into port
  Would be jolly good sport,
If the rest of the fleet hadn't *been.*"

1948.

403

Inserting one's sex in Miss Mavern
Is like poking a cane in a cavern.
  Were it in my possession
  I would rent a concession:
What a place to install a big tavern!

1965.

404

Say! Have you heard about old Henry Miller,
Whose specialty's the sexual thriller?
Though his ego (see *Sexus*)
Is as big as all Texas,
Can his prick really be such a killer?

1954A.

405

Said a plucky young girl in Monticello,
When she saw the big cock on a fellow:
"That oversize pecker
Looks like a cunt wrecker,
But let's try it, man—I ain't yellow!"

1965.

406

There was a young lady named Mudge,
All day long she ate candy and fudge.
Her ass was so fat,
It went *splat* when she sat,
And no one could get her to budge.

1967A-1975.

407

There was a young fellow from Munich
Who everyone thought was a eunuch.
But loudly he cried,
With a note of hurt pride:
"Just look at that bulge in my tunic!"

1948.

408

A pubescent young lady from Murray
Sighed, "I sure wish my cunt would get furry.
Each day with great care
I count every hair,
But, darn it! the fur just won't hurry!"

1965.

409

There was a young lady of Nantes
Whose figure was *très élégante.*
    But her cunt was so small
    It was no good at all,
Except for *la plume de ma tante.*

1954U.

410

It seems that a harlot in Natchez
Was blessed from birth with two snatches.
    With half her appliance
    She services clients—
The other is stuffed with book matches.

1966.

411. THE METER-PETER

There never was anything neater
Than the Bishop of Colchester's peter.
    In the heat of a clinch
    It would stretch from an inch
To just a bit short of a meter.

1948.

412

There was a suave swinger named Nello
With balls like a great, luscious jello.
    He'd screw, chew, and shunt
    Each available cunt—
A peculiarly randy-arsed fellow.

1971*ff.*

413

The penis of Ethelbert Nevin,
When on earth measured just inches seven.
    But when he reached Hell
    It started to swell,
And the head of it now pierces Heaven!

1954J.

414

A lady from lower New Hyde
Had a cunt so enormously wide,
Every fucking companion
Who fell in that canyon
Was lost for a fortnight inside.

1958.

415

A geologist down in New Mex'
Found a fossilized dinosaur's sex.
They're short, and all tend
To bend near the end,
And they're *covered* with funny brown specks.

1965.

416

A tit connoisseur from North Ealing
Said, " A flat-busted babe ain't appealing.
What you want's a BIG gland
You can knead with your hand,
And evoke groans and moans when you're feeling! "

1965.

417

A cunt-happy coot of North Galion
Is hung, so they say, like a stallion.
Effecting insertion
Takes grease and exertion,
And he drives the girls nuts with his dallyin'.

1966.

418

There was a young girl from Pei-tou
Who almost never said " No! "
She met up with a Winger,
Took one look at his stinger,
And said, " I'd prefer your big toe. "

1950R.

419

A young doctor peripatetic
Was testically very pathetic.
    The poor boy tried to swallow
    The balls of Apollo . . .
I hope you are all sympathetic.

1948.

420

The pendulous pecker on Pete
Protrudes to great length when in heat.
    This protuberant treasure
    Gives pussies great pleasure—
It's a fabulous pantsload of meat!

1965.

421

An unfortunate lady named Piles
Had the ugliest bottom for miles.
    A great surgeon took pity
    And made it quite pretty :
All dimples and pouting and smiles.

1966A.

422

There was a young man of Port Said
Whose penis grew tattered and frayed,
    Thus earning the jeers
    Of his Sadistic peers,
And complaints from the women he laid.

1945-1970A.

423. BACKYARD ASS-TRONOMY

There was a young fellow named Primmer
Whose arsehole was all of a skimmer.
    On a cold, frosty night
    It would sparkle quite bright,
But in daylight 'twas only a glimmer.

1956U.

424

There was a young lady named Pritchett
Who had a diminutive twitchet.
He stuck in ten inches ;
She squealed, " How it pinches!
Pray cut it in half, ere you bitch it. "

1950.

[425]

Another young lady, named Puckett,
Had a twitchet as big as a bucket.
An elephant's nose
Or a stiffened firehose
Were the only things able to fuck it.

1950.

426

There once was a handsome young punk
With a prick like an elephant's trunk.
When this prick pachydermatous
Sprayed a shower of sperm at us,
You could bathe head to foot in the spunk.

1957J.

427

There was a young man of Purdue
Who had not just one dick, but two.
He'd fuck two girls at once ;
And two dicks in two cunts
Gives a really phenomenal screw.

1956.

428

There once was a soldier named Purvis
Whose cock was the pride of the service.
They'd come in on trucks
To watch one of his fucks,
Though he always said, " Crowds make me nervous. "

1945.

429

In choosing the High King of Quong,
They measure the length of his dong.
    If he's nagged by his harem,
    The band plays to scare 'em,
And " God Save the Queen " is the song.

ff. 1970.

430

" Would I like some nookie? Well, rah-ther!
Are you the Smith son, or his father?
    Any small whippersnapper
    I prop in the crapper,
So unless you've nine inches, don't bother. "

1965.

431

That man is undoubtedly rare
Who can stare at a bare *derrière,*
    And be so unimpressed
    By Sweet Fanny, undressed,
That his flag doesn't wave in the air.

1965.

432. OH MANI ! PADMI HOKUM

Wise Hoagy, the yogi from Rawls,
Toots away as he sits on his balls.
    Thus parked on his glands,
    His vast penis stands,
The sight of which shocks and appalls.

[433]

Said the yogi, " My twisted position
Has deep meaning—it's not exhibition.
    My aura expands,
    Giving glow to my glands,
Thus increasing my powers of coition. "

1966.

434. ANOTHER MYSTERY SOLVED

Pubic hair is put there for a reason
That is evident in the cold season :
For the balls it's a muff,
For the rod it's a ruff,
And it keeps the vagina from freezin'.

1958.

435

A long-peckered midget named Red
Said, " I'm a hot cock on a bed!
Though sawed off for height,
Me pecker's a sight—
So get on that bed, kid, and *spread*! "

1966.

436

There was a young man of Regina
Who sampled all kinds of vagina.
Some were fat, some were thin,
Some were blacker than sin,
And some sideways (on ladies from China).

1975.

437

There was a young fellow named Rod,
Renowned for the size of his prod.
He attempted to stuff it
Up little Miss Muffett,
And the last words she spoke were : " My God! "

1975A.

438

To the aid of those impotent rummies
Whose tools dangle under their tummies,
Came a genius named Gardner
Who devised such a hardener
It erects even long-deceased mummies.

1966.

439

A little old man from St. Chester
Decided to tackle his sister.
    But all that he packed
    Was a wrinkled old sack,
And all that she had was a blister.

1932-1952L.

440

A horny young man from St. Jude
Carried both of his balls in a snood.
    They were so big and round
    That they dragged on the ground;
He was scared to go out in the nude.

1968.

441

A sinful old monk of Saint-Lô
Used to cool his jappáp in the snow.
    But no matter how frigid,
    The darn thing stayed rigid,
And *popped* when it got two below!

1970A.

442. OLYMPIC TRYOUT

An oversexed man from St. Paul
Had a cock as long as he was tall.
    When he had a wet dream
    He awoke with a scream,
As he pole-vaulted into the hall.

1949.

443

There was a young girl of Salina
Who had such a tiny vagina
    Men entered and left
    That diminutive cleft,
And now they have had to reline her.

1948.

444

There was a young fellow named Schmutz
Who was able to rotate his putz,
An aptitude queer
Which made him the dear
Of the girls, and the death of his nuts.

1948.

445

A well-equipped fellow in school
Has the whole class admiring his tool.
This magnificent dong
Is just twelve inches long,
But he don't use it much—as a rule.

1975A.

446. ACCEPT NO SUBSTITUTES

There was a young fellow named Schwartz
Who was hounded by girls of all sorts.
He tickled them good
(Like no other brand could)
For his penis was studded with warts.

1967A-1975.

447

A virile young villain of Scone
Had a pecker as hard as a stone.
This made things quite nice ;
He could thrust it in twice
And still there'd be starch in his bone.

1948.

448

Hermaphrodites cause a sensation
By their odd, two-in-one combination.
Concave and convex
They are partly each sex,
And a *dilly* at self-fornication!

1965.

449

The difference between the two sexes
Is the same in both China and Texas,
    Korea, Valbonne,
    Cairo, Crete and Athlone,
For the same genitalia connexas.

1965.

450

There once was a goon from Sheepshit
Who proved to be only a half-wit.
    His girlfriend he bumped,
    And seeing her cunt,
" My God, " he cried, " I've cracked it! "

1932-1952L.

451

Said a whore in a house in Shit Falls :
" While they ain't very stylish, men's balls
    Are delightful to feel ;
    If you squeeze 'em they squeal,
But *don't* twist their balls, 'cause they squawls! "

1965.

452

The penis of Scrabbleton Skink
Was set in a curious kink.
    So he cut off the end
    Where it started to bend,
And used it for mixing his drink.

1967A-1975.

453

Said a haughty old lecher named Sloan,
Who had naught but five inches of bone :
    " I feel no deep urgin'
    To consult any surgeon—
A poor thing, perhaps, but my own! "

1970A.

454

An innocent bride, all shy smiles,
Asked the old family medic, Doc Wiles :
  " Now what things are these
   That hang down to his knees? "
Said the doctor, " On me, they'd be piles. "

1953.

455

It is said that a fellow from Spitz
Was frightened half out of his wits.
   What caused such a fright
   Was the sight in the night
Of a phantom with ninety-nine tits!

1966.

456

A strange-looking fellow named Stan
Met a woman as big as a van.
   He wed her on Monday
   But not until Sunday
Found where her pudenda began.

1971 *ff.*

457

Nothing prompts a man's member to stand
Like the feminine mammary gland.
   Those unadorned dugs
   Drive us titmen all bugs,
And we *grab* with a big hairy hand.

1965.

458

There once was a coed from State
Who had a desire to mate.
   When her skirt would flutter,
   The boys they would shudder ;
She had, not a box, but a crate.

1961*

459

There was a young shop clerk of Stoke
Who said to her boss : " It's no joke.
This working in china
Has moved my vagina—
I have to lie crossways to poke. "

1968A.

460

There was a young lady named Stone
Whom the boys let severely alone,
Because she had thighs
Of preposterous size,
And an arse such as elephants own.

1948.

461

Said a girl as she walked down the Strand,
To her friend who was too plainly manned :
" Dear, it's catching the eye
Of each girl we pass by.
Can't you cover it up with your hand? "

1973.

462

The asses you pass on the street
Often heat up your genital meat.
Though you know you can't screw 'em,
It's great just to view 'em ;
For us ass-men, it's life's greatest treat.

1965.

463. MAMMÆ !

A busty young biddy named Suggs
Remarked of her bounteous dugs :
" The way fellows get fresh,
And go mauling my flesh,
I'm afraid soon they'll droop like two jugs. "

1966.

464

Every time Lady Lowbodice swoons
Her bubbies pop out like balloons.
But the butler stands by,
With hauteur in his eye,
And pops them back in with warm spoons.

1966A.

465

There's a popular doxy from Syria
Whose front view could scarcely be drearier.
But your day she would cheer,
If observed from the rear :
Her success rests upon her posterior.

1972.

466

There was a young girl from Taipei
Who was voted the Queen of the May.
But the pole she went 'round
Wasn't stuck in the ground,
But attached to a young man named Wei.

1950R.

467. REMEMBRANCE OF THINGS PAST

Big redheads run mostly to tits,
Which drives some men out of their wits.
A big, wobbly bust
Stirs men's animal lust,
And she fucks 'em until they have fits!

1966.

468

An Abo his tribesmen all toast
Has a penis so long he can boast
It will glide out alone
Late at night on its own,
Seducing young girls of the coast.

1970.

469

Said a practical female, Tombigger :
" Reserve your cunts, girls, for a nigger.
His trigger is bigger—
More rigor—more vigor—
And he's sure a deep digger as frigger! "

1950.

470

There once was a eunuch from Tonga
Who spent all day dancing the conga.
Said the queen, " This here dance
Stirs the ants in my pants,
But I *do* wish your conga were longer. "

1974A.

471

There was an old sculptor named Tony
Whose joystick refused to get bony.
It writhed and it wriggled,
Until his girl giggled :
" Now I know where they get macaroni. "

1950.

472

To Joe Dong said the well-spread Miss Tootle,
Whose sex bouts so far had been futile :
" Up to now, men I've tried
Left me unsatisfied,
But if any root can, why your root'll! "

1965.

473

Down in Dixie a lecherous trollop
Said, " My crack packs a helluva wallop!
You may think it's funny,
But it's dangerous, Sonny,
For it's likely to swallow you-all up! "

1965.

474

The tool of the Bishop of Truro
Was a rich *colorado maduro.*
And the real cognoscenta
Said his balls were magenta,
Shot through with chiaroscuro.

1959*

475

The wife of El Hassan the Turk
Fell in love with a fellow named Burke.
When he got to the palace
So long was his phallus
He had to stand back from his work.

1945.

476

Abreast of the times, our Miss Twitter
Has a torrid career as a titter.
Her magnificent dugs
Lure to bed endless lugs
To a twathole so vast few can fitter.

1965.

477. STEIN SONG

The pink buds refuse to unclose.
The aroma's not much for the nose.
Gardening's been luckless
For Alice B. Toklas,
But a rose is a rose is a rose.

1970A.

478

At the auction of Mabel's vagina,
All her lovers bought parts they thought fine: a
Coal miner, a rajah,
Bought labia major,
And a major her labia minor.

1974.

479

Girls' cunthair grows strange in variety,
And one deeply regrets that society
    Thinks it vulgar or lewd
    To show the stuff nude—
To hell with all prudes and propriety!

1965.

480

Sobbed a guy, "Though for sex I am vaunted,
A horrible hex has me haunted.
    In the sexual tussle
    I can stiffen each muscle
Except the one muscle most wanted!"

1965.

481

If hard questions stump Webster-Merriam,
He rather adroitly can parry 'em.
    When asked for the weight
    Of eight balls, he said, "Wait!
I don't know, but it takes four men to carry 'em."

1954J.

482

The tits, legs, and ass on Miss Weir
Cause the cults of all three parts to cheer.
    She's a sensual delight
    To lascivious sight,
Down to and including the queer.

1966.

483. UNISEXUS VEX US

Now wouldn't the women look weird
If they all grew a mustache and beard?
    And if men grew effeminate
    For lack of a stem in it,
I think the whole game would be queered.

1970A.

484

There was a young lady of Wells
Whose cervix was festooned with bells.
  Whenever she'd come
  Her vagina would hum,
Just like the *Boléro*—Ravel's.

1953-1960.

485

Our topless bartender, Miss West,
Serves mixed drinks direct from the breast :
  The right tit yields cherry,
  The left one strawberry,
And there's Moxie, by special request.

1966A.

486

The tits on Miss Fitts of West Cape
Bulge forth in such sensuous shape,
  Titwatchers all drool
  (Nothing more, as a rule)
And frustratedly fantasy rape.

1965.

487

It's well known that the men of Westphalia
Have unusually large genitalia,
  And spend much of their lives
  Hunting wives the right size—
A search often ending in failure.

1953.

488

Said a young tennis player named Whipp,
Adjusting his unruly zip :
  " It wasn't her face
  That I fell for, in Grace,
But the bubbies that bounced in her slip. "

1973.

489

A Negro possessed of a whopper
Was disturbed on the job by a copper.
When caught in the light,
He withdrew in a fright
With an audible *plonk,* like a stopper.

1973.

490. RULE OF THUMB

Said a cynical doxy named Wimple :
" To classify clients is simple.
You can tell at a glance
When he pulls off his pants
If a man's got a prick, or a pimple. "

1965.

491

There once was a sailor named Wingy
Whose flagpole grew ragged and stringy.
And his balls got so calloused
He used them for ballast,
And sailed 'round the world in a dinghy.

1945.

492

There was a young lady named Wise
Whose ass would have won a First Prize,
But you needed a swatter
And an oversize blotter
To get past the juice and the flies.

1975.

493

There was a young lady named Witt
Whose cunt was a fifteen-inch slit.
It seemed like a sin,
When you laid your jock in,
That the hole should reach up to her tit.

1959A.

494

A Chinese coolie named Wong
Had the longest dong in his tong.
His fellows all voted
To have him promoted,
And used it for striking a gong.

1952A-1970.

[495]

So here was this fellow named Wong,
Attached to this monstrous great dong.
Said his girl, "Yes, your prick
Is remarkably thick,
But *why* must it be so darn long?"

1968.

496

There was a young fellow of Wooster
Who'd a red-hot Rhode Island rooster.
But when he grew old,
His rooster grew cold,
And could no longer peck like it useter.

1972A.

497

Quoth a lady when asked if she would:
"I suppose, in a pinch, that I could,
But a vulvular tumour
Keeps me in ill humour,
So I don't think you'd like it so good."

1955M.

498

A luscious, lewd negress named Zoe
Had hardened the prick of her beau.
She said, "Though it pinches,
I'll take all twelve inches.
Come on, honey, slip me Ol' Black Joe!"

1948.

III

STRANGE INTERCOURSE

499

There was a young fellow named Ades
Whose favorite fruit was young maids.
    But sheep, nigger boys, whores,
    And the knot holes in doors
Were by no means exempt from his raids.

1948.

500. CLERIHEW

A man with an affinity
For his daughter's virginity,
    Said, as he pressed her
    And finally possessed her :
"To Hell with consanguinity!"

1948.

501

A dolly in Dallas named Alice,
Whose overworked sex is all callous,
    Wore the foreskin away
    On uncircumcised Ray,
Through exuberance, tightness, and malice.

1965.

502

In Chicago a lady named Anna
On her torso wore just a bandanna.
    When she met some Fifth Liners
    (They're much worse than Shriners)
She was last seen sprinting through Montana.

1966-1970A.

503. THE BEY OF ALGIERS

The randy old Bey of Algiers
Who'd confined his cock-poking to queers,
Tried a cunt for a change,
And remarked : " It felt strange . . .
Just think what I've missed all these years! "

[504]

The sore-peckered Bey of Algiers
Told his harem next evening : " My dears,
Last night's round of screwing
Has proved my undoing,
So you may not get fucked for TEN YEARS! "

[505]

This spermless old Bey of Algiers
Said : " Back in my more potent years,
I begat brats by dozens
On my sisters and cousins,
Besides oiling the hips of fat queers. "

[506]

" But alas! " said the Bey of Algiers,
" I've gone impotent now, it appears.
If the eunuchs won't suck you,
I'll have puppydogs fuck you,
So don't pee in your pants or shed tears. "

1965.

507

Exuberant Sue from Anjou
Found that fucking affected her hue.
She presented to sight
Nipples pink, bottom white ;
But her asshole was purple and blue.

1966A.

508

A wench from the Lesser Antilles
Says dog fashion gives her the willies.
    Except big, long cocks
    That stay hard as rocks,
But it's seldom she's fucked by such dillies.

1965.

509

When you fuck little Annie in Anza
You get a great bosom bonanza :
    Sucking Annie's soft tits
    Makes her throw fifty fits,
And the fuck is a sextravaganza!

1965.

510

Shirley's face appears careworn and ashen,
And it's all due to sexual passion.
    Though she knows it ain't right,
    She shacks up day and night,
Like nookie might go out of fashion.

1966.

511. THE HORRIBLE HUN

There once was a Hun named Attila,
Whose life was a genuine thrilla.
    From village to village,
    He'd rant, rape, and pillage,
Seldom spending two nights on one pilla.

[512]

His neighbors objected, it's true,
To the way he would plunder and screw.
    But he'd say, " 'Tain't my fault,
    'Cause it's all the resault
Of a trauma I suffered at two. "

1972.

513

Those scared kangaroos in Australia
Can blame it on oversexed Thalia.
For they heard the babe screaming
When Tim started reaming
In her bedroom on Cunt Street, Sedalia.

1966.

514

A wealthy young man of Bagdad
Has morals excessively bad :
He keeps seven Circassians
As a vent for his passions,
And on Sundays he buggers a lad.

1968A.

515

A town girl spread sex by the bale,
Specializing in students from Yale.
They spent gala nights
Sampling *her* nude delights,
Which kept half of Yale mighty pale.

1965.

516

There was a young girl from Balmoral
Whose habits were highly immoral.
For the price of a dime
She took three at a time :
One fore, and one aft, and one oral.

1945R.

517

A woman from southern Banquillo
Calls her husband an old armadillo :
His prick is so rough,
And his manner so bluff,
When he's finished she hardly can pee-o!

1948.

518

There was an old lady of Barking
Thought life and its cares were too carking.
She could not approve
Of the way events move,
And frowned upon laughing and larking.

[519]

Her daughter went down to the creek,
And had her cunt licked by a peke,
Her bottom enjoyed
By sixteen unemployed,
And her mouth crammed with spunk by a Greek.

1937C.

520. OLD RAPES FOR NEW

There was an old lady named Barr,
Defiled by six men in a car.
They were hellbent on rape
And she could not escape,
So she stayed and outfucked them by far.

1967A-1975.

521

A musician who played the bassoon
Complained sex sprees ended too soon.
He got busy on Mary
One cold January,
But gave out on the nineteenth of June.

1965.

522

One day as I slept on the beach,
Up onto my balls crawled a leech.
When I lay with my bride
The leech got inside—
But *she* didn't fuss ; she's a peach.

1953.

523. NO JEWS

There was an old whore from Bengazi
Who'd been laid by a Frog and a Nazi,
And a Wog and a dog,
And a razorbacked hog,
But she drew the line at the Pinkerton brothers.

1953.

524

Being raped, a fat girl named Bernice
Ups and yells for the local police.
Who, to her dismay,
Would not go away
Until each had knocked off a free piece.

1965.

525

A sexless old lady named Beth
Polished up her false teeth and her breath,
Till her smile was so white,
Just from Peppermint-Brite,
That sixty men banged her to death.

1970A.

526

A much-diddled dolly named Beverly
Goes about her sex bouts so darned cleverly,
She services three
At a time—all for free—
Positioned about herself severally.

1965.

527

A riot was caused in Big Sur
By the genital itch in the fur
Of a lady with ants
In the crotch of her pants,
Who screwed dozens without a demur.

1966.

528

A dike on the Bay of Biscay
Frigs herself with her thumbs twice a day.
  But a bitch in Australia
  Prefers male genitalia,
And fucks 'em in scores without pay.

1965.

529. SEMPER FI!

Said a sex-starved marine, Sergeant Blake,
Whose lust no six wenches could slake:
  "On the sea for my nation!
  But for my vacation
Gimme a week on Veronica Lake."

1948.

530

There was a young lady named Blanche
Who took on all the boys at the ranch.
  When they'd fucked her all day,
  Till their pricks wore away,
She demanded nocturnal *revanche*.

1948.

531

An oversexed satyr named Bluxom
Likes babes who are big, bare, and buxom.
  "Them gals," the guy said,
  "Are the best ass in bed,
And when *I* gets 'em spread, man, I fuxom!"

1965.

532

An oversexed fellow named Bode
Remarked as he shot his ninth load:
  "Being sexually deft,
  I have one load still left,
So spread, baby.—One for the road!"

1966.

533

There was a young lady from Boston
Who thought she'd been raped in an Austin.
But the truth is, I fear,
She had sat on her gear,
And a pickle truck knocked her exhaust in.

1970A.

534

There was an old fellow named Boze
Who fucked a young kid in the nose.
Sex needs, he admits,
A choice of two slits :
Plus ça change, plus c'est la même chose!

1948.

535

Said a foolish old lecher named Brannigan :
" My dear, I *don't* think I can again.
That dozen last night
Were just a delight,
But lord knows when I'll be a man again. "

1966.

536

There was a woman named Brewer
Who boasted that no one could screw her.
Along came a fink
With an iron-alloy dink,
And rammed the thing all the way through her.

1965*

537. DEFROSTED BRIDES

A frigid young lady named Bryce
Thought sex just a low form of vice,
Till she met Captain Baker,
Who had sailed an icebreaker,
And he plowed a wide path through her ice.

1975.

538

There was a young lady named Bunch
Who much loved to wriggle and scrunch.
On the Citadel green
She was screwed by sixteen ;
Then she sucked off the Sergeant for lunch.

1948.

539

There was a young lady named Bundy
Who was fucked by a Belgian on Sunday.
On Tuesday a Uhlan
To her twat put his tool in—
SIC TRANSIT GLORIA MUNDI.

1919E.

540

A young dancer who worked in burlesque
Used to fuck in a manner mauresque.
With her lover she'd jibe
So her ass would describe
A shockingly cute arabesque.

1948.

541

There was a young girl with a bust
Which roused a French cavalier's lust.
She was since heard to say,
About midnight, " *Touché!*—
I didn't quite parry that thrust. "

1970.

542

Theodora the queen of Byzance
Was known for her royal hot pants.
At one *soirée de luxe*
She took on six dukes,
An ape, and two tropical plants.

1970A.

543

A fisherman out from Calais
A mermaid ensnared in the bay.
    He searched back and front,
    But found nary a cunt,
So he sucked on her titties all day.

1975.

544

There was a young man from Cape Hatteras,
When he saw a girl, first he would pat her ass,
    Then strip her chemise
    From her tits to her knees,
And at last let his weapon get *at* her ass.

1950.

545

In the gravel pit, young Miss Carruthers
Gets their rocks off for all of her brothers.
    Since she's got eight or ten,
    And all big husky men,
There's no pussy left for us others.

1965.

546

There was a young maid from Cathay
Who, when asked if she knew how to lay,
    Said, "You're damned right I can,
    With my quiff or my can,
Or my mouth—or a three-way parlay."

1945R.

547. A TOAST TO HOLLYWOOD

A starry-eyed starlet named Charlotte
Said: "Hollywood! home of the harlot,
    Where cute split-tail bitches
    Take a quick ride to riches,
If their sins are sufficiently scarlet!"

1966.

548

Two spectres who screwed in a chasm
Had a simultaneous spasm.
With a howl of despair
The invisible pair
Was splattered with ectoplasm.

1958.

549

The pantyhose style is first-class
For revealing the shapely young lass.
All the better to view her,
But damn hard to screw her,
With those stockings up over her ass!

1970A.

550. THE FOUR SEASONS

To the sound of his beat-up old clavier,
A satyr in Xenia named Xavier
Pops girls' maidenheads
In rumpled broad beds,
With his highly unmusical behavior.

1965.

551

Ten thousand GI's with hard cocks
Lined up around town for ten blocks,
For a chance to fuck Millie;
Half the gang fucked her silly,
And the rest shot their wads in their socks.

1965.

552

That curvaceous cutie, Miss Coker,
Regrets ever playing strip poker.
When she lost she soon found
She was rushed bedroom bound,
With seven guys drooling to stroke her.

1966.

553

There was a young matron of Coosa
Whose spouse would do nothing but goose her.
While he watched through a crack,
She bared for a black,
And, boy! did that bastard seduce her!

1950.

554

There was a young lady named Cruller
Whose sex life got duller and duller,
Till she sampled the nectar
Of Hector's erector,
In stereo, three-D, and color!

1967A-1975.

555

A frantic young lady named Crumb
Thought her lover too naïve and dumb.
She gave him no rest
Till he straddled her chest,
And then she was all over-come.

1945.

556

That lovely young lady, Culard,
Met a coon whose prick measures a yard.
Although he was black
She would lie on her back
As long as his nine inches were hard.

1930-1956A.

557

There was a young lady from Dallas
Whose conduct in coitus was callous.
But this stopped on the night
When her man, out of spite,
Used a fireman's axe for a phallus.

1954A.

558

A gold-digging doxy from Darien
Laughed at Seth, the old coot she was marryin'.
On their wedding night Seth
Screwed the poor girl to death—
Quite a feat for an octogenarian.

1972.

559. FUCK FREUD!

There was a young fellow named Dave,
Had a prostitute out of her grave.
He said, "I confess
I'm a hell of a mess,
But it's a lot better than going to an analyst, ain't it?"

1973A.

560

Her pickup fucked Fanny for days,
Altogether some forty-eight lays!
Though her cunthole feels sore,
She could use a few more,
But the fellow's just left in a daze.

1965.

561

Said a potentate gross and despotic:
"My tastes are more rich than exotic.
I've always adored
Making love in a Ford—
They say I'm an auto-erotic."

ff. 1959*

562

There once was a faddist of Devon
Who said, "I have raped only seven
Young women to date,
But I'll soon make it eight,
And shortly thereafter eleven."

1948.

563

A pubescent Girl Scout of Dewar
Was raped by two cops and a brewer,
A postman, three sailors,
And a shopful of tailors,
And next week I'm going to . . . interview 'er.

1965.

564

" Indeed, " said an actress named Dix,
" We played safe when we toured in the sticks.
In case men attacked us,
We wore panties of cactus—
Is life *just* a succession of pricks? "

1965.

565. MY BLUE HEAVEN

Fucking hot Mrs. Diddle next door
Is getting to be quite a chore.
There's the milkman and me
(Her hubby makes three)
And she's putting out feelers for more!

1966.

566

Said an angry young bride down in Dover :
" Now your minuteman spasm is over!
Well, I'm still in heat,
So go down in the street,
And bring me some big guy—or Rover! "

1966.

567

The wife of an absent dragoon
Begged a soldier to grant her a boon.
As she let down her drawers,
She said, " It's all yours—
I could decant the whole damned platoon! "

1973.

568. SAN QUENTIN QUAIL

There's San Quentin quail out in droves,
With fuzzy cunts hotter than stoves.
    If mounted with care,
    There's no cunt can compare
With those hot, underage treasure troves!

[569]

If you like your cunt young, tight and tender,
For a really wild sexual bender,
    You'll find the best tail
    Is on San Quentin quail,
So pick a young chick and up-ender!

[570]

Seeing San Quentin quail in the nude
Makes senile old peckers protrude
    That have dangled for years ;
    Such effects, it appears,
Make us Dirty Old Men—also lewd.

[571]

She proved to be San Quentin quail
When bed-spread by the hot-blooded male.
    She said, " My name is Nita—
    It isn't Lolita—
But it gets you the same time in jail! "

[572]

Us *Cherryhawks* swear naught will swerve us
From gang-shagging luscious Miss Purvis.
    I've the yen, but I fail
    When I think about jail ;
That San Quentin quail makes me nervous!

1966.

573

So slow was the horny old duchess,
She could never keep out of men's clutches.
She was fucked, as she ran,
By a one-legged man,
Who managed to crotch her on crutches.

1975.

574. AD ASSTRA PER ASPERA

Said a coed from Duke University,
When asked about sexual diversity:
"Screwing's O.K.,
In the old-fashioned way,
But I *do* like a touch of perversity."

1970A.

575

A stodgy game warden named Dunn
Nabbed a pair at the height of their fun.
He caught them bare-ass,
Out in the tall grass,
In the wrong season for shooting a gun.

1954-1976A.

576

A long-peckered sailor from Durham
Made all the girls holler and squirm.
He withdrew, letting fly,
Saying, "Mud in your eye!"
Which is where he deposits his sperm.

1948.

577

Somehow you don't think of the Dutch
As given to lewdness and such.
But they pour on the sex
With terrific effex
When a Dutch *maisie* gets you in her clutch.

1965.

578

You really can't blame our Miss Ealing
For moaning and groaning and squealing.
    She sat down on Bill's frame,
    And his wad, when he came,
Blew both dame, wad and blast to the ceiling!

1966.

579

There's a passionate young lady named Eleanor,
So wild they all say she's got hell in 'er.
    But this doesn't bother
    Her amorous father:
"Here's *one* thing," says he, "will look well in 'er!"

1950.

580

Hell's Angels on the way through Emporia
Gang-banged a virgin named Gloria.
    That was two weeks ago,
    But as far as we know
She is still in a state of euphoria.

1965.

581

An acrobat lewdly enwrapt
Went wild as Tom's testicles slapped.
    "Your great balls need sucking,"
    She yelled, and *while* fucking
She drove Big Tom mad as she lapped!

1971 *ff.*

582

When Oedipus entered, erect,
Jocasta screamed, "Stop! I object.
    You're a Greek! Screw some other—
    A goat, or your brother—
Mother-fucking's a little suspect."

1970A.

583

I Caesar, when I learned of the fame
Of Cleopatra, I straightway laid claim.
    Ahead of my legions
    I invaded her regions—
I saw, I conquered, I came!

1954J-1973.

584

A man with venereal fear
Had intercourse in his wife's ear.
    She said, "I don't mind,
    Except that I find
When the telephone rings, I don't hear."

1948.

585

There was a young fellow who fell in
An affair with an old whore named Helen.
    And now his prick itches
    For all kinds of bitches,
Or even a burro to swell in.

1948.

586

Like cats out at night on a fence,
Our newlywed neighbors they yentz.
    With the light on upstairs
    They have rare sex affairs,
And the view from our attic's immense!

1965.

587

There was once a young lady of Fez
Who had thighs like Maria Montez.
    She was raped on the floor
    By a brutal señor
In Madrid, Marrakesh, St. Tropez.

1969.

588

There was a young man with a fiddle
Who asked his best girl, " Do you diddle? "
    She replied, " Yes, I screw,
    But prefer to with two—
It's twice as much fun in the middle. "

1955A.

589. EROTIC BAROQUE

An abnormal young fellow named Fishes
Had a penchant for pleasantries vicious.
    He took two of his nieces
    And fucked them to pieces :
The whole thing was simply delicious.

1964A.

590

There was a young man from Fort Knox
Who was singularly blessed with two cocks.
    When used in rotation,
    Neither stopped copulation,
But always brought on a hot box.

[591]

He finally gave up the hunt
For a gal with a twin-barrelled cunt,
    And forgetting compunction,
    Used both in conjunction :
One behind and the other in front.

1953.

592

There was a wild youth of Fort Sumter
Lured a gal up the creek and then jumped 'er,
    Whistling " Dixie " meanwhile
    In rock-&-roll style,
All the time that his love-muscle pumped 'er.

1965.

593. THE AMOROUS PHANTASM

In a spooky old château in France
The chatelaine slipped off her pants.
For a bold apparition
Was demanding coition,
And she'd try anything once—even ha'nts!

1965.

594

"Have you met the bedworthy Miss Frings,
Who knows all those sexual things?
Her double *vibrato*
And plucked *pizzicato,*
And that candy ass—jello on springs!"

[595]

"Yes, I knew that great sex job, Miss Frings,
Who loved joys that cohabiting brings
(In a score of odd ways)
But she died in a daze
On a bed fixed with overdrive springs."

1966-1976A.

596

High on a hilltop in Frisco,
With his pecker greased lightly with Crisco,
A lecher named Whitney
Raped a girl in a jitney,
While she casually munched a Nabisco.

1965.

597. NEVER ON SUNDAY

Greek passions are carefree and furious,
And their excesses, sometimes injurious.
Though they're blessed with great zest,
On the Sabbath they rest,
In a manner Melina Mercurious.

1972A.

598

There once was a girl from Galahad
Who fancied her father—too bad!
She then caught her brother
Going down on their mother,
Who remarked, " Not in the same class as dad. "

1967A.

599

We're tickled as hell to hear Gertie,
That frigid bitch, got it so dirty.
For little Jack Horner
Got her trapped in a corner,
And fucked her from ten to five-thirty!

1965.

600

There once was a lady named Gloria
Whose lewdness was such it would worry ya.
She fucked only niggers—
They've much bigger triggers—
I'd say more, but I don't want to bore ya.

1950A.

601

There was a young fellow from Goshen
Caused a scandal this side of the ocean.
He raped both his aunts
Who had Saint Vitus dance,
And explained, " I like *plenty* of motion! "

1975A.

602

An Idaho gal named Miss Grange
Roamed the hills for a purpose quite strange.
When she found a young hick
She would measure his prick,
And, if long, drive it Home on the Range.

1948.

603

A farm girl ten miles south of Granger
Was fucked all one night in the manger.
She claims not to know
Who diddled her so,
But she says that it *felt* like a stranger.

1965.

604

An incestuous bastard named Grant
Remarked while ass fucking his aunt :
" Dear, somehow or other
It isn't like Mother,
Though the difference is actually scant. "

1965.

605

A free-lancing artist named Greeley
Had a model who suited him ideally :
At the first scent of paint
She would fall in a faint,
And would only revive when frewed screely!

1953-1966.

606

There's an avid young woman in Gunnison
Who's always around when the fun is on.
And all she demands
Is a hold for her hands,
And a firm seat to settle her cunnus on.

1948.

607

We feel sorry as hell for this guy,
For he gave it the Old College Try.
Still, a nympho from Livermore
Kicks because he won't givermore,
And *that* when his pecker's wrung dry.

1966.

608

In an area ten miles around Gypsum,
Once a gal's caught by Hal, the guy strips 'em.
He gives fillies rare fun
As he gets off his gun
In the sport for which Nature equips 'em.

1965.

609. THE LAST TUPPER

An ancient Greek harlot named Harriet
Would take on two men in a chariot,
Six monks and two tailors,
Nine priests and ten sailors,
Doubting Thomas and Judas Iscariot!

1966A.

610

Miss Nympho was in such a heat
That ten times my quota of meat
Couldn't hope to appease her.—
Though I *did* fail to please her,
The ten bangs I got were a treat.

1965.

611

A musical Imam of Héjaz
Taught his favorite eunuchs to play jazz.
So his fucks *pizzicato,*
Staccato, legato,
Made his harems Arabia's rages.

1948.

612

A sprightly young woman of Hellas
Made all of the other girls jealous.
In a pastoral region
She screwed half a legion,
And asked, " Where are the rest of the fellas? "

1945.

613

An extraordinary fellow named Hilary
Was blessed with twin sexual artillery.
    When you get off one gun
    Your fun is all done,
But *he* drives home his pulsing auxiliary!

1965.

614

The word's out that little Miss Hintz
At the mention of sex now will wince.
    A student from Corning
    Kept it in until morning,
And Miss Hintz hasn't been the same since.

1965.

615

A cheerful young chap from Hong Kong
Had a truly fantastic oolong :
    It would swell into place
    For a twelve-day embrace,
And none would complain 'twas too long.

1971 *ff.*

616. WALLFLOWER AT THE ORGY

An oversexed young girl named Hooker
Says life has just up and forsooker.
    At a party in Taft
    She felt every man's shaft,
But not a damn fellow there tooker!

1966.

617. AMERICAN CULTURE

A perverted young pair in Hot Springs
Delight in peculiar sex things.
    They fuck in a daze
    In a dozen freak ways
With the swingers their three-line ad brings.

1966A.

618

Oversexed is the word for friend Howe,
Who in one day twice mounted his frau,
Several sluttish she-neighbors,
The maid at the Tabors,
Two sheep, and an old brindle cow.

1965.

619

A hot-pussied dolly named Hunt
Remarked to friend Joe in her cunt:
"Keep up that hard poking
To keep my cunt smoking,
And after you come—you can bunt!"

1966.

620

A nervous young nympho in Hyatt
When laid simply *will* not keep quiet.
In the midst of a reaming
The wench starts in screaming,
Till she sounds like a five-alarm riot.

1965.

621

Once a girl had a skiing instructor,
But she fell down everywhere he'd conduct 'er.
Since she couldn't say "No"
With her mouth full of snow,
The instructor quite frequently fucked 'er.

1972.

622

I kissed her red lips with intention
Of proceeding to things I won't mention.
Now who could suppose
That her pretty pink toes
Would grip onto my virile extension!

1973.

623

It somehow seems highly ironical
That a Londoner laid Miss McGonickle,
And, having no rubber,
The sex-crazy lubber
Whipped out and inserted his monocle!

1965.

624

A cute little coed named Jean
Evoked the dismay of the dean
By flooding the college
With intimate knowledge
Of subjects perverse and obscene.

1967*

625

On their wedding night Sadie told Joe :
"There's something I think you should know.
I've scraunched sixty guys,
Poodle dogs and horseflies,
And the cop on the beat down below!"

1966.

626

Have you heard of the boxer named Jules
Whose hunger for rape never cools?
He pays no attention
To social convention,
Or the Marquis of Queensberry rules.

1945.

627. DIETETIC NOTE

A haggard old harlot named Keating
Had taken a terrible beating :
She was stewed, screwed, tattooed,
Also buggered and blued,
And her pussy was *not* fit for eating.

1975A.

628

There was an old fellow from Kent
Who on pleasure was always hell-bent.
He fucked far & wide
Till of v.d. he died,
But he claimed that his life was well *spent.*

1960.

629

A lesbian down in Khartoum
Runs a whorehouse for freaks in her room.
But a bitch in Bombay
Daisy-chains it away,
While she's frigging her ass with a broom!

1966.

630

I came on a lady named Kitchener
As her lover was fucking the niche in her.
So I pulled out my prick
And stuck it in quick,
And buggered the son-of-a-bitch in her.

1950.

631. TOUJOURS GALANT!

There was a young cocksman named Krupp,
Whom a harlot got awfully keyed up.
He unzipped in great style,
But outstripped her a mile;
Then paused so that she could catch up.

1967A.

632

An astonished young bride named LaFong
Found her husband abnormally strong.
She knew about sex
And its heady effects,
But thought thirty-two times *might* be wrong.

1966.

633

Said Miss Farrow on one of her larks :
" Sex is more fun in bed than in parks.
You feel more at ease,
Your ass doesn't freeze,
And passersby *don't* make remarks. "

1965.

634

There was a young girl named LaRue
Who thought it great fun just to screw.
She was never particular
And performed perpendicular—
An art known to only a few.

1971.

635

There once was a Communist lass
Who made liberal use of her ass.
There is no comrade yet
To whom she has said " Nyet! "—
It was fully reported in *Tass.*

1972.

636

There was a young lady of Lassen
Who was raped by a loony assassin.
For an hour or two
He tried to unscrew,
But found that he couldn't unfasten!

1966.

637

There once was a monk of La Trappe
With a strength that no harlot could sap.
In the midst of a stand,
With a wave of his hand
He could turn the thing off, like a tap.

1954A.

638

Have you heard about Toulouse-Lautrec?
Though at first flush an ambulant wreck,
He could hitch up his nuts
And follow his putz
Into twitchets right up to his neck!

1941-1948.

639. GONE, MAN, GONE!

The orgy was held on the lawn,
And we knocked off two hours before dawn.
We found ourselves viewing
Twenty-two couples screwing,
But by sun-up they'd all come and gone.

1965.

640

The Abode of True Wisdom called Lawrence,
To the godly's a vicious abhorrence,
For the prexy gets stewed,
And the faculty screwed,
And the semen runs streetward in torrents.

1948.

641

Strong men have begun to be leery
Of taking on lissome Miss Dearie.
While her tail's a delight,
It needs plugging all night,
And by morning a guy's mighty weary.

1965.

642

The exploits of sexy Miss Lecks
On men have such wearing effects,
That a night of embraces
Turns sexual aces
Into limber-kneed, quivering wrecks!

1966.

643. HUMAN, ALL TOO HUMAN

There was a young fellow named Leif
Whose erection was swollen but brief.
He would end in despair
With a handful of hair,
And a big bite of tit in his teeth!

1953-1966.

644

A circus midget named Lew
Once asked the fat lady to screw.
Said she, " I don't mind,
But I think you will find
Your father-in-law's not quite through. "

1948.

645

There was a young lady named Liston
Whose cunt was as big as a piston.
But an able mechanic,
Who was not one to panic,
Fucked her twice with his foot and his fist in.

1975.

646

An old window washer named Luigi
Was screwing a lady from Fiji.
When she started to sweat,
He said, " Hold it, my pet, "
And squished off the sweat with his squeegee.

1975.

647

A hard-peckered lecher named Lutz
Had his prick in a bitch to the nuts.
She remarked, " My friend Hunt
Has more fun in my cunt ;
He goes three times as deep when he butts. "

1966.

648

A passionate damsel of Lyme
Always takes on two men at a time.
Cried she, " What a blast!
With one up my ass,
And a straight-man up front—it's sublime! "

1965.

649

There was a young lady called Mabel
Who liked it best on the table.
What a cunt of a whore!
She'd take hundreds or more,
And invite any back who were able.

1963*

650

There was a young girl named McGarrity
For whom sex had for years been a rarity.
At an orphanage dinner
She let six guys in her,
But more from hot pants than real charity.

1966.

651

A rapacious young man named McGee
Who was out on a big screwing spree,
Said, " Let those who don't fuck
Take a quick, quiet duck—
The rest better pass it out free. "

1948.

652

A candid young girl named McMillan
Replied to an arrogant villain
Who leered, " Now I'll rape you! "
With, " I can't escape you,
But rape me you can't—I'm too willin'. "

1948.

653

There was a young plumber, McNary,
With erection that hardly would vary.
    In a girls' school, one night,
    Before morning light,
He knocked up the whole seminary!

1950.

654

A happy old hag named McPherson
Was really the *busiest* person :
    Spent her days, for a fact,
    In the sexual act,
And all of her nights in rehearsin'.

1945.

655

A nympho from Bangor in Maine,
Who runs more to cunt than to brain,
    Performs odd sex functions
    Without qualms or compunctions—
But then, who am I to complain?

1965.

656

Quite sordid and most maladroit
Was the neighborhood studsman's exploit :
    He fucked like Old Scratch
    At the cinched-up old snatch
Of my ugliest aunt from Detroit.

1965.

657

In Great Neck, Old Lyme, and Manhasset,
Copulation's an important facet
    Of suburbian life,
    And a hot, willing wife
For trading is a valuable asset.

1966.

658. A TRIP AROUND THE WORLD

Have you aphrodisiacal mania?—
Then hightail it to Rumdum, Rumania,
Where a gypsy in rut
Will, for weeks in her hut,
Instruct you in sex miscellania!

[659]

Are you looking for wenching and rumming?
In India you'll find things are humming.
With those Hindu gals, sex
Is so totally complex,
You won't know if you're going or coming.

[660]

An itchy-hipped hussy named Jane
Hitchhiked from Vancouver to Maine.
The whole Santa Fe trail
She paid for in tail,
Before resting her messy membrane!

[661]

It occurred when she crossed the Atlantic,
But the screw made young Mamie half frantic.
It wasn't losing her cherry
That upset her—not very—
But the aisle of a plane's *not* romantic.

[662]

A streetwalker, working the Strand
Propositioned that tightwad, Durand.
He said, " At that price,
My reply is : *No dice!*—
My sex needs I have well in hand. "

[663]

A summer in England did vex
Three American girls from South Hex.
Excessively British,
The men were quite skittish,
And much preferred dartboards to sex.

[664]

A fussy old maid from Vancouver
Messed her pants while touring the Louvre.
Guards trailed her a bit
By her spoor of soft shit,
Then proceeded to quietly remove 'er.

[665]

The ants in the pants of Miss Morse
Would dance with such passion and force,
That when in southern France
She just left off her pants,
And let nature take its own course.

[666]

Said a virile young tourist from Galion,
Who was hung like a champion stallion :
" I've fucked girls from Fort Worth
To the ends of the earth—
None match the hot female Eyetalian! "

[667]

A young tourist girl from Toledo
Just went plumb to hell on the Lido.
Under a big beach umbrella
She was bunged by a fella,
In a game he called " Lido Torpedo. "

[668]

In a ratty bordello in Venice,
An oversexed tourist named Ennis
Found they'd stolen his money
And swiped his do-funny,
Which the girls now employ to play tennis.

[669]

A tourist in Rome, from South Bend,
Decried sodomy to an old friend.
Leered a visiting Bulgar:
"Sir, you may say it's vulgar,
But you'll find that it's fun, in the end!"

[670]

It was on the south bank of the Po
That a young lady tourist named Flo
Laid a husky Italian
With balls like a stallion,
Who was oddly named Roger—not Joe.

[671]

A prudish young tourist named Kay
Was a virgin when she sailed away.
But she ceased acting prissily
After bandits in Sicily
Worked her over, one long summer day.

[672]

"Sex is the same everywhere,"
Said a round-the-world tart from Montclair.
"The prick and vagina
In South Carolina
Do the same as in Spain or Mayfair."

[673]

In a back street down in San Maduro
A tourist from Trenton named Truro
  Tried to make sweet Conchita,
  But the chaste señorita
Had her sex parts at home in the bureau.

[674]

On an outing with seventeen Czechs
A girl tourist supplied the free sex.
  She returned from the jaunt
  Feeling more or less gaunt,
But the Czechs were all absolute wrecks!

[675]

On an island off Naxos in Greece,
A girl tourist wanting a piece
  Was raped on the beach—
  It was useless to screech—
Her bungholers were all Greek police.

[676]

On the cruise ship in port at Stamboul,
Said the nymph on the purser's big tool :
  " What magnificent fucking,
  And reaming and sucking—
It's the best that I've had since high school. "

[677]

A tourist from Nyack named Durkee
Found a small, cut-rate harem in Turkey.
  Their exotic technique
  Kept him spinning for a week ;
Even now, a year later, he's jerky.

[678]

A Turk caught Joe Blow in his harem,
And snarled, " Man, are *you* harum-scarum!
I'm calling my wranglers
To bite off your danglers—
From now on you ain't gonna wear 'em! "

[679]

A tourist who stopped in Tangier
Bedded down with the fat old Emir.
She remarked, " His great weenie,
With which he's no meanie,
Beats all the darned sights they have here. "

[680]

A passion-struck tourist named Eunice
Was laid by the Emir of Tunis.
She said, " Very few guys
Can approach him for size,
Which makes his a prize by its fewness. "

[681]

A taxicab driver in Tiflis
Told his fare, " Hookers here are so shiftless,
Few tourists rejoice
Though they have a wide choice
Between itches, gon, crabs, clap and siflis. "

[682]

A highly confused tourist named Kapps
Had to trace out his trip on the maps.
He discovered that Tiflis
Was where he got syphilis,
And London was where he caught claps.

[683]

A sex-mad young satyr named Toby
Set up shop in the town of Nairobi,
Where, to worn-out old tarts,
He sold brand-new sex parts
Which he cleverly made of adobe.

[684]

A hot tourist gal in Zambezi
Said, " Attracting the men is damned easy :
Don't wear any pants,
And at every chance
Stand somewhere that's frightfully breezy. "

[685]

In Uganda a tourist named Ryan
Had his manhood nipped off by a lion.
He cried, " Now I'm sorry
I made this safari,
For my great virile days are fast dyin'! "

[686]

Raped by four apes in Rangoon,
A torrid young tourist named June
Said, " I dug the wild screwing
Those heathens were doing,
But why did they all come so soon? "

[687]

Said a timid young girl in Hong Kong
On seeing her cabdriver's dong :
" I have heard about sex
And its heady effects,
But must I use *that* to go wrong? "

[688]

Said the black-bearded Raj of Johore
As he turned Miss Tuppeen from his door:
 "I've just swived four wives,
 And a nautch girl with hives—
No thanks, I can't use any more."

[689]

While seducing the Queen of Siam,
An imprudent American named Sam
 Was deprived of his nuts
 By two deftly placed cuts,
And what dangles there now is a sham.

[690]

A round-the-world traveler named Ann
Shacked up with a Tokyo man.
 She was diddled and swived,
 And her baby arrived
With its bottom stamped: MADE IN JAPAN.

[691]

Said a worn-out old tourist in Nome:
"Travel may broaden one, in Rome,
 But you don't need a passport
 If you're looking for ass-sport—
There's all you can take right at home."

[692]

Few girls beat the record of June,
Who was laid in Bangkok and Rangoon,
 Hong Kong and Vallejo, France, Montevideo,
 Melbourne, Shigachi, Kabul, and Karachi,
 Kowloon, Saskatoon,
And in a cold-water flat, right on her prat,
Out in back of Petrucci's saloon!

1965.

693

A fastidious girl in Manila,
Whose panties were lined with chinchilla,
    Said, " One thing money brings
    Is a taste for fine things,
And *fabulous* screws in my villa. "

1966.

694

The lewdest of voyeurs named Max,
While watching two sex maniacs,
    With cock all bespattered
    Had his optic nerve shattered
As they all had their thousandth climax.

1971 *ff.*

695

A young fairy who'd eaten raw meat
Maintained sex relations discreet :
    He received Eskimos
    In the holes in his nose,
And buggered a horse with his feet.

1955A.

696

There once was a master mechanic
Whose skill with the girls was satanic.
    The tool that he used
    Never left the girls bruised,
And his oil-and-grease job was a panic.

1956.

697

Said a fisherman fishing in Michigan :
" Here comes that sweet little bitch again! "
    So he hoisted her anchor,
    And spanked her and thanked her,
And went back exhausted to fish again.

1966.

698

There was a young lady named Miller,
Not a man in the navy could fill 'er.
She was tied to the stern,
When the wheel took a turn,
And was near fucked to death by the tiller.

1948.

699

A certain young priestess of Ming
Said, " Concerning the rape of Nanking:
Every Jap in North China
Has explored my vagina—
It's so sore, I can't powder the thing! "

1953.

700

There was a young man from Missouri
Who screwed a French dame in a brewery.
As he dressed in the dark
His wand started to spark . . .
He said, " That must've been Madame Curie. "

1948.

701. SEXUAL STATISTICS

There was a young man from Molapida
Whose rebound was rapid or rapider.
In an hour and three-quarters
He fucked eight farmers' daughters,
Which is 'way above average per capita.

1948.

702

There was a stout whore from Montrose
Who could go off whenever she chose.
One day she went blooie
Ninety times in St. Louis—
If that ain't a record, it's close.

1948-1970A.

703

A young southern lady, Miss Muller,
Eloped with a gemp'mun of color.
She said, " Please keep it dark,
But this isn't a lark—
My doughnut's just right for his cruller. "

[704]

Another young lady named Munger
Said, "Since I've been fifteen or younger,
I've relished a poke
From a nice naked smoke.
It's perfect for clitoris hunger. "

1950.

705

There was a young whore in Nantasket
Who would fuck (for a price) in a basket.
She could make it spin 'round,
And jounce up and down,
While her client below blew his gasket.

1951R.

706

A waterfront wench who's from Natchez
Likes to sample her pricks in big batches.
So she frequently screws
The mates and the crews
While the captains are safe under hatches.

1948.

707. TRUE ENTHUSIASM

There was a fat lady named Nelly
Whose bosom hung down to her belly.
She enjoyed copulation
With such animation
That she mashed all her partners to jelly.
—*Squashed 'em like flies!*

1948.

708

Said a sexy young nymph of Newcastle :
" A fuck's at least partly a wrassle,
From the spread of your thighs,
Through the humping and sighs,
To the slow easing out his wet tassel. "

1965.

709

A damsel from far Newport News
Was a pushover when she would booze.
So men filled her with whiskey,
To keep her cunt frisky,
And used her for suck-offs and screws.

1950.

710

A maker of condoms was Newsom,
And the one he designed was quite gruesome :
It seemed strangely confused
But was meant to be used
By three people instead of a twosome.

1967A-1975.

711

Three whores took on nine men at once,
In their mouths and their assholes and cunts.
Only on a golf green
Can gen'rally be seen
Eighteen balls and nine holes at such stunts.

1954J.

712

The last time I had an orgasm,
It came with a spine-tingling spasm.
In the midst of our thralls
It busted my balls,
And I smeared all the walls with my plasm!

1969A.

713

A damsel who sailed the Pacific,
When the cocks in her cunt grew prolific,
Exclaimed, " This is fun,
But it's wearing on one :
The strain on my twot is terrific! "

1950.

714

In a broken-down Indian pagoda,
One hears the Ranee of Baroda
Serviced ten sexual bandits,
Including two pandits,
Afterwards blowing each who'd bestroda.

1966.

715

The sexual demands of Miss Payne
Cause even strong men to complain.
Two chaps on a spree
Started Wednesday at three,
And were carried out Sunday—insane!

1965.

716

It seems that all our perversions
Were known to the Medes and the Persians.
But the French and the Yanks
Earn our undying thanks
For inventing some modernized versions.

1962.

717

A gent who spoke fluent pornography
Met girls who mixed sex with choreography.
The flicks they created
Were triple-X rated—
Set records for filth in photography.

1971 *ff.*

718. THE INCA

The Inca, in ruling Peru,
Had really but little to do.
Supplied with fresh virgins,
He'd assuage his sex urgin's,
And spent life in a perpetual screw.

[719]

When the Inca found virgins grew rare,
There were always fresh llamas, or bear!
What prudes view as bestial
He declared was celestial,
And fucked every hole in his paradise terrestial.

[720]

In erection within the royal palace
The Inca, with Incaic malice,
Would bugger his wives
Till they broke out in hives,
And his Regal Pud grew a great callus.

[721]

Whoever said " No " to the Inca
Was flung in a crater extinca,
Leaving behind genitalia
To adorn his regalia—
This Inca was really a stinca!

1966.

722

Her pubic hair Pam pats with pride,
Though it's gummed up with semen that's dried.
Her lover, young Ewing,
Gets nervous when screwing,
And goes off before he's inside.

1965.

723

The mere sight of horny Miss Pringle
Causes male genitalia to tingle.
    Every cocksman in town
    Has roped that girl down—
We all hope to hell she stays single.

1966.

724

The belly on Tillie protrudes,
Due to hipshots from twenty male nudes.
    At that party at Lear's
    She laid all but three queers,
Six impotent guys, and two prudes.

1965.

725

The crotch of Miss Gotch of Purdue
Is the cunthole us guys love to screw.
    She takes *so* many peckers
    We're now all wet-deckers,
And slide in on the other guy's goo.

1965.

726

Beware of a fate such as Queenie's,
Whose downfall was due to martinis.
    Ten got her so drunk
    She'd give sex to a skunk,
And all the men pickled their weenies.

1966.

727

There once was a coed named Rath
Who dreamed she got screwed in her bath.
    She woke up perspiring,
    And said, "How inspiring!—
And more fun than doing my math."

1962A.

728

Said an unashamed satyr named Rex,
Unabashedly showing his sex:
  " My bollocks are brimmin',
  I hanker for wimmen—
This display better have some effects!"

1965.

729

A boisterous cocksman named Rind
Stuffed a firecracker up his behind,
  And screwed sweet Miss Pearl—
  A decent young girl—
Out of what she had used for her mind!

1965.

730

An opera tenor in Rio
Had vocal chords where he did pee-o.
  As he dabbled his dong
  It broke into song,
Rendering " O Sole Mio " *con brio!*

1966.

731

There was an old sadist named Rip
Who made love to his wife with a whip.
  He'd tease and provoke her,
  And finally choke her,
As he shot her a fuck in the hip.

1971 *ff.*

732. MARRIED MAN'S RUST

There was a young man so robust
That he suffered from Married Man's Rust.
  When he slipped girls the missile
  It made their ass whistle,
But the blast of his ass gave him thrust.

1975A.

733. SMOG ON CAPITOL HILL

" Where're my rubbers? " cried Phog with a roar.
" The junk here could stock up a store!
Can't you half-witted shits
Lay your hands on those kits—
Those French ticklers I bought for Miss Shore? "

[734]

Said the page at the Senator's door :
" They want you at once on the floor. "
" You damn, whey-faced shit,
Go say I can't quit ;
Just tell them I'm fucking my whore! "

[735]

" Holy Jesus! " cried Phog, " something's tore.
Here's a mishap I greatly deplore.
Three cheers for motherhood!
And all of that other crud—
I've just shot my bolt in Miss Shore! "

[736]

Since Phogbound must go on the floor,
And hasn't quite brought off his whore,
He endeavors by proxy
To finish his doxy :
The Sergeant-at-Arms gets the chore.

[737]

Said Phogbound : " I'm poor at retarding.
When attempted, it just leads to farting.
No slow pokes for me—
Let the jizz flow like pee!
I'm no Warren Gamaliel Harding! "

1969.

738. WIFE-TRADING FROM A TO Z

My wife has an elegant rump.
Whenever a man has a hump,
He's invited to hug her,
And drug her, and bugger
The hole that is used as her dump.

[739]

My wife is a glorious lay,
She'll take it in any old way.
You may bugger or French her,
Or fuck her and drench her
Hot womb with your genital spray.

[740]

I've always loved buggering brother,
And licking the cunt of my mother.
But the joy of my life
Is to see my sweet wife
Suck pricks off, one after another!

[741]

My wife, in her best bib and tucker,
Will ask men to please give her succor,
Though each man she met
Found her ovary wet
From the last man who happened to fuck her.

[742]

My wife is a filly of wit.
She'll say, " Go ahead, suck my tit ;
Beat my ass black and blue,
And then you may screw
Till you've squirted your spunk in my slit. "

[743]

There was a young man from Point Hunt,
My wife asked him, " What do you want?
A tail, juicy, fine?—
Why don't you try mine? "
So he shot off his prick in her cunt.

[744]

A man asked my wife, " May we fuck? "—
" I'm flowing. Your cock let me suck.
You can knock up at will
My daughter—maid still—
And cream off my sons, just for luck! "

[745]

My wife is ideal for screw'n,
By kike, polack, mick, wop, or coon.
Though we men much prefer
When enjoying of her,
To use it for pot or spittoon.

[746]

A burglar named Willy O'Bangeller
Said, " Cash, or your wife! Man, I'll mangle her,
And rape her! Quick—which? "
I said, " Rape the bitch,
And I'll suck off your prick if you strangle her. "

1950.

747

Said a steaming young lady named Russell,
As she piled into bed for a tussle :
" I've got a hot oven,
So get busy shovin'—
Start pushing in *yards* of love-muscle! "

1965.

748

The rapists who rape around Salem
Hope their genital organs won't fail 'em.
    It'd look rather silly
    To tip over a filly,
Lacking that which one needs to assail 'em.

1965.

749

A philosopher known for sarcasm
Took a tart to his bed for orgasm.
    He found to his horror
    He had a limp jarrer,
And denounced her as naught but phantasm.

1971 *ff*.

750. MACHINOMANIA

To the penis of feeble old Schuster
Was attached an electrical booster.
    In a screw with Miss Drew
    His main rheostat blew,
And she felt like a snowplow had goosed 'er!

1966.

751

When Cupid loved Psyche, it seems,
Their sex life was one of extremes.
    Their performance in bed
    Exceeded, it's said,
The wildest sex orgies of dreams.

1973.

752

It is rumored in Seneca Falls
That when horny young Engelbert calls,
    He gets stewed, he gets blewed,
    He gets screwed and tattooed—
These modern kids just climb the walls!

1966.

753

There was a young lady named Sentry
Who claimed to be raped by some gentry.
But the judge said, " Dismissed! "
When he looked where she pissed,
And saw *no* signs of forcible entry.

1975.

754

The horrible snake-goddess, Set,
Was fucked by a man on a bet.
When he tried to get near 'er
She became a chimera—
It's something he'd rather forget.

1970A.

755

There was a young lady named Seward
Who claimed she had never been skewered,
Till the time she was trapped in
The hold by the captain,
And was fucked by the purser and steward.

1975.

756

Sigmund Freud's discussion of sex
Centers much around Oedipus Rex :
A stupid young sucker
Who turned mother-fucker,
And placed quite a hex upon sex.

1971A.

757

Two dollies aboard a cruise ship
Men found mighty easy to trip.
But their sexual excesses
So wrinkled their dresses,
That next time they're planning to strip.

1965.

758

On good old Malaya's shore
Lived a queen with the tastes of a whore.
When asked to cohabit,
She would fuck like a rabbit
'Gainst the side walls, the ceiling, or floor.

1944.

759

To the eunuch, the Queen of Siam
Cried, " Fuck me, O nutless Big Sam!
Behind or in front,
Either arsehole or cunt,
One or both—I don't give a goddam! "

1966.

760

It's a wonderful pleasure to sin
With the bountifully lusty Miss Quinn.
But her love-screams and crying
Are terribly trying—
Twice last week the cops busted in.

1965.

761. POCKET VENUS

She looked terribly fragile and small,
As she stood with her back to the wall.
But she opened her sluices,
And let out her juices,
And bloody near flooded the hall!

ff. 1970*

762

A saucy young lady of Spitz
To some boys showed a full pair of tits.
One she let fondle,
To another gave suck,
But the last one she couldn't stop having a fuck.

1953U.

763. TALES OF MY LANDLORD

The Blonde on the Bar-stool thus spoke :
" I prefer the unusual poke.
I like it, when able,
Bent over a table,
Or spread-eagled under an oak. "

[764]

Said one of the Boys in the Band :
" I never have done it by hand. "
Spurred by contumely,
Laughing most gloomily,
He added : " I hear that it's grand. "

[765]

The Bartender reeled out his whang,
An instrument stiffened with bhang :
Of Old Adam's family,
Oozing so clammily,
A veteran of arse, cunt, and fang.

[766]

With a leap on the Lady named Lou,
He flamed up her arse with his goo.
Ere her limbs frigidly
Stiffened too rigidly,
He dealt her a murderous screw!

[767]

Said mine Host : " This will not do a bit.
You are getting me arse-deep in shit.
Touch her not scornfully,
Lift her up mournfully,
Pinch her once more on the tit! "

1976A.

768

There was a young lady from Spain
Who liked it now and again.
By " Now and again, "
Please let me explain,
I mean now and *again* and AGAIN!

1950R.

769

A stringy food-faddist named Sprat
Wed a maid who was billows of fat.
After strenuous tries
At exposing her prize,
He farted so hard that he shat.

1971 *ff*.

770

On a mattress with superspeed springs
Nan found that by using the things,
With her lover astride,
It was like a high ride,
While the guy felt as though he had wings.

1965.

771

Sweet nymphomanic Miss Stainer
Finds most male sex organs now pain her.
" I guess that I've blundered, "
She said, " seven hunderd
Are too much for one little container. "

1966.

772

An impotent fumbler named Starrett
Lured a kitchenmaid up to the garret.
Intent upon sexing,
He found it damned vexing
To hear " Foul ball! " shrieked by the parrot.

1966.

773

A sweet Georgia peach of high station
Became overnight a sensation,
When she took on Fort Benning
And charged not a pfenning,
Saying, " Who could do less for her nation? "

1972.

774

In case you like sexual stunts,
Don't take on five cunts all at once.
All wise men eschew
Overdoing a screw ;
It can shrink mighty peckers to runts!

1965.

775

A whore had the notion sublime
To take on seven men at a time :
One on top, one beneath,
In each hand, in the teeth,
And two with her toes—for a dime!

1953.

776. THE OLDEST JOKE

Said Jim to his sweet sister Sue :
" Mom's much better fucking than you. "
Said Sue, " What a bore!
I have heard that before,
From Daddy and Gran'pappy too. "

1948-1975A.

777

Said a worn-out young fellow named Tabor
To his nymphomaniacal neighbor :
" In sex I delight,
But a dozen a night
Comes under the head of slave labor. "

1965.

778. REVELRY

A froward young fellow named Tarr
Had a habit of fucking his Ma.
"Go pester your sister,"
She said when he kissed her;
"I have trouble enough with your Pa."

1966A.

779

At the corner of Sutter and Taylor
Lay a girl being fucked by a sailor.
From the crowd came loud cheers
(Except for two queers)
As they watched his great instrument nail 'er.

1965.

780

In the army and navy the toast is:
To the talented USO hostess,
Who was diddled by scores
Who could not afford whores—
Of hostesses she was the mostest!

1945A.

781

An elderly harlot from Trings
Has fucked the last four Spanish kings.
Says she, "They're all short,
And no good at the sport,
But the queen is a lezzie, and swings."

1971B.

782

A roundly raped girl of Tulane
Cried, "It may not be nice to complain,
But why can't I ever
Get raped in good weather?
I *always* get raped in the rain!"

1966.

783. RAPE ! !

As a hobby, rape helps to kill time,
So why the law calls it a crime
Us rapists can't see—
It's the Land of the Free,
And with rape you don't pay a damn dime.

[784]

An agile young rapist named Jay
Who settles for five rapes a day,
Says : " Rape's great for erections,
But takes fast connections,
And one *helluva* fast getaway! "

[785]

A rapist who raped in West Lunt
Made this interesting comment on cunt :
" Every dame has a twat,
But I rapes just the hot,
So it's that kind of cunt that I hunt. "

[786]

A rapist who practiced near Nice
Was cautioned severely to cease.
He was not to be doing
That promiscuous screwing—
Such stuff is reserved for police.

[787]

" As to rape, " mused Joe Blow in Cell 9,
" I'll take any cunthole for mine :
Dogs, sheep, mares, or squirrels,
Or, if nothing else, girls—
As long as it *stinks,* man, it's fine! "

1965.

788

At the orgy I humped twenty-two
And was glad when the whole thing was through.
    I don't find it swinging
    To do all that change-ringing,
But at orgies what else can you *do*?

1965.

789

A couple named Big Dick and Valerie
Were hired at fabulous salary
    To make love on the stage;
    Though the censors all rage,
It sure pleased us bums in the gallery.

1965.

790

There was a young lady from Vassar,
At screwing none could surpass her.
    So she went up to Yale
    And peddled her tail
From the Bulldog up to the Headmaster.

1953.

791

A machine-built-for-love is Miss Vector,
So at times her subsexual sector
    Just comes to a boil
    From a shot of hot oil,
And that last lubrication nigh wrecked 'er!

1966.

792

A vibrant and virile young Viking
For intercourse had a great liking.
    He would shatter the asses
    Of sweet Viking lasses
As though he were lightning a-striking.

1958.

793. LO! THE WELL-HUNG INDIAN

A Blackfoot whose pecker was vast
Made the silent squaws scream when he'd blast.
    When he hankered to screw
    He'd select twenty-two,
And their first fuck was often their last.

[794]

To his squaw said the Iroquois stud :
" It's full moon, and your cunt's running blood.
    For a nighttime of joys
    I've picked two fat white boys,
With assholes like roses in bud. "

[795]

She's a chaste Hopi virgin no more
Since two bucks got her spread on the floor.
    Her career as a tart
    Ended right at the start,
For she made just two bucks and no more!

[796]

A passion-swept Seminole buck
Wouldn't pay a red cent for a fuck.
    Shunned by Indian girls
    He resorted to squirrels,
And in one extreme case to a duck.

[797]

Beware of that sensuous Sioux,
For no one can get her to screw!
    She gave no relief
    To her favorite chief,
Until both of his balls had turned blue.

[798]

A proper young tourist in Taos
Had her panties trimmed neatly with lace.
    But a Navaho buck
    Roped her down for a fuck,
And left them pure panties in chaos!

[799]

An Arapaho given to screwing
Laid a lush tourist dolly from Ewing.
    As he slowly withdrew,
    He said : " Heap good cunt, you.
Now douche yourself, babe, and quit stewing. "

[800]

A Nez Percé squaw from the prairie
Of sex and such nonsense was wary,
    Till a well-hung Apache
    Got her down in Wenatchee—
Now he milks her along with the dairy.

[801]

A hot Piute squaw in Nevada
Got madda and madda and madda.
    What so much dismayed her
    Was the Injun who laid her,
For he'd poked his vast pud in her bladda.

[802]

When Chief Long-Pecker has an erection,
Small boys view the sight with affection.
    His delight is to pillage
    Virgins, village by village—
Squaws, head in the other direction!

1966.

803. THE ROMANTIC AGONY

In bed the Romantics were vile—
Lord Byron apart, Shelley's style
Was to lick his wife's belly
While poor Mary Shelley
Wrote *Frankenstein* grimly meanwhile.

[804]

If Byron laid his half-sister Augusta,
'Twas but to give the gossip columns lustre,
And should not nowadays, in practice,
From his poetry distract us—
Get on with reading *Manfred,* will you, Buster?

[805]

'Twas a trait of small Thomas Love Peacock's
And his brother to sink both their wee cocks
Into fish, snake, or bird,
But the tail they preferred
Was the one that made Thomas love peacocks.

[806]

Swinburne—he of the multiple rhyme—
Was a victim of nursery crime.
To make his little pinny stir
His nurse used to administer
Treatment so sweet and sinister
It still made Swinburne burn when in his prime.

[807]

Ivy Compton-Burnett's irritations!
And the titles she gives her narrations!
All those misses and misters,
Those " Brothers and Sisters "—
They all sound like sexual relations!

1974.

[808]

No wonder that Lord Bulwer-Lytton
With the penning of novels was smitten:
Every morn in a trice
His wife sucked him off twice—
The Coming Race had to be written.

[809]

No urine was ever pristiner
Than the piss of Rossetti, Christina.
So claimed Ford Madox Brown
As he quaffed a tot down,
In a cup of her priceless bone china.

1974-1976A.

810

Though he tried many times, many ways,
To fuck his beloved with *sauvaise,*
He'd constantly fail
To find the detail
That would send her right off in a blaze.

1971*ff*.

811

An innocent virgin was wed
To a man with one thought in his head:
He wanted to futter
His wife into butter,
But the first time he creamed her, she fled.

1971*ff*.

812

There was a young fellow named Weft
Whose movements were rapid and deft.
While his girl ate her dinner,
He got his prick in her—
She was still in the throes when he left.

1975.

813

There was a grass widow out west
Whose manner of fucking was best.
  She could raise up and hone
  A skeleton's bone—
And had *done* it one time, on a test.

1965.

814

They say that the natives of Wheeling
Prefer to go at it while kneeling.
  It does give a crick
  In the shank of the prick,
But oh! what a glorious feeling!

1950.

815. ONE WHO KNOWS

A sizzling nympho named Whitely
Demanded a workover nightly.
  You'd fuck her for hours
  With all of your powers,
Then creep home all limp and unsightly.

1965.

816

The genital itch of Miss Wing
Caused a riot last week in Big Spring.
  Ten men dropped their pants
  For a go at her ants,
But they didn't calm down a damned thing.

1965.

817

The sight of three tits on Miss Witt
Causes hard-peckered lechers to shit.
  When she pulls off her pants
  Guys haven't a chance,
For the bitch never *does* wanta quit.

1966.

818

There was a young lady named Wright
Who claimed she gave Turkish delight.
  Her cunt was the juiciest,
  Hottest and gooseyest—
One man who survived said, "Quite right."

1967A-1975.

819

A sheik from far-off Xanadu
Had not just one penis, but two.
  He wailed, "Woe is me!
  If I only had three,
I could masturbate, bugger, and screw."

1948.

820

There's a passionate lady of Yorick
Whose temperature's always caloric.
  As a general rule
  She deep-fries a guy's tool.
For him, screwing *her* is historic!

1965.

821

A newlywed bride, Mrs. Young
Asked the doctor to fix her torn lung.
  When asked how it ripped,
  She replied, as she stripped:
"That man that I married is *hung!*"

1954J.

822

Impatient and passionate youth!
They got laid in a telephone booth.
  When he pressed button "C"
  She exploded in pee—
The onlookers thought it uncouth.

1970A.

IV

ORAL IRREGULARITY

823

Said the cunt-lapping Bey of Algiers,
In a cunt halfway up to his ears:
  " This nautch is delicious,
    And without doubt nutritious.
She's my best-tasting wife in ten years! "

1965.

824

There was a young chap in Arabia
Who courted a widow named Fabia.
  " Yes, my tongue is as long
    As the average man's dong, "
He said, licking the lips of her labia.

1948.

825

A linguist at old Balmoral
Lay down one day on his Laurel.
    He said, at the end :
  " Better gargle, dear friend,
You've just passed your middle French oral. "

1965A.

826

A loquacious cocksucker named Bassett
Had mastered his art in each facet.
    He delighted to rave
    Of the pleasure it gave,
But was happiest when he was *tacit.*

1955J.

827

Young Frederick the Great was a beaut.
To a guard he cried, " Hey, man, you're cute.
If you'll come to my palace,
I'll finger your phallus,
And then I shall blow on your flute. "

1970A.

828

A cocksucking steno named Beeman
Remarked as she swallowed my semen :
" On my minuscule salary
I must watch every calorie,
So I get *ahead* eating you he-men! "

1966.

829

There was a young man of Belgrade
Who remarked, " I'm a queer piece of trade.
I will suck, without charge,
Any cock, if it's large.
If it's small, I expect to be paid. "

1954A.

830. NO SMOKING, PLEASE

That rotten old person named Biggem,
He likes to have little girls frig him.
The big girls he fuckses,
Their panties he muckses,
And trains 'em to swallow and swig him.

1976A.

831

There once was a guardsman from Buckingham
Who said, " As for girls, I hate fucking 'em.
But when I meet boys,
God! how I enjoys
Just licking their peckers and sucking 'em. "

1950.

832

A newlywed husband named Bynum
Asked his bride to please sixty-nine him.
When she just shook her head,
He sighed sadly and said :
" Well, if we can't lick 'em, let's jine 'em! "

1970A.

833

There was a young girl of Cape Town
Who usually fucked with a clown.
He taught her the trick
Of sucking his prick,
And when it went up—she went down.

1955A.

834

There was a young man named Carruthers
Who sucked off the cocks of his brothers.
He cuntsucked just dozens
Of sisters and cousins,
And knocked up both his grandmothers!

1950.

835

There was a young fellow named Case
Who entered a cunt-lapping race.
He licked his way clean
Through Number Thirteen,
But then slipped and got pissed in the face.

1975.

836

There was a young girl of Catalina
Who had a peculiar demeanor :
Either she'd fuck,
Or else she would suck,
And I'm not quite sure *which* was the cleaner.

1948.

837

There was a young slattern of Cette
Who was devilishly fond of a bet.
    She wagered she'd suck
    Twenty cocks for a buck,
And she's cleaning the kitchen up yet!

1954A.

838

A clergyman's bride, very chaste,
Who wanted a child in great haste,
    Said : " Mother, I grieve,
    But I'll *never* conceive—
I just can't get used to the taste. "

1968A.

839

A charming *jeune fille* of Châteauneuf
Had a rep for knowing her steuf :
    She did *à cheval*,
    This remarkable gal,
And specialized in *soixante-neuf*.

1954A.

840. CHRISTMAS PARTY

There was a young girl from the coast
Who, just when she needed it most,
    Lost her Kotex and bled
    All over the bed,
And the head and the beard of her host.

1958A.

841

A lecherous barkeep named Dale,
After fucking his favorite female,
    Mixed Drambuie and scotch
    With the cream in her crotch
For a lustier, Rusty-er Nail.

1971*ff*.

842

The cunthole on Kate in Detroit
Was the size and shape of a quoit.
    It proved hopeless, on viewing,
    For conventional screwing,
And lapping lured just the adroit.

1966.

843

There was a young fellow named Dick
Who had a magnificent prick.
    It was shaped like a prism
    And shot so much gism
It made every cocksucker sick.

1948.

844

Said sneering Mohammed el-Din :
" Only infidel dogs put it in.
    Back home in Arabia
    We nibble the labia
Till the juice dribbles off of our chin. "

1965.

845

There's a social-psych coed at D.U.
Who'd just as soon suck you as see you.
    Veblen gave her a taste
    For conspicuous waste :
Are the other girls jealous? Miew!!

1948.

846

There was a lewd fellow named Duff
Who loved to dive deep in the muff.
    With his head in a whirl
    He said, " Spread it, Pearl ;
I cunt get enough of the stuff! "

1966.

847

" Fucked by the finger of Fate! "
Bewailed a young fellow named Tate.
" Since dating Miss Baugh,
My whole tongue has been raw—
It must have been something I ate. "

1965.

848

There was a young lady of Fez
Who was known to the public as " Jez. "
Jezebel was her name,
Sucking cocks was the game
She excelled at (so everyone says).

1969.

849. ONCE OVER LIGHTLY

A fagged fornicator named Flynn
Said, " Concerning my yearning to sin :
When my doodad goes dead
I just use the old head,
And work off the bitch with my chin! "

1965.

850

There was an old man from Fort Drum
Whose son was incredibly dumb.
When he urged him ahead,
He went down instead,
For he thought to *succeed* meant succumb.

1953J.

851

A boardinghouse floozy named Glubb
Loved sucking off cocks in the tub.
Her midnight ablutions
Were filled with pollutions
Of men coming home from the pub.

1960.

852

There was a young lady named Grace
Who would *not* take a prick in her " place. "
Though she'd kiss it and suck it,
She never would fuck it—
She just couldn't relax face-to-face.

1953.

853

A happy old hooker named Grace
Once sponsored a cunt-lapping race.
It was hard for beginners
To tell who were winners :
There were cunt hairs all over the place.

1975.

854

An amusing young lady named Greer
Was always dispensing good cheer.
Her favorite trick
Was to suck on the prick
Of a guest who was serving her beer.

1948.

855

There was an old bastard named Grimes
Who bragged of his sexual crimes :
One in bed with a whore,
Sixty-nine on the floor—
For a total of seventy times.

1975.

856

That hearthrug-pie fancier, Hicks,
Prefers young girls fresh from the sticks.
Says he : " For the tongue,
Get 'em dewy and young.
It's then you get in your best licks. "

1966.

857. DEEP THROAT

The star of that X-rated hit
Plays a nurse with a throat full of clit.
  This serves as a palace
  For each turgid phallus—
Some say that the plot is pure shit.

1974A.

858

A corpulent young man named Hyatt
Sowed all his wild oats on the quiet.
  He was caught on a wharf
  Bending over a dwarf,
But explained he had gone on a diet.

1950R.

859

There was an old nudist named Ikey
Who had a disconcerted psyche.
  He fell arse-to-face
  On a Chinese named Grace,
Who chortled, "No movee, me likee."

1971 *ff*.

860

A legman for Research Immoral
Got hung up, it appears, on the oral.
  Asked to do the statistics
  On cunnilinguistics,
He said, "I might give it a whorel!"

1970A.

861

There was a young twirp of Ishkooda—
I never knew anyone lewder.
  She sucked off the chauffeur,
  The African loafer,
And worried his cock till he screwed her.

1950.

862

There was an old rounder named Jack
Unable to cream in a crack.
    But with a cocksucking hag or a
    Boy, he'd Niagara,
Even while flat on his back.

1950.

863

Pearl's panties came down with a jerk,
As she bared her fair bottom for work.
    Said she, " Pants are silly,
    But the men like 'em frilly,
And *chewing* 'em drives men berserk! "

1965.

864

There was a young fellow named Jewett
Whose prick was too short, and he knew it.
    He said as he stuck it
    In where she could suck it :
" But darling, you don't need to chew it. "

1948.

865

There once was a man named Jim
Who had a girl who ate hymén.
    It wasn't her size
    That attracted his eyes,
But the crystallized cum on the rim.

1963*

866

There once was a fellow named Keith
Who liked it above and beneath.
    His nights were so harried,
    As positions were varied,
That he woke up with hair in his teeth.

1960.

867

A juggler of women I knew
Had a tongue that would oft go askew.
    While chomping hair pie
    (Both her legs in the sky)
He would double-tongue wrong—up her flue!

1971A.

868

There was a young lady named Lees
Whose tits were as small as two peas.
    When a boy started kissing,
    He thought they were missing,
So he kissed in the place where she pees.

1968A.

869

Said a lass to a lecher named Legman :
" Get up off your knees, and don't beg, man.
    With your tongue in my pussy,
    And your necktie all juicy,
You look like a butter-&-egg man. "

1955A.

870

She grabbed both my ears and cried, " Lissen!
You're driving me wild with your kissin'.
    So close, but oh my!
    Just a few inches high—
Move down, or you'll make me start pissin'! "

ff.1970*

871. DENTAL FLOSS

There was a young Scotsman named Leith,
Caught gobbling the goop on the heath.
    But he broke jail, by Jove,
    With a rope that he wove
Out of hairs that he plucked from his teeth.

1956A.

872

A twelve-year-old nymphet, Lolita,
Was an expert at eating a peter.
She demurely would say :
" I could nibble all day—
I'm a slow but fastidious eater. "

1970A.

873

A cocksucking whore in Long Prick
Said : " Semen gulped straight is too thick.
But it gets nice and thin
If you cut it with gin ;
A Croatian dwarf taught me that trick. "

1965.

874

A full-breasted girl named Louise
Had a habit of pulling her chemise
To a point well above
Her object of love
For any sucker who'd get on his knees.

1946A.

875

There once was a jenny from Luxor
Who said to her sheik, " Don't let's fuck, sir!
My cave is so large
It would swallow your barge—
Dive in for an old-fashioned suck, sir! "

1950.

876

Of her first sex encounter, Miss Lyme
Said : " I had a delirious time!
I'd have paid any money
To suck all that honey,
But nobody charged me a dime. "

1966.

877

A sexual wreck was MacDougall ;
He ceased all relations con*ju*gal.
So his wife sadly said,
" Since your pecker is dead,
I'll blow ' Taps ' on your battered old bugle. "

1975.

878

Have you heard of Professor McFigg,
That awful, male-chauvinist pig?
All the coeds he screws,
Feeds 'em reefers and booze,
And teaches them semen to swig.

1976A.

879

There was a young man from Madrid
Who discovered when only a kid
That by lying supine,
And twisting his spine,
He could suck his own cock—so he did!

1948.

880. ONE-DOWNMANSHIP

There was a young actor named Mallory
Who gobbled his boss in the gallery.
He said, with some wit,
" I may be a shit,
But look at the size of my salary. "

1953.

881

Joe is just one of the masses
Of guys quite inept with the lasses.
He remarked in a fright,
As he kissed her good-night :
" Spread your legs, dear, you're breaking my glasses. "

1953.

882

A couple named Carmen and Matteo
Found their organs were quite incompatio.
Said he, with a snicker:
"Since mine is no thicker,
We'll have to resort to fellatio."

1960.

883

Quoth the sage: "If Mankind can mature,
Will sexual perversions grow fewer?
Until cunnilinctus
Is almost extinct as—"
(*Pause*.) "Malady's better than cure!"

1974.

884

There was a young fellow named Menzies.
Whose kissing sent girls into frenzies.
But a virgin one night
Crossed her legs in a fright,
And fractured his bifocal lenses!

1968A.

885

A tongue-happy chappy named Mingus
For his sex kicks prefers cunnilingus.
One babe whom he savored
Remarked, as he slavered:
"It sure beats a bang with your dingus."

1965.

886

There was a black whore from Montrose
Whom a man told to suck off his hose.
When she started to chew it
He quickly withdrew it,
And gave her his load up the nose.

1956J.

887

There was a young couple from Mucking
Who disapproved strongly of sucking.
So they spent day and night
In chaster delight,
Just fucking, and fucking, and fucking.

1950.

888

A playboy who came to New York
Coaxed a bunny to kiss his p'dork.
It rose up so huge
It shot a deluge
Before the poor girl got her fork.

1971 *ff*.

889

There was a young maid named O'Hare
Whose cunt was so juicy and rare
That her date, if you please,
Simply fell to his knees,
As he paused for a moment of prayer.

1975.

890

There was a young lady of Ophir
Whose mother said, " That girl's a loafer!
I don't like her trick
Of nibbling the prick,
And sucking the balls of the chauffeur. "

1950.

891. TOO OLD TO CUT THE MUSTARD?

You men who are not up to par,
And no longer in sex seem to star,
There's no need to get flustered
If you can't cut the mustard,
You always can lick out the jar.

1975.

892

A truculent guy from Pawtucket
Inquired of a girl if she'd suck it.
She exclaimed with surprise,
" Why, it makes my gorge rise! "
He replied with a snarl, " Well then, fuck it! "

1971*ff*.

893

A young midget couple named Pfaff
Engage in sex play with a laugh.
When lust raises its head
They lay on the bed,
And perform thirty-four-and-a-half.

1963B.

894

Wept Nell to the Sarge, " I'm no pickup.
I've been stranded out here by a stickup. "
As they bounced down the trail
In his jeep, she turned pale,
And moaned, " Sir, shall I crap, COME, or hiccup? "

ff.1969A.

895

A wealthy young squaw, a Piute,
Thought cocksucking utterly cute.
And if you lacked succor,
She'd laugh while you'd fuck her,
And tip you a dollar, to boot!

1950.

896

The French are a race among races,
They screw in the funniest places.
Any orifice handy
Is considered just dandy,
And that goes for the one in their faces.

1948.

897

A toothless old wench named De Roncelles
Was acquainted with numerous consuls.
They'd come to be gummed,
And she'd gum as they'd come ;
She really had overworked tonsils.

1953.

898

Two dykes went their separate routes :
Said one, " I just *don't* give two hoots.
No common tie linked us
Except cunnilinctus,
And a penchant for Brooks Brothers suits. "

1953A.

899

There was a young Frog from the Saar
Who went down on a boy's prick too far.
And he near had a spasm
When a sudden orgasm
Inundated his uvular " R ".

1948.

900. TOGETHERNESS

As she sucked on Pete's peter, Pam said :
" It's that big squirt of come that I dread.
That thick baby goo
Tastes a lot like cheap glue—
I'd prefer it vanilla instead. "

[901]

As he sniffed at her snatch, Peter said :
" Woman, something down there sure smells dead.
Perhaps I seem hasty,
But I doubt if it's tasty,
So I'll settle for fucking, instead! "

1965.

902

A big bull-dyke, surly and sallow,
Cried, "Pricks are just wicks without tallow!
    Why, all men admit
    They'd prefer a clit."
(That's something I find hard to swallow.)

1970A.

903

There once was a poetess Sapphic
Who wrote about things pornographic.
    She would daily entwine
    In the old sixty-nine,
And indulge in nefarious traffic.

1956-1967A.

904

There once was a jolly young satyr
Who when seeing a lass would then mate her.
    But when one grew with child
    His ardor grew mild,
And the next one he saw, well, he ate her.

*ff.*1968A.

905

There once was a bridegroom named Schmidt,
Could never divine his wife's clit.
    She complained all disgruntled:
    "I love to be frontalled—
Cunniling-is my favorite bit!"

1971*ff.*

906

There was a young stripling from Selma
Who sucked off his mother, named Thelma.
    "I never did dream
    A cunt held so much cream,
But God! what a terrible smell, ma!"

1950.

907

There once was a gay señorita
Whose pleasure was munching a peter.
She said, " It's much neater,
And certainly sweeter,
And æsthetically, somehow, completer! "

1973A.

908

There once was a maiden seraphic
Who doted on attitudes Sapphic.
She anointed her cunny
With essence of honey—
There's nothing like gumming up traffic.

1950.

909. PHONE : SNARK-6969

Her husband's a pimp, and will share
(For a lucrative fee) the quite rare
Connubial privilege
Of licking the dribblage
That oozes from 'round her cunt hair.

1969.

910

A versatile girl from the South
Of erogenous zones had no drouth.
When she opened her chasm
She would have an orgasm,
And ten when she did it by mouth!

1975.

911. MATH FOR THE MILLIONS

Four fairies once met in the street,
And arranged an exceptional treat :
Soixante-neuf was impractical,
So the only thing tactical
Was something like *cent-trente-huit.*

1960.

912

There once was a daring young stripper,
And a young man decided to flip her.
He thought he would kiss her
Right smack on the pisser,
But his necktie got caught in her zipper!

1973A.

913

The old crocodile sampled his tool
As he lay on his back in the pool.
And he spat and said, " My!
But I taste rather high.
Am I flavored like this as a rule? "

1965.

914

There was a wine taster named Trilling
Who thought he knew all about swilling.
With his tongue up the ass
Of a bright girl in class,
He murmured, " This vintage is thrilling! "

1956A.

915

There was an old fellow named Tuckem
Who liked little girls and would suck 'em.
When their cunts were hirsute
They would tickle his snoot,
And he'd rip off their panties and fuck 'em.

1975.

916

There once was a zealous old Turk
Who drove all the ladies berserk.
It was not with his prick,
Which was three inches thick,
But his tongue which he worked with a jerk.

1975.

917. RED RIDER

I came home at a quarter past two,
And there spread in bed was my Sue,
With my neighbor, old Fife,
Going down on my wife
The day that her period came due.

1965.

918

A frustrated boy on vacation
Could only cause girls consternation.
It seems that his dong
Was excessively long,
So he settled for autofellation.

1971 *ff*.

919

Said the beautiful, bountiful Venus
To a youth with a too-softened penis:
"You must stiffen your dingus,
Or else cunnilingus,
Or all will be over between us."

1952A.

920

There once was a girl named Veronica
Whose vagina was like a harmonica.
When blown the right way
The darn thing would play
A solo for Jew's harp on Chanukah.

1958.

921

That pretty young lady, Miss White,
Ran off in the still of the night
With a wealthy young Turk:
Now she need do no work,
She just lies and sucks Turkish delight.

1973.

922

There was a young man who said, " Why
Can't I suck my own cock, if I'm spry?
    Twist up like a worm,
    And lick off all the sperm?—
You never can tell till you try! "

1950.

923

The oral technique of Miss Wren
Appeals greatly to all virile men.
    This Southern-fried chicken
    On gism don't sicken,
And goes family-style, now and then.

1965.

924

Said a candid young lady from York
To a Frenchman who gnawed at her fork :
  " My cunt is dripping,
    So stop your sipping,
And use your cock as a cork! "

1963*

925

There was a young fellow from France
Who waited ten years for his chance.—
    Then he muffed it . . .

[*The only three-line limerick.*]

1948.

V

BUGGERY

926

The Grecians were famed for fine art,
And buildings and stonework so smart.
  They distinguished with poise
  The men from the boys,
And used crowbars to keep them apart.

1975.

927. THE BEY OF ALGIERS (II)

The long-peckered Bey of Algiers
Loved to spear chubby lads in their rears.
  A demon for semen,
  This buggersome he-man
Shot the chute till it seeped from their ears.

[928]

This two-balled old Bey of Algiers
Sent his head eunuch shopping for queers.
  "Mohammed," he smirked,
  As he casually jerked,
"Just be sure they have overdrive rears!"

1965.

929

A cretin who lived in an attic
Was fallaciously rated as static.
  But how little they knew,
  His knob was not blue,
But hoary—and necrophilatic.

1955.

930

There once was a fairy named Avers
Who encircled his cock with lifesavers.
    Though buggers all claimed
    That their asses were maimed,
Sixty-niners all cheered the new flavors.

1960.

931

In the back room of Frogsnipper's Bar,
Calmly puffing a two-bit cigar,
    The owner was browned,
    With his chin on the ground,
By a lad with a lavender car.

1966.

932

When it comes to the birds and the bees,
The Greeks excel others with ease.
    With a frontal attack
    Or an end run 'round back,
They impale any hole that they please.

1972.

933

There was a young man of Belgrade
Who slept with a girl in the trade.
    She said to him, " Jack,
    Try the hole in the back ;
The front one is badly decayed. "

1975.

934

Being buggered by big burly Ben,
Said a dolly in Almadén :
  " I'm tired of you queers
    Who only spear rears—
I'd like my cunt plugged now and then! "

1965.

935

It seems a fat homo of Bentree
Trafficks nightly with pederast gentry.
　It may strike you as frightful,
　But *he* finds it delightful,
As they vaseline up his rear entry.

1966.

936

" In my salad days, " said Lady Bierley,
" I took my cocks fairly and squarely.
　But now when they come,
　They go right up my bum—
And that only happens but rarely. "

1955.

937

A perverted young husband named Bligh
Tried to bugger his wife on the sly.
　In his lecherous haste
　He used library paste,
And now they are bound, hip & thigh.

1948.

938

There was a young fellow named Blum
Who was always too quick on the come.
　When he slept with a lass,
　As he felt for her ass
He would fill up her bum with the scum.

1948.

939. IN A PIG'S ASS

There was a young fellow named Butler
Who took out a girl to backscuttle 'er.
　She exclaimed : " Oh! what luck!
　I expected a fuck,
But this is a bloody sight subtler. "

1948.

940. WUFF TRADE

Said a hairless young homo from Butte:
"I detest being such a weird fruit."
He was frequently stomped,
So male hormones he chomped,
And he's now an effete, hairy brute.

1972.

941

Said a lady who lived on Cape Fear:
"I prefer being screwed in the rear.
Sailors like it that way,
And there's never a day
When the coast isn't perfectly clear."

1972.

942

There was a young man of Cape Town
Who acquired European renown
By sucking his come
From his bugger-boy's bumb,
Swallowing it, and keeping it down!

1904C.

943

There was a young man named Carruthers
Who buggered two crippled twin brothers.
And he felt some surprise,
As you may surmise,
When they both announced: "We are mothers!"

1948.

944

As Professor B. wiped his prick clean,
He cried, "Henry! your shit is obscene.
Next time, move your bowels,
Or I'll go back to fowls,
For I've punctured the piles of the Dean."

1966.

945

The passionate ass on Miss Coker
Requires wild prods from my poker.
You can hear her a block
When I ram in my cock,
And *ten* blocks when I start to butt stroke 'er!

1965.

946

The English are creatures quite cold,
Though one of them ventured so bold,
As to say to his bride :
" Please turn on your side,
I believe I have gotten arse-holed. "

1953.

947

Said a lecherous damsel named Cole,
When I complained about greasing my pole :
" Don't be so meticulous,
Honey man, it's ridiculous—
Let it slide into *any* old hole! "

1965.

948. ESOTERICA AMERICANA

Said the Doc to J. Fenimore Cooper :
" Son, something's gone wrong with your pooper.
Them Injuns, I fear,
Have attacked from the rear,
While you lay in inebriate stupor. "

1970A.

949

There was a young fellow of Crete
Who picked up a girl in the street.
Her cunt was so roomy
He became rather gloomy,
So she offered her asshole petite.

1975.

950

An intense dick addiction is Dan's :
He stands at the piss trough in cans,
    And avidly scans
    Every man's exposed glans,
While a book on the subject the son of a bitch plans!

1957J.

951

So I says to this mermaid, " My dear,
I've thought about this for a year :
    Since it's no use to hunt
    For a cunt in your front,
By chance, is there one in your rear? "

1965.

952. SADIE-MAISIE SPEAKS

The S. & M. bar, oh my dears,
Is a place to get stomped on, for queers.
    To get beaten and spat on,
    And pissed on and shat on—
The *thrill* of your gayest young years!

1972A.

953

The fastidious Count De la Rue
Fucked his servingman up the rear flue.
    " Nevermore, " the Count snapped,
    When the servingman crapped,
" Will I bugger a beggar like you! "

1958.

954

A well-buggered boy named Delpasse
Was cornholed by ten in his class.
    Said he, with a yawn :
    " Now the novelty's gone,
It's only a pain in the ass. "

1966A.

955

Let Spellman no longer detain us,
With his flexible glottis-*cum*-anus :
Not behind, you will note,
But in front of his throat,
Where it's far more likely to pain us.

1956A.

956

A sensible girl, name of Dexter,
Told the queer in her rear that he vexed 'er.
Why pick her arsehole
For his sexual goal,
When her cunt was right next?—it perplexed 'er!

1965.

957

A gallant young fellow named Dick
Was blessed with a galloping prick.
But the thing was quite blind
And went in from behind—
" This is, " said the lad, " rather thick. "

1955A.

958

A perverted scoutmaster named Dike
Loved to bugger a boy on a hike.
He felt pederasty
Was not really nasty,
But the judge said : " Ten years up the pike! "

1976A.

959. EMINENT STATESMEN

Said an Eminent Statesman named Dixon :
" I'll screw them *all,* now that my prick's in!
Let the voters complain
That their rectum's in pain—
Them assholes could sure use some fixin'. "

1974A.

960

The dissolute doings of Doris
Once shocked, but now only bore us.
    This concupiscent frail
    Is so hot in the tail
That her asshole has now become porous.

1965.

961. AFTER MARTIAL

There are those who profess honest doubt
At your claims to be virgin, Miss Trout.
    You refuse men your cunt,
    But if I may be blunt,
Your asshole is almost worn out.

1959J.

962

That transvestite Peter Doyle
Adored ruffles and tuffles and voile.
    Just to see his pink tool,
    Through a veil of dink tulle,
Rarely failed to provoke change of oil.

1957J.

963

The Hungarian charm of young Drill
Gives gals who love goosing a thrill.
    Before thumbing their bum
    He warms up his thumb,
So the goose is all thrill and no chill.

1966.

964

There was a young man from El Paso
Whose penis was shaped like a lasso.
    He presented this phallus
    To a lady from Dallas,
And roped a turd out of her asshole.

1948.

965

There was a young fellow named Eric
Who fucked in a manner Homeric:
Which means 'twixt the cheeks,
In the way of the Greeks,
Since he deemed other methods barbaric.

1953.

966

While the big shots along the Euphrates
Held to riches and slaves and *penates,*
In their measure of might
Was included delight
In steatopygious brown *nates.*

1960A.

967

The lovers of kooky Miss Fay
Her neighbors believe are all gay.
For none, when they call,
Use her front door at all:
They always go in the back way.

1965.

968. THE MAMMOTH COD

"Mark Twain," said wise Dr. Feebler,
"Never took out a nymphet to wheedle'r.
Like Whitman, 'twas buggery
And other hugger-muggery
That excited his tired old tweedler."

1976A.

969

A nearsighted fellow named Fender
Said: "Pardner, I think I surrender.
I've had more than enough,
And the going is tough,
And I fear you are of the wrong gender."

1975.

970

A big bugger-&-egg man named Field
Reaped the pleasures young boy-asses yield.
Now he's known as a queer
Since early last year,
When his favorite ass-istant squealed.

1965.

971

Said Dumas the *père* to the *fils* :
" I really am getting obese.
No longer a runt,
I project so in front
That I scarcely can bugger my niece. "

1969.

972

There was a young physicist named Fisk
Who was termed a security risk,
For acts of perversion
Were his only diversion,
At which one can only say " Tsk. "

1962.

973

A Tennessee faggot named Fleers
Remarked as he balled with some queers :
" As God is my witness,
If this ain't the shittenest
Gangbang that I've been on in years! "

1970A.

974

On a date with a lad, young Miss Flo,
When asked for a fuck answered, " No!
You can go second class—
Shove your prick up my ass—
I'm saving my cunt for my beau. "

1975.

975

An Indian of old Fort Duquesne
Had the oddest job ever seen :
It sparkled at night
Like the light of a sprite,
And after the ream turned to green.

1940-1957J.

976

An effete young esthete, Fruity Fred,
To a faggoty friend sadly said :
" When I woke up last night
Just imagine my fright
When I found a nude *girl* in my bed! "

1966.

977

A certain young lady named Freitas
Developed an anal pruritis,
The result (thus her claim)
Of her boyfriend's bad aim,
On repeated attempts at coitus.

1953.

978

A smooth-bottomed fellow named Fritz
Contracted a case of the shits.
Now with asshole distended
His future is ended—
He can't find a penis that fits.

1948.

979. TALES FROM BOCCACCIO

An Italian painter named Giotto
Seduced an old nun in a grotto.
To her shrivelled-up cunny
He preferred her fat bunny :
" Any port in a storm! " was his motto.

1945-1970A.

980

An aspiring young fellow named Grant
Unwillingly buggered his aunt.
He said, " On my uncle's
Backside are carbuncles :
I wish that I could, but I can't. "

1945C.

981

An athletic young cowgirl named Harriet
Keeps her boyfriend in line with a lariat.
Though she keeps a tight rein,
All her effort's in vain,
'Cause she isn't aware he's a farriet.

1972.

982. DIE WACHT AM RHEIN

An anal erotic named Herman
Had a passion for buggering mermen.
He'd lure the poor swine
From their haunts 'neath the Rhine
With songs in exécrable German.

1955A.

983

Said a chippie to Buggerby Hoke :
" I'm sure what you said is a joke.
Of course I've a pair
Of apertures there—
Just make *sure* it's the top one you poke! "

1965.

984

A tousled old harlot named Hough
Lost her trade on account of her muff.
But the men came in flocks
With inquisitive cocks,
When she broke out her virginal duff.

1956J.

985

Full of lust, a gym teacher named Howard
Was screwing a girl while she showered.
He said : " Listen, I hope
You're still holding that soap,
Or else it's your ass I've deflowered. "

1970A.

986

A sodomist, fresh out of jail,
Was desperate for some sort of tail.
Though it wasn't his type
He buggered the pipe
Of a truck clearly marked U.S. MAIL.

1971.

987

A midnight cowboy named Jervis
Said, " Long-peckered guys make me nervous.
With a shit-eating grin
They shove it all in,
And my asshole's a wreck giving service! "

1966.

988

There was an old man with fat jowls
Who said, as he spread out the towels :
" I know pederasty
Is sometimes thought nasty,
But think how it loosens the bowels. "

1948.

989

We all hate that pratt boy named Jules
Who fucks by the Queensberry rules.
His rectum is proper,
His prick is a whopper,
But oh! when he lets go his stools!

1976A.

990

It seems the Rajah of Kashmir
Is more than a little bit queer.
Nowadays his sex joys
Come from fat-bottomed boys,
And he ain't topped his wife for a year.

1966.

991

A hermaphrodite fairy of Kew
Offered boys something new in a screw,
For they both looked so sweet
On the front and back seat
Of a *bisexual built for two.*

1970A.

992. GOOD-BYE TO ALL THAT

A fat fetid fart named Laval
Served Hitler instead of a gal.
One night down at Vichy
Adolf said, "It's too itchy—
Your moustache, my bisexual pal."

1948.

993

There was a young bride named LaVerne
Who found she'd a great deal to learn.
The man she had wed
Took young boys into bed,
And she didn't know which way to turn.

1945.

994

A sad-eyed young pimp named Leander
Found it rather hard going, to pander.
For queer after queer
Cocked an eye at *his* rear,
Which they'd price with the greatest of candor.

1966.

995

There once was a tweetle called Lee,
Whom B***** invited to tea.
He was promptly debagged,
And buggered and shagged
Till his tool simply grew like a tree.

1920*

996

Squire Tupham, the bailiff of Leith,
Buggers pixies who dwell on the heath.
But his runcible dong
Is so terribly long,
He urinates right through their teeth.

1945.

997

There was a young fairy named Lessing
Whose fastidiousness was distressing.
He met many a lad
Who could have been had,
But found their prepuces unprepossessing.

1957J.

998

A queer fellow went bumming at Lloyd's,
But now all his friends he avoids.
As a gay homosexual
He was most ineffectual,
And is now nursing wet hemorrhoids.

1965.

999. — F.A.G.

A three-letter man on Long Guyland
Did a four-letter word on Fire Island
With disastrous effects—
Now he's practicing sex
With a five-letter gal out in Thailand.

1966.

1000

A serious-minded young lugger
Surprised all when he went out for rugger,
    Till they found he spent hours
    Stripped off in the showers,
Persuading the whole team to bugger.

1948.

1001

A perverted policeman, McClasty,
Excels at one sport—pederasty.
    He'll bugger with joy
    Any underage boy,
But thinks fornication is nasty.

1956A.

1002

Two gobs from the cruiser McFoys
Came ashore on the prowl for new joys.
    It was well understood
    They esteemed womanhood—
So they struck out in search of small boys.

1953-1966.

1003

There once was a priest named McGrath
Who would fuck anything in his path.
    With speed most uncanny
    He ravished the fanny
Of his granny bent over her bath.

1958P.

1004

There was a young girl named McNavity
Who was born with no vaginal cavity.
    She was no good for fucking
    But an expert at sucking,
And superior for asshole depravity.

1975.

1005

Pity poor seaman McQuig,
Who is spending his life in the brig.
At Captain's inspection
He had an erection
When the skipper bent over the gig.

1953.

1006. THE MIDNIGHT INTRUDER

There is an old maid named Magruder,
Nightly screwed by a Midnight Intruder.
In a state of euphoria
In the town of Emporia,
Each night she gets nuder and screweder.

[1007]

Till one night this old maid named Magruder
Remarked to her Midnight Intruder:
" I must turn on the light
To make sure you aim right—
The *last* time you went up my tooter! "

1965.

1008

An up-to-date homo, Maguire,
Hung a signboard out : " ASSHOLE FOR HIRE.
For sale by the piece,
Or on quarterly lease :
For clerical rates, please inquire. "

1970A.

1009

There once was a Renaissance man
Who modeled his conduct on Pan.
" I will " was tattooed
On the tip of his rood,
And " I will if I must " on his can.

1970A.

1010

A Fire Island pixie called " Mary, "
Whose erogenous zones were quite hairy,
    Said, " That last guy, I'll swear,
    Is still in there somewhere,
So I want to warn *you* to be wary. "

1965.

1011

There was a professor of math
Who was thrilling his girl in her bath.
    The soap slipped from reach
    And plugged up her breech,
So he finished the job in her ath.

1950R.

1012

The treatment by old Mr. Mears
Of small chubby boys and their rears
    Appears to his God
    As unnatural and odd :
Can it be he is one of those queers?

1965.

1013

Let Us Now Praise Famous Men,
Such as existed now and then.
    The current crop
    Are all assholes and slop,
With a *very* marked buggery yen.

1976A.

1014

Of that terrible King Mithridates,
His subjects along the Euphrates
    Used to say in great scorn :
    " He's of no woman born,
But extruded from fatherly *nates.* "

1970.

1015

There was a young fellow whose mode
Was taking it up the dirt road.
He maintained pedication
Cured acute constipation,
And no enema beat a good load.

1957J.

1016

There was a young man in Monette
Who went out with a dainty soubrette.
He spent the whole night
Up her ass, which was tight—
His doctor makes calls on him yet.

1948.

1017

There was an old bastard named Mott,
By the vilest of fates he was wrought :
He was born of skulduggery,
A product of buggery,
And was born through the ass, not the twat.

1975.

1018. THE MACHO POSE

A self-confessed sex hound named Nailer
Dragged a girl to his room to assail 'er.
He swore he would screw 'er,
And make her his whoo-er,
But at all but a bum-fuck did fail 'er.

1972A.

1019

Another young man from Nantucket,
His prick was so long he could muck it.
He would twist back his pole
Till it met his asshole,
And then he would tenderly fuck it.

1950.

1020

There once was a tailor named Naylor
Who measured the pants for a sailor.
As he started to crotch it,
The sailor said, "Watch it,
Or I'll buy my clothes from a wholesaler."

1954J.

1021

A young man who feared he was neuter
Fed his vital details to a computer.
The machine, in a flash,
Printed out: "FORGET GASH . . .
YOU'LL BE FAG-OF-THE-YEAR AS A FRUITER."

1970A.

1022

Have you heard of the man from New York
Who held up his balls with a fork?
In an asshole he'd bugger
Without any rubber,
This sanitary man from New York.

1956A.

1023

There was a young bugger named Nick
Who remarked, "I feel dreadfully sick.
The last man I buggered
I thought was a sluggard,
Till a fart of his blew off my prick."

1948.

1024

The cunt of a cutie in Niles
Attracts all the cocksmen for miles.
She likes her coition
In any position,
Except in the rear (she has piles!)

1966.

1025

There was a young fellow named Nutz
Who would rut as the pederast ruts.
His physician said, " Solon,
There's more in your colon
Than ever got in through your guts. "

1948.

1026

A lickerish octogenarian
Once raped a protesting librarian.
Between MED and MUM
He buggered her bum—
The conskited old bawdy vulgarian!

1965.

1027

There was an old Greek named Onossus
Whose pego was quite a colossus.
He'd sneak up behind
With buggery in mind :
He'd a penchant for tight brown crevasses.

1971 *ff*.

1028

There was once an effeminate Ottoman,
For the fair sex, I fear, he was not a man.
He was all up in arms
Against feminine charms :
" Quite frankly, " he said, " I'm a bottom man. "

1974A.

1029

A prince with a temper outrageous
Had a palace replete with young pages.
They were used for skulduggery
And much Royal buggery,
And he castrated some in his rages.

1953.

1030

There once was a decadent Persian
Who had a peculiar perversion :
His subtlest joy
Was an idiot boy,
On whom he performed " The Excursion. "

1948.

1031

A young fairy with habits perverse
Found that beatings made life just a curse.
So each time he went hence
He assured his defense
With a dildo he kept in his purse.

1972.

1032

Don Rodriguez del Mar y Posada
Commanded the Spanish Armada,
But was quite indiscreet
With a lad in the fleet,
And was hanged by the . . . er . . . neck in Granada.

1948.

1033

There once was a student of Queens
Who haunted the public latrines.
He was heard in the john
Saying," Bring me a don,
But spare me those dreadful old Deans. "

1974A.

1034. PERMISSIVE PARENTHOOD

As the idiot son, rather queer,
Tried to bugger his dad in the ear,
Said the father, " Fun's fun,
But I really must run.
Be quick now and come ; that's a dear. "

1948.

1035

Said a queer captain, name of Ramnugger:
"I shipped a whole crew just to bugger.
While the chubby first mate
And the bosun are great,
The cabin boy's arsehole is snugger."

1965.

1036

Our ship's captain, nicknamed Old Randy,
Makes advances to any girl handy.
But when shipwrecked a while
On a bleak desert isle,
He made do with midshipman Sandy.

1973.

1037

The lovers of young Mrs. Ray
Used her front door all during the day.
But a perverted old doctor
Sewed her up as he cocked her,
And now they come in the back way.

1966A.

1038. PLAIN TALK FROM TRUTHFUL MAME

When he tried fucking Mame from the rear,
She cried, "What are you, a man or a queer?
You pick for your pole
My dirty asshole,
When my cunt is so hot and so near!"

1965.

1039

There once was a bugger named Russell
Who adored a tight anal muscle.
To enter with ease
Required bear grease,
With that tool 'twas a real hustle-bustle.

1971 *ff.*

1040. MISS ROTTENCROTCH EXPLAINS

Said a gabby old queer in Saint-Lô :
" We sophisticates bugger and blow.
Women just bore me,
I need niggers to gore me—
I'm a bit of a *bisexual,* you know. "

1970A.

1041

There once was a villain named Seagress
Who tried changing his luck with a negress.
But her cunt was as loose
As the balls on a moose,
So he ended up her rear egress.

1954A.

1042. LAST TANGO IN ANUS

Said an innocent girlie named Shelley
As a man rolled her onto her belly :
" This is not the position
For human coition,
And *why* the petroleum jelly? "

1965-1975A.

1043

There was an old fellow of Skokie
Who had spent a long time in the pokey.
He spent so many years
In his cell with the queers
That his asshole was all charred and smoky.

1975.

1044

There was a Greek ruler named Solon,
With a fondness for joys that were stolen.
He claimed Alcibiades,
Whom he buggered on Fri-a-days,
Had the nicest tight ass for cornholin'.

1948.

1045. SIAM

First spoke the King of Siam :
" For women I don't give a damn.
I get all my joys
From fat juicy boys,
I'm a cocksucking monarch, I am! "

[1046]

Then said the King of the Czechs :
" I, too, have a problem in sex.
The men of my nation
Prefer masturbation,
My women are physical wrecks. "

[1047]

Then arose King Alphonso of Spain,
A monarch both haughty and vain :
" When a woman comes nigh
I take Spanish fly,
And I jazz her again and again! "

[1048]

Then said Prince —— of Wales :
" I know what marriage entails,
So I don't want a girl
But a jolly young Earl,
To solace my passion for males. "

[1049]

Next spoke the venerable Pope :
" In my youth I learned how to grope.
Now, though old and infirm,
I still seek the worm
That hides 'neath the chorister's cope. "

[1050]

Then said the Prince Palatine :
" Of course fornication is fine,
But I entertain 'em
Per os et per anum,
A sport I consider divine! "

[1051]

Then spoke the headmaster of Rugger,
A most accomplished old bugger :
" I spend half each night
With a smooth catamite.
My wife? I don't even hug 'er. "

[1052]

Then spoke up an old Maharajah :
" When I get a new wife I dodge her,
And so tease her a bit
If she's too tight a fit,
Till someone has made her hole larger. "

[1053]

Then spoke the Sultan himself,
A monarch of great power & pelf :
" I take thirty whores
And lock all the doors,
And proceed to enjoy myself. "

[1054]

Then spoke the Grand Duke of Lorraine :
" Your worries give me a pain.
I don't worry at all,
But retire to my hall
And beget new blacks for my train. "

[1055]

An Episcopal Bishop coadjutor
Proclaimed that he liked persons neuter:
" For so long as they're tender
The question of gender
Is a relative one to a fruiter."

[1056]

Then they questioned the King of the Cannibals
If 'twere true that he did it with animals?
" Oh, I boast of the same,
For I say to your shame
That they have far superior genitals."

[1057]

And they asked the Nippon Mikado,
A monarch well pinned in bravado,
If the men of his land
Ever did it by hand,
To which he replied, " Oh my God no!"

[1058]

Then they paused while the Persian Shah
Tried to settle a bet with the Czar,
That the tip of his tool
Was much the less cool—
But neither could reach quite that far.

1930*

[1059]

Then up spoke the Shah of Iran:
" All women from court we must ban.
They haven't the clutch
Or the velvety touch
Of the orotund arsehole of man."

1975.

1060

A young lady, uncommonly stacked,
On the street from the rear was attacked.
When the foul deed was done,
She said, " Frankly, it's fun,
And provided a background I lacked. "

1972.

1061

Said a madam named Mae down in Taft :
" We'll take on a man fore and aft.
But we *don't* think it's smart
In the rear—when you fart,
A big pecker will cut off your draft. "

1965.

1062

A neurotic young fellow named Tatum
Found regular sex didn't sate 'im.
But wherever he went
He was more than content
When he found some big guy to phallate 'im.

1972A.

1063

A great surgical genius named Taylor
Grafted tits on the back of a sailor.
If his ass had held out,
There is hardly a doubt
That the cash would have filled up a whaler.

1954A.

1064

An Italian instructor called Ted
Was wonderfully active in bed.
But one night he'd a virgin
With aversion to mergin',
So he buggered her bum till it bled.

1948.

1065

A randy young student called Teddy
With his acolytes used to make ready,
    Till the snoopy old Head
    Caught the bugger in bed,
Up the arse of his thirteen-year-old steady.

1970A.

1066. SOMEBODY'S SON

A young Harvard man, sweet and tender,
Went out with some queers on a bender.
    He came back in two days
    In a sexual haze,
No longer quite sure of his gender.

1967A-1975.

1067

Said an angry young lady from Texas:
"I wish there were only two sexes.
    Today, it appears,
    There are four—counting queers—
And they grab off the men just to vex us!"

1965.

1068

There was a Greek sailor from Thalia
Who knew several ways to regale ya.
    His principal trump
    Was his cute little rump,
Just behind his huge male genitalia.

1970A.

1069

Have you met our staff psychopath, Totter?
A typical shite and a rotter:
    His idea of fun
    Is to bugger a nun
Or else some impoverished squatter.

1976A.

1070

"Though sodomy many find trite,
To us sodomites it's a delight!"
Thus from deep in a ghetto
Came a plaintive falsetto
From a eunuch whose sphincter was tight.

1965.

1071

A matron of fashion in Utah
Once said to a devoted suitah:
"This is all on the sly,
But let's give it a try . . .
We'll find out what's such fun for a fruitah."

1948.

1072

There was a young sailor from Uttocks
Who had the most beautiful buttocks.
They were used by large crowds
In the middlemost shrouds,
Which were afterward known as the futtocks.

1970.

1073

There was a young man from Vancouver
Who claimed to have buggered Herb Hoover.
'Tis plain, whether he
Was fuck*er* or fuck*ee,*
'Twas a most impolitical maneuver.

1948.

1074. BISEXUAL BUILT FOR TWO

A vivacious young lady of Vedder
Said, "You'll find I'm a good two-way spreader:
Before or behind—
Either hole—I don't mind—
Or go for a nice double-header."

1965.

1075

There was an old doctor of Vere
Whose *forte* was Disease of the Rear.
His treatment was crude,
And forthrightly lewd,
But suppose he were treating the ear!

1954A.

1076

There once was a warden of Wadham
Who approved of the folkways of Sodom.
For a man might, he said,
Have a very poor head,
But be a fine fellow at bottom.

1953-1957*

1077. LEAVES OF GR-ASS

There was an old fellow named Walt
Who used to take Eno's Fruit Salt.
With a fellow named James
He played Oscar Wilde games,
And often would win by default.

1950.

1078

Said a gruesome grave-robber from Wapping:
" A mummy's not rummy for clapping.
It's a bit of a bust
With the dirt and the dust,
And your penis gets caught in the wrapping."

1958.

1079

A lonesome young man of White Plains
Waves the mark of his manhood at trains.
It's made queer engineers
Mess their denims for years,
And makes brakemen have inguinal pains.

1965.

1080

When the groom found the bride's cunt too wide,
And suggested her ass, she replied:
  "I've shit many a stool
  Twice as big as your tool,
So I doubt you'll be more satisfied."

1956J.

1081

That famous old pederast, Wilde,
Felt sure a boy stayed undefiled
  If you handled his penis
  With no trace of meanness,
Whenever you sucked off the child.

1960.

1082. PREMATURELY GAY

A visiting scholar at Yale
Was in search of a fresh piece of tail.
  He found in his classes
  Both girl and boy asses—
Now he spends all his spare time in jail.

1965.

1083

A pretty young fairy named Yussel
Has the pederast world all a-bustle.
  It's his darling pink hole
  And amazing control
Over his sphinctereal muscle.

1948.

VI

ABUSES OF THE CLERGY

1084

The bishop of Alexandretta
Loved a girl and he couldn't forget her.
So he thought he'd enshrine her
As the Holy Vagina
In the Church of the Sacred French Letter.

1962.

1085

A contrite acolyte of Friar Ansel
Said, " Last night by mischance in the chancel,
Lured by carnal desires
I had sex with Miss Myers.
Are there vows such a whimsy might cancel? "

1966.

1086

There was a young fellow named Baker
Who seduced a vivacious young Quaker.
And when he had done it,
She straightened her bonnet
And said, " I give thanks to my maker. "

1956.

1087

A preacher once lived in Bangkok
Who had an adjustable cock :
A remarkable feature
That enabled this preacher
To satisfy all of his flock.

1945R.

1088

A fervent young maid of Bermuda
Embraced all the doctrines of Buddha.
But in six weeks, all told,
She returned to the fold,
When the Anglican archbishop screwed her.

1945.

1089

A crepitant person named Birch
Often farts right out loud during church.
Said the pastor, " Dear friend,
You'll be blessed in the end—
But it won't be an end without smirch. "

1966.

1090

You've heard of the Bishop of Birmingham,
Well, here's the new story concerning 'im :
He buggers the choir
As they sing " *Ave Maria,* "
And fucks all the girls whilst confirming 'em.

1950.

1091

Saint Peter was once heard to boast
That he'd had all the heavenly host :
The Father and Son,
And then—just for fun—
The hole in the Holy Ghost.

1958.

1092

There was a young friar named Borrow
Who eloped with two nuns to his sorrow.
They lived on an isthmus,
And one he called *Christmas*—
The other he christened *Tomorrow*.

1968A.

1093

The fearless old bishop of Brest
Put his faith in the Lord to the test.
He fucked whores in the apse
With chancres and claps,
But first they were sprinkled and blessed.

1975.

1094

A wicked stone cutter named Cary
Drilled holes in divine statuary.
With eyes full of malice
He pulled out his phallus,
And buggered a stone Virgin Mary.

1960.

1095

An eclectic young cleric named Casey
Favors underthings pink, silk, and lacy.
Though his vows are quite strict,
They don't seem to conflict
With his sex life, both D.C. and A.C.

1972.

1096

Said a divinity student named Cass:
"I should never be fit to say Mass,
If I kissed the Pope's toe
And then failed to bestow
A like sign of respect to his ass."

1969.

1097. ESCHATOLOGICAL PROBLEM

As he came in his chubby choirboy,
Father Burke said, "There's no greater joy!
If no sodomy leavens
Any possible heavens,
Existence will merely annoy."

1966.

1098

The Mater of Convent Colchester
Did sate her with Brother Sylvester,
Who cried, " Sainted God!
She has tainted my cod! "
When later it started to fester.

1948.

1099

Mused the deacon, in deepest dejection,
As he passed 'round the box for collection :
" If it comes to the worst
Can a curate be cursed,
Or a rector be wrecked by erection? "

1945.

1100

" Given faith, " sighed the vicar of Deneham,
" From the lusts of the flesh we might wean 'em.
But the human soul sighs
For a nice pair of thighs,
And a little of what lies between 'em. "

1973.

1101

There was an old harlot from Dijon
Who in her old age got religion.
" When I'm dead & gone, "
Said she, " I'll take on
The Father, the Son, and the Pigeon. "

1971B.

1102

There was a young lady named Dot
Whose cunt was so terribly hot
That ten bishops of Rome
And the Pope's private gnome
Failed to quench her Vesuvial twat.

1975.

1103

A bashful young priest once, a Druid,
Would run from a nun when pursuèd.
One kissed him with zest
Which left him distressed,
And he lost all his seminal fluid.

1975.

1104. SECRETS OF THE CONFESSIONAL

A responsive young girl from the East
In bed was an able artiste.
She had learned two positions
From family physicians,
And ten more from the old parish priest.

1975.

1105

Did you know that the Bishop at Eton
Schemes at nothing but getting his meat in?
He has whores by the scores
And can undo his drawers
With no hands, while a girl he is greetin'.

1953.

1106

The discerning old Bishop of Ewing
Observed that his nuns had tattooing
So loathsome and crass
On their belly and ass
That he wore his dark glasses while . . . viewing.

1975.

1107

There was a young Jew of Far Rockaway
Whose screams could be heard for a block away.
Perceiving his error,
The Rabbi in terror
Cried, "God! I have cut his whole cock away!"

1953.

1108

The visiting Bishop of Fife
Had a nymphomaniacal wife.
    While he exhorted the pews
    She was out in the mews,
Bringing stodgy young vicars to life.

1953.

1109

An eccentric young curate named Flicker
Once had an affair with the Vicar.
    He frigged him, butt fucked him,
    Shit buggered and sucked him—
'Twas under the influence of liquor.

1959A.

1110

There was a young choirboy named Gene
Whose sex life was somewhat unclean.
    He received Extreme Unction
    Through anal conjunction—
Gave his asshole an unwonted sheen!

1954A.

1111

There once was a monk of Gibraltar
Who buggered a nun on the altar.
    "Good God!" said the nun,
    "Now look what you've done:
You've gummed up the leaves of the Psalter."

1948.

1112

In his pulpit the Reverend Goff
During sermons delights to jerk off.
    It seems quite ironical
    Something so uncanonical
Parishioners pick on to scoff!

1966.

1113

In the midst of an anthem of grace
The choirmaster slipped from his place,
To goose the soprano
In lingering manner,
And returned with a smile on his face.

1945.

1114

Father Donnelley lay in the grass
With a dornicker probing his ass.
When the fellow proved slow,
He said, " Look, come and go ;
For I've got to get back and say Mass. "

1966A.

1115

A soldier rewarded for gunnery
Invaded the halls of a nunnery.
He taught the nuns joys,
And the secrets of boys—
Now it's a coeducational funnery.

1948.

1116

A nun of an order inferior
Entertained priests upon her posterior.
She grew greater in girth,
Gave Immaculate Birth,
And now she's a Mother Superior.

1958.

1117. GLADLY THE CROSS-EYED BEAR

As Offkey the priest sang Introit,
At his first springtime mass in Detroit,
Lightning crashed through a pew,
And a couple mid-screw :
God blasting them for their exploit.

1966.

1118

There was an old priest of Jablonica,
Cunt-struck was the poor bastard's monicker.
In the middle of Mass
He grabbed a girl's ass,
And sucked her off like a harmonica!

1974A.

1119. BIBLE STORIES

A Shinto priest out in Japan
Has a horrible sexual plan :
His soul burns and festers
For the ghosts of ancestors,
And he writes all their names in the can.

1946A.

1120

Said the Reverend Archbishop Jones
As he rammed a choirgirl to the stones :
" You may trust and believe
That you will not conceive,
So stifle your moans and your groans. "

1971A.

1121

The agèd archbishop of Joppa
Said, " I think circumcision improper
If the organ is small ;
But I don't mind at all
About cutting a slice off a whopper. "

1962.

1122

Said the head lama of Katmandu :
" These American kids never screw.
They drop out on hash,
And are useless for gash—
This is strictly between me and you. "

1972A.

1123. THE BISHOP OF KEW

Have you heard of the Bishop of Kew
Who preached with his vestments askew?
A lady named Morgan
Caught sight of his organ,
And fainted away in her pew.

1974A.

[1124]

That selfsame young lady of Kew
Remarked as the Vicar withdrew:
"The Verger's emerger
Is longer and lurger—
And he gets his bollocks in too."

1962.

[1125]

That impenitent lady of Kew
Observed as the Bishop withdrew:
"I prefer the dear Vicar,
He's longer and thicker—
Besides, he comes quicker than you."

[1126]

Said the Bishop, "My dear, you are right:
The Vicar's a man of great might.
But he hasn't my flash,
My vigor and smash,
And he can't come eight times in one night!"

1950R.

1127

A young novice priest of Lahore
Ogled nuns in the convent galore.
He climbed in and defiled one,
Who proved such a wild one
That he stayed to defile her some more.

1975.

1128

A pious young nun from La Plata
Was blessed with the Holy Stigmata.
They appeared on the rim
Of her virginal quim
When she did what she shouldn't have atta.

1960.

1129

There was a young monk of La Trappe
Who had shooting pains in his jappáp.
He said, "Jesus Christ!
This don't feel nice—
Methinks Sister Maud hath the clappe."

1973A.

1130

A Quaker bartender named Lee
Avoided all raucous melee.
But he got up his ire
At religious inquire,
And quietly murmured, "Fuck thee!"

1953.

1131

There was a young lady from Leigh
Who slipped into church for a pee.
Without any malice
She pissed in the chalice
While singing the *Agnus Dei*.

1950.

1132. THE OPHITE HERESY

A horny old priest named McGinnity
Has his doubts about Mary's virginity.
For he thinks that Old Nick
Has a much longer prick
Than all three (combined) of the Trinity.

1971B.

1133

A divine by the name of McWhinners
Held classes each evening for sinners.
    They were sectioned and graded
    So the very degraded
Would not be held back by beginners.

1953.

1134

I know a young priest of Mayence
Whose pecker is simply immense.
    He's unable to fuck
    Unless by good luck
The brothers have extra-large vents.

1948.

1135

There was once a Dominican monk
Who was shut up so long that he stunk.
    And that wasn't all,
    (If I rightly recall)
There was something about him that shrunk.

1953.

1136

A whore working down in Montgomery
Said, "Preachers bore me with their mummery.
    Once given the chance,
    They are into your pants,
And forget all their sanctified flummery!"

1965.

1137

On the slopes of Mount Ananias
A nun whom all thought highly pious
    Ran wild in the nude,
    And was so soundly screwed
That today her cunt lies on the bias.

1966.

1138. THE CHORISTER SPEAKS

You made love to me first, last November,
Snug in a box pew, remember?
    Removing your cassock
    You adjusted my hassock,
And prayed for my soul and your member!

1973.

1139

A rotten old harlot of Oregon
Had hoped to be pure to the core again.
    She sought help from some priests,
    But they fucked her, the beasts—
She was glad to be back as a whore again.

1975.

1140

As the verger explored her hot pants,
A Sunday school teacher in Hants
    Cried, " I don't think that God
    Approves vergers who prod,
But you *must* now, to quiet my ants! "

1966.

1141

Now here was St. Paul's peroration :
" Love Jesus ; avoid fornication.
    Far better is buggery,
    Or sucking a dug, or re-
Vival of joint masturbation. "

1950.

1142

There was a young rabbi named Pete
Who circumcised youngsters quite neat.
    But during the Passover
    They kicked his ass over,
For selling the clippings as meat.

1948R-1953.

1143. PAGES OF PAPAL HISTORY

Alexander, the Borgian pope,
Remarked to his cardinals, " Nope,
I'd rather fuck Lucy,
My daughter, than goosey
A priest with his ass full of soap. "

[1144]

So here was this popular pope,
With a prick he could knot like a rope.
He baptized this rarity
With his balls, Faith and Charity,
And his asshole as Christendom's hope.

[1145]

Then filled with ambition, the pope
Once bound his huge cock with a rope.
If once he could thin it, he
Could bugger the Trinity,
And fill Mary's cunt with soft soap.

[1146]

Alas, our dissatisfied pope
Would stretch out his cock with a rope.
He used it on foresters,
And virginal choristers,
Which made all the cardinals mope.

[1147]

When an old vegetarian pope,
He shot off in a ripe cantaloupe.
The seeds produced scores
Of sanctified whores,
And a priest with a prick for a cope.

1950.

1148

A religious young lady named Pitts
Lets lechers ram home where she splits.
  Later on, at confession,
  She lists in succession
All the lewd, lustful acts she commits.

1966.

1149

There once was a neophyte priest
Attending a holy day feast.
  In a trance he went forth
  With his asshole to north,
While the knob of his dong pointed east.

1967A-1975.

1150

There was a teenager named Pryor
Who felt her insides were on fire.
  "I don't mind," she exclaimed,
  "This feeling inflamed,
But *who'll* fuck me here in the choir?"

1965.

1151

A bishop in Rome named Puccini
Has fathered one hundred bambini.
  He says, "Nookie sizes
  Are often surprises,
But they all give a thrill to my weenie."

1966.

1152

The awful old Bishop of Purvis
Would wiggle and scratch during service.
  His balls and his boredom,
  And his attitude toward them,
Made all his parishioners nervous.

1953.

1153

As the acolytes bared their fat rears,
The Reverend Father McQueers
Said, unsheathing his tool :
" Rectums still make me drool,
Though I've buggered them daily for years."

1966.

1154. VATICAN ROULETTE

Said the Pope, as he read from the Roll :
" True religion saves only the soul.
We must have further study,
And then *more* further study,
Of further study of birth control."

1967A.

1155

" The conception," the archbishop said,
" Of a personal Tempter is dead."
But a meek little curate
Begged leave to demure : it
Was something he fought with in bed.

1955A.

1156

There was a fat priest of St. Giles
Who was much too wide for the aisles.
Passing to and from mass,
The pews pinched his ass,
And gave him a bad case of piles.

1953.

1157

Have you heard of the dean at St. Paul's
Who had no hair on his balls?
When asked why was this,
He whispered, in bliss :
" The rector, my God how he mauls!"

1945R.

1158

There once was a shepherd named Sam
Who for hellfire cared not a damn.
His religion was deep
For he fucked pregnant sheep,
And washed in the blood of the Lamb.

1960.

1159

A blasphemous bastard named Skougaard
Had a horrid contempt for the true God.
One Sunday in chapel
With his balls he did grapple,
And buttered his penis with rhubarb.

1948.

1160. IMMORTAL EROSTRATUS

Greek sculptors attired in smocks
Nude statues created from rocks.
But their names are forgotten,
We recall just the rotten
Old bishops who knocked off their cocks.

1975.

1161

When the Reverend Frogdiddle Stead
First saw his new bride bare in bed,
He knelt at his prayers,
But his nose bumped some hairs,
So he hopped on and fucked her instead.

1965.

1162

There once was a rounder from Syria
Who entered a convent's interior.
Ere they loosed him—what luck!—
The dear man had to fuck
All the nuns and the Mother Superior.

1950.

1163

There's a priest, quite perverse, in Tangier
Who is fond of an Arab boy's rear.
Though it surely would shock
All the folks in his flock,
Ecumenically speaking, he's queer.

1972.

1164

A deacon of Tartary-Crim
Whose notions of fucking were grim
Used to get lots of fun
Out of stuffing a nun,
With the Sign of the Cross on her quim.

1962.

1165

Saint Anthony, in his temptation,
Was urged to enjoy fornication,
By bitches with nipples
Like colliery tipples,
And clefts like the Cunt of Creation.

1950.

1166

After having a wonderful tilt,
Miss Crockett had feelings of guilt.
So she went to a priest
Who was hung like a beast,
And he straightened her out 'neath the quilt.

1975.

1167

When the archbishop sprinkled their tools,
They broke all episcopal rules,
And piddled right back at him,
Took quite a whack at him,
Smeared him all over with stools!

1969.

1168

There once was a student of Trinity
Who shattered his sister's virginity.
He buggered his brother,
Had twins by his mother,
And now he's a Dean of Divinity.

1955.

1169

There was a young curate of Twickenham
Whose pants had a wonderful prick in 'em.
He thought it great guns
To disrobe all the nuns,
And this marvelous object to stick in 'em.

1950.

1170

There once was an old Jewish villain
Who would screw any girl who was willin'.
This orthodox louse
Had a nearsighted spouse
Who thought he was just laying *t'fillin.*

1960.

1171

That maiden who lost her virginity
To a lustful D.D. in Divinity,
Was heard to exclaim :
" He's to blame with his claim
That the penis and balls are the Trinity! "

1958.

1172

When they found the luscious Miss Wall
Being raped in the drafty church hall,
The Rt. Reverend Vance
Went off twice in his pants,
And two vestrymen felt their balls crawl!

1966.

1173. A MUSICAL PEAL

A militant Mormon of Wells
Said, " Decent polygamy quells
Lust—'twould bring pious ease
Back to the diocese
With a musical peal of ten bells.
Tintinnabula omnia, give me insomnia!
—A musical peal of ten bells. "

[1174]

Said a Yankee who visited Wells :
" Say, these ecclesiastical swells
Seem grand at contriving
To manage their swiving
To a musical peal of ten bells. "

1937C.

1175

The rector of West Constipation
Created an awful sensation :
It was often his wont
To jerk off in the font,
And three virgins are far in gestation.

1965.

1176

An ardent young acolyte named Xavier
Dedicated his soul to the Saviour.
Then a bitch taught that boy
Matrimonial joy—
My God! how the Saviour's lost faviour!

1948.

1177

A simple young lady of Ypsi
Was fucked every time she got tipsy,
By the chief of police
And the justice of peace,
And a preacher disguised as a gypsy.

1975.

VII

ZOOPHILY

1178

A young taxidermist from Ada,
Whose wife claimed that he had betrayed her,
    Was sued for divorce
    For mounting a horse
A moose and a goose and a 'gator.

1948.

1179

One night a girl had an affair
With a fellow all covered with hair.
    His enormous red whang
    Gave her a wonderful bang—
She'd been diddled by Smokey the Bear.

1963A.

1180

Said a mermaid, " No matter what ails me,
There's one cure I find never fails me :
    I've got me a gob
    Who does such a good job,
I'm in heaven each time that he scales me. "

1972.

1181

Once a farmhand outside Alexander
Attempted to goose a big gander.
    But the gander got even—
    Shat all over Stephen!
Moral : Don't rile a big gander's dander.

1966.

1182. — GIRLS ! !

Don't copulate with alligators,
Especially not in elevators.
But once in a while,
With a mild crocodile,
It's a sure cure for wild woman-haters.

[1183]

And don't *ever* try screwin' a bruin,
For while it may love what it's doin',
It shoves with such force,
Just like a stud horse,
You're left with your cleft in a ruin!

1965.

1184

That learned old pundit named Babbitt,
I found prick-to-arse with a rabbit.
I asked, with a choke,
" Is it not hard to poke? "
He said, " No : the great trick is to grab it. "

1948.

1185

A sailor boy, tall and banale,
Met up with a *femme fatale.*
Though he tried every ruse
She denied him her mews—
She preferred a *ménage à cheval.*

1971 *ff.*

1186

There once was a Duchess of Beever
Who slept with her golden retriever.
Said the potted old Duke :
" Such tricks make me puke!
Were it not for her money, I'd leave her. "

1974A.

1187. BIRDS : A FOUL BROOD

The absurd and antique Annie Besant
Accosted an innocent pheasant.
It said, " Of a surety
I'll tell Krishnamurti,
And that would be very unpleasant. "

[1188]

[Said a] young dude who decided to bribe his
Mammá to procure him an ibis :
" Don't get me a crane,
It would give me a pain
If you knew how exclusive the tribe is. "

[1189]

" Rate, did you say, " cried Cadger, " rate?—
I fuck at the regular spadger rate!
Bring me a duck!
I'll teach you to fuck :
I swear I would scorn to exaggerate! "

[1190]

On the duck he did excellent work, he
Destroyed it, he never got jerky.
He smoothly went on
To a goose and a swan,
And we left him untired with a turkey.

[1191]

A professor of Ethical Culture
Once said to his class, " 'Twould insult your
Intelligence if
I said I got stiff
For anything less than a vulture. "

[1192]

Paul Proper vowed virtue a cinch is :
His tool was a foot and four inches.
He thought it was legal
To bugger an eagle,
But utterly wrong to fuck finches.

[1193]

His twin brother, Puritan Peter,
Whose prick measured one millimetre,
Thought Hell would break loose
If one got on a goose,
But a saint may be stuck on a skeeter.

[1194]

She said, " There you go! False alarm again!
You bally old bounder, get calm again!
I once taught a starling
To answer to 'Darling,'
But I'm usually faithful to ptarmigan. "

[1195]

A fellow who fucked as but few can
Had a fancy to try with a toucan.
He owned like a man
The collapse of his plan :
" I can't—but I bet none of *you* can! "

[1196]

[Oh a] frantic, fanatical friar,
In love with a large lammergeier,
In spite of his sins
He knew why, when it spins,
Is a mouse—for the fewer the higher.

[1197]

A clergyman said to a girl, " You
Love fucking : Jehovah will hurl you
To Hell if you love it
So much that you covet
The criminal cock of a curlew! "

[1198]

Like the virgin who pouted, " By jingo,
I never yet fucked a flamingo! "
We bought him a bride,
But he fumbled and sighed :
" Here, damnit, I can't make my thing go! "

[1199]

The hoary old sinner named Sinnet
Took his prick out and started to skin it.
He muttered, " Though that's key
Was fat old Blavatsky,
I could do in a pinch with a linnet. "

[1200]

The boy who buggered a sea mew
Was tempted to tackle an emu.
He said, when he lost :
" Though our love has been crossed
I shall always sincerely esteem you. "

[1201]

The son of a merciful Mandarin
Once said, " Could I but get a gander in
The family way,
I should openly say
I considered it fancy philanderin'. "

1920C.

1202

A madam named Fay of Black Pubes
Said, " We lay city fellows—not rubes.
The hicks from the sticks
Have sheep pills in their pricks
And they plug gals' Fallopian tubes. "

1965.

1203

Did she douche when his long penis blew
All that semen that shot into Sue?
The little fool was too lazy ;
Now she's caught and half crazy,
For she laid a buck gnu at the zoo!

1965.

1204

There was an old feminine blighter
Who trained a Chow dog to delight her.
She would cream her own pool
While she sucked off his tool—
How his cock in her cunt would excite her!

1950.

1205. ORTHO-DOXY

When Pan, full of classical bonhomie,
Met a maiden, she cried, " Don't get onna me!
And the goats I keep, too,
I forbid you to screw :
I have just read a book—*Deuteronomy!* "

1970.

1206

There once was a Russian named Boris
Fell in love with a stuffed brontosaurus.
Each night you could see him
In the Moscow museum,
As he diddled that Stone Age clitóris.

1959A.

1207

After tippling two six-packs of brew,
Willie staggered and swayed to the zoo.
His bestial ways
Caused gossip for days,
For he ravished a she-kangaroo.

1966.

1208

While fucking an ostrich, young Buck
Said, "They're *ten* times more fun than a duck.
As you'll notice, Miss Moultrie,
I'm queer for all poultry,
So glue on some feathers—we'll fuck!"

1966.

1209

There once was a timid bull calf,
Thought heifers too virtuous by half.
So he trekked to the Niger
To diddle a tiger,
And bugger a kneeling giraffe.

1950.

1210

With bribes of small cookies and candies,
Joe lured and laid goats in the Andes.
Said he with a leer:
"I'm repeating next year—
Those Andes sure spawn some jim dandies!"

1966.

1211

There was a fair wench of Capri
Who tumbled one day in the sea.
She returned from her splash
With a fish in her gash,
And her face was transfigured with glee.

1945.

1212

A wistful young lady named Carr
Divulged her perversions bizarre :
  " Though this *may* sound preposterous,
  I have fucked a rhinosterous,
But a unicorn's better by far. "

1975.

1213

That famous old painter, Cézanne,
Fucked a hole in an old frying pan :
  " I just love rough edges!
  I fuck all the hedges,
And cats on the Island of Man. "

1950.

1214. THE PLAYGIRL PHILOSOPHY

Nude 'neath her coat of chinchilla,
Miss Richbitch set forth from her villa,
  Saying : " James, to the zoo!
  I have nothing to do,
So I'll service their bachelor gorilla. "

1966.

1215

As dull as the life of the cloister
(Except it's a little bit moister)
  Mutatis mutandum,
  Non est disputandum,
There's no thrill in sex for the oyster.

1945.

1216

There was a young man named Colquhoun
Whose pet was a red-arsed baboon.
  His mother said, " Cholmondeley,
  It isn't quite comely
To wank off your pet in a spoon. "

1966A.

1217

Said a cowpuncher punching a cow:
"I wish that somehow they'd endow
My frau with a bogey
As good as this dogie,
Or as fine as that suckalin' sow!"

1965.

1218

It seems that our neighbor, Miss Gray,
Has odd sex desires, so they say.
She delights in her folly
With a pedigreed collie,
And each year gives a litter away.

1965.

1219

We know now that Ichabod Creep
Makes sexual use of a sheep.
He patronized whores
In our local love stores,
Till he found out a sheep was so cheap.

1966.

1220

Old Mother Hubbard went to the cupboard
To get her poor doggie a bone.
When she got back
She got knocked on her back—
The poor dog had a bone of his own.

1953A.

1221

A breeder of dogs—what a dastard!—
A chastity belt for dogs mastered:
A device to ensure
That the breeds remained pure,
And no son of a bitch was a bastard.

1975.

1222

The birdwatcher stares in despair,
As birds 'round him fuck everywhere.
Though he strains through his glasses
For a look at their asses,
He can't see just what goes in where!

1975.

1223

In her travels a lady named Dinah
Harbored several white mice in her vagina.
When asked for her reason,
She quipped, "They're in season,
And men like to eat them in China."

1953.

1224

A critter of charm is the djerbil,
Its diet's exclusively herbal.
It browses all day
On great bunches of hay,
And farts with an elegant burble.

1974A.

1225

It's dollars to doughnuts that Dolly
Will someday regret her low folly.
This nympho craves men,
But is known, now and then,
To borrow the neighbor's big collie.

1965.

1226. TO THE CONQUISTADORES

Up sabres! Salute Don Quixote!
His instincts were raunchy and goaty.
He screwed llamas and camels,
And other small mammals,
And a rattlesnake once, on peyote.

1970A.

1227

There was a young lady from Dover
Who said, as she lay in the clover:
"I don't give a damn
For the penis of man—
(Whistle: *Tweedle-dum-deedle*) Here, Rover!"

1948-1974A.

1228

There was a young lady named Dyson
Who conceived a mad love for a bison.
After sexual fruition
Her snatch's condition
Was never again so enticin'.

1945-1970A.

1229

There was a young lady called Emily
Who was not understood by her femily.
She acted so rummily
The head of the fummily
Had her crossed by a greyhound from Wembley.

[1230]

He feared she would breed a facsimile:
Bring utter disgrace on the fimily!
So he read her a homily
In front of the fomily—
And the Devil flew out of the chimily!

1944C.

1231

When the cows spied the bull in erection
They observed, with soft moos of affection:
"Bulls are sure heifer shockers—
Get a load of them knockers!
They hang to the ground in perfection."

1966.

1232

A somnolent damsel in Ewing
Dreamed her Great Dane was on her and screwing.
She awoke and discovered
The beast had her covered,
And her asshole was plastered with blueing!

1965.

1233

There was a young virgin named Fairdale
Whose cunt would, when she was unbared, ail
For cock ; at this itch
The virginal bitch
Got her maiden cunt screwed by an airedale.

1950.

1234. THE CAT'S ASS

The he-cat sat on a high board fence,
The she-cat sat on the ground.
The tom made a pass
At the pussycat's ass,
And the world went around and around!

1919-1952L.

1235

A maritime gent named Fiorello
Maintained an aquatic bordello.
There you'd roger a seahorse
On a bed of soft sea gorse,
Or fuck mermaids in pools of fish jello.

1954R.

1236

Said Rover, backscuttling Miss Fitch :
" While I greatly prefer a hot bitch,
My normal delight
Is a cunt, hot and tight,
And it doesn't make *much* difference which."

1966.

1237

Hats off to the orthdox flea
Who attempted to bugger a bee,
 But emerged from the fray
 In a family way . . .
Which is why we do things so fee-bly.

1930E.

1238

There was a young lady named Fleagle
Who had an affair with a beagle.
 But she couldn't have sinned
 For he ran out of wind,
And the act was not likely illegal.

1975.

1239

A honey who hookers in Florida
Lays her customers in a dark corridor.
 One night in the dark
 She fucked an aardvark,
And claims that no fuck could be horrider!

1965.

1240

In the weak mind of Frighamyoung Freep
His one thought of sex is with sheep.
 But each time, when he's through,
 He gobbles lamb stew—
What a half-cannibal, half-crazy creep!

1965.

1241

The anger of Dribblecock Frouse
We excuse, for he found in the house,
 A Great Dane astride
 His lovely young bride,
Who cried, " Fuck you, Frouse! " to her spouse.

1965.

1242

A stalwart young fellow named Galion
Was given the Pervert's Medallion,
For he buggered a cow
As he stood on a sow,
While he sucked off a Percheron stallion.

1975.

1243

There was a young lady named Gish
Who was filled with a passion for fish.
Five minutes of lovin'
Put a bun in her oven,
And she gave birth to a platter of squish!

1976A.

1244. GOSSIP, GOSSIP

Two she-camels spied on a goat,
And one jealously said, "You will note
She leaves the sheik's tent
With her tail oddly bent,
And hanks of hair pulled from her coat."

1965.

1245

Drop a tear for charming Miss Gotch
Who camped on a mountainous notch.
She was raped by an eagle—
Or perhaps 'twas a seagull—
Which then built a nest in her crotch.

1970A.

1246

A shepherdess high in the Grams
Had a beautiful slit 'twixt her hams.
One day an old buck
Got her down for a fuck,
And now she's the mother of lambs.

1953.

1247

While fucking a chicken, young Greg
Said, " The best thing's, I don't have to beg.
She's open and clear
All the time, in the rear,
Except when she's laying an egg. "

1966A.

1248

There was an odd fellow named Gropper
Who was famed as a maidenhead popper.
When he couldn't get girls,
He was known to chase squirrels—
A whimsy some felt was improper.

1965.

1249

With his shoes some two feet off the ground,
The farmhand one morning was found
With his prick, to the belly,
In the ass of old Nelly,
But he said: " I'm just horsing around. "

1966A.

1250

In the forests of wild Guatemaya
Lived a girl who was always on fire.
She would screw the day through
With the gnat and the gnu,
But the cobra did most satisfy her.

1960.

1251

High up on her rump, red with heat,
With his cock in an elephant, Pete
Said, " I like to shoot sperma
In this hot pachyderma,
Which I've done twice this week—what a treat! "

1965.

1252

At the zoo, a young fellow named Heeper
Asked the price of a screw from the keeper.
Said the keeper, " A gnu
Is ten bucks a screw.—
The rhino and camel are cheaper. "

1975.

1253

It seems a lewd lady named Hines
Loves to fuck all the larger canines.
It's a manlike sensation,
Without procreation,
Which fits in with her feelthy designs!

1965.

1254

Pity the poor hippopotamus ;
His sex life is sadly monotonous.
His lady friend, Gyppo,
Is a twenty-ton hippo,
And her face is as broad as her bottom is.

1974A.

1255. POLITICAL NOTE

A southern hillbilly named Hollis
Used possums and snakes as his solace.
The children had scales
And prehensile tails,
And voted for Governor Wallace.

1968A-1970.

1256

A vicious young lady named Ida
Loved feeling her pet beasts inside 'er.
The result of this whim
Was one broken-down quim,
Three pups, and a circumcised spider.

1950-1974A.

1257

Erat miles olim in Italia
Qui magna habebat genitalia.
    Cum puella negabat
    Coitum : copulabat
Elephantos aliaque animalia.

1956J.

1258. OCTOPUSSY!

A libidinous pissant named Jack
One time with a spider did shack.
    You may get oddball kids
    Sleeping with arachnids,
But oh! those eight legs 'round your back!

1958R.

1259

A lusty farm lad, for a joke,
Gave the hens in the barnyard a poke.
    But his vice was betrayed
    When the eggs that they laid
Were nothing but whites with no yolk.

1956J.

1260

There was a young lady named Jolly
Who spread wide her thighs to a collie.
    The girl, as she spent,
    Went nuts with content,
And the collie certainly felt Jolly.

1950.

1261

There was a young shepherd named Jones
Who developed an ache in the stones.
    But he knew what to do,
    So he screwed an old ewe
Till the hillside re-echoed her groans.

1956J.

1262

A damsel in Kalamazoo
Found her sexual life far too few.
She let a spotted retriever
Get into her beaver,
And today her first litter is due.

1965.

1263

A lecherous damsel named Kelly
Loved the feel of a seal on her belly.
She sighed, " It's celestial,
Though horribly bestial,
And when coming in heat, are *they* smelly! "

1966.

1264

A captious young woman named Kewin
Snapped : " Listen, I know what I'm doin'.
As a vice, dogs are nice,
But I've had poodles twice—
From now on I'll frig, and no screwin'! "

1966.

1265

The monarch of ancient Kowloon
Was known to be struck by the moon.
At the full moon he'd creep
In the jungle, asleep,
Attempting to fuck a baboon.

1970A.

1266

You'd think nothing happens in Kzyltu,
And godnose there's hours to kill too.
But those randy Kazaks
Bugger long-suffering yaks—
There's always a way, when there's a will to!

1976A.

1267

A young lady climbed up on a ladder
And attempted self-rape with an adder.
She gave a wild grasp
At the tail of the asp,
As its head penetrated her bladder.

1948.

1268

There once was a delicate lass
Who loved getting layed in the grass.
Till a toad hopped inside her,
Pursued by a spider—
Now she's an insane piece of ass.

1950A.

1269

A foolish young cowboy named Lear
Put Spanish fly into his beer,
After drinking this potion,
Overcome with emotion,
He buggered six cows and a steer.

1970.

1270

There was a young lady from Leeper
Who was raped by an ape in a sleeper.
When nine months were through
She called up the zoo,
And gave the results to the keeper.

1965.

1271

There was a young girl named Lenore
Who liked to be screwed by a boar.
They brought her battalions
Of Percheron stallions,
But always she hollered for more.

1953.

1272. MYTHOLOGICAL MYSTERIES

Leda, thinking no Swan could make love,
Laid two white eggs : warmed by the stove,
One hatched Helen of Troy,
Whilst her double-yolked joy
Produced Castor and Pollux—by Jove!

1973.

1273

An innocent chap named McBean
In sex ways is terribly green.
With a choice between girls
And all else, he picks squirrels,
Which in parks makes for quite a rare scene!

1965.

1274

Concupiscent young Miss McGarrity
Finds men who can please her a rarity.
So she uses bologna
And a small Shetland pony,
Both of which get her off with celerity.

1966.

1275

" This plot, " said old Farmer McGraw,
" I hold in great reverence and awe.
For here on the grass
I had my first piece of ass,
While her mother stood by and said 'Baa'. "

1975.

1276

An old misanthrope named McRoyster
Spent most of his life in a cloister,
Because, in his youth,
He'd attempted, forsooth,
To bugger the R's of an oyster.

1942A.

1277

There was a young man of Madrid
Who had an affair with a squid.
As he wore off his rod
In this cephalopod,
She squirted her ink—yes she did!

1950.

1278

The pig-fucking girl of Malmö
Said: "How many teats will I grow?
Most girls are through
After growing just two,
But now under each arm I've a row!"

1965.

1279

A horny zoo keeper named Mapes
At the apes often lustfully gapes.
He avers: "All the flunkies
Get to diddle the monkeys.
Us zoo keepers should rate the she-apes."

1965.

1280

There was a sad singer named Mick
Whose penis was but a mere stick.
But then he proceeded
To find what he needed:
A skunk who required a small prick.

1970A.

1281

There was a young girl of Milan
Who never had sinned with a man.
But she fucked in a bog
With a St. Bernard dog,
A pig, and an orangutan.

1975.

1282

A cavernous cutie named Miller
Finds very few fellows can thrill her.
So she goes for a pony
With a big red baloney—
Too bad for us chaps that can't fill her!

1966.

1283. MY SWEETHEART

My sweetheart's a mule in the mines :
I drive her without reins or lines.
On the bumper I stand
With my jock in my hand,
And ram it up my sweetheart's behind.

1948A.

1284

A messy old maid named Miranda
Corrupted a meek giant panda,
Who rogered her bum
Till it toppled off numb,
Every evening upon her veranda.

1965.

1285

A round-bottomed babe in Mobile
Longed for years to be screwed by a seal.
But out at the zoo
They insist, " No can do! "
Though the seal is all hot for the deal.

1965.

1286

Consider the noble Mohican,
He gets all his jollies from peekin' :
From watching while bears
Carry on their affairs,
And the rooster seducing the chicken.

1970A.

1287

Then there was an old Lady Moncrieff
Who was wealthy beyond all belief.
She spent much of her boodle
On a long-peckered poodle
Whose bollox she hid with a leaf.

1967A-1975.

1288

There once was a girl named Monique
Whose sex life was rather unique,
For her large, well-trained parrot
(For a radish or carrot)
Would diddle Monique with its beak.

1972.

1289

There was a young maiden named Muffett
Who sat on a dildoform tuffett.
Along came a spider,
Who offered to rider 'er,
But she sneered at the size of his stuffett.

1971*ff*.

1290

There was a young lady from Nattick
Whose sex life was very erratic.
She dodged every feller
From third floor to cellar,
But fucked all the bats in the attic.

1953-1966A.

1291

There was an old maid from New Haven
Whose desires were unhealthy and craven.
She scattered live ants
On the seat of her pants,
And had them pecked off by a raven.

1953.

1292

Said a crocodile far up the Nile:
"While our habits are crude as to style,
We crocs wish to say
We have fun in our way,
And it beats human screwing a mile!"

1965.

1293

Shed a tear for wild Miss O'Flynn
Who jumped from a boat for a swim.
A squid slipped inside her
And started to ride her—
Now seaweed grows out of her quim.

1970A.

1294

There was a young fishwife from Ongar
Who used to make love with a conger,
Which she kept in a creel
Till that willy old eel
Tried her asshole and found it was longer.

1973.

1295

Another young girl, named O'Shea,
Liked sex in an aqueous way.
When out for a swim
She opened her quim,
And the eels had a great holiday.

1960.

1296. ALL ROADS LEAD TO ROME

Lewd ways have led lecherous Otto
Deep down in a moss-covered grotto.
From the barks and the squeals,
One undoubtedly feels
That Otto has ravished a potto!

1966.

1297

A yogi named Parminahanda
Thought love with a cobra just dandy,
    Till a flick of the fang,
    In the shank of the yang,
Left him dead upon the veranda.

1953.

1298

An octopus, purple with passion,
Said, " Sex in the sea they can't ration.
    Octopussy, when wet,
    Is the best I've found yet—
I sure hope it don't go out of fashion! "

1966.

1299

Said a man with a turbulent penis :
" I wish the whole world could've seen us!
    For I stood on a stool
    And buggered a mule,
And produced an entirely new genus. "

1948.

1300

That queerest of queers, named Petrillo,
Has a yen for a girl armadillo.
    With hot words of affection
    He effects sex connection,
With the beast on its back on a pillow!

1965.

1301. THE PIG-SHIT STOMP

When performing with human pig fuckers,
Most pigs demand cash when they puckers.
    They don't take a chance—
    They get paid in advance—
Pig fucking's killed plenty of suckers.

1976A.

1302

There was a young man from Point Pleasant
Who once tried to diddle a pheasant.
It squeezed out his prick
To a reg'lar toothpick,
And it's on vacation, at present.

1950.

1303

There was a young lady named Pratt
Who caught in her attic a bat.
This she kept in the loo
With a tomcat and gnu,
So all four shared the hole where she . . . sat.

1973.

1304

The habits of Dilkington Prodd
Are horribly gruesome and odd:
He dabbles small snails
In his ladyfriends' tails,
And lets them creep over his pod.

1965.

1305

A naturalist we know is a queer.
Of women he has a strange fear.
He spurns their advances,
And takes his own chances
On buggering male sheep and deer.

1948.

1306

A venerable Indian rajah
Once decreed that all cunts be made larger,
And, until it was done,
That he'd have his fun
With the arse of his favorite charger.

1957A.

1307

There's a shepherd stuck out on the range
With a malady wondrously strange,
For he slept with his flock
Till he found that his cock
Had been badly affected by mange.

1972.

1308

A venerable dame from Rangooser
Had a tapeworm that used to amuse her.
When she'd lie on the bed,
It would stick out its head,
And tickle her lallapaloozer.

1953.

1309. KING KONG EXPLAINS

King Gorilla, the monarch of roarers,
Warned his mate : " Stay away from explorers.
If they fuck like we do,
They'll be sure after you,
And I don't want no half-human horrors. "

1965.

1310

There was a young artist named Royce
Who tired of women and boyce.
Said he with a sigh,
" I fear I must try
Wiggly worms for my sexual joyce. "

1948.

1311. A HERO REMEMBERS

Oh, you and me, and old Uncle Sam,
We brought Democracy to Vietnam.
We fucked monkeys and yaks,
Little girls in black slacks,
And smoked pot till we gave not a damn!

1977A.

1312

There was an old man of Santander
Who said, "You be goose : I be gander."
The shaft of his tool
Was soon covered with stool—
Shitty time he had trying to land her!

1950-1974A.

1313

An old miser was once heard to say,
After roll Number One in the hay :
"This is nowhere as cheap
As my usual sheep,
Yet I think sex may be here to stay."

1967A.

1314

A German explorer named Schlichter
Had a yen for a boa constrictor.
When he lifted its tail,
Mein Gott! 'twas a male :
The constrictor, not Schlichter, was victor.

1966A.

1315

A vainglorious diver in his scuba
Tried to rape a small whale south of Cuba.
But she-whales are grim,
And what *she* did to him
Would make a Dead March on the tuba.

1965.

1316

There once was a man from Seattle
Who had screwed a lot of cattle.
His balls hung so low
He tied both in a bow,
And swung them over his saddle.

1961*

1317

That sow Dick was trying to sell us,
His wife hates the sight of, they tell us.
For he diddles this pig
With a stick or strong twig,
Till the *smile* on its face makes her jealous!

1973.

1318

Said a zoo keeper's wife in Shalott,
As she stuffed some live ants up her twat:
"Of all sexual sensations
The eccentric gyrations
Of an anteater's tongue beats the lot."

1971 *ff*.

1319

Two monkeys, a he and a she,
Were naughty as naughty could be.
A twelve-year-old kid
Watched to see what they did,
Then he went in the closet to pee.

1888.

1320

On his knees at the back of a sheep,
The shepherd was getting in deep.
He said, "Gosh, what a breeze!
For I save the stud fees,
And all of the lambs I can keep."

1966A.

1321

The tiniest mammal, the shrew,
Is known for its three-second screw.
He'll repeat it at will,
On any molehill
Till the tip of his weenie turns blue.

1970A.

1322. SID THE SQUID

There was a young seaman named Sid
Who decided to bugger a squid.
    But the squid squirted ink
    On the pink of his dink,
And went down in the bilges and hid.

1953.

1323

There was a young farmer named Sig
Whose prick was too long and too big.
    His perverted passion,
    Contrary to fashion,
Consisted of fucking a pig.

1948.

1324

No man has yet filled the vast slit
In the lush, hairy crotch of Miss Witt.
    As a matter of course
    She now fucks a small horse,
And is starting to kick about *it!*

1965.

1325

A dairyman working at Slough
Fell madly in love with his cow.
    He made love in bed
    With this beast, it is said,
But no one has quite explained how.

1973.

1326

Another old person from Slough
Fucked rabbits and snakes and a sow.
    It may not be relevant,
    But he tried a small elephant—
They're dredging to find his corpse now.

1967A-1975.

1327

Cried a hopeless young nympho in Spain,
Who nightly took on a Great Dane :
" ¡Caramba! señor,
I am just a dog whore,
So what is the use to complain? "

1965.

1328

There was a young sparrow named Spark
Who went hunting for cunt in the park.
He came back to the nest,
Kissed his mate and confessed
He had only gone off on a lark.

1975.

1329

There once was a human spittoona,
Fucked a llama—also a vicuna.
He then knocked on the door
Of a dirty old whore,
And reamed the poor bitch without scruna.

1950A.

1330

There was an old nympho named Spruce
Who wished to get banged by a moose.
Though he sweated and tried
She was unsatisfied—
The shank of his crank was too loose.

1971A.

1331

A man climbed a tall milking stool
To ram his long horn in a mule.
But just as he started,
The animal farted,
And blew all the gas up his tool.

1950.

1332

A lazy old rat, for a stunt,
Built a nest in a prostitute's cunt.
  The cat, with much laughter,
  Came tumbling in after,
And got himself lost in the hunt.

1948.

1333. MAN'S NOBLEST CONQUEST

Said the horse, who was almost in tears,
To the cowboy who herded the steers:
 "I beg of you, mate,
  If you *must* masturbate,
Please try not to come in my ears."

1958.

1334

Though Nell's belly is swelled, and she ain't telling
With whom or with what she's been helling.
  But that nasty Miz' Boggs
  Claims the girl diddles dogs,
And it's due to a poodle from Snelling.

1965.

1335

The infamous Richard the Third
Found the fashionable fuck was a bird.
  The hole of a sparrow,
  So dry, pink, and narrow,
He oiled up with hummingbirds' turd.

1955.

1336

At Christmas a lady named Thrasher
With three drinks got bolder and brasher.
  First she screwed Santa Claus,
  Then without any pause
She had Donder and Blitzen and Dasher.

1975.

1337

Lady Jane longed for sex through and through,
But her offering was sampled by few.
Life is now wild and glad
Since the night she was had
By a blue-bottomed ape in the zoo!

1966.

1338

There was a young fellow named Tony
Who once tried to bugger a pony,
Which he blithely confessed
He preferred to Miss West—
A statement I think is boloney.

1948.

1339. THE HELICAN!

A marvelous bird is the toucan,
Who, when engaged in a screw can
Stand on his head,
Shove his beak in instead—
If you think that's a cinch, see if *you* can!

1953.

1340

A horrid old whore of Uttoxeter
Had all the dogs waving their cocks at her.
She'd stuffed up her cunny
With dog-rose and honey,
But it did her no good, for the pox et' her.

1870-1976A.

1341. PRECIOUS BANE

Our perverse old scribbler, Vladimir,
Was stroking a butterfly's femur.
"I prefer this," he said,
"To a lady in bed,
Or even a velvet-eyed lemur."

1948.

1342

While forming my coming year's vows,
I promise to stop fucking cows.
    To stand on a stool
    Is playing the fool,
And it's easier buggering sows.

1971A.

1343

The deacon, unhappily wed,
Once smuggled a pig into bed.
    The prick of the pig
    Was what you'd call big,
And he raped the old deacon instead.
(Cork-screwed 'im!)

1971A.

1344

Young Jack has a pet habit, which is
The cause of his always-damp breeches.
    He masturbates gaily
    A dozen times daily,
And screws hens and heifers and bitches.

1950.

1345

A sheep-herder said to a whore :
" Oi don't buy me cunt in a store.
    For I bugger me sheep—
    They're clean an' they're cheap,
An' they don't make me Old Faithful sore. "

1965.

1346

A young flea exploring a zone,
By a rich growth of hair overgrown,
    Was surprised to discover
    The balls of a lover,
And that he and his host weren't alone.

1973.

VIII

EXCREMENT

1347

There was an old man of Alsace
Who played the trombone with his ass.
    He put in a trap
    To take out the crap,
But the vapors corroded the brass.

1948.

1348

There was an old man from Arcola
Who didn't know shit from Shinola.
    He pined and he pined,
    For his shoes were unshined
When hernia stopped up his hole-a.

1948.

1349

There was an old fellow named Art
Who awoke with a horrible start,
    For down by his rump
    Was a generous lump
Of what should have been just a fart.

1953.

1350

It takes little strain and no art
To bang out an echoing fart.
    The reaction is hearty
    When you fart at a party,
But the sensitive persons depart.

1965.

1351

It's my own fault I've only one ball,
And it's lucky I *have* one at all.
While sittin' and shittin'
I should never have written
My phone number up on that wall!

1970A.

1352. THE POOTMOBILE

Our staff proctologist, Dr. Barr,
Has invented a new kind of car.
With a tank full of shit
There's no stopping it—
For short trips, two poots take you far.

1976A.

1353

At an opera performance the bass,
Much to his despair and disgrace,
Farted with violence
In a moment of siolence,
And a rosy blush flushed every face.

1965.

1354

An eccentric old coot from Bel Air
Was accused of passing hot air.
Said he : " It's right smart
To fire off a fine fart.
'Twould be louder if my ass were quite bare. "

1968.

1355

A flatulent Cockney named Billy
Could fart like a two-year-old filly.
He did it so well
That he soon blew to hell
Every shithouse in old Piccadilly.

1948.

1356

There was a young man from Biloxi
Whose bowels responded to Moxie.
Drinking glass after glass,
He would tune up his ass,
Till he played like the band at the Roxy.

1948.

1357

Said a decadent wench of Bombay:
"This has been a most wonderful day.
Three cherry tarts,
At least twenty farts,
Two shits, and a bloody fine lay."

1955-1956.

1358

There was a young lady from Bristol
Who went to the Palace called Crystal.
Said she, "It's all glass,
And as round as my ass,"
And she farted as loud as a pistol.

1888.

1359

An observant old codger named Browder
Said, "Now, between bean soup and chowder,
You'll find, my good friend,
That bean soup—in the end—
Will prove to be several times LOUDER!!"

1966.

1360. INDUSTRIAL ASSPIONAGE

The office brown-noser named Bunky
Would claim he was nobody's flunky.
But when the chips were all down,
His proboscis was brown,
And there hung many strands which were gunky.

1975.

1361

The morals of a fellow named Burke
Brand him as a low sort of jerk.
For he shits in the halls
Of the homes where he calls,
And scuffs it around with a smirk!

1965.

1362

A fat-headed female called Burt
Was an artist in sexual dirt.
She devotedly shat
In her shoes or her hat,
And wiped her backside with her shirt.

1941C.

1363. THE FARTING CONTEST

At a contest for farting in Butte
One lady's exertion was cute :
It won the diploma
For fetid aroma,
And three judges were felled by the brute.

1975.

1364

A playful young chemist named Byrd
Had an urge that could not be deferred.
So to irritate Knox
He shit in his sox,
And plastered the walls with his turd.

1948.

1365

If you find for your verse there's no call,
And you can't afford paper at all,
For the true poet born,
However forlorn,
There is always the lavat'ry wall.

1973.

1366

Said a gaseous old laddie named Carter,
Well known as a helluva farter:
"It's that bad sauerkraut
That I've eaten, no doubt,
So here goes a blast for a starter!"

1965.

[1367]

So glib with his asshole was Carter,
No man with his mouth appeared smarter.
But what issued ethereal
From that venthole sphinctereal
Transcended the Farter from Sparta.

1975.

1368

A shiftless old coot of Cayuse
Had bowels abominably loose.
His quick defecation
Was a sickening sensation—
He was nine times as loose as a goose.

1966.

1369. SAINT FARTRE

There was an old *roué* of Chartres
Who had to stoop over to fartre.
He'd oft burst his britches,
Which put folks in stitches,
But proved most inspiring to Sartre.

1954A.

1370

There was a young woman named Chase
Who pissed in a Florentine vase,
And gave as excuse:
"My God, what's the use
Of tramping all over the place?"

1945.

1371. TRIANGULAR ASSHOLE

A flatulent fellow named Cooper
Is known as a blue-ribbon pooper.
  Them as knows, says it means
  He's a glutton for beans—
Well, he sure bangs 'em out like a trooper!

1965.

1372

When he lets fly a foul crepitation,
Gassy Gus must create a sensation.
  It's worse than just silly—
  He's been gorging on chili,
In an effart to gas the whole nation!

1966.

1373

'Twas the whimsy of a fellow named Crump
To package and peddle his dump.
  But the odor o'er-fetid
  Made sales rather tepid,
And his business went into a slump.

1976A.

1374

In a whorehouse on Pee Street in Dallas
A popular trollop named Alice
  Is today in disgrace:
  Shitting in Madam's face
Was *no* way to show ire and malice!

1965.

1375

A bashful young lady named Dee
Sings loudly all during a pee.
  She sings, for that matter,
  To drown out the splatter,
And not as a mere *jeu d'esprit*.

1965.

1376

A philosopher once, named Descartes,
Was explaining himself to a tart.
    " Since I think—I exist, "
    He remarked, as he pissed ;
" But what does it mean when I fart? "

1948.

1377

A flatulent floozie named Dinah
Said : " No pecker shall prod my vagina! "
    But, seduced to a screw,
    Her arse when she blew,
Propelled Dinah across Carolina.

1965.

1378

" I really don't know what to do, "
Said the woman who cleans up the loo.
    " In Number 1 closet
    Someone's left a deposit
Of arrears that were long overdue. "

1973.

1379

A sailor who'd been ashore drinking,
Dreamed he'd slipped overboard and was sinking.
    Indeed he was sunk,
    And he smelled like a skunk,
As he lay in the urinal stinking.

1973.

1380. TRUTH WILL OUT

There was a young girl from East Lansing
Who shit down her left leg while dancing.
    It slid down her nylon
    And left a great pile on
The floor upon which she was prancing.

1948.

1381

May the fame of Archduchess Eliza
Outlive that of Pope and of Kaiser!
She has placed a pierced chair
In the *pissotière* ;
Now one's bowels need no longer play miser.

[1382]

These *chalets de nécessité,*
Improved in a quite basic way
(Many vents, so I've heard),
By a great Royal Turd
Will be opened on Saint Swithin's Day.

1969.

1383

There once was a man in a fit
Who just wasn't able to shit.
He struggled and cursed,
But he swelled up and burst—
A hell of a fate, you'll admit.

1953A.

1384

A nervous young maiden named Fitt
Remarked as I fondled her tit :
" I feel very funny,
So skip the tits, honey,
I'll get so hot and bothered, I'll *shit*! "

1966.

1385

There was a young woman of Florence
Who was looked on with general abhorrence.
In the amorous crush
Her bladder would flush,
And the stuff would come out in great torrents.

1945.

1386

With saxophone, trombone, and flute,
A costive old codger named Newt
Sailed into the can,
For this was his plan :
If he couldn't crap he could toot!

1966.

1387

A madman who murdered in France
Was elected our Prexy by chance.
When he storms into class
The cadets suck his ass,
And the faculty shits in its pants.

1948.

1388

Odette, nationality French,
Was quite a remarkable wench.
She excelled at the art
Of stifling a fart,
But never could manage the stench.

1954.

1389

The dung of a fellow named Frink,
Unlike dung *we* void, doesn't stink.
If he'd only shit faster
He could sell it for plaster,
So he really should try, don't you think?

1965.

1390

A food-faddist fellow from Frisco
Lived on nothing but peanuts and Crisco.
He not only shat
After eating this fat,
But you just should've seen the guy's piss go!

1966A.

1391. BEANS

Beans, beans, the musical fruit,
The more you eat, the more you poot.
    The more you poot
    The better you feel,
So why not eat beans with every meal?

1954A.

1392

There was an old virgin of Ghent
Whose pooper was horribly bent.
    And thus was her ailment
    The lack of impalement,
For she shat at each sexual attempt.

1976A.

1393

A young Highland gillie named Giles
Was badly afflicted with piles.
    His mother's herb ointment
    Proved a sad disappointment—
The deer smelt him coming for miles.

1973.

1394

A nefarious Nazi named Goebbels
Once loaded his anus with pebbles.
    The slightest suspicion
    Or hint of sedition
Found him farting a broadside at rebels.

1948.

1395

For his birthday a chap from Great Britain
Was given a rocker to sit in ;
    A knob for his door,
    A brass cuspidor,
And a blue chamberpot, just to shit in.

1975A.

1396

If the Concorde ever gets off the ground
'Twill produce the most ungodly sound.
  Those aeronautical darts
  Blast out cosmic farts
That will level any poorly built town.

1971.

1397. THE HIPPOCRITIC OATH

Those doctors who cut up your guts
Are out for the money, not nuts.
  When they scrape out your pooper,
  It's the dough they find super :
The *money!*—no if's, and's, or but's!

1976A.

1398

The foible of Frimbleton Hake
Of farting at fish in a lake
  Seems rather far-fetched,
  And though several fish retched,
It is *fart* too much trouble to take!

1965.

1399

A phoney pop artist named Hart
In a jug kept a large purple fart.
  He said, " Yes, I did it,
  But it ain't right to kid it,
Who are YOU to say it ain't Art? "

1966.

1400

The dignified Duchess of Howell
Examined the turd from her bowel,
  And announced, rather miffed,
  That she never had sniffed
An odor so fetid and foul.

1975.

1401

'Twas a notion of William Dean Howells
That a man should have ultraclean bowels.
He would swallow pipe cleaners
The size of small wieners,
With a chaser of pink paper towels.

1965.

1402

When your sphincter nips off the last issue,
And you reach for a handful of tissue,
And then comes the dawn—
The last sheet is gone!—
"O tissue, do I ever missue!!"

1965.

1403

There was a young fellow named Jack
Who ate his girl's snatch—from the back.
He developed the art
Of avoiding a fart,
But got hit in the face with the flak.

1975.

1404

There was an old lady from Kent
Who farted wherever she went.
She went to the fair,
And dropped a few there,
So they plugged up her ass with cement.

1948.

1405

There was a food faddist named Keynes
Who ate only carrots and beans.
At night, on the prowl,
He could see like an owl,
But he farted all day in his jeans.

1975.

1406

A foolish geologist from Kissen
Just didn't know what he was missin',
    By studying rock
    And neglecting his cock,
And using it merely for pissin'.

1948.

1407

There was a young lady named Kit
Who went out in the garden to shit.
    But the stretching and straining,
    And underwear staining
Left her sure that her asshole was split.

1975A.

1408

An *alte kacker* named Klartz
Stinks everyone out with his farts.
    Posed like " The Thinker, "
    He fires off a stinker
To China and more distant parts.

1976A.

1409

An attorney who practiced at law
Wed a bright, cultured girl with one flaw :
    She farted so foul
    He'd let out a yowl—
Though asleep, he would rush out the daw!

1971 *ff.*

1410. A LITTLE CLEAN PEE?

All rivers that water the lea
Are quite pestilential with pee.
    But the gallons of sperm
    Spread nary a germ :
In rubber they sail out to sea.

1970A.

1411

There was an old farmer named Lear
Who possessed a fine cow that gave beer.
Budweiser and Schlitz
Could be tapped from her tits,
And pretzels came out of the rear.

1970.

1412. BLOWJOB

An unfortunate girl named Louise
Lets a vast ventral blast with each sneeze.
She attracts quite a crowd
When they rip out real loud,
And she blushes clear down to her knees.

[1413]

But oho! for our girl named Louise,
Who broke wind every time she would sneeze:
The blast from her ass
Is all high-octane gas,
And she goes jet-propelled on her skis!

1965.

1414

There was a young lady of Lynn
Who could pee on the head of a pin,
By filling her bladder
With a quart of Salada,
And letting it out very thin.

1966A.

1415

The bed manners of Mrs. McCart
I find more offensive than smart,
For each time I come
She arches her bum,
And lets fly with a wall-shaking fart!

1965.

1416

A peculiar young Scot named MacDougal
Delights to break wind in a bugle.
Otherwise he is sane,
Comes in out of the rain,
And is hardworking, kindly, and frugal.

1966.

1417

Unpredictable Mrs. McGrady
Has a rep both unsavory and shady.
Her poops during service
Make communicants nervous,
Though she *eases* them out like a lady.

1966.

1418

A curious old maid named McKesson
Walked in while a man was undressin'.
He said with a sneer,
As he pissed in her ear:
"I guess that'll teach you a lesson."

1945.

1419

There was a young man named McSidney
Who secreted Scotch in his kidney.
When he wanted to drink
He pulled out his dink,
And pissed out a shot of pure whiskey.

1948.

1420

The flatulent Mrs. McTweek
Kept her rear end corked up for a week.
She expected a blast,
But when the time passed
She could manage no more than a squeak.

1965.

1421

There was an old whore of Madras
Who was bushed with a liner of brass.
When you clappered the bell,
She would tinkle like hell,
And played the bass notes with her ass.

1970A.

1422

A Good Humor man in Manila
Stuck a freezer inside a gorilla,
Which when frequently screwed
And fed the right food,
Shat chocolate, lemon-ice, and vanilla.

1970A.

1423

There was a young fellow named Martin
Whose favorite pastime was fartin'.
But one day, alas,
What he thought to be gas
Was something you shovel and cart in.

1948.

1424

A lousy lieutenant named Martin,
Of habits—dad nabbit!—unsartin,
Would brag of his wit,
Which was nothing but shit,
For his mouth he used mainly for fartin'.

1948.

1425. LET WELL-ENOUGH BE

An insane inventor named Martz
Can stop odor from underarm parts.
He has pussies de-stunk,
And a potion that's drunk
To impart a high flavor to farts.

1975.

1426

A silly young virgin named Mary
Who watched her pudenda grow hairy,
  Remarked in high glee:
  "Now I fizz when I pee!
A pastime I *do* like to vary."

1965.

1427

There was a young fellow named Max
Who avoided the gasoline tax.
  It was simple, you see,
  For his scooter burned pee
From his grandfather's herd of tame yaks.

1966A.

1428. FAREWELL, CRUEL WORLD

A prissy young girl named Melissa
Shut the powder-room door . . . A loud hissa . . .
  Then a screech! And a hush . . .
  She was caught in the flush,
And Heaven knows all of us missa!

1966.

1429

There was a young fellow named Mose,
An expert at picking his nose.
  He extracted a clinker
  That was really a stinker,
For it dangled right down to his toes.

1967A-1975.

1430

There was a young lady named Nell
Whose stretch pants were holey as hell.
  She said, "When I fart,
  My shoes fall apart,
And my knees unaccountably swell."

1970A.

1431

A nancy boy of Newcastle
Once wrapped up a turd in a parcel.
'Twas not to offend
But to send to a friend,
To show him the size of his arsehole.

1948U.

1432. AROUND THE HORN

There was a man from New York State,
The more he drank, the more he ate.
The more he ate,
The more he shit—
Vicious circle, isn't it?

1950.

1433

An upstart who gained notoriety
Is shunned by the cream of society,
For his foul ventral breezes
He voids as he pleases,
In tones of fantastic variety.

1965.

1434

A miner from Scranton, P.A.
Swallowed anthracite dust every day.
When burdened with debts
He shits coal-dust briquets,
Which he peddles to eke out his pay.

1953.

1435

A pathetic old virgin of Pau
Fell in love with a dashing young beau.
To attract his regard
She would squat in his yard,
And appealingly pee in the snow.

1966A.

1436

There was a young man from Penn State
Who could fart at a terrible rate.
Rips, rattles, and growls
Came forth from his bowels—
He maintained it was something he ate.

1948.

1437

There was an old farmer named Pitt
Whose cart a big boulder did hit.
His load of manure
So so insecure,
He was up to his neck in the shit!

1968A.

1438

Miss Jane was extremely provoking,
With her halitositical sucking.
She'd stink in her kissing,
And fart when she's pissing,
And pee in the midst of her fucking!

1950.

1439

A crepitant cutie named Puckett
Loves to fart in B-flat in a bucket.
This rare sphincter tune
Gets her cheers in Rangoon,
But a fast trip to jail in Nantucket.

1965.

1440

In Tacoma a girl named Ramona
Let a fart with such fetid aroma,
That her panties corroded,
Her asshole exploded—
But it won her a Fine Arts diploma.

1975.

1441. L'HOMME PÉTOPHONE

A crafty old bugler of Rheims
Would feast upon chocolate creams,
Then fart a toccata
Or a Mozart sonata
On seventeenth-century themes.

1945.

1442

A discerning young fellow named Rickwid
Said, "Chili is one dish I'll stick wid.
For there's quite an art
To predicting which fart
Will be gas, and which one will be liquid."

1953.

1443

There was a young lady named Rose
Who filled not one po, but twelve poes,
With piss, sweat, and come,
Thick slime from her bumb,
And snot from her bloody old nose.

1904C.

1444

A torpedoed seaman named Rowell
Was flagging a ship with a towel.
As the rescuers started
He excitedly farted,
And blew himself back to Rabaul.

1948.

1445

There was a young artist named Saint
Who swallowed some samples of paint.
All the shades of the spectrum
Flew out of his rectum
With colorful lack of restraint.

1950.

1446. THEN THERE WAS THE . . .

Poor old boatman who plied in St. Giles
Who suffered severely from piles.
If he ever sat down
His drawers were stained brown,
So he had to row standing for miles.

1974A.

1447

There was an old man from St. Kitts
Who was troubled with galloping shits.
One morning at last
He let loose a blast
That tore his old asshole to bits!

1953A.

1448

There once was a canny old Scot,
Too stingy to piss in the pot.
So late every night
When his bladder got tight,
He filled up his old lady's twot.

1955A.

1449

An eccentric young fellow named Scott,
His intelligence wasn't too hot.
So small was his wit
That he started to shit
With his trousers draped into the pot.

1954A.

1450

It is useless for people to seek
A pisser like Dribblepuss Beek :
He'll sit for a year,
Drinking oceans of beer,
Then knock off and piss for a week.

1965.

1451. WOMEN'S LIB

There was an old lez of Seringapatam,
Who always wore pants and did not give a damn.
No bra cramped her titty,
Her ass was all shitty,
And whenever she piddled she strode like a man.

1974A.

1452

Said the Queen of Rumania while shitting:
"This nauseous act I'm committing
Suits only the common herd.
That we Royal must turd
I consider both gross and unfitting."

1966.

1453

In the land of Pisuerga they sing
Of how their beloved late king
Would step right up and pee,
If caught short, on a tree,
And the hell with exposing his thing!

1969.

1454

A long-peckered fellow named Slaughter
Wished to hell he'd been born a daughter:
If he hiccuped a bit
While taking a shit,
He siphoned the whole bowl of water.

1952J.

1455

A millionaire miner named Slatter
Had manners folks say do not matter.
He used a Spode teapot
Instead of the peepot,
And shat in a Crown Durham platter.

1950.

1456

Alas for a statesman named Smuts,
Whose shit was all stuck in his guts.
He farted a blast,
Left his hearers aghast,
Yet nothing emerged but some nuts.

1948.

1457

There was a young lady named Sneed
Who flooded the place when she peed.
People put in new plumbing
When she said she was coming,
And everyone ran who could read.

1948.

1458

Said a fart smeller living in Snell :
" I judge a fart's power by the smell.
A small, scentless popper
Ain't really improper—
It's those big greasy blasts that raise hell! "

1965.

1459. THE FARTER FROM SPARTA

You've heard of that fellow from Sparta,
Renowned as musician and farter ;
He could fart pizzicata,
With flute obbligata,
And boom out the bass of Bach's B-flat toccata.

[1460]

He could blow stately themes in organlike styles,
Such as "Ein Fester Burg," with his sphincter in smiles ;
He could fart " Dulciana "
Or a soft *vox humana,*
With tremolo stops from his piles . . .

1951R.

1461

We avoid that lush maiden from Spitz,
Due to vile ventral gas she emits.
    In the midst of a dinner
    This unconscionable sinner
Hops up on the table and shits!

1966.

1462

In her lover's bed, Edna was spread
As *in* went his pecker's red head!
    Did his long diddling-bone
    Make the girl moan and groan?
No, the bitch farted loudly instead.

1965.

1463

There was a young scholar of Spy Hill
Who retired after lunch to a high hill.
    Said his friends, " Well, how was it?
    A healthy deposit? "
He sighed, " *Vox, et præterea nihil.* "

1904C.

1464

Long turds of most horrible stench
Are voided by a person named Dench,
    Who sneaks out after dark
    To Whoremonger Park,
And smears them about on a bench!

1965.

1465

In this world there is one thing that's sure :
For eating there's really no cure.
    What you chew as fine chow
    Wanders through you somehow,
And ends up as human manure.

1966.

1466

There once was a Kensington strumpet
Whose arsehole would bray like a trumpet.
Besides which gift, she
Had one art, repartee,
As tasty and crisp as a crumpet.

[1467]

So when her pa proved " a mere scum pit
Your cunt is, and as for your rump, it
Is all out of tune! "
She laughed, " Yer baboon!
Yer don't like it? All right! yer can lump it! "

1904C.

1468

There was a young woman of Surrey
Who wanted to piss in a hurry.
She went 'round the back
And opened her crack,
And a fellow backed in with his lorry.

1948U.

1469

A crepitant cowhand named Sweezy
With his blasts made the countryside breezy.
Accomplished by means
Of big meals of red beans,
To Sweezy these breezes came easy.

1965.

1470

Our schoolteacher drank so much tea,
She went to the can for to pee.
When she jerked on the chain
She was flushed down the drain,
And by now she's ten miles out to sea!

1965.

1471

Lord Sniffnose was brought up to think
That the stools of his class did not stink.
Nothing changed his beliefs
Till he sullied his briefs,
And rinsed them himself in the sink.

1973.

1472

There was a young lady of Thrace
Who was woefully lacking in grace.
In the midst of a kiss
She'd start in to piss,
Which was neither the time nor the place.

1954A.

1473. A HERO'S LIFE

Richard Strauss won't let Bach steal his thunders;
What his next work will be, the world wonders.
Musicians who know him
Predict a tone poem
Scored for flush toilets, horns, and *gesunders!*

1973.

1474

There was a rash man in Toledo
Who swallowed one day a torpedo.
He fell off a cart
And the folks heard him fart
Just a mile and a half from Toledo.

1888.

1475

There was a young man from Turin
Who had sugar galore in his urine,
Which made him right handy
For makers of candy,
And he got paid extra for stirrin'.

1953.

1476

There was an old spinster of Tweed
Who was prudish in thought, word, and deed.
    Yet she held it no scandal
    To squeeze on the handle
Of the vessel in which she wee-weed.

1970A.

1477

An unhappy young filly from Vassar
Has a terrible rep as a gasser.
    She knows what it means
    When she fills up on beans,
But she'll never let pork-&-beans pass 'er.

1965.

1478. MY SECRET LIFE

There was a young fellow named Wattie
Who drove every girl he met dotty.
    He explained, " I'm the boy
    Who fucks women with joy,
And delights when they rattle the potty. "

1971*ff*.

1479

An impolite lady named Welch
Remarked of an earth-shaking belch :
    " Well, I knew all along
    'Twas a poop headed wrong,
But *either* is damned hard to squelch. "

1966.

1480

Said Jonah, as he crept through the whale :
" I'm hip-deep in shit in this jail.
    I'll shoot through its ass
    In a mass of hot gas!— "
And he whizzed in a fart through its tail.

1970A.

1481

There was a young lady from Wheatley
Who perfumed herself so discreetly,
From her head to her toes
She offended no nose,
But her rectum, alas, smelled less sweetly.

1967A-1975.

1482

There was an old lady from Wheeling,
The skin of whose hind end was peeling.
When she sat at the stool
Her anus would drool,
So she had to defecate kneeling.

1948.

1483

A lady of beauty and wit
Remarked as she squatted to shit:
"Are there *no* polite words
Used to designate turds?—
Just plain shit doesn't please me one bit!"

1965.

1484

There was an old girl up at Yale
Who filtered her shit through a veil.
She would have used cotton
But her asshole was rotten,
And she splattered all over the pail.

1948.

1485

A bitter old hermit named Yewer
Complained, as he sat in a sewer:
"I *hate* my own species!
It's only with feces
That I feel both relaxed and secure."

1965.

IX

GOURMANDS

1486

A necrophile named Ab
Sneaked into the coroner's lab.
  He went down on a stiff
  Who had died of the syph,
And choked to death on a scab.

1960.

1487

There once were two cooks from Barbados
Who dated two buxom tomatoes.
  After lengthy maneuvers
  They said, " That's the *hors d'œuvres* ;
Now prepare for the meat and potatoes! "

1975.

1488

A gourmet from Ghana who'd been
Introduced to cannibal cuisine
  Said, " Those Texans I favor
  For texture and flavor,
But aren't they a nuisance to clean! "

1967A.

1489

A madam who ran a bordello
Put come in her pineapple jello,
  For the rich, sexy taste
  And not wanting to waste
That greasy kid stuff from a fellow.

1965.

1490

There was a young man of Calais
Who considered himself a gourmet,
    Eating crocodile roast
    Or flies' eggs on toast—
His sex life was more *recherché*.

1970.

1491

A nasty old drunk in Carmel
Thinks it funny to piss in the well.
    He says, " Some don't favor
    That unusual flavor,
But I don't drink the stuff—what the hell! "

1965.

1492

The vulva of Lord Byron's daughter
Was served at a feast with iced porter,
    And heartily praised :
    It was boiled first, then braised,
With plenty of herbs in the water.

1974.

1493

It seems that a Miss Delehanty,
Whose morals are putrid and scanty,
    Picked crabs from a fellow,
    Which she put in lime jello
And fed with great glee to her auntie.

1965.

1494. ROOTY-TOOT-TOOT

There was a young girl from Dundee,
From her fanny there grew a plum tree.
    No one ate the nice fruit,
    To tell you the truth,
Because they knew it came from her tooty-toot-toot.

1954A.

1495

A brooding, neurotic young fellow
Went into a low-class bordello,
    Where he ordered four whores
    All with chancres and sores,
And ate them with strawberry jello.

1975.

1496

To his bride said economist Fife:
"The semen you'll launch as my wife,
    We will salvage and freeze
    To resemble goat's cheese,
And slice for *hors d'œuvres* with a knife."

1966.

1497

Said a happy young man of Fort Drum:
"What care I for this shortage of gum?
    My favorite chew
    Is a condom or two,
With a goodly amount of fresh come."

1945.

1498

A man on the isle of Great Thatch
Kept a woman diseased in the snatch.
    By her breasts she was hung,
    And down poured the mung—
He was heard to exclaim, "Down the hatch!"

1959A.

1499. GOLDEN SHOWERS

Having picked out a whore from the group,
He asked her for douche-water soup.
    Cried the girl in surprise:
    "You damned fetish guys
Make my ass so damn tired I could *poop!*"

1965.

1500

The son of a cheesemaker, Little Hans,
Was known far & wide for his *grosse Schwanz.*
It looked nice and clean
And had a grand sheen,
But under the foreskin was Liederkranz.

1971 *ff.*

1501

A lazy young houri named Hayes
Said, " I don't mind giving guys lays,
If they bring vaseline
Or plain margarine,
But I hate to use good mayonnaise! "

1965.

1502

There was a young man named McNabs
Who lived on pox-pickings and scabs.
If he got sick on the spew,
Which he often would do,
His wife's monthly blood brought the son of a bitch
through. 1963A.

1503

In his back-alley shack in Mattoon,
Rumor has it an ignorant goon
Gathers feces from snakes
For the icing on cakes,
Which he spreads on quite thin with a spoon.

1965.

1504

There was an old lady named Mott
Who lived on the cheese from her twat,
Snot from her nose,
Jamb from her toes,
And the Devil almighty knows what.

1942A.

1505

For fear she might have a child, Nelly
Rarely let a man into her belly.
She would eat it instead,
And spread it on bread
With guaranteed spermacide jelly.

1957J.

1506

There was a right royal old nigger
Who ate the *somethings* of the reverend MacTrigger.
His five hundred wives
Had the time of their lives,
It grew bigger and bigger and bigger.

1918-1922*

1507

A cranky old woman from Nottage
Lived alone by the sea in a cottage.
She ate solely sea food,
But it did her no good—
She died eating homemade crap pottage.

1973.

1508

There was a young jaygee named Pitt
Whose anus refused to emit.
This terrible curse
Put his bowels in reverse,
And filled up his jowls with shit.

1942A.

1509

It is best to avoid Pocatello,
Where the women weewee in the jello.
It's a great recipee,
But not my cup of tea,
Though they *do* say it makes your balls mellow.

1965.

1510

Hear the sad tale of foolish young Post
Who cut off his manhood to roast.
    Said he, "Though it's tasty,
    Perhaps I was hasty—
It's the slice I'll be missing the most."

1966.

1511. THEOBROMA PAPAO

A ragoût of virgin posteriors
Is a dish fit for papal interiors:
    On holy days, baste
    And garnish to taste
With the hymens of Mother Superiors.

1974.

1512

The mayor of Boston, it seems,
Was troubled with repeating beans.
    With commendable wit
    He encased them in shit,
And sold them as chocolate creams.

1963A.

1513

There was a young man from the South
Who taught girls to pee in his mouth.
    He explained, "It's a taste
    We oughtn't to waste,
And essential in case of a drouth."

1950.

1514

That exquisite barman at Sweeney's
Is famed for his ale and free wienies.
    But I thought him uncouth
    To gulp gin and vermouth,
Chill the glasses, and piddle martinis.

1956.

1515

A bitchy young girl of Valhallad
Says, " Honey chile, family-style's pallid! "
This erogenous wench
Loves to work 'em off French,
And use the results in her salad.

1965.

1516. SOUTHERN COMFORT

A drip who delights in low vices
Spent a hectic weekend with the Rices.
In a state of elation
He performed masturbation,
And dribbled his sperm on the ices.

1966.

1517

A moody young pervert called Walter'd
Moan, " My coprophilia's faltered.
A tasty supply
Is so hard to come by.—
Shit! I wish that my life-style was al-tered. "

1974.

1518

From Rectum-on-Pot in West Bum
All sorts of wild rumors have come :
Limp-peckered old fools
Have cut off their dead tools,
And already have barbequed some!

1965.

1519

An anatomy student at Yale
Sliced off many a cadaverous tail.
Carefully pickling each clyde
In formaldehyde,
He discovered they have little sale.

1966.

1520. THE DIRTIEST DOZENS

The world is so full of a number of things,
I'm sure we should all be as happy as kings.
    I'll tell you a story—
    It won't take me long—
Of a brother and sister whose *tale* is my song.

[1521]

There was an old fellow and what do you think?
He lived on the cheese that he scraped from his dink.
    He whacked it, he hacked it,
    He ate it with glee—
Was there ever a fellow so happy as he?

[1522]

This charming old chap had a sister as well :
She was ugly and gaunt, with a horrible smell.
    Her cunt was so dirty
    It stank like a beast,
And the odor killed flies as they gathered to feast.

[1523]

What a wonderful family! What marvellous style!
I'll bet you and I aren't close by a mile.
    Their odor and diet
    Won't soon be forgotten,
And one day you and I may be equally rotten.

1976A.

X

VIRGINITY

1524

Young virgins who sigh for affinity
And yearn to be loved to infinity,
All their troubles would pass
If they'd struggle for ass
Just as hard as they fight for virginity.

1975.

1525

Sighed a neat little package named Annie :
" I've the tits and the twat and the fanny,
Plus the yen, but the men
Only call now and then—
Can it be I've B.O. in my cranny? "

1965.

1526

An old maid who had a pet ape
Lived in fear of perpetual rape.
His red, hairy phallus
So filled her with malice
That she sealed up her snatch with Scotch tape.

1953.

1527

A frigid young lady named Bates
Was accursèd from birth by the Fates.
She was dying to screw,
When the men asked her to,
But always refused when on dates.

1970A.

1528

Shed a tear for poor brainwashed Miss Beek
Who, though blessed with a glorious physique,
    Hot-blooded and passionate,
    As to sex she would ration it
On some crackpot Liberation mystique.

1977A.

1529

A boastful young virgin from Boulder
Swore no man on earth ever rolled her,
    But was highly dismayed
    When her ass was displayed
On a Vegas massage-parlor folder.

1970A.

1530

An uptight young lady named Breerley
Who valued her morals too dearly
    Had sex, so I hear,
    Only once every year,
And she strained her vagina severely.

1975.

1531

There was a young fellow named Brewer
Whose girl made her home in a sewer.
    Thus he, the poor soul,
    Could get into her hole,
And *still* not be able to screw her!

1954A.

1532. THE BALL O' KILLIECRANKIE

A sweet Scottish lassie named Bude
Was debauched on a hilltop quite nude.
    In some crude hanky-panky
    Above Killiecrankie,
She was buggered, stewed, screwed, *and* tattooed.

1974A.

1533

A hidebound young virgin named Carrie
Would say, when the fellows got hairy:
"Keep your prick in your pants
Till the end of this dance—"
Which is why Carrie still has her cherry.

1965.

1534

A good Jewish mamma most chary,
Found her daughter in love most unwary.
"What a boy!—but a Goy!
He's a positive joy!
So screw if you must, but don't marry!"

1971 *ff.*

1535

A desperate spinster from Clare
Once knelt in the moonlight all bare,
And prayed to her God
For a romp on the sod—
'Twas a passerby answered her prayer.

1962A.

1536

A precautious *jeune fille* named Colette
Parked her prat on a purple bidette,
And remarked with a wince:
"It is nonsense to rinse
When I ain't even been diddled yet."

1965.

1537

Poor Alice who lived in Corvallis
Had heard of, but not seen, the male phallus.
At her first sight of one
She started to run,
And last was seen sprinting through Dallas.

1966.

1538. MAKE WAR, THEN LOVE

Said President Jobcock one day :
" War's better than love, I should say.
Instead of a virgin,
It's murder I'm urgin'—
You get lots more blood that-a-way. "

1971B.

1539

There was a young lady of Dee
Whose hymen was split into three.
And when she was diddled
The middle string fiddled :
" Nearer My God To Thee. "

1959A.

1540

An old electronic designer
Had designs on a minor named Dinah.
He couldn't carry them out
For his prick was too stout,
And too small was the minor's vagina.

1954.

1541

Cried a silly old maid of Devizes :
" Mercy me! My tits are two sizes.
Still, there's no one to see
How they look, except me,
And I'm rather above such surprises. "

1966.

1542

The maidenheads popping next door
Are getting to be quite a bore,
For it's only with virgins
Neighbor Jock has sex urgin's—
We long ago quit keeping score.

1966.

1543

An inquisitive virgin named Dora
Askèd the man who started to bore 'er :
" Do you mean birds and bees
Go through antics like these,
To supply us our fauna and flora? "

1965.

1544

At the marriage bureau at Dover
A finicky fellow named Stover
Said, " I want for a bride
One whom no one has tried,
Not a widow you have to warm over. "

1976.

1545

A Greek scholar who walked like a duck
Had a habit of running amuck,
Till little Miss Royster
Lured him out of his cloister,
And taught the old codger to fuck.

1948.

1546. A LA RECHERCHE DU TEMPS PERDU

There was an old maid of Duluth
Who wept when she thought of her youth,
And the glorious chances
She'd missed at school dances,
And once in a telephone booth.

1945.

1547

A captious young girl of Dundalk
At belly-to-belly would balk.
When a swain became pressing
And started caressing,
She'd say, " Let's just sit here and talk! "

1974A.

1548

An ignorant maid of Durango
Didn't know where to make a man's whang go.
    But she picked up this knowledge
    At her first dance at college,
With a sigh you could play as a tango.

1970A.

1549. NEVER OVERDO

An innocent virgin named Fletcher
Succumbed to the wiles of a letcher.
    She found it so glorious
    At last to be whorious!—
Well, they carried him out on a stretcher.

1965.

1550

Of her " opening night " near Fort Bliss
She explained, " It began with a kiss.
    Then it ended in bed
    With a torn maidenhead,
And my eyeballs both rolling like THIS! "

1965.

1551

Still a virgin at age forty-two,
An unhappy old maid of Purdue
    Trapped a midnight intruder
    Who reluctantly screwed 'er,
Then charged her ten dollars when through.

1966.

1552

Oh, there are no virgins left in Foster Hall!
I thought there were, but when I went to call,
    I found there was no chance
    That I'd not been in their pants,
For I personally had fucked 'em one and all!

1953A.

1553

" Watch out! " warned a damsel in France ;
" Let his hand reach the fuzz in your pants,
While his other hot mitt
Clamps onto a tit,
And your maidenhead don't stand a chance! "

1965.

1554. THE HARD-BOILED VIRGIN

An erudite spinster named Frances
Who delighted in ribald romances,
Resolved to find out
Beyond physical doubt
What the point of the joke in men's pants is.

1930-1956A.

1555

A charming young lady named Gail
Was having her first piece of tail.
And this girl, sweet and pure,
Felt completely secure
With this scabby old scrofulous male!

1967A-1975.

1556

Said a much-diddled dolly named Gissing :
" Virgins don't know what they're missing!
Though I'm not very lewd,
I enjoy being screwed—
That's what a cunt's *for,* besides pissing. "

1966.

1557

There was a young lady named Gloria
Whose boyfriend said, " May I explore ya? "
She replied, " What a sap!
I will draw you a map
Of where others have been to before ya. "

1957A.

1558

A well-bred young girl of Gomorrah
Would never let any man bore her :
    Neither back nor in front,
    Not in mouth nor in cunt,
And she viewed their stiff pricks with horror.

1956J.

1559

Though American girls are good-looking,
Their husbands get a terrible rooking,
    And learn with surprise
    That their partners are wise
In fooking rather than cooking.

1957M.

1560. THANK YOU ! !

Said a nervous old maid in Grant's Pass :
" I must stop taking walks through the grass.
    When I think I'm alone
    I hear some girl moan,
And step on some man's heaving ass. "

1965.

1561

Sighed a sensual virgin named Griffin :
" I've longed all these years for a stiff 'un.
    Why, even a short 'un
    Would start me to snortin'—
Do I pray for a lay? You ain't whiffin'! "

1966.

1562

To his bride said the nervous young groom :
" Girls would beg, but I never would scroom. "
    She replied : " I'm a virgin,
    But once, Nature urgin',
I worked myself off on a broom. "

1966.

1563

There once were three girls from Hohokus
Who cried to some swimmers, " Please poke us!
Use your tools so gigantic
To drive our twots frantic—
Spray ahead ; we don't care if you soak us. "

1950.

1564

An astonished ex-virgin named Howard
Remarked after being deflowered :
" I knew that connection
Was made in that section,
But not that it's so darn *high-powered.* "

1965.

1565

There was a dry virgin named Hunt
Who said, " Yes, I'm rough up in front."
But a man greased his borer
With Fnerk's Hair Restorer,
And gave her an ermine-lined cunt.

1968A.

1566. VOX CLAMANTE IN DESERTO

A desperate spinster named Hyatt
Got the cops coming out for a riot.
" After years an old maid,
And at last getting laid, "
She explained, " I just couldn't keep quiet. "

1966.

1567

An elderly maid, inauspicious,
Was raped by a robber quite vicious.
She came out of her faint
To file a complaint,
But admitted the whole thing was delicious.

1975.

1568

A hardy old spinster named Jane
Was raped by a man on a train.
She enjoyed it so much
He could scarce break her clutch,
But he fought his way free with his cane.

1975.

1569

To a shy little miss from Kentucky,
A man said, "Say, kid, this is lucky!
Do you think that we *could*?—"
"If I just understood—"
"Spread your thighs double-quick! I feel fucky!"

1950.

1570

There was a young lady named Kitchener
Who had a most terrible itch in her.
A lad offered relief,
But he ran like a thief
When he saw the great size of the ditch in her.

1975.

1571

There was a young coed from Knox
Who had no experience with cocks.
She dated a sailor
Who started to tail her,
And left her to nurse a sore box.

1953.

1572

An eager young bride of Lahore
Found her husband a terrible bore.
She'd expected of *him*
That he'd tickle her quim,
But the bastard did nothing but snore.

1971.

1573

Gossips yak in Kuala Lumpur
That virgins there feel insecure.
  For fat rajahs in heat
  Stalk such unsullied meat,
Which daily gets fewer and fewer.

1965.

1574

A comely young woman named Laura,
Thinking wedlock tyrannical horror,
  And *sub rosa* screwing
  The passport to undoing,
Stayed a virgin intact, to her sorrow.

1948.

1575. GERSHON'S GIRLS

Said a free-love professor named Legman,
To a passel of virgins just beggin' him :
  " Strip down to the nude
  If you want to get screwed,
Or the sheets will get mixed blood and egg in 'em. "

1965A.

1576

There was an old lady of Lissing
Who discovered what she had been missing
  When laid on the sod,
  And she cried : " Oh, my God!
All these years I just used it for pissing! "

1975.

1577

There was a lewd fellow named Long—
Short on wit but immense in the prong.
  He preferred to fuck virgins,
  And with his carnal urgin's
He'd helped scores of young ladies go wrong.

1966.

1578

A sensitive virgin of Lynd
Observed when she'd sexually sinned:
"If I chance to beget,
This *soirée* I'll regret,
But my virtue is Gone With the Wind!"

1965.

1579

A hesitant virgin named Mabel
Remarked: "Though I'm not sure I'm able,
I am willing to try,
So where shall I lie—
On the bed, or the floor, or the table?"

1974A.

1580. LAY ON, MCDUFF!

"Great God!" bemoaned playboy McDuff,
"What *is* all this purity stuff?
You twiddle my prick,
Get it stiff as a stick,
Then deny me the use of your muff!"

1955A.

1581

There was a young girl named MacNeal
Who fashioned her panties of steel,
For diverting the thrust
Of a thumb filled with lust,
And deflecting the unwanted feel.

1975.

1582

Innocent young Miss Mahoney
Heard that love was a lot of baloney.
But the lass never knew
It was literally true,
Till fed the baloney by Tony.

1954J.

1583

There's a coed at college named Mary
Who technically still has her cherry.
For she claims it's not sin
Till ten inches is in—
Her vagina is very short, very!

1948.

1584

There was a young girl named Matthias
Who was so exceedingly nice,
That one night on the farm
She awoke in alarm,
Having lost her virginity twice!

1950.

1585

The maidenhead young Mistress Meggs
Guarded chastely by crossing her legs
Went the way of all flesh
When six satyrs got fresh
And, one by one, polished their pegs.

1966.

1586. ORIGINAL SIN

There was a young girl from the Mission
Who was seized with an awful suspicion
That sexual sin
Didn't matter a pin
In the era of nuclear fission.

1971*

1587

A randy young lass of Mount Barry
Used a candle to rupture her cherry.
And she smirked, "Who will know?
Inside *me* it won't show—
And outside, that spot is all hairy!"

1965.

1588

Oh where, oh where is my nightie?
For I surely must look quite a frightie.
To be caught in the nude
And deliciously screwed
Is as good as a flight in a kitie.

1967K.

1589. CAVEAT EMPTOR

There was a young lady named Pelt
Who wanted her genitals felt.
But no one was wont
To play with her cunt,
Because of the way that it smelt.

1948.

1590

There was a young maiden of Perth
Whose vagina was sealed up at birth,
All because her fond mother
Feared some man or other
Would carnally alter her girth.

1948.

1591

Said Miss Primly, " I kiss and I pet,
But that's all the sexy I get. "
So she thought till one night
She got screwed out of sight,
With her navel just brimming with sweat!

1965-1974A.

1592

At death's door lay old lady Phipps ;
No man had yet mounted her hips.
But one intern tried her,
And God! did he ride her—
She died with a smile on her lips.

1948.

1593

" It's *Pony Express,* " said Miss Pound,
" A wonderful game that we've found.
Like *Post Office,* " she said,
" But you play it in bed,
And there's a little more horsing around. "

1967A-1975.

1594

Arabella's a terrible prude :
She says, " Men are beasts. Men are lewd.
A girl has to watch
Or a hand's in her crotch,
And the next thing she knows—she is scrude! "

1965.

1595

A passionate virgin named Pruitt
Was raped in the woods by a druid.
She cried, her breath bated :
" Oh, God! how I've waited!
I don't CARE what you do—just *do* it! "

1974A.

1596

A frustrated virgin named Pugh
Once dreamed she was having a screw.
Repenting her sin,
She awoke with chagrin
At finding it perfectly true.

1962.

1597

Virgins are now so damned rare,
The mere sight of one makes you stare.
Such babes seem to dread
Losing their maidenhead—
What the hell! it won't show through the hair.

1965.

1598

There was a young lady from Reading
Who was constantly wetting the bedding,
    Till her mother one day,
    In an insolent way,
Suggested a man and a wedding.

1953.

1599. PROMISES! PROMISES!

A spinster who came from the Ruhr
Was grasped by a vulgar young boor.
    This detestable varmint
    Unfastened her garment,
But she found he was just a voyeur.

1975.

1600

An ex-virgin wept in St. Louis,
After being bedridden by Hughie,
    That she felt quite dejected
    For what he'd ejected
Had made her new panties all gooey.

1966.

1601

There once were three maids from St. Mary's,
Who sold all their milk to the dairies.
    They sold beans and tomatoes
    For meat and potatoes—
Soon all they had left were their cherries.

1967A-1975.

1602

A prudish young girl of St. Paul
Dreamt she'd undressed on the Mall.
    The best of the joke
    Was when she awoke,
And found mud on her backside and all.

1948A.

1603

There was a young miss from St. Simon
Who sighed to her gentleman, " Why, man,
I've torn underwear,
And you've worn off the hair,
And you've not even punctured my hymen! "

1950.

1604

There was a young matron named Sally
Who went with her groom up an alley.
She was quite out of luck,
The young boy didn't fuck,
And she muttered, " How Green Was My Valet. "

1948.

1605

There was a young girl from Samoa
Who said to a sailor named Noah :
" You can kiss me and squeeze me,
But remember, to please me,
I'm allergic to spermatozoa. "

1945R.

1606

There was a young lady from Sark
Who would only make love in the dark.
But her boyfriend said, " Hon,
Could you loosen your bun?
I can't tell if I'm hitting the mark. "

1959A.

1607

A lustful old codger from Sheds
Delights to pop girls' maidenheads.
He claims, " Virgins long,
Oftentimes, to go wrong—
It's that first painful POP a girl dreads. "

1966.

1608

There was a young fellow called Simon
Who for years couldn't pierce his wife's hymen,
    Till he hit on the trick
    Of sheathing his prick
In a steel condom studded with diamond.

1948.

1609

Seducing shy virgins to sin
Takes more than sweet talking and gin :
    An all-out seduction
    Is a major production,
And it may take you *hours* to get in.

1965.

1610. THE BOOSTER

A careless young virgin named Slattery,
Led astray by martinis and flattery,
    Became so unwary
    She was robbed of her cherry
By a fiend with an overcharged battery.

1966.

1611

She came as a maiden from Spitz,
But was fucked half the night by Big Fritz.
    Her cunt, chaste and tight,
    Nowadays is a sight :
It's so stretched that a marrowbone fits.

1966.

1612

Where cowards buy their sex in love stores,
Real men want virgins, not whores.
    Like that satyr, old Burroughs,
    Who prods virgin furrows,
And now counts his bastards in scores!

1965.

1613

It seems the ex-virgin Miss Storr
Is flavored with cherry no more.
For a maidenhead buster
Warmed up her cold custard—
She's now known as Pussy Galore!

1966.

1614

For years all the young men had striven
To seduce a young lady named Ruthven,
Till a fellow named Bert
Poked a hole in her skirt.
(In Heaven such sins are forgiven.)

1974A.

1615. HOLD BACK THE DAWN

An eager young virgin named Strong
Thought that passion would last all night long:
That her lover's capacity
Would match her voracity—
She found out, alas, she was wrong.

1977A.

1616

I once had a hot-tempered sweetie
Who resented, in spades, spermaceti.
The real thing that galls
Is, she'd cut off your balls
Before she'd sign a piece treaty.

1961A.

1617

There was a young lady of taste
Who kept herself virgin and chaste,
And stoutly defended
With bear traps suspended
By filigree chains from her waist.

1945.

1618

Cried a bride as she came the first time :
"How *can* you contain so much slime?
I'm not really a prude,
And I'm glad I've been screwed—
I find all but the slime is sublime! "

1965.

1619

When he raped a young maid on the train,
They arrested a fellow named Blaine.
But the ex-virgin cried :
"That's for *me* to decide,
And I'd be the last to complain. "

1965.

1620

A luscious young thing named Miss Trevor
Was cute and exceedingly clever.
To damp her beau's ardor
She put pins in her garter,
And spiked the poor fellow's endeavor!

1958P.

1621

Said a loose-moralled lady at Trinity :
"The date when I lost my virginity
I cannot remember,
But there's been a male member
Ever since in my genital vicinity. "

1966.

1622. YOU NEVER KNOW

There was a young man from Troy
Who went out with a lady of joy.
But he came back nonplussed,
Not to say somewhat fussed,
For *he* wasn't that kind of a boy!

1959*

1623

A professor teaching at Vassar
Was implored by a student to pass her.
    So the ill-tempered grouch
    Threw her down on a couch,
And punctured her antimacassar.

1970A.

1624

A fellow named Teeter in Vaughter
Popped the cherry on his hostess's daughter.
    Life then became boring,
    So she's gone in for whoring
With the techniques that damned Teeter tawter.

1965.

1625

Said the blushing young girl, slightly vexed :
" I am practically certain I'm sexed.
    So, if you don't mind it,
    Let me know when you find it,
And we'll figure out what to do next. "

1965.

1626

I once fucked a respectable virgin
Who needed a damn lot of urgin',
    But she'd always react
    With more vigor than tact
When she felt the hot semen come surgin'.

1948.

1627

Said a guy to his girlfriend, " Virginia,
For ages I've courted to win ya.
    But my point of frustration
    Has reached saturation—
This evening I gotta get in ya! "

1972.

1628

There was a young girl from The Waste
Who filled her vagina with paste.
Her reasoning ran :
" I'll hold onto my man,
Or else I will damn well stay chaste! "

1954A.

1629. PERIOD PIECE

What he asked for (a four-letter word)
Badly frightened the frigid Miss Byrd.
But gin and insistence
Wore down her resistance,
And that four-letter word then occurred.

1966.

1630

A loose-moralled fellow at Yale
Worked his will on an underage frail.
The gal was beguiled,
And was gotten with child,
And *he's* been transferred to a jail.

1965.

1631

If a woman waits thirty-six years,
No wonder sex stirs her to tears.
Full of hope, in her pants,
Sit old gray-headed ants
In cunt juice clear up to their ears!

1965.

XI

MOTHERHOOD

1632

There was a young girl from Alaska
Who'd do anything that you'd ask her.
She'd go out in the woods
And deliver the goods,
And be ready again nine months after.

1952A.

1633

After Joe shot his wad into Ann,
She thought she'd douched out in the can.
But she missed by a myriad
And is now past her period,
And old Joe's on his way to Japan!

1965.

1634

An angry young girl named Arbutus
Said, " I'm fed up on fellows who root us.
It's not the bed-bouncing
That I am denouncing ;
It's that Extract of Kid the brutes shoot us. "

1966.

1635

A young lady, unruly and arrant,
Did the things that more proper girls daren't.
She both hoped and expected
'Twould go undetected,
But she's slowly becoming *apparent.*

1972.

1636

Said a shameless young girl of Bagdad,
Concerning the twins she'd just had:
  "At the party, while tight,
  Fellows used me all night,
So how can I know who's the dad?"

1965.

1637

A big-busted biddy of Beeman
Likes all about sex except semen.
  She knows girls produce
  From that harmless white juice,
But she still goes for sex like a demon.

1965.

1638

A certain young rascal from Bicester
Told the court of a girl—how he'd kissed her.
  But he did not divulge
  That 'twas he caused the bulge
In the front of her underage sister.

1973.

1639. THE CALL OF THE WILD

When a lady returned from Big Moose
Her husband exclaimed, "What the deuce!
  I am quite reconciled
  To the Call of the Wild,
But where did you get that papoose?"

1948.

1640

Said a gloomy young lady named Bloomer:
"I do hope this lump is a tumor.
  I'd be very dismayed—
  Since I *did* once get laid—
To find I'm with child by my roomer."

1966.

1641

His nude model moaned to Botticelli,
As he bounded with glee on her belly :
  " Though you're driving me wild,
    Please recall I'm with child,
And you're beating the brat to a jelly! "

1965.

1642. WEAR YOUR BUTTON, BOYS

A nervous young lady named Cheryl
Said in bed, when she'd shed her apparel :
  " I'm sick of you lubbers
    Who forget to bring rubbers,
So I sure as hell hope that you're sterile. "

1965.

1643

These figures should give you a chill :
The little space left on Earth still
    Folks are fucking away
    With that twice-a-week lay,
So it's either The Bomb or The Pill!

1975A.

1644

There once was a virgin named Claire,
Who would do anything on a dare.
    But some dares, she soon found,
    Make one's tummy quite round,
And she now has a visitor there.

1972.

1645

In the ocean, Puerto Rico's a cork ;
Its national bird is the stork.
    There the natives deploy
    To share natural joy,
And then send the results to New York.

1972.

1646

Though warned that Joe Doakes was a dastard,
Who would rape her on getting her plastered,
Now, alas! Fannie's fecund
For she finally weakened,
And she'll soon have that dastard's li'l bastard.

1966.

1647

That oversexed guy, Delehanty,
Whose morals are terribly scanty,
Badly shocked Peyton Place
And is now in disgrace
For fathering twins on his auntie.

1965.

1648

An irate young damsel of Delhi
Exclaimed as come flowed on her belly :
" Damn your spouting cock, Sikhi,
That goo's not just sticky,
It is horribly messy and smelly! "

1965.

1649

She awoke in the night to discover
That the person who pulled off her cover,
And made her maidenhead shatter
Was the dad who begat her—
Now he's grandfather, father, and lover!

1965.

1650

Poor little Joan was dismayed,
A month after first getting laid.
Her belief he was sterile
Got her over a barrel,
For *one sneaky sperm* made the grade.

1966.

1651

A young girl felt forced to divulge
The reason her belly did bulge :
  " It is not pie and cheese
  Which expand my chemise.
I suspect it's the sport I indulge. "

1975.

1652

An eminent Harley Street doctor
Had a visit from little Miss Proctor,
  Who had to find out
  Beyond any doubt
Just how far up her boyfriend had knocked her.

1954A.

1653

A cynical dolly named Dunn
Said, " The shot in a guy's zipper gun
  Is ghastly : when plastered
  It loads you with bastard,
And fucks up what started as fun. "

1965.

1654

Sighed a foolish young lady named Dunning :
" Your two little balls are so cunning.
  Can it be they've made me
  A mother-to-be?
' Cause this week my monthly ain't running. "

1965.

1655

Said a whore to the doc, in Duquesne :
" This bastard is hard to explain.
  I douche and I douche
  After every darn poosh—
It must be a damned sturdy strain! "

1966.

1656

There was a young girl at Ferranti's
Who spent all her money on panties.
  Then she went to Met-Vickers,
  Where the girls wear no knickers,
And now all her sisters are aunties.

1954.

1657

A Boy Scout was having his fill
Of a Brownie's sweet ass on a hill.
  "We're prepared ; yes, of course,"
  Said Scoutmistress Gorse,
"My Girl Scouts are all on the Pill."

1974A.

1658

The "Pregnant Girl Scout" is fine,
Though some think her quite out of line.
  The fruit of her womb
  Is starting to bloom—
She's the Virgin of Troop Sixty-Nine.

1971.

1659. ABORTION, ANYONE?

The passionate pussy on Fran
Wears out the most virile young man.
  Now and then—just a maybe—
  This results in a baby,
But she flushes them all down the can.

1965.

1660

A cautious young filly of France
Said, "*Non, m'sieu,* I no take ze chance.
  I once try ze tail,
  And my luck . . . *zut!* she fail,
So keep your mitts outa my pants!"

1966.

1661. PEOPLE POLLUTION

The world population's a fright ;
Its numbers soar right out of sight.
Who's to blame?—bear the brunt?
It's the prick and the cunt,
And the shortage of electric light.

1971.

1662

That nympho, my neighbor's wife Gail,
Is forever at me for tail.
Half the kids that girl's had
Should be calling me dad—
Those sperms that I shoot never fail.

1965.

1663

There was a young lady named Gert
Who was heard on occasion to blurt :
" It wasn't so bad
My just getting had,
It was having the baby that hurt. "

1967K.

1664

The Vassar girls cocked up a girdle
Of plastic as tough as a turtle.
Between these and locked knees,
And their A.B. degrees,
It's a wonder the bitches get fertile!

1955M.

1665

Said our Little Nell of Glen Ellen,
On finding her midriff was swellin' :
" I've only used candles,
Hot dogs and broom handles,
So what I will have is hard tellin'. "

1965.

1666

When diffident Milquetoast makes hay,
He first kneels to ponder and pray.
    Then rubber and diaphragm
    Protect *him* and his nervous ma'am,
But by then his yen's gone away.

1965.

1667

A fertilized lady with headaches
Decided to try Dianetics.
    When she found that the fœtus
    Could take notes of coitus,
She shot dead the night man with Nedick's.

1950A.

1668

A nervous young woman in Herts
Complained as she hoisted her skirts :
  " It ain't the skarooing
    That's proved my undoing,
It's that viscous emission you squirts. "

1965.

1669

To an unmarried lady named Hintz
The mention of sex brings a wince.
    In a burst of exuberance
    She sheathed Peter's protuberance,
And she's just been aborted of quints!

1966.

1670

A small population increase
Is due to a dolly in Greece,
    Who spread on a bed
    For a cocksman named Ed
Full many an interesting crease.

1966.

1671. FÜR VOLK UND FÜHRER FICKEN

Artificial insemination
Some say will replace fornication,
  But perish the day
  When the old-fashioned way
Can't supply kids enough for the nation!

1965.

1672

There was a young girl in Japan
Who went for a ride in a tram.
  The dirty conductor
  Got up her and fucked her,
And now she's wheeling a pram.

1963.

1673

To her ma said a proud girl in Keyes :
" I'll do all the fucking I please! "
  But to pay for her sins
  She had interlocked twins,
And oh! did those two bastards *squeeze*!

1965.

1674

A cautious young girl of Khartoum
Always kept a large frog in her womb.
  She said, " I'd be wild
  If I *did* have a child,
And this way there just isn't room. "

1966.

1675

Though full nine months pregnant, Miss Kitchener
Found sexual passion still itchin' her,
  And in spite of the pain
  She laughed like a drain
At the thought of that son of a bitch in 'er.

1974A.

1676

There was a young girl of Lahore,
The same shape behind as before.
    Since no one knew
    Which side to screw,
It baffled the spermatozoa.

1945R.

1677

There was a young girl of Lapland
Whose belly began to expand.
    She cried, " It's a baby! "
    Her boyfriend said, " Maybe—
From now on we'll do it by hand. "

1954A.

1678

A medical student named Lea
Once ravished a taunting P.T.
    She sobbed, " How I rue
    Taking a rise out of you ;
Now please take the rise out of *me*! "

1968A.

1679

An obliging young lady of Leeds
Thinks life should be filled with good deeds,
    But regrets the sequelæ
    Of free gillie-gillie,
For her kids are ten shades and three creeds.

1965.

1680

A naïve teenager, Miss Lewis
Asked : " What is it fellows do to us
    That makes babies come—
    Or am I just being dumb? "
Her sister's reply was : " They screw us. "

1966.

1681

Nearly nine months along with her load,
Big Bertha, about to explode,
Cried, " I loved all the sexing,
But these pains are most vexing ;
I would never of fell if I'd knowed! "

1965.

1682

A careless young girl named McMinns
Was loaded with twins for her sins.
The doc mixed an elixir
He told her would fix her,
But McMinns is *still* loaded with twins.

1966.

1683

The passionate Lady McTidd
Is sadly awaiting a kid.
Says she, " To stay heirless,
One mustn't be careless—
Not even just *once,* as I did. "

1966.

1684. THE NEW GALLANTRY

Said man-hater, Clito McWilde :
" Goddammit, I find I'm with child!
But the worst of the bother
Was telling the father—
The son of a bitch merely smiled! "

1970A.

1685

There was a young girl of Madrid
Who found she'd be having a kid.
She swallowed a rubber
To kill the poor bugger,
And out came a Dunlop non-skid.

1970A.

1686

A lusty young man named Malone
Knocked up every girl in Athlone.
    Their doom had been fated
    When he masturbated
On top of the old Blarney Stone.

1953.

1687

It seems I impregnated Marge,
So I do sort of feel, by and large,
    That some dough should be tendered
    For services rendered—
But I can't quite decide what to charge.

1965.

1688

There was a young lady named Martha ;
Where other girls went far, she went fartha.
    The affairs were good fun,
    The result was a son,
But it hardly seemed worth so much bartha.

1948.

1689

When Fay missed her last menstruation,
'Twas a highly unpleasant sensation.
    And it's getting me down,
    I'll not only leave town,
But the county, the state, and the nation!

1966.

1690

There was a young girl of Milpitas,
Exceptionally fond of coitus,
    Till a halfback from State
    Made her periods late,
And now she has athlete's fœtus.

1948-1965A.

1691. HEAVENLY DISCOURSE

"Since parthenogenesis misses
The rapture of previous kisses,
One is apt to inquire
As to what might inspire
Such a singular stunt by the Mrs."

1967A.

1692

There was an old man of Mongolia
Who suffered from strange melancholia.
His penis turned blue,
His testicles too,
And his asshole produced a magnolia!

1975.

1693

A thoughtless young girl said, "Oh my!
My apron is rising quite high.
Since I carefully douched
Every time that we pooshed,
I really am wondering why."

1963A.

1694

An Old English princess named Myrtle
Was so fruitful and fecund and fertile,
That Sir Christopher Wren
Put an egg in this hen
Through a crack in her chastity girdle.

1970A.

1695

A nigger from old New Orleans
Used to smear his big cock with baked beans.
With this, and salt pork,
He avoided the stork
And annoying Caesarean scenes.

1950.

1696

There was a young girl from New York
Who said, "I'm expecting the stork.
I don't know the father;
It's just too much bother
In a city the size of New York."

1953A.

1697

Since the days when old Adam and Noah
Had a corner on spermatozoa,
Those wee potent critters
Have given girls jitters,
But they keep right on begging for moah!

1965.

1698

Said a fuddled young girl of North Bend:
"I was just being nice to a friend.
He slipped his red schlong
Up my purple sarong—
But God! to get caught in the end!"

1966.

1699

There was a young lady of Ocquerk
Whose menses were steady as clockwork.
But they failed to appear
For nearly a year,
On account of some young fellow's cockwork.

1955J.

1700

There was a young lady from Ottawa
Whose husband, 'twas said, thought a lot of her.
Which, to give him his due,
Was probably true,
For he'd sired twenty brats, all begot of her.

1973.

1701

An insatiable satyr named Pacer
Is known as a wild woman-chaser.
He's the main cause of myriads
Of overdue periods,
For to him " rubber " means an eraser.

1966.

1702

The deliciously sexy Miss Pate,
Who'd been screwed seven times on a date,
Said, " No, I don't mind it—
I take life as I find it,
But forgetting my douche bag, I HATE! "

1965.

1703. OEDIPUS REDIVIVUS

An eccentric young man of Penzance
Madly tore down his grandmother's pants.
He knocked her up properly,
Broke the bed and the crockery,
And must now be called " Dad " by his aunts.

1976A.

1704

There was a young lady of Perth
Who said, " Lord! I'm increasing in girth! "
And her lovely young figure
Got bigger and bigger
And BIGGER—till after the birth.

1974A.

1705

Lil is always forgetting The Pill,
And those babies she has make me ill.
She's great fun in bed—
It's those bastards I dread,
For she always socks *me* with the bill.

1965.

1706

I finally had Adeline plastered,
Her quibbling and delaying all mastered.
    All my systems said "Go!"
    When she hollered, "Oh, no!!
I forgot my Pill—pull out, you bastard!"

1966.

1707

A Mexican wench of Point Reyes
Missed her period by seventeen days.
    Cried she, "My first screwing,
    She is my undoing—
I scarcely can lace up my stays!"

1966.

1708. OH, DOCTOR!

"If you'll just take the knee-chest position,
I can tell more about your condition.
    I'll tune up your womb
    To make room for the groom,
For I gather, you're planning coition."

1965.

1709

There are few things that Nature produces
With the kick of man's genital juices.
    But besides making kiddies
    In concupiscent biddies,
The stuff has but few other uses.

1965.

1710

That sexy young teacher in Prother
Says having a baby's a bother.
    Promiscuous Miss Prudence
    Yentzed all her male students,
So damned if she knows who's its father!

1965.

1711

Her spouse was of passionate race,
So she kept a coil always in place.
  But he thought it was better
  To use a French letter
When the moon was at full—just in case.

1973.

1712. BAD DAY COMING

Give no help to poor bastards who roam,
Seeking food in the trash cans they comb.
  It is courting disaster ;
  They'll just multiply faster,
And they'll fuck you right out of your home!

1975.

1713

A tenor who warbled in Rome
Had to pack up and quickly leave home.
  He'd messed up the lives
  Of ten knocked-up wives—
Now he fucks Eskimaidens in Nome.

1966.

1714

There was a young woman named Rose
Who had bunions all over her toes.
  But the worst of it was,
  She was childless because
She had warts in worse places than those.

1952A.

1715

A well-poised young lady named Sawyer
Claimed nothing could vex or annoy 'er.
  But the baby I fathered
  Got her all hot & bothered,
And I get nasty calls from her lawyer.

1965.

1716

Mae's resistance when fondled was scant,
So her cherry went west with young Brant.
Now her brother, Garfunkel,
Is a much-surprised uncle,
And Annie her sister's an aunt.

1966.

1717

A satyr named Anton in Scranton
Can even get cautious babes pantin'.
Today there's no telling
How many are swelling
From the baby-juice Anton's been plantin'.

1966.

1718

When Carol was told about sex,
She said, " Mama, it sounds so complex.
Do you mean you and father
Went through all that bother,
And I'm just the after-effects? "

1965.

1719

Since her baby came, little Miss Snow
Won't diddle—she just hollers *No!*
She thinks a fat senator
Was its likely progenitor,
But having laid ten, she can't know.

1966.

1720

A seamstress divulged 'midst her sobbin'
She'd been pricked by a tailor named Robin.
The result of her sins
Was a paper of pins,
And some red and white thread on a bobbin.

1975.

1721. JODY SPEAKS

I am happy to help all wives spawn,
And the last ten I've helped are far gone.
    To inoculate Sally
    I must sneak through the alley,
While her louse of a spouse mows the lawn.

1966.

1722

There's a dance-mad young matron of Sterling
Who can't be well fucked except whirling.
    If the music's too mild
    You can get her with child,
But the little thing's hair will need curling.

1948.

1723

A traveling salesman named Strother
Claims he never has yet been a father,
    Unaware that Miss Johnson
    In Combined Locks, Wisconsin,
Had his twins, since to douche was a bother.

1966.

1724

A certain young lady who stuttered
So wobbled her breasts when she uttered,
    It was later revealed
    That her milk got congealed,
And the brood she brought forth was half-buttered.

1973.

1725

An improvident girl from Syosset
Had a baby while locked in the closet.
    The noise of her labors
    Brought out all the neighbors,
Which wasn't quite nice of her, was it?

1950R.

1726

Have you heard of the blonde in Tahoka
Who lost her first game of strip poker?
    In nine months to the day,
    She'd a baby, they say;
" Well, " said she, " I've discarded the joker. "

1965.

1727

Making love is no longer a thrill
When my girl keeps forgetting her Pill.
    The hours seem myriad
    Till it's time for her period—
If she misses, it's me for Brazil!

1966.

1728

Though she looks upon sex as unclean,
Scores of satyrs have mounted Miss Bean.
    Each time that she's weakened
    She's found herself fecund,
And her bastards now number sixteen.

1966.

1729

There was a young lady named Winnie
With a pain just under her pinny.
    Hoped it was wind—
    Recalled that she'd sinned—
Had it removed for a guinea.

1948U.

1730

There was a tan miss from Zambezi
Whose twat was capacious and cheesy.
    She was always in scrapes
    From perpetual rapes:
Like *all* girls, she raped pretty easy.

1950.

XII

PROSTITUTION

1731

It's the whore with the swivel-hip action
That gives a man real satisfaction ;
Who knows what she's doing
All the time that you're screwing,
And leaves you limp with reaction!

1965.

1732

There was a young wench of Adowa
Whose face was as fair as a flower.
She couldn't say " No, no! "
To General De Bono,
So they called off the war for an hour.

1936A.

1733

Il y avait une demoiselle d'Aix
Qui demanda, " Mais qu'est-ce que c'est—SEX?"
Une vieille dit, " Je sais!
C'est ce que cherchent les Anglais,
Mais n'acceptez pas travellers' cheques! "

1974*

1734

There was a young whore of Alicante
Whose morals were notably scanty.
When overdressed
She was not at her best,
So she wore neither brassière nor panty.

1974A.

1735
A reticent lady named Alice
Returned from a long trip to Dallas.
She refuses to say
What she did while away,
But complains that her fanny's all callous.

1965.

1736
The town's leading trollop, Miss Barkus,
Rents the genital parts of her carcass.
To lust she must thank
Daily trips to the bank
And a sable fur coat (Neiman-Marcus).

1965.

1737
There was a young lady named Bastor
Who always said " No " when they asked her.
But she took down her britches
For rich sons of bitches
Like Morgan and John Jacob Astor.

1948.

1738
Unattractive as Mabel may be,
What she has that I want, she gives free.
The local love stores
Charge too much for their whores,
So it's Mabel, dear Mabel, for me!

1966.

1739. THE VOICE OF EXPERIENCE
Opined an old trollop named Beasley :
" I can handle most clients quite easily.
Now and then there are guys,
Oversexed or outsize,
But the average is just barely measly. "

1965.

1740

Rumor has it a satyr named Ben
Keeps twenty fat whores in a pen.
  "They're real handy," he'll say,
  "When I want a quick lay,
Or for loaning to friends now and then."

1966.

1741. LEGISLATIVE PERQUISITE

A flighty young floozie named Bennett,
On checking her cunt's current tenant,
  Found the randy old Governor
  Was frantically shovenor,
And waiting was half of the Senate!

1966.

1742

A would-be young harlot was Bess,
But had nothing at all to caress.
  Her titties were small,
  She had no ass at all:
She could hardly do business with less.

1975.

1743

The big, bulbous boobies on Blanche
Set the hired hands wild, on our ranch.
  Lured away by skunk Morehouse,
  Who runs the town whorehouse,
He'll use her to open a branch.

1966.

1744

A belligerent hooker (while blewing)
Said, "I snigger and snort when I'm screwing.
  It bothers the gents,
  With their genitals tense,
And fucks up the screwing they're doing."

1965.

1745

A prostitute, Priestess of Blow,
Wears a cunt meter: START—STOP—and SLOW!
With a musical chime
To keep track of the time,
Which allows you to pay as you go.

1970A.

1746

I'd much prefer glamorous Miss Blum,
But she yammers for dough till you're numb.
So I bang cute li'l Nevis
Who donates her wet crevice,
Being hot and incredibly dumb.

1965.

1747

One look at the whore of Bombay
Would turn a man ashen and gray.
The mere sag of her tits
Gives strong men the fits,
And she carries her cunt on a tray.

1975.

1748

There is a young lady in Brussels
Who keeps her spare cash in her bustles.
When she runs out of food
She stops being good,
And takes off her bustles and hustles.

1956A.

1749

Said a tired old trollop named Bryant,
After ten days with nary a client:
"Can it be that the men
Hereabouts lack for yen?
Or perhaps my equipment's gone pliant."

1966.

1750

There was an old madam named Bryce
Whose college for harlots was nice :
While the young girls would learn
How to handle their stern,
You could fuck them at very low price.

1967A-1975.

1751

There was a young trucker named Bryerder
Who found a good harlot and hired her
To fuck between trucks,
But to truck between fucks
Made him tireder and tireder and tireder.

1948.

1752

That luscious young harlot, Miss Burks,
The pick of our local sex-works,
Attracted the mayor,
The judge, a surveyor,
And a newsboy who normally jerks.

1965.

1753. MAKE LOVE, NOT WAR !

Old Mars in a fit of caprice
The mad dogs of war did release.
But young Xaviera
On the French Riviera
Unleashed all the pussies of piece.

1975.

1754

A whorish young lady named Cass
Tried to make a young fellow of class.
When she showed him her stunt
He called her a cunt,
And stuffed two dollar bills up her ass.

1971A.

1755. DIRTY GERTIE SPEAKS

"Well, I only charge ninety-nine cents,
And get fucked by no end of hot gents.
It lures passels of peckers—
They're mostly wet deckers—
And the payoff, per night, is immense!"

1965.

1756

How sad for a girl called Charlotte,
That her name is so close to harlot.
She may have the rep
And even the pep,
Though she never has crotched a varlet.

1913*

1757

There was an old lady of Cheltenham
Said, "Cunts? Why of course, dear, I dealt in 'em.
I thought it my duty
To make 'em so fruity
My clients used simply to melt in 'em."

1933C.

1758

A charitable harlot from China
Declared, "I never felt finer.
And so poor men won't holler,
I'll just charge a dollar,
And twenty-five cents for each minor."

1953.

1759

A young gal who was semi-Chinese
Had taken up screwing for fees.
Would the proper approach,
If one dared to encroach,
Be exactly *half* ninety degrees?

1953.

1760

A horny young sailor named Clark
Once picked up a slut in the park.
She was ugly and crude,
And a horror when nude,
But was good for a fuck in the dark.

1975.

1761

There was a young harlot of Clyde
Whose doctor cut open her hide.
He misplaced all the stitches,
And sewed up the wrong niches—
She now does her work on the side.

1966A.

1762

There was an old fellow named Coombs
Who rented apartments and rooms.
His rents were reduced
For the girls he seduced,
And were free to the ones with tight wombs.

1975.

1763

A tired old tart, name of Corrigan,
Told the madam : " I'd sure like to whore again.
If you'll gimme a bed
I'll whore till I'm dead,
But *not* on the bare, wet, cold floor again! "

1965.

1764. TIGER IN YOUR TANK?

A girl on a countryside course
Found a brand-new natural resource :
She traded her ass
For anti-knock gas
At the Sign of the Flying Red Horse.

1970.

1765

There was an old harlot named Cushing
Whose trade for long years she'd kept pushing.
She'd turned so many tricks,
With all manner of pricks,
That she needed a pussy rebushing.

1975.

1766

Said a streetwalker bold to Big Dan:
"I'll take you on *any*where, man!
If you're in a big rush,
There's the park underbrush,
Or how 'bout a quick blow in the can?"

1965.

1767

A lady named Rose had a daughter
Who did things no lady had ought'er.
The good folks confessed
She was none of the best,
But I noticed they all of them bought her.

1904*

1768

There was a young lady named Dawes
Who went out without any drawers.
Her mother said, "Celia,
Let nobody feel yer—
One'd think you was one of them whores."

1948U.

1769

Another young lady named Dawes
Went out to a dance without gloves.
Her ma said, "Amelia,
Should anyone dance with you,
He'll take you for one of those actresses."

1954A.

1770. YAMA : THE PIT

There once was a whore most *de luxe,*
All the perverts adored her lewd fucks.
She'd beat their tools off,
Let them cunt lap her froth,
Or she'd shit in their face, for two bucks.

1948.

1771

" Give in to your feelthy desires?
I should say not! " cried snotty Miss Myers.
" The only thing free
I do with it is pee—
As for fucking, I've dozens of buyers. "

1966.

1772

In a whorehouse in Cunt Lane, Devizes,
They take on men's cocks of all sizes.
From one inch up to ten,
It depends on your yen ;
For still bigger knobs, there's free prizes.

1965.

1773

There was a young whore named Diana
Who would have anyone for a tanner.
Amidst roars of applause
She would let down her drawers,
And tighten her cunt with a spanner.

1945R.

1774

In spite of a wasting disease,
O'Reilly went down on his knees
Before altars of gods,
Whores, boys, and small dogs—
And all this for very low fees.

1955.

1775

To a whore said the cold Lady Dizzit:
"Lord D.'s a new man since your visit.
As a rule the damned fool
Can't erect his old tool;
You must have what it takes, but what *is* it?"

1965.

1776

A businesslike harlot named Draper
Once tried an unusual caper.
What made it so nice
Was you got it half-price
If you brought in her ad from the paper.

1975.

1777

"I just can't be bothered with drawers,"
Said one of our better-known whores.
"There isn't much doubt
I do better without,
In handling my everynight chores."

1966A.

1778

A street bawd arrested in Drury
Cried after the trial, in great fury:
"I didn't begrudge
A free grind to the Judge—
The hard part was gamming the jury!"

1965.

1779. LAST TANGO

A tearful old tart of Durango
Bewailed as she saw her last man go:
"Well, it looks like I'm through—
That's my last living screw—
And there's nothing can beat a bed tango!"

1965.

1780

The madam on Ball Street, East Mott,
Said : " Our stock in trade here is twat.
We are famous as wreckers
Of pulsing red peckers,
So drop in next time you are hot! "

1965.

1781

A worn-out old hooker named Ewing
Remained in the business of screwing
With a pussy brand-new,
Which she stuck on with glue,
But it couldn't withstand the shampooing.

1975.

1782

A woman who was quaintly called fallen,
On a Russian big-shot went a-callin'.
She took in all his root,
But the brute wouldn't shoot—
Was she mad when she found he was stallin'!

1948.

1783

There was a young woman named Fay,
Who took on crotch boarders for pay.
She wore out her insides
With one-dollar rides,
At a hundred and one rides a day.

1948.

1784

Said an impotent, mellow old fellow,
As he mooched into Mamie's bordello :
" I'd sure love to do it,
But I'm just not up *to* it,
So I'll just have a smell, and say Hel-lo! "

1965.

1785. FIFE'S WIFE

I did feel obliged to friend Fife
For the overnight use of his wife.
    But he dropped in today
    And insisted on pay—
Such sordidness sours me on life.

[1786]

The passionate ass on Fife's wife
Should provide me free fucking for life.
    The notch on that bitch
    Gets so hot it'll twitch:
It will wear out both me and friend Fife.

[1787]

I think I must speak to my wife,
For she's giving free tail to old Fife.
    It isn't the screwing
    I mind the fool doing,
It's the " free " bit that's causing the strife!

1966.

1788. GYNECOLOGICAL GAZETTE

A floozie-type filly named Flo
Will do any damn thing that pays dough.
    Offer her enough salary,
    And she'd pose in a gallery
With her legs spread as wide as they go.

1965.

1789

There was an old seamstress forlorn
Whose pussy was tattered and torn.
    But she didn't much mind—
    It was far worse behind,
For her asshole was weathered and worn!

1975.

1790

There was a young lady from Foynes
Who collected pounds, shillings, and coins.
The tuppeny bits
She earned with her tits,
But the shillings she earned with her loins.

1950R.

1791

An oversexed nympho in France
Finds it useless to try to wear pants.
Few hookers can match
The mob after her snatch,
So her pants never had a real chance.

1965.

1792

The harlots of London are frightful,
And the fairies—those barstards—so spiteful!
But I'm not in heat,
For I happened to meet
A sheep in Hyde Park. Quite delightful.

1970A.

1793

Sweet innocent little Miss Frome
Thought sex hunters off in the dome.
But old man Prohaska
Spread her legs in Alaska—
Now her home is a *house* up in Nome!

1966.

1794

A harlot did not think it funny
To hear the bad jokes told by Bunny.
" I will not, " she said,
" Have such filth in my bed! "
And she cursed him and gave back his money.

1975.

1795

A homely old hooker named Gert
Used to streetwalk until her corns hurt.
    But now she just stands
    Upside down on her hands,
With her face covered up by her skirt.

1953.

1796

There was a young lady of Glomms
Who'd undress without any qualms.
    She would strip to the buff
    For enough of the stuff,
And freely dispose of her charms.

1974A.

1797. STUDS FOR BLOODS

The frigid old Duchess of Gloucester
Once hired a gigolo named Foster.
    She was fucked by this pro
    Seven weeks in a row—
It took nearly a month to defrost her.

1975.

1798

"Of my clients, I like best the go-getter,
Who is rich and disdains a French letter.
    Some men think a lot of me,
    Who profess to like bottomy,
But for *me* frontal twatomy's better."

1973.

1799

A Parisian harlot named Grace
Detested the Teutonic race.
    For when the army of Germany
    Made her all verminy,
The gendarmes shut down her place.

1948.

1800

From Penobscot in Maine to Grant's Pass,
One finds many a girl in the grass
    Donating for free
    What undoubtedly she
Could exchange for hard cash, on her ass.

1966.

1801

A haunter of hookshops named Guy
Remarked with a glint in his eye:
  "I've found amongst hookers
    Damn few good lookers—
But it's ass, and not face, that I buy."

1965.

1802. OLD AGE PENCHANT

"No, Grandma, you can't whore while you're here,
Like you did on your visit last year.
    It's too hard to explain
    When the neighbors complain,
And the fine for streetwalking's severe."

1965.

1803

A harried old hooker named Hicks
Remarked of the guys in the sticks:
  "They give me arse pains,
    For they bring in Great Danes
And watch 'em dog fuck me for kicks!"

1966.

1804

A red-headed lass from Hoboken
Claimed she'd do aught for a token.
    I viewed with suspicion
    The words of this Titian,
But I'm here to say she warn't jokin'.

1945A.

1805

Said a horrid old hag, " Look here, honey,
I know that I'm frowsty and funny ;
    But get me in bed
    With a sack on my head,
And I'll give you a run for your money! "

1965.

1806

A worldly-wise tart named Miss Hunt
Said, " Girls! vaseline in your cunt
    Makes the big peckers slide
    With great ease inside,
And the darn things won't cause you to grunt. "

1965.

1807

The erotic desires of Miss Hyers
Required a great many suppliers.
    When she found, in late years,
    Far too few volunteers,
She got her a pimp, who got buyers.

1966.

1808

The neighborhood house of ill-fame
Will never again be the same,
    Since virile young Booker
    Wore out every hooker,
And then buggered the madam, Old Mame!

1965.

1809

An indolent lass from Iraq
Spent a great deal of time in the sack,
    Where she'd earn a month's pay
    In a night and a day,
Without once getting up off her back.

1967A.

1810

Those geisha who live in Japan
Exist just for pleasing a man.
They give you fellatio
As you lay on their patio,
And muffle their farts with a fan.

1970A.

1811

There was a streetwalker named Jones
Who felt a deep chill in her bones.
She performed for humanity,
Interspersed with profanity,
And the whole night was pierced with her groans.

1975.

1812

A vulgar sex kitten of Kent
Exclaimed when her husband's prick bent:
"Well, I wanted a fuck,
But I'm shit out of luck—
Ain't there hard cocks some place I can rent?"

1965.

1813

There was a young madam named Kline
Who kept whorehouse prices in line.
She did not deal with tramps,
Gave S. & H. stamps,
And she charged just a buck eighty-nine.

[1814]

Another young madam named Garrity,
The brothel she ran was a rarity.
She ran newspaper ads,
Charged half-price to young lads,
And was open on weekends for charity.

1967A-1975.

1815

There once was a whore from Kilkenny
Who peddled her ass for a penny.
    She would holler out loud
    At the men in the crowd :
"Hello, dear! You been gettin' any?"

1955A.

1816

Only Joey ever will know
How he got his petoot into Flo.
    Though she looks and acts hot,
    Free twat she gives not—
Was it Joey's sweet talk, or his dough?

1965.

1817. NOSTALGIE DE LA BOUE

How low can a girl get? Well, who knows?
Once she has peeled off her clothes,
    And spread flat on her back
    With your cock in her crack,
You don't *care* how low the bitch goes!

1966.

1818

Your average French girls are no ladies ;
They'll do anything to get a Mercédes.
    In private or whore-office
    They peddle each orifice,
Nor care if they end up in Hades.

1974A.

1819

A sordid old slut from Lahore
Would fuck till her asshole was sore.
    Her cunt was more hairy
    Than wheat on the prairie,
And she never got pregnant, what's more!

1975.

1820

A loose-hipped young lady of Lyme
Who started streetwalking part-time,
    Found, at five cents a sale,
    She sold oodles of tail.
Now she's whoring full-time for a dime.

1965.

1821

There was a strip-teaser named Mabel
Who began her career in a stable.
    She was young and in doubt—
    The hired man tried her out—
Now she's ready and willing and able!

1948.

1822

Another young lady named Mabel
Was so ready and willing and able,
    And so full of spice
    She could name her own price.
Now Mabel's all wrapped up in sable.

1956.

1823. BUTTERBALLS

That irate old Madam McCall
Got a grip on a deadbeat's left ball.
    And she cried : "Either pay
    For two blows and a lay,
Or you'll leave here with *no* balls at all!"

1966.

1824

A tired old whore named McDuff
Once said, "I have had quite enough
    Of men far past forty,
    And nasty and dorty—
What I need is that greasy kid stuff."

1970A.

1825

That happy old hooker, McFink,
Her pussy was rotten, I think.
    She was fucked for an hour
    By Admiral Bower—
That's all he could take of the stink.

1975.

1826

There was an old rounder, McGee,
Who thought he could dip his wick free.
    But a harlot named Charlotte
    Remarked with a snarl, " It
Is business, not pleasure, for me. "

1966.

1827. PLAY FOR PAY

An ambitious young trull named McPherson
Leased the sexual rights to her person
    To rich Arab sheiks
    And other sex freaks,
And left the rest of us ravin' and cursin'.

1974A.

1828

The cunthole in cute Miss McWright
Is not only juicy and tight,
    It is FREE, man ; it's FREE!
    Which is why you'll find me
Inside Miss McWright every night.

1965.

1829

The cop in the callhouse said, " Madam,
Where are all of your whores? You sure had 'em! "
    Said the madam, " Oh, balls!
    They are all out on calls,
Supplying what Eve had for Adam. "

1965.

1830

There was a young girl from Madrid
Whose fucking was worth but a quid.
    When her cunt was ajar
    You could go just as far
As Byrd on his polar trip did.

1948.

1831. THE PURPLE PASSION

Mysteriously smiling, said Mame,
When a new whorehouse customer came :
  " If you'll double the dough
    I'll give you a slow blow,
And from then on life won't be the same! "

1965.

1832

Said a professional gal from Manhattan :
" Concerning this business of cattin',
    If I had my picks
    Of the world's finest pricks
I'd take neither this'n nor that'n. "

1968.

1833

A greedy young whore of Marseille
Would fuck by night or by day.
    She sucked the men's cocks
    To buy Kimberley rocks,
And swore to make every lay pay.

1954A.

1834

A young college student named Mätthaus
Studied up for exams at the frat house.
    But the boning done there
    Didn't start to compare
With the boning he did at the cathouse.

1957J.

1835. LES FLEURS DU MAL

There was an old trollop of Mayence
Renowned for her nasty defiance.
She would curse you and spit on you,
Piddle and shit on you—
This pleased only few of her clients.

1976A.

1836

Said a maudlin old madam of Mears:
"I've peddled hot cunt fifty years,
And I'm sure by now men
Never run out of yen—
If they can't find a whore, they prod queers."

1966.

1837

A Yank in Vietnam named Moe,
Once said, "It is painful to know
That what these girls sell
Is expensive as hell—
They'd have done it for nothing for Hô."

1971B.

1838

A trollop named Mae in Montclair.
Would only take tricks in a chair.
When questioned, she said:
"It's too tiring in bed.
If you don't like a chair, go elsewhere!"

1965.

1839. HOUSEWIFE HARLOTRY

"Of my husband I do not ask much,
Just an all mod. and con. little hutch;
Bank account in my name,
With a checkbook for same,
Plus a small fee for fucking and such."

1973.

1840

Said a foot-weary waitress in Nashville:
"Sure, and ruin my arches this hash will.
  I'm tired to the bone—
  I'd much rather work prone—
Make an offer, love, please don't be bashville."

1972.

1841

A pimp toured his whore through ten nations,
Selling various and sundry sexations.
  When asked his position,
  He said, "Pushing coition—
I handle her pubic relations!"

1966.

1842

An incredible old harlot named Nellie,
Repugnant, foul-spoken, and smelly,
  Owes all her success
  To an adman's finesse,
Selling media space on her belly.

1975.

1843

A perverted boss-whore in North Durham
Said, "Hiring new whores, I de-fur 'em.
  A closely shaved twat
  Gets the men twice as hot,
And our aim is to sexually stir 'em."

1965.

1844

There was a young lady of Norwood
Whose ways were provokingly forward.
  Her mother said, "Dear,
  Please don't wiggle your rear
Like a tart or a trollop or whore would."

1974A.

1845

A sex-crazy girl named O'Dwyer,
Who felt that her crotch was on fire,
Played the tart in bordellos
Where horny young fellows
Brought the thing only men could supply 'er.

1966.

1846. ROSE ORMESBY-GORE

They call her Rose Ormesby-Gore,
An elderly, better-type whore.
In clothes soiled and mucky
She'd call old men " Ducky, "
Yet wince when the working class swore.

[1847]

She paraded a pitch near the Strand,
Where she took it in mouth, vag', or hand.
And for a small extra sum
One could finger the bum
Of that elderly Rose Ormesby-Gore.

1965*

1848

There was an old man of Pelagie
Who fucked an old harlot so scroggy
That he asked the old hag
To put some in a bag,
And took a piece home to his doggy.

1975.

1849

There was a young woman named Pellett
Whose cunt was immense, but she'd sell it.
Though Jack's penis was tall,
He felt nothing at all ;
" Well at least, dear, " he said, " I can *smell* it. "

1948.

1850

To old codgers who live on their pensions,
To barkeeps and drunks at conventions,
To studs on the street
Mabel sold her arse meat
In a way one reluctantly mentions.

1965.

1851. PICCADILLY

Sister Lily is a whore in Piccadilly,
My mother is another in the Strand,
My father hawks his arsell
'Round the Elephant & Castle—
We're the *finest* fuckin' family in the land!

1948U.

1852

Up the street sex is sold by the piece,
And I wish that foul traffic would cease.
It's a shame and improper,
And I'd phone for a copper,
But that's where you'll find the police!

1965.

1853

Wept a blowsy old bawd of her plight:
"Where I once was excitingly tight,
Now I'm loose as a goose
From continual use—
Night after night after night!"

1965.

1854

That elegant gigolo, Price,
Said: "Screwing's a terrible vice,
But one thing I know,
This fucking for dough
Is a thing that's exceedingly nice."

1948.

1855. THE SLAP-HAPPY HOOKER

Said a happy young harlot named Prue,
As her bank account mushroomed and grew:
"Milking prick's a delight
When the customer's right—
It's a business doing pleasure with *you*!"

1965.

1856

A hardy old whore of Quebec
At the end of the night was a wreck,
From the moans and the trials
Of old farts with piles,
And the bastards who breathed down her neck.

1975.

1857

Matilda, the sportinghouse queen,
Does most of her work in Moline,
A form of employment
Which gives no enjoyment
To Archbishop Fulton J. Sheen.

1970.

1858

There was an old madam named Rainey,
Adept at her business and brainy.
She charged ten bucks or more
For a seasoned old whore,
But a dollar would get you a trainee.

1975.

1859

There was a young harlot of Rheims
Who took on the soldiers in teams.
After ten thousand diddles,
Plus widdles and piddles,
Her ass fell apart at the seams.

1975.

1860. ZZ'S EYES

Oh, it's nice to be awfully rich,
And to pander each feminine itch.
It's well worth being called
By the men you've enthralled,
" That scheming, unfaithful, cold bitch! "

1973.

1861

All income that's earned in the sack
The prudish delight to attack.
" But as all of it's profit, "
Says sexy Miss Moffett,
" I spend all my time on my back. "

1966.

1862

A meticulous madam named Sax
Proceeded to fill out her tax.
She totalled the wear
On each girl's derrière,
And deducted the wrinkles and cracks.

1975.

1863

A clever young harlot named Scott
Had a trick that would make the men hot:
On the streets she'd solicit
In a manner explicit,
And hand you her card with her twat.

1975.

1864

If bargains are what you are seeking,
Madam X. has harlots from Peking.
She has dead ones on ice,
And some covered with lice,
And some with foul odors are reeking.

1975.

1865. GIRLS! CAREERS IN WHORING

It pays to play Sex-in-a-Bed,
For those peckers so turgidly red
Bring Gash Cash to a honey
(A Fun Way to make money)
With just bugs and bastards to dread!

1966.

1866

Said perturbed Madam Mae, up Shit Creek:
"We ain't sold a fuck for a week.
We have cunt, we have bingo,
With a bottle of stingo—
If *that* won't lure men, it's a freak."

1966.

1867

A hot little lady named Sission
Developed wild needs for coition.
She gave it away
Until yesterday,
When she learned men will pay for admission.

1965.

1868

Said a sexual athlete named Snell:
"These girls do not satisfy well.
I'm happy that passion
Is still all the fashion,
But I'd like to stop buying, and *sell*."

1965.

1869

I was asked by that lecher named Spicer,
"Is there anything, really, that's nicer
Than a neat bit of crumpet
With an amiable strumpet
Who doesn't expect you to splice her?"

1973.

1870

Since daughter's gone in for streetwalking,
It keeps the whole neighborhood gawking.
In addition, we've said,
There's the wear on the bed,
But our comments are just wasted talking.

1966.

1871

" Goddammit! " cried a harlot named Strong,
" I regret now I ever went wrong.
It ain't the straight tail,
It's the slashing toenail
That knocks a girl out before long! "

1966.

1872

The cathouse on Stuckzipper Lane
Is the place about which I complain.
They go in for strange vices
At exorbitant prices,
And my bank account's feeling the strain.

1965.

1873

A randy old tart of Tacoma,
When diddled would sing " La Paloma. "
Her price dropped to dimes
If a guy shot five times,
And she'd give him a special diploma.

1966.

1874

There was an old girl of Tarentum
Who couldn't get men, so she'd rent 'em.
She invariably said,
As they got out of bed,
" Now, didn't you like my placentum? "

1948.

1875

There was an old whore in Times Square
Who went 'round with her genitals bare.
But the Union said, "Stop!
You can't keep open shop.
We consider such practice unfair."

1948.

1876. EMPLOYEE RELATIONS

When he felt his stenographer's tits,
She said, "Though I'm game, Mr. Fritz,
If you're planning a screw
I'll want overtime too—
Whatever our Union permits."

1965.

1877

The sex sale next door ends today,
And I've no dough to pay for a lay.
The Madam has said it:
She'll give me no credit,
For I *still* owe for lays from last May!

1966.

1878

A luscious young trollop named Troll
Has a crotch that is many a man's goal.
Most clients go crackside,
Though some prefer backside—
She charges the same either hole.

1965.

1879

The whorehouse nearby in Tucson
Lays their overflow trade on the lawn.
The cock-&-cunt fights
Are a sight summer nights,
And we dread the quick coming of dawn.

1966.

1880

An elderly harlot of Twitting
Received an award upon quitting:
    An elephant's cock
    Well-preserved in a crock—
All agreed the award was most fitting.

1975.

1881

Phryné was a harlot unchaste
Whom Greek playwrights futtered in haste.
    What delighted Euripides
    Were her swelling *callipyges,*
And her asshole assorted (to taste).

1976A.

1882. IN THE PARLOR, GIRLS!

"Our price, you will find, rather varies:
From Angie, who often miscarries—
    She's a buck for a lay—
    To ten bucks for Big Mae,
And a hundred for virgins with cherries."

1965.

1883

There was a young widow named Verity
Who peddled her ass just for charity.
    She'd bugger or fuck,
    And occasionally suck,
Which accounted for her popularity.

1953.

1884

There was a young maid from the Vosges
Who laid men in dark theatre loges.
    A Paris success,
    She got into a mess
In a cross-channel pew at Stoke Poges.

1954A.

1885

A randy old granny named Ward
Cried, "Back in my youth, when I whored,
Life gave me both treasure
And a crotchful of pleasure,
Which I dream about now when I'm bored."

1966.

1886

There once was a nubile young whore
Who laid every soldier she saw.
But she thought it obscene
To bed down a Marine:
She was rotten—rotten to the Corps!

1948-1976A.

1887

Maud, for a lifetime, just whored,
Till her hole grew so big, men got bored.
So she sewed up the thing
With a long piece of string,
And now they just pull on the cord.

1953.

1888

Said a whoremonger, mongering whores:
"When mongering whores, nothing bores.
I love testing tails
In a batch of new frails,
Before they get loose on the floors."

1965.

1889

There've been many illustrious whores—
Salomés, Nell Gwyns, Pompadours—
But none so notorious,
So lovely and glorious
As the mistress of Louis Quatorze.

1945A.

1890

A cheerful young girl who was willing,
Used to lay all the boys for a shilling,
    Till a man deep in vice
    Gave her double the price—
Though still willing, a shilling's not thrilling.

1953.

1891

In the park, in the dark by a yew,
Ten flatfeet proceeded to screw
    The town trollop, Mae,
    And of course didn't pay,
But they *did* run her in, being through.

1966.

1892. THE CATHOUSE OF TIME

We miss the fat trollops of yore—
The doxy, the trull, and the whore ;
    The bawd and the chippie,
    Well-padded and hippy,
The likes of whom peddle no more.

[1893]

Oh, the whorehouse of yore is no more,
And its passing we deeply deplore.
    Its lack leaves the horny
    Reading all that bad porny,
Full of murder and rapine and gore.

[1894]

All hail, in our fond, foolish rhyme
To the plush whores of yore in their prime!
    To the millions of dollies
    Whose sexual follies
Ring down through the cathouse of Time!

1965.

XIII

DISEASES

1895

The poxed-up old Bey of Algiers
Viewed his pecker amidst scalding tears.
    And he said to it, " Pete,
    You're now nothing but meat,
But you've pleasured me nobly for years. "

1966.

1896

There once was a harlot called Annie
Who had fleas, lice, and crabs in her fanny.
    Getting into her flue
    Was like touring the zoo :
Wild beasts lurked in each nook & cranny.

1967A.

1897

A brilliant young girl from Ann Arbor
Strange to say, went at night to her barber.
    There with tweezers and comb,
    And much sweat on his dome,
He chased crabs in the hair 'round her harbor.

1948.

1898

From the shade of two mountainous balls
A crab to its mate softly calls,
    And cautions, " My love,
    Watch out when they shove,
For a death drowned in cuntjuice appalls. "

1965.

1899

He was happy as hell to hear Bee
Hotly pant he could fuck her for free.
    But since then, poor old Zapp
    Finds himself with the clap,
And he curses at Bee with each pee.

1966.

1900

A neat, but not gaudy, lewd bitch
Is the way that I thought of Miss Fitch.
    But I quit going 'round
    To her crib when I found
It took weeks to get shet of that itch!

1966.

1901. NIGHT THOUGHTS

On the Piedmont, the nocturnal breezes
Bring reminders of various cheeses,
    And make inhabitants prattle
    Of multiform skatole,
And Potomac-engendered diseases.

1959*

1902

There was a young lady named Brewer
Who poxed all the men getting through 'er.
    One whiff of her pratt
    Killed a bloody great rat
Who'd lived all his life in a sewer.

1948U.

1903

As she sucked off the Reverend Brock,
Mae noticed odd pits on his cock.
    She inquired, with a sniff:
  "Is it clap, Sir, or syph?
You should drag that pocked cock to a doc!"

1966.

1904

There was a young girl from Cardiff
Who publicly fingered her quiff.
    When asked why, she would say
    In a truculent way:
"Well, it's better than getting the syph."

1948.

1905

There once was a heathen Chinee
Who went in the backyard to pee.
    He said: "How is thisee?
    My cockee no pissee!
Hellee! God-dammee!! Chordee!!!"

1888.

1906. ON ELEPHANTIASIS

I view with no end of compassion
Any fellow bedecked in this fashion.
    Such a horribly odd piece
    Would call for a codpiece,
And sitting down slow to save mashin'!

[1907]

The drawback to elephantiasis
Is your failure to flee in a criosis.
    You're chained by your balls—
    A thought that appalls,
To the point where some guys avoid vi-oces.

1965.

1908

On a business trip to D.C.
Jack picked up a case of V.D.
    For ten bucks a shot
    He was saved from crotch rot—
Changed his style to celibacy.

1971 *ff.*

1909

As he fucked the lewd bitch in a ditch,
He said, " Something keeps making me itch.
So you either have crabs
Or venereal scabs,
But I won't take time now to see which. "

1966.

1910

In the house of ill-fame that's next door,
I've sampled the snatch of each whore.
But one of those drabs
Gave me both clap and crabs,
So I *won't* whore next door anymore!

[1911]

No, the rotten old crotch of each whore
Will feel my John Thomas no more.
Some bitch that I mounted
Had crab lice uncounted,
And, ke-rist! is my genital sore!

1966.

1912. THE REDS!

We feel sorry as hell for young Dot,
Now her boyfriend can't probe in That Spot.
For unfortunate Roscoe
Got the clap while in Moscow—
He claims it's a Communist plot!

1965.

1913

Though the practice of poor Eloïse is
To play with whomever she pleases,
She admits the one hitch is
She suffers from itches,
And various social diseases.

1958.

1914

A frantic young filly named Fitch
Cried, " That last fuckin' sonofabitch
Musta gimme his bugs ;
From my snatch to my dugs
I am simply one great flaming itch! "

1965.

1915

There was a young man from Fort Knapp
Who boasted a cock full of sap.
He said with a snigger,
" It gets bigger and bigger—
Or, Christ! is it only the clap? "

1948.

1916

There was a young lady from France
Who found twenty-nine bugs in her pants.
She asked : " Am I dirty?
I'm sure there were thirty ;
Can one have crawled up, by mischance? "

1948.

1917

There was a young lady named Freed
Who said that it hurt when she peed,
And this was because
Of immutable laws
Concerning contaminate seed.

1948.

1918

A grimy young fellow was Gus,
His pecker was slimy with pus.
But his girlfriend was grimier,
And her pussy was slimier,
So she didn't kick up any fuss.

1975.

1919

An impatient teenager named Hitchin
Was screwed on the floor of the kitchen.
  This short, hot romance
  Left her ants in her pants,
And a twitch in her twatch that keeps itchin'.

1965.

1920

An airline hostess honeybun
Screwed a sore-peckered son of a gun.
  Now our lovely young sylphess
  Is corroded with syphilis,
Till her cunthole and bunghole are one!

1966A.

1921

Venereal disease is insidious,
And the end results truly are hideous,
  So the pure and ethereal
  Try to shun the venereal,
Though they're *not* really all that fastidious.

1965.

1922

There once was a Spaniard named Jesus
Who seduced his two virginal nieces.
  To the first he gave twins,
  To the second one quins,
And to both of them, frightful diseases!

1974A.

1923

Syphilophobiac Jules
Lives according to hygienic rules.
  He has never been seen
  At a public latrine,
Or in coëducational schools.

1945A.

1924

There once was a pilot from K-2
Who buggered a girl down in Taegu.
He said to the doc,
As he handed him his cock :
" Will I lose both my testicles too? "

1958P.

1925. ON THE DELTA

There was a young lady named Kay
To whom v.d. had caused much dismay.
What had once been hirsute
Was now bald as a coot,
So she wore a triangle toupée.

1975.

1926

A luetic young man from Kentucky
Felt most unappeasably fucky.
He persuaded a dame
Who was halt, blind, and lame ;
And, at that, he was damnably lucky.

1948.

1927

There was a young lecher named Knapp
Who thought using condoms was crap.
Said he : " Us real he-men
Like to scatter our semen! "—
Six months later he still has the clap.

1970A.

1928

There once was a cowboy named Leo
Met a fast señorita in Rio.
A full night and a day
They rolled in the hay,
And now the poor cowboy can't (*yodel* :) Pee-O!

1970A.

1929

There was a young fellow named Linus,
An expert at eating vaginas.
But he made a bad slip
And ate one with a drip;
Now he's got a bad case of the sinus.

1975.

1930

There once was a virgin of London
Who said to her lover, " I'm *un*done!
I've gon' in my chute,
And I'm pregnant, to boot—
Just see what your idea of fun done! "

1950.

1931. FLORA AND FAUNA

There was a young lady named Lorna
Whose mother neglected to warn her,
Till some uncleanly eremites,
Infested with termites,
Corroded her flora with fauna.

1948.

1932

Said the Duke to the Duchess of Lotham,
Who had crabs, but couldn't say where she'd got 'em :
" My dear, you're too generous
With your *mons veneris,*
And equally so with your bottom. "

1942A.

1933

" Although I'm not rich, " said Miss Lowell,
" One gift is within my bestowal :
A kick in the rear
Every day for a year,
For the bugs some slob left in my hoewell. "

1965.

1934

There was an old man of Manchuria
Who suffered from painful dysuria.
It was not (yes, you thought it)
From a girl that he caught it,
But from trying to read Browning's *Luria.*

1904C.

1935

Then there was a girl from Manchuria
Who said, when her lover was scruinga :
" The head of your penis
Is quite a bit greenis ;
Step around to the doctor—he'll curia. "

1968.

1936

A lascivious gentleman, Martin,
After a fuck would swiftly be parting.
Did anyone here
See him piss in my beer?—
My *membrum virile* is smarting.

1970A.

1937

The crabs that so irritate *me*
I got in sex-congress with Bee.
So I paid for the tail
That I got from that frail,
With the crotch-pheasants thrown in for free.

1966.

1938. ABELINA

Oh Abelina, that old gal of mine,
With her ass full of shit and her cunt full of slime!
When she got started
She pissed and she farted,
And shat yellow maggots all over the carpet.

1935*

1939

There once was a traveling miser
Who lay with a dame called Eliza.
    Now he takes no more trips ;
    He takes shots in the hips—
He's a sadder old miser, but wiser.

1948.

1940

There was a sad damsel named Mitchener,
Who cried when her thing began itchiner.
    For she'd picked up a bug
    From some unwholesome lug,
Which she gave to the next sonofabitchiner.

1965.

1941

A lady from Morningside Crescent
Could never make men acquiescent
    To a lewd proposition,
    For they knew that coition
Wasn't safe with a cunt so putrescent.

1948.

1942

There was a young man fron Nantucket
Who soaked his sore cock in a bucket :
  " Oh, never no more
    Will I fuck a whore!
I'd rather have somebody suck it! "

1919-1952L.

1943

Said a fellow named O'Shea
Who was cursed with gonorrhea :
  " *Mama mia,*
    Papa pia—
This is worse than diarrhea! "

1976A.

1944. URBAN AMENITIES

Punctilious Park Avenue Paul
Pulled off a piece in the hall.
    In neglecting to choose, he
    Wound up with a floozie
And one great big indigo ball.

1956.

1945

A Rajah who ruled in Penang
Felt a terrible itch in his whang.
    Cried he, " By my life!
    I must have a poxed wife,
But which one can she *be* in my gang? "

1966.

1946

There was a young man who said, " If Phyllis
Has really given me syphilis—
    I know she's had tabes,
    Clap, shankers, six babies—
What the hell is there left I can *give* Phyllis? "

1948.

1947

An historian named Poppencott
Got infected with tropical rot.
    While gathering data
    He smeared his spermata
All over a Red Cross girl's cot.

1944.

1948

There once was a doorman punctilious,
Whose manner was most supercilious.
    He opened his door
    For a world-famous whore,
And now has a case of syphilious.

1971 *ff.*

1949

Said the Queen, bedspreading her Queenness :
" Dad, I notice your Right Royal penis—
I don't wish to offend—
Has a dull purple end.
Is it buboes, or just plain old meanness? "

1965.

1950. A WORD TO THE WISE

According to latest reports,
If you hope for venereal warts
Go in for connection
With a sneer at infection,
And they'll gather upon you by quarts.

[1951]

You'll find things begin to get rough
When the bugs begin gnawing your stuff.
It *hurts* when those gnawers
Get into your drawers ;
When you end with no knockers, that's tough!

[1952]

I suppose you will think I'm sarcastic
About sexual poses too plastic,
But many a fool
Has been led by his tool,
And has ended syphilitic *and* spastic.

1966.

1953

The wandering singer did say
That, much as he wanted to stay,
She had buckets of crabs,
Running sores and old scabs,
And she'd be that lost minstrel's last lay.

1970A.

1954

Velasquez of Spain took a ship
To see all the East in one trip.
  But a cheap whore in Tiflis
  Gave him crabs, clap, and siflis,
And he henceforth mixed paints with the drip.

1966.

1955

Down with Gandalf, the wizard of Shoreditch!
He gives gals who refuse him the itch ;
  And he works his low spells
  On sex-shy young belles—
He is really a son of a bitch!

1965.

1956

There was a young playboy named Shorty,
Who thought of himself as quite sporty.
  He had plenty of moxie
  But he clapped up each doxy,
For chancres and clap were his forte.

1967A-1975.

1957

A woman from Sleepy Hollow
Got all of the menfolks to follow.
  They played with her crack
  But she took all their jack,
And gave the blueballs to them all-o!

1932-1952L.

1958

A horny young man named Sylvester
Took a whore to his room and caressed 'er.
  He was proud of his skill,
  But the joke was on Syl,
When his pecker proceeded to fester.

1959

A tearful young girl of Terrazzo
Cried, " Why does clap torture a twatzzo?
It bites like a flea,
And it's murder to pee—
I'm amazed that one's cunthole can rotzzo! "

1965.

1960

A bawdy young houri of Tiflis
Gave all of her customers syphilis.
She said, " I intend
To come clean in the end,
But so far I've been mighty damn shiftless. "

1965.

1961

There was a young lady named Tunney
Whose cunt was a little bit runny.
Since she'd taken a nap
With a guy who had clap,
This was not unexplainably funny.

1953.

1962

There was a young fellow named Vinal
Who thought his affliction was spinal.
But medical examination
Disclosed contamination
From sources more likely va*gi*nal.

1945R.

1963. POKAHONTAS SPEAKS

Said an itchy young squaw of Wenatchee :
" You sexum me—no chief can matchee.
Me feelum bad—ugh!
You givum squaw bug?
Alla time me feel itchy, me scratchee. "

1965.

1964

There once was a girl from Westchester
Whose boyfriend, on impulse, undressed her.
But this action, so coarse,
Filled him deep with remorse,
For his penis soon started to fester.

1954A.

1965

A scrupulous man from Westminster
Went out on a date with a spinster.
To make sure she was clean
He douched her machine,
And thoroughly washed out and rinsed her.

1967A-1975.

1966. SNOWDROPS FROM A GARDEN

There was an American whore
Whose cunt was a festering sore.
She caulked it with pitch
Till the bloody old bitch
Was A-1 at Lloyd's evermore.

[1967]

But with earthly success not content,
She grew pious—to Heaven she went.
Son, Father, and Ghost
And the heavenly host
Have all got the double event.

1904C.

1968

Mrs. Baker was known to be wild,
For her husband was built like a child.
Seeking manlier cocks
She contracted the pox . . .
It all came to light at the trial.

1948.

XIV

LOSSES

NOTE

[*Losses through the agency of animals and through masturbation will be found in Chapters VII, "Zoophily"; and XV, "Sex Substitutes." For interplanetary losses, see Chapter XVII, "Science Fiction."*]

1969

There once was a wicked old actor
Who waylaid a young girl and attacked 'er.
    In reply to this trick
    She bit off his prick,
And thus remained *virgo intacta.*

1968A.

1970

He approached her with gentle affection
And a prominent outthrust erection.
    But the love of his life
    Grabbed a large carving knife,
And—(see Diagram 6 : Conic Section).

1967.

1971

A stalwart of Stalin named Adam
Took a potshot at splitting the atom.
    He blew off his penis,
    And now, just between us,
He's known 'round the Kremlin as "Madam."

1953.

1972

There once was a sadist named Alice
Possessed of considerable malice.
She'd open up wide,
Let the man get inside ;
Then her grip would clip off his whole phallus.

1948.

1973

There was a young lady alluring,
Said : " A ditch digger's cock is enduring. "
But the rigger's was bigger,
And he fucked with such vigor
That her asshole was torn from its mooring.

1975.

1974

There was a young girl from Alsace
Who could pick up a dime with her ass.
As her muscles contracted
Her chest was retracted,
And her teats both fell off in the grass.

1953.

1975

There was a young lady named Annie
Who slipped on a peel of bananny.
She saw stars of blue,
And every known hue—
The bananny flew up Annie's fanny!

1949A.

1976. WILDE PARTY

Salomé! Salomé! where art?
Thou Biblical strip-teasing tart!
I'd have thought that instead
Of Jokanaan's head,
Thoud'st have asked a more pertinent part. "

1948.

1977

A swami in far-off Assam
Was caught by a man-eating clam.
    This accounts for the nick
    On the end of his dick,
And each testicle's shape like a cam.

1947R.

1978

There was a young woman named Astor
Whose clothes fit her tight as a plaster.
    When she happened to sneeze
    She felt a cold breeze,
And knew she had met with dis*ast*er.

1945.

1979. MISS GIFT

In Boston, a young maiden aunt
Entered into an amorous entente
    With a neophyte draftsman,
    A blundering craftsman,
Who rendered her promptly *enceinte.*

[1980]

Showing no sense of fatherly pride,
And displaying a greedier side,
    Our draftsman (Sicilian)
    Shagged a comely Brazilian,
And was caught by his common-law bride.

[1981]

Now our mother-to-be was so miffed
That her mental estate went adrift.
    She embarked on a scheme
    Not quite proper, 'twould seem,
For the fine Boston family of Gift.

[1982]

She went up to her paramour's pad
And dispatched him ; but having gone mad,
She, with surgical skill,
Amputated the quill
Which qualified him as a dad.

[1983]

Gracious! How this bizarre sequence grew!
When from love nest our murderess withdrew,
For with passport in hand
(In her luggage, his gland)
On a jet down to Rio she flew.

[1984]

Though the customs men had quite a start
On discovering this eerie spare part,
She excused its appearance,
And gained rapid clearance
By declaring it : " GIFT—Work of Art. "

[1985]

As the terminus of her design,
She, in action uniquely benign,
Gave the Latin pretender
Their dead sweetheart's pudenda,
Saying, " Here, dear, you left this behind! "

[1986]

Now Miss Gift's in a jail in Back Bay
Where she'll languish for many a day.
You see, morally, Bean Town
Is a dreadfully clean town
In which crime of this sort doesn't pay.

1969.

1987

In Turkey the vicar of Avery
Was captured and sold into slavery.
    He escaped with his life,
    But distresses his wife,
And his sermons are high-pitched and quavery.

1970.

1988

A pimp with elliptical balls
Went out for his afternoon calls.
    But an indignant whore
    Got them caught in a door,
And splattered his seed on the walls.

1955A.

1989. COME, SWEET DEATH

We miss that lean guy with the beard
Whose experience with women was weird :
    In South Carolina
    He fell in a vagina,
Screamed, struggled, and then disappeared!

1965.

1990

We were took by our teacher, Miss Beeham,
To see statues in't British Museum.
    We girls were in fits
    'Cos the interestin' bits
Of the boys were broke off—you should see 'em!

1973.

1991

There was a young fellow named Blunt
Who was such a pitiful runt,
    That when he assayed
    To hump a fair maid
He smothered himself in her cunt.

1948.

1992

His sweetheart so deftly scratched Boyd
As to render him sexually void.
She is now serving time
For the heinous crime
Of using the nails to de-Freud.

1945A.

1993

I once knew a terrible bragger
Who walked with a clump and a swagger.
The reason, they say,
That the guy walked that way
Was, his dick was cut off with a dagger.

1961A.

1994

There was once a young basso bravura
Who went swimming one night at Ventura.
A fun-loving shark
Nibbled him for a lark,
And now he sings coloratura.

1955A.

1995

A maiden with heavenly busts
Parried a married man's thrusts.
They finally did fuck,
But the goddamned thing stuck ;
Said she : " It stays there till it rusts. "

ff.1955A.

1996

A hot-tempered wench of Caracas
Shook her tits like she'd shake the maracas.
When her man tried to cheat her
With a dark señorita,
She kicked him right smack in the knackas.

1966A.

1997

There was a young girl named Charlótte
Who lived on toe-jam and snot.
She slipped on some shit,
Broke open her tit,
And crabs crawled out of her twat.

1963A.

1998

A peckerless person named Chuck
Said : " Sex is a pastime I duck.
With a gal I can neck 'er,
But, having no pecker,
I'm not the best choice for a fuck. "

1966.

1999

A myopic young fellow named Clark
Raped a large poplar tree in the dark.
What a splendid surprise!—
Such tightness and size!—
But his foreskin got scraped on the bark.

1945-1970A.

2000

A callous soprano from Crete
Men find is no great sexual treat.
In erotical frenzy
With poor young MacKenzie,
She ripped off his balls with her feet!

1965.

2001

A political planner named Danner
Once planned to seduce a Japanner.
Though he diddled for days
He could not get a raise,
From his pecker which hung in this manner.

1975.

2002

A very keen cyclist named Dash
Once jumped on his bike, and the crash
  Of his balls sounded worse
  Than his curse to the nurse
As she bandaged his sausage—and mash.

1948U.

2003

Said the horrible harlot of Dayton :
" I'm getting tired of all this waitin'.
  Fuck me, you fool!
  Or I'll cut off your tool,
And send it to someone in Place Peyton. "

1968.

2004. THE LAST TRUMP

When Lazarus rose from the dead
He still couldn't function in bed.
  " What good's Resurrection
  Without an erection? "
Old Lazarus testily said.

1958.

2005

Though in fucking I dearly delight,
Now I'm surely the town's saddest sight.
  For the hair on my belly
  Wore off fucking Nellie,
And my balls are half-frozen at night!

1965.

2006

There was a young girl from East Wrangle
Who got her snatch caught in a mangle.
  It tore off the hair
  And left her cunt bare,
And at a *most* pecu-li-ar angle.

1948.

2007. VAGINA DENTATA

There was a young lady named Fabia
With hooks on the flaps of her labia.
    She was fucked by young Flynn
    But she ripped his foreskin,
And she laughed and said, " How does this grab ya? "

1975.

2008

A careless young man of Far Rockaway,
At the zoo folks heard screaming a blockaway.
    He got apes in a rage
    Jerking off near their cage,
And they ripped both his balls and his cockaway.

1966.

2009

An unhappy young musical fellow
Complained as he fiddled his cello
    That its rumbling vibration
    Impaired copulation,
For what he comes now is lime jello.

1966.

2010

A hermaphrodite once, in a fever,
Amputated his cock with a cleaver.
    Now all she has left
    Is a hot, humid cleft,
Concealed in the bush of his beaver.

1971 *ff*.

2011

As the elevator car left our floor
Big Sue caught her teats in the door.
    She yelled a good deal,
    But had they been real
She'd have yelled considerably more.

1948-1976A.

2012

Said old Madam Flo, in Fort Erie,
To the new whore she hired, " Lissen, dearie,
I have one strict rule :
You must squeeze the guy's tool,
And if it pulls off—you be leery! "

1965.

2013

A raffish young rowdy from France,
His zipper got caught in his pants.
And his friends all agreed
That the way that he peed
Was purely a matter of stance.

1963A.

2014

An aquarium keeper named Frank
While pissing fell into a tank.
Cried a girl who was viewing :
" Gad! what is he doing?
He let go a pink fish as he sank! "

1973.

2015

Oh, pity poor Corporal Frost,
Whose troop was ambushed as they crossed
The lands of the Sioux ;
He lived, it is true,
But most of his privates were lost.

1971B.

2016

When Smith caught his cock in some gears,
They grafted on skin from his ears.
And now the poor guy
Can hear through his fly,
But fucking just bores him to tears.

1960.

2017. INCIDENT IN RACINE

An electronic inventor named Gene
Perfected a fucking machine.
    In a horrible manner
    It grabbed his banana,
And all that was left was a scream!

1962A.

2018

A Chicago nymphette, name of Gloria,
On a kick of real zany euphoria
    Took into her bed
    An atomic warhead—
Bits of Gloria were seen over Peoria.

1948-1971A.

2019

A Bennington student named Grace
Slipped a barbed-wire pessary in place.
    When her Chinese instructor
    Frenched rather than fucked her,
He moaned through torn lips, " I *roose* face! "

1965A.

2020

A deep baritone from Havana,
While singing, slipped on a banana.
    He was ill for a year,
    Then resumed his career
As a coloratura soprana.

1954*

2021

" I was proud of my pecker, " said he ;
" ' Twas the liveliest portion of me.
    But the last girl I screwed
    Was so thoroughly stewed,
That now it's been pickled in pee! "

1955A.

2022

Explaining a gash on his head,
" I was fucking dog fashion, " he said ;
" When, with consummate cunning,
My gal started running,
And dragged us both under the bed. "

1950R.

2023

There was a young fellow named Hitchin
Who was screwing the maid in the kitchen.
When his ass got too close to
The red-hot stove toaster,
He woke up the house with his bitchin'.

1945.

2024

A dwarf Kike who called himself Houghton :
His balls in his boyhood were caught on
His mother's false teeth
In a foul slum in Leith ;
She stewed them with truffles and Corton.

1933C.

2025. UNOSEX

An effete little fellow named Hunt
Said, " I hate being such a weird runt. "
At his best buddy's urgin'
He went to a surgeon,
And asked, " Can't you guess what I wunt? "

1972.

2026

Her husband is in the Hussars,
A colonel all covered with scars.
But it isn't his weals
For which nightly she feels ;
It's those privates he lost in the wars.

1973.

2027

There was a young man from the Isthmus
Whose bride had acute vaginismus.
On their very first fuck,
They found themselves stuck,
And had to stay that way till Christmas.

1953.

2028

There was a romantic Italian
Who conducted himself like a stallion.
Too much horsing around
Put him under the ground,
And his tomb is a phallic medallion.

1955J.

2029

There was a young man from Johore
'Oo was grievously 'urt in the War.
So he painted his front
To resemble a greenhouse,
And let himself out as a jobbing gardener, eh wot?

1953.

2030

I know a young lady named Kitty :
There she lies on the beach, very pretty.
" Say, listen, " she blurts ;
" Pull it out, please ; it hurts!
You've been laying in the sand and it's gritty. "

1948.

2031

There was an old fellow named Kling
Who fucked with a kink in his thing.
When screwing a tart,
She let go a fart—
Now he wears the poor thing in a sling.

1953.

2032

There once was a man from Larang
Whose bladder blew up with a bang.
His prick flew back
With a god-awful whack,
And his asshole whistled and sang.

1958P.

2033. GOD BLESS OUR HAPPY SADISM

A seamstress we'll call Miss Levine
Caught her breast in her sewing machine.
And she found, with a shudder,
That stitched on her udder
Was " God Bless Our Home " done in green.

1945.

2034

There was a young man of Loch Ness
Whose sexual life was a mess.
Then the Beast in the Loch
Bit the head off his cock,
Which solved his sex problems, I guess!

1970A.

2035

That wily whoremaster, McBeer,
Laid cheating wives nightly all year,
Till caught in the bed
Of a frau from Burnstead,
And her husband cut off his career.

1966.

2036

A foolish young man named McClain
Fell beneath the wheels of a train.
It sliced off his nuts
With no if's, and's, or but's,
And caused him a horrible pain.

1949.

2037

There was a young man from Madras
Who made a French Safe out of brass.
    It didn't expand
    As fast as his gland,
And he blew out the cheeks of his ass.

1950*

2038

There was a young fellow named Martin
Whose penis was painfully caught in
    A nigger whore's butt,
    Till the bloody old slut
Ejected the damn thing by fartin'.

1948.

2039. FLEETING FAME

You have heard of the Greek named Melitus,
And his " Ode on the Nubian Fœtus. "
    But *who* now recalls
    How he fractured his balls
In research on Egyptian coitus?

1945.

2040

There was an old dame from Miami
Who fucked herself with a sledgehammer.
    But the hammer was blunt
    And stuck in her cunt,
And that was her finish, goddammer!

1948.

2041

There once was a maidenly mystic
Whose habits approached the sadistic.
    While kissing a chum,
    With one thumb up his bum,
She bit off the end of his piss-stick.

1950.

2042

Stormy night at the royal palace:
When the Queen, in a moment of malice,
Filled her cunt up with acid
And lay there quite placid,
Dissolving His Majesty's phallus.

1958.

2043

When she danced at the Easter Parade,
Such a sexy impression she made,
That some lads from St. Paul's
In tight jeans, hurt their balls,
And had to be given first-aid.

1973.

2044. THE KIDNEYCRACKER

As she squatted to ride on Dick's pecker,
A luscious blonde nympho named Decker
Said, "I seldom meet guys
With kidneycrackers this size,
So I hope yours won't prove a cuntwrecker!"

1966.

2045

A fuddy old duddy named Purvis
Disrupted a solemn church service.
In the town of South Nevis
His sex caught in a crevice—
Remembering, his screams still unnerve us!

1966.

2046

We warned Herman about that big quim,
But he'd only wink at us, and grin.
It's hard to determine
What happened to Herman,
But we more or less think he fell in.

1965.

2047

There was a young fellow named Rawls
Who slipped from the Dome of St. Paul's,
    But two angels of grace
    Sped thither apace,
And lowered him down by the balls.

1945.

2048

In front of the fire sat Rose
Attempting to thaw out her toes.
    It was thirty below,
    Where she'd rolled in the snow,
And her pussy was fucking near froze.

1975.

2049

There was a young man of St. Paul's
Who dreamt of Niagara Falls.
    When he woke the next day
    It was "Anchors aweigh!"
For his penis, his ass, and his balls!

1945.

2050

A pilot who flew to Salinas
In one of those old Catalinas,
    Pulled back on the yoke
    With a hell of a stroke,
And fractured his co-pilot's penis.

1953A.

2051

After lunch at her manor in Schweck,
The duchess remarked, "In effect,
    We've found a man's tool
    In the garden fish pool,
So will all of you gentlemen *check*?"

1965.

2052

A knot hole he happened to see,
So he stuck his dink through it to pee.
    Then he gave a loud yell :
  " Whoop! Damnation!! Hell!!! "
(On that side of the fence was a bee.)

1888.

2053. WOMB RETURN

A daring young midget named Shaw
Went to bed with a very large whore,
    And—God rest his soul!—
    He fell into her hole,
Screamed twice, and was heard of no more.

1962.

2054

An obese old washwoman named Singer
Once caught her big tit in the wringer.
    Said the sow in the sty,
    As the milk squirted by :
" Some boar must have slipped her a dinger! "

1953.

2055

When the last victim's groaning was stifled,
He moaned : " I'da never have trifled
    With Hortense the whore—
    Got my pore penis sore—
If I'd known her vagina was *rifled.* "

1970A.

2056

An elderly dean at Sweet Briar
Tried to stiffen his penis with wire.
    It worked till it rusted,
    Then twisted and busted,
And skewered the Directress of Choir.

1965A.

2057

It was hard on Apollo, I thought,
When the workman who shifted him caught
And broke off his penis,
Out of malice or meanness,
And shipped him to England with naught.

1973.

2058. GREAT EXPECTATIONS

There was a young girl of Tobruk
Who had the most terrible luck:
She went out in a punt
And fell over the front,
And was pecked in the dunt by a cuck.

1954A.

2059

Said the groom to his best man, " That's torn it:
I've been stung on the cock by a hornet,
Right under my prepuce,
And it hurts like the deuce,
But the sting's out—the hornet's withdrawn it. "

1973.

2060

A young university tutor
Fed his sex history to a computer.
Due to pulse-circuit stalls
It reprogrammed his balls,
And he ended up totally neuter.

1970A.

2061

A minister of the Church in the Vale
Was chasing a bevy of quail.
He slipped on a rock
And damaged his cock,
And from then on was not very male.

1949.

2062

Said a soldier, just back from Viêt,
To his sweetheart : " Be patient, my pet.
I will fondle your breast
And your twat without rest,
But my pecker I left with the Tet. "

1973A.

2063. BALLS!

There was once a sad hunter named Ware,
Had his manhood snapped off by a bear.
Sobbed he, " That damn bruin
Caused my sexual ruin—
Do you think I could glue on a pair? "

1965.

2064

Said a young man named George, " I've a whim :
I'd rather be *her* than be *him*.
I'll just change my goal,
And my pole for a hole,
With serum and surgical trim. "

1952A.

2065

There was a young fellow most willing
To teach all the gals about squilling,
Till he met a virago
Who bit off his pago,
The while she was trilling, " How thrilling! "

1971 *ff.*

2066

Lamar got too close to a winch,
And was caught you-know-where in the pinch.
Bystanders deplored
While he screamed, yelled, and roared,
And his sex life went west, inch by inch!

1966.

2067

A careless young laundress in Wrangel
Got both her tits caught in the mangle.
    They turned off the juice
    While they pried her pair loose,
But now, where they dingled, they dangle!

1965.

2068

There was a young student of Yale
Whose features were sickly and pale.
    He was caught in a frost
    And his balls were both lost,
While his pecker was battered by hail.

1975.

2069

A dashing, fine fellow named Young
On the gallows stood, hooded and strung.
    Though everyone saw
    A miscarriage of law,
The ladies liked how he was hung.

1970A.

2070

There once was a drunkard named Zack
Who puked all his guts in a sack.
    As he needed them soon,
    With a long-handled spoon
He managed to stuff them all back.

1953.

2071

The dangers of zipping a zipper
Keep fat fellows watching that nipper.
    For that fiendish device
    Can take off a real slice—
Beats a *mohel,* hands down, as a clipper!

1965.

XV

SEX SUBSTITUTES

2072

A bumpkin behind Albuquerque
Was discovered while jerking his turkey.
Said he with a grin:
"Some say it's a sin,
But it's better than goin' berserky!"

1965.

2073

A feminine queer of Algiers
Loves to fondle small boys' chubby rears.
When finished with those,
Frigs herself with her toes,
And then douches out with two beers.

1966.

2074. PRACTI WITH CACTI

There was a young widow named Alice
Who lived in the desert near Dallas.
Each day, just for practice,
She'd gather up cactus,
And use them instead of a phallus.

1954A.

2075

There was a young girl from the Amazon
Preparing to put her pajamas on,
When she had an orgasm,
And out from the chasm—
Well, *she* had to put her mama's on.

1948.

2076. SYNTHETIC PROSTHETICS

A eunuch who lusted for ass
Made him a dong out of brass.
    Two balls made of gold
    Were a sight to behold,
And oil was injected by gas.

[2077]

A prick could be made of cement,
And could certainly never be bent.
    Two balls made of leather
    Could go off together,
And the thing was equipped with a vent.

1952.

2078

A shapely young lass with a very big ass
Had a dildo made out of the very best brass.
    She had little instruction
    In its use or construction,
And her friends mostly thought it quite crass.

1968.

2079

There was an old maid of Balaclava
Who made a great dildo of lava.
    It rasped and it scraped
    As her pouty lips gaped,
And an old Peeping Tom yelled out, " Brava! "

1971 *ff*.

2080

On your sixty-fifth birthday your balls
Shrivel up, and your prostate gland falls.
    But you still get your kicks
    Feeling stoned hippies' pricks,
Phoning strangers, and writing on walls.

1970*

2081

Said the man-hater buying baloney:
" Of course, it is only a phoney.
    But with self-service sex
    I get better effects
Than poor women *trapped* in matrimony! "

1965.

2082

The eminent Doctor Barnard
Has labeled " A baseless canard, "
    That injecting epoxy
    Into older men's jocks, he
Can cause them once more to get hard.

1970A.

2083

An expert onánist named Bart
Tutored many a man in his art,
    Till in desperation
    A great delegation
Of neglected wives tore him apart.

1971*ff.*

2084

The first fuck she had, a Miss Bickles
Cried, " Oh, but that prick of yours tickles!
    I've never had meat
    In my cunt when in heat—
It's always been carrots or pickles. "

1965.

2085

A hot-pants young lady named Biddle
Cried out in her passion, " Oh, fiddle!
    Did you come from Eau Claire
    To jerk off in that chair?
Well, cut out the doodling—let's diddle! "

1966.

2086

There was a young man from Biloxi
Who got all his screwing by proxy.
His girlfriend—how sad!—
Was equally bad,
She got hers by douching with Moxie.

1952A.

2087

A naïve young fellow named Blore
Tried to buy rubber cunts in a store.
The storekeeper's wife
Explained Facts of Life ;
Now Blore's fucking *her* more and more.

1966.

2088

Priapus, god of gardens and bowers,
Liked to stand out in sunshine and showers.
Without any toga—
The randy old roguer—
He would play pocket rugby for hours!

1973.

2089

There was a young man from Brazil
Who said, " My wife screws when I will.
But I'd much rather neck her,
And play with my pecker—
Eet's my way of deriving a thrill. "

1953.

2090

A dashing young fellow named Bream
Every night had a juicy wet dream.
His wife, quite annoyed,
Called a student of Freud,
Who cured him—which really was mean.

1970A.

2091

A flatulent fellow named Breuil
Fell into a cave as a boy.
On a warm limestone shelf
He played with himself
With speleological joy.

1966M.

2092

There was a young lady named Bright
Whose passions were faster than light.
She set her dildoe
To "Medium Slow,"
And creamed on the walls half the night.

1976A.

2093. INSTANT JOCK

A young nymphomaniac named Brock
Devised something she called Instant Jock.
With its power so mighty
It singed off her nightie,
And turned her tits green from the shock!

1965.

2094

A gorgeous young fay of Budapest
Just adored to de-pants and transvest.
With things between legs
He'd take ostrich eggs,
And achieve a coq-succulent breast.

1953A.

2095

Of unstable morals, young Burke
Always sits on a park bench to jerk.
To the idlers, in shock,
He waggles his cock,
And says, "Folks, it's more pleasure than work."

1966.

2096

There was a young fellow of Calais
Who took his best girl to hear Hallé's.
When the music got flat
He played with her twat,
And she did the same with his alleys.

1944*

2097

A golfer who came from Calcutta
Had thoughts much too pungent to utter,
When his wife he once found,
Ere commencing a round,
Sitting diddling herself with his putter.

1953.

2098

A worried young bridegroom named Carson
Observed his bride had every farce on.
He was not shook a bit
By her wig and false tit,
But he begged her to please keep her arse on.

1975.

2099. MUMBLINGS AT MIDNIGHT

Said Otto, the ghost of the castle,
As he fiddled and fooled with his tassel:
"This chain-rattling's old.
With no clothes I catch cold.
What I need is a she-ghost to rassle."

1945.

2100

There was a young man of Cawnpore
Whose tool was so awfully sore,
From the slapping and rubbing
And pulling and drubbing,
It was useless for what it was *for*.

1948.

2101

There was a young girl from Cheyenne
With a horrible loathing for men.
Instead, 'twas her pleasure,
In moments of leisure,
To gentle herself with a pen.

1950.

2102

There was a young lady *très chic*
Who kept her hair shining and sleek
By rubbing it nightly
With stuff that she lightly
Jacked off from her beau of the week.

1945.

2103

While awaiting the season of Christmas,
A man on the Panama Isthmus
Formed a phallus of holly
To make his gal jolly,
But it caused her to have vaginismus.

1971*

2104

A boy with whom I was once chummy
Was told if he'd lie on his tummy,
It would not be so bad
For a habit he had,
That we used to call flogging his dummy.

1950.

2105

A remarkable fellow named Clarence
Had learned self-control from his parents.
With his wife in the nude
He would sit there and brood,
And practice the art of forbearance.

1945.

2106

There was an old lady named Clarke,
Most surely a maiden of mark!
  She made her fat womb stick
  Astride of a broomstick—
And ho! for a lark in the dark.

1945C.

2107

Inventive, ingenious young Clyde
Perfected a Mechanical Bride:
  Without fear or compunctions
  It performed all sex functions,
While a permanent virgin beside.

1975.

2108

A young nurse and a colonel named Crandall,
To be sure and avoid a great scandal,
  After taking a drink
  He pulled off in the sink,
And she diddled herself with a candle.

1944.

2109. OBSCENE PHONE-CALLS, ANYONE?

The sport of a sexy-voiced crone
Is calling strange men on the phone.
  First she'll picture to him
  Her hot little quim—
Then finish herself off alone.

1971 *ff.*

2110

A lovely fiancée had Croylett,
But his morals said: " Do not despoil it! "
  So when love and desire
  Welled up like hot fire,
He flushed every drop down the toilet.

1975.

2111

Poor old Robinson Crusoe!
He had no woman to screw, so
He sat on a rock
And played with his cock,
And shot it all over the seashore.

1915-1952L.

2112

A cuddly young creature named Cupp,
In bed with me feeling her up,
Said : " Man, you're a dinger
At playing stinkfinger,
But I'm past that since Heck was a pup! "

1965.

2113

There was a young man bade defiance
To the vaunted advances of science.
His manhood he'd lost
Because of whore frost,
So he fucked with a plastic appliance.

1967A-1975.

2114

The Work Manager gets his delight
From a game he plays every night :
With his penis in hand
He feels really grand,
Switching from left hand to right.

1965*

2115

Oh, it's hard to wake up from a dream,
To the fact things are not what they seem :
That you've no mate at all,
And an aching left ball,
Both your sheets messed and chilly with cream!

1973.

2116

I fucked her in my dreams,
I listened to her screams.
When I awoke
The bed was soaked,
For I had fucked her in my dreams!

1939-1952L.

2117

A quick-triggered man from Duluth
Was phoning his sweetheart named Ruth.
When he got his connection
He had an erection,
And foamed at the mouth in the booth.

1953-1966.

2118. MADE IN JAPAN

Drugstores today are fantastic,
They sell battery-run dildoes of plastic.
They come red, white, or spade—
All Japanese-made—
As well as in Slow, Fast, and Spastic.

1970A.

2119

There once was a stupid young fellow
Whose balls were all slimy and yellow.
'Twas not from disuse,
Nor too much self-abuse,
But from trying to fuck lemon jello.

1948.

2120

A fast-frigging fellow named Fess
Kept his prick in a hell of a mess.
He could hit any hole,
From an ass to a bowl,
And his balls went from little to less.

1948.

2121

An impotent fellow named Fife
Had little to do with his wife.
She dreamt in her slumbers
Of giant cucumbers,
Which greatly enhanced her love life.

1974A.

2122

There was an old woman of Filey,
Who valued old candle ends highly.
When nothing was doing
She used them for screwing :
" It's wicked to waste, " she said dryly.

1948.

2123

At Newlyn a furious filly
Cried, " Christ! I have frigged myself silly.
I cannot get Granny
To tickle my fanny ;
I'll marry that bugger, Bodilly. "

1924C.

2124

For a pickup, Pete's pecker was fine,
And the way he fucked Fay was divine.
Peeking thru the wee keyhole,
As he prodded her peehole,
Made me wish that his peter were mine!

1966.

2125

To those lovers onstage who sit flirting
It must be, I'd think, disconcerting,
When from dimly lit stalls
An angry voice calls :
" Sod! Let go my balls! Damn, you're hurting! "

1973.

2126

I've always enjoyed fornication
With maidens of ev-ery station ;
    And sucking of tits
    And cunts gives me fits,
But I prize most a joint masturbation.

1950.

2127

There was a young lady named Fox
Who planted an acre of cocks.
    They grew up firm and strong,
    Nearly twelve inches long,
And she stuffed them all into her box.

1975.

2128. RUGGED BUT RIGHT

There was a young lady named Fran,
Had a short-peckered lover named Dan.
    In bed the poor runt
    Would fire up her cunt,
But she cooled it with an electric fan.

1968.

2129

The morals of this fellow from France
Have us savages looking askance.
    His superior smile
    Is a bore after while,
And *why* is his hand in his pants?

1965.

2130

Said an angry young lady of Frandel :
"Your sexual effort's a scandal!
    That short, feeble poke
    Was a horrible joke—
Now I'm sorry I burned up my candle!"

1966.

2131

There was a boy named Frank
He had a hearty wank.
His prick came out
As stiff and stout,
That learned him not to swank.

1935*

2132

There was a young fellow named Franz
Provoked by his gonadal glands.
He tried various whores
But found them all bores,
And now he is using his hands.

1948.

2133. SO FAR IN, YOU'RE OUT

Said a tired old playboy named Fred
To the eager young matron in bed :
" The weather's too sultry
For committing adultery ;
How about an interpersonal body-contact
psychological hot-oil massage instead? "

1976A.

2134

A nasty young widow named Garrity
Once said, with angry asperity :
" I'd have cut off his gherkin
To use when I'm perkin',
But he willed the damned thing to some charity. "

1970A.

2135

There once was a foreman named George
Who beat out his prick on a forge.
He made it too big
And had nothing to frig,
So he fucked the Grand Canyon gorge.

1957A.

2136

There was a young fellow named Gish
Who used to jack off in a knish.
He dreamt that Venus
Was nibbling his penis,
And woke up with a handful of slish.

1945R-1976.

2137

A man like an ancient Greek god
Blocked a girl from the door with his cod.
She grabbed it and shook it,
And said, " Golly, lookit! "
As his essence flew out of his rod.

1971 *ff*.

2138

When a virile young butcher named Gossage
Catches ladies purloining a sausage,
He offers his own—
Not a gift but a loan—
It cuts down his big sausage-lossage.

1965.

2139. THE UNSCREWABLE BRIDE

There was a young lady of Guelph
Who would daily assemble herself :
Rubber tits, a glass eye,
A blonde wig all awry,
And her cunt which she kept on the shelf.

1967A-1975.

2140

There was a musician named Handel,
Whose intimate life was a scandal.
When he fugued with his bass
He grew red in the face,
And buggered himself with a candle.

1948.

2141

A prissy old maid named Miss Hannah
Wrote Burbank a note in this manner:
  "Could you spare a few hours
  From your shrubs and your flowers
To perfect a pulsating banana?"

1945.

2142

An impatient young girl from Havana
Once screwed herself with a banana.
  She jumped into bed
  And stood on her head,
And farted "The Star-Spangled Banner."

1958P.

2143

There was a young lady named Hopper,
Owned twelve dozen dildos of copper.
  The Army reclaimed 'em,
  You can't really blame them
For branding her hoarding "improper."

1960A.

2144

Laundresses at honeymoon hotels
Get so heated by bridal-suite smells
  That by day in a frenzy
  They read up on Kinsey,
And by night practice all the book tells.

1954J.

2145

There was a thin lady of Hungary
Who had something pushed up her bungery.
  But it wasn't the size
  That brought tears to her eyes—
She'd a dildo that big of ironmongery.

1942M-1976.

2146

The balls of a man from Jerusalem
Were as dead as those of Methusalem.
But by splinting his prick
With an odd length of stick,
He'd fool all the girls and bamboozle 'em.

1953.

2147

Nymphomaniacal Jill
Used a dynamite stick for a thrill.
The cheeks of her ass
Landed up in Madras,
And bits of her tits in Brazil.

1962A.

2148

There was a young lady named Joan
Who got all her thrills from the phone,
Secreting the bell
And receiver as well
Where you wouldn't believe if not shown.

ff.1970.

2149

When they probed a young lady named Kannel
Who complained she felt choked in her channel,
They found shoehorns and spoons,
Six busted balloons,
And a horsecock wrapped up in red flannel.

1970A.

2150

Three elderly spinsters of Kent
Gave up copulation for Lent.
This included door handles,
Perfume bottles and candles,
And anything else hard and bent.

1968A.

2151

There once was a man from Kent
Who gave up masturbation for Lent.
His hand never played
Till the Easter parade,
And millions were drowned when he went.

1961*

2152

There was a young lady named Kerr
Whose pussy had ultra-thick fur.
She delighted to stroke it,
And pat it and poke it,
For the pleasure of hearing it purr.

1970A.

2153

A college professor named Klees
Had a whang which hung down to his knees.
When it bounced on the floor
He would beat it some more,
Till it came with a hell of a wheeze.

1948.

2154. THE SLEEVE-JOB

An old Chinese poet named Koo
Fell asleep in a rubber canoe.
He was dreaming that coolies
Were tickling his goolies,
And woke up with a hatful of goo.

1963A.

2155

There was a young girl of Las Palmas
Who, having discarded pyjamas,
Said : " Dear sister Sue,
We could share a blow-through,
But YES! we have no bananas."

1948U.

2156

A botany student named Lee
Fell madly in love with a tree.
  Each knothole with care
  He embellished with hair,
And went wild on a tree-fucking spree.

1975.

2157

Our blessed Saint Rosa of Lima,
When bothered with anal eczema,
  Found relief from the pain
  Of the itch in her drain
By tickling her cunt with her femur.

1950.

2158

A lonely old maid named Loretta
Sent herself an anonymous letter,
  Quoting Ellis on sex,
  And *Oedipus Rex*,
And exclaimed, " I already feel better! "

1945.

2159

Lubricious young Lulu just loves
To jerk off men's peckers with gloves.
  She's in no position
  To consider coition,
Being pregnant from previous shoves.

1966.

2160

An old nymphomaniac's lust
Was for iron bolts covered with rust.
  One day in a passion
  She exceeded her ration,
Gave birth to a shipwreck, and bust!

1959A.

2161. THE PLEASURE OF PORNO

A perverted old person named Lux
Said, " I have to feel *pain* when I fucks :
To get whipped and eat shit
While I fingers the clit—
(This stuff really brings in the bucks!) "

1972A.

2162

There was an old maid named McCall
Who liked her men handsome and tall.
She could even make do
With a finger or two,
Or the newel post out in the hall.

1945.

2163

A fat old inventor, McCawdell,
Complained : " The girls fiddle and dawdle. "
So he hid in his lab
Where he hoisted his flab
Aboard a mechanical model.

1975.

2164

There was an old Scot named MacDushan
Whose tool had an odd convolution.
This filled him with guilt,
For the tilt of his kilt
Caused frequent nocturnal pollution.

1970A.

2165

A horny young seaman, McGee,
Gave live-meat injections for free.
He shot it in dozens
Of his aunts and his cousins,
Then went it alone while at sea.

1965.

2166

The sex drive of old man McGill
Gives fortunate ladies a thrill.
    They say his technique
    Is delightful—unique!—
He uses an electrical drill!!

1966.

2167

A madam in town named Maloney
Taught new whores how to fuck with baloney.
    She said : " That's the way,
    But of course, in a lay,
You get poked with a prick, not a phoney. "

1966.

2168

There once was a damsel quite middling,
Whose interests soared far above piddling.
    She loved masturbation,
    Adored tit-illation,
And fucking and screwing and diddling.

1950.

2169. WASTE NOT, WANT NOT

A self-serviced old maid of Montclair
Often plays with herself in a chair,
    Which produces more juice
    Than for which she has use,
So she just leaves the leftover there.

1965.

2170

Petunia, the prude of Mount Hood,
Devised an odd object of wood,
    Which, employed on hot nights,
    Gave her carnal delights
Far beyond what the average man could.

1965.

2171

A neurotic young girl from Natchez
Wrote in weird Freudian snatches.
    Her doc was impressed
    Till she finally confessed
That she wrote with her cunt and burnt matches.

1958P.

2172

A horny professor named Ned
Dreamed off on a buxom coed :
    He grabbed her, he sucked her,
    He scuttlebutt fucked her—
But alas! it was all in his head.

1966A.

2173

There was a young girl from New York
Who got all her fun with a fork.
    She said, " It won't beat
    Six inches of meat,
But why be scared of the stork? "

1953.

2174

A technical virgin, Miss Nichols,
Has never used candles—just pickles.
    She doesn't like men,
    But gets hot now and then,
And rubs off them hot, sour prickles.

1965.

2175

A plant down in North Carolina
Makes a pink plastic bird's-nest vagina.
    It fits worn-out trulls,
    Fairies, geese, and sea gulls,
And they use them for soup in Red China.

1965.

2176

There was a young lady from Nyer
Who, in her extreme desire,
In lieu of man's handle
Had played with a candle,
And set her vagina on fire.

1948.

2177

A rapid young jeweler named Oak
Fixed clocks that were damaged and broke.
He opened the face
And in very short space
He'd change hands without missing a stroke.

1948.

2178

Said old Zeus as he sat on Olympus :
" Even Gods find that old age will crimp us.
So far as sex goes,
What once boldly arose
Now requires the aid of a wimpus. "

1965.

2179

An elderly gent named O'Maundry
Had his sheets partly starched at the laundry,
For they served to remind him
Of his youth now behind him,
When wet dreams kept his mom in a quandary.

1957J.

2180

A passionate schoolgirl named Parrott
Made indiscreet use of a carrot.
Said her mother, " When through,
Throw it into the stew ;
We've got so darn few we can't spare it. "

1966.

2181

There was a young sailor named Peck
Who kept his brute passions in check
By thinking of bloomers,
Testicular tumors,
And beating his meat below deck.

1945-1970A.

2182. GUYS AND DOLLS

There was an inventor named Perkin
Who perfected a mechanized merkin:
Wholly inflatable
With vagina dilatable,
It sure as hell beats this jerkin'!

1956J-1976.

2183

There was an old spinster named Perkins
Whose gardener gave her some gherkins,
And times without number
She tried his cucumber,
Which pickled her internal workin's.

1968A.

2184

A sorry young soldier was Pete:
Some shrapnel had blown off his meat.
And his arms were just stumps,
But he still got his lumps
For he diddled his girl with his feet.

1975.

2185

An introvert lad named Pierre
Who played with himself in the square,
Said, "I must confess,
When I come it's a mess,
But I let it lay there—I don't care."

1965.

2186

A perfectly miraculous new plastic
Has been used to perfect this prophylactic.
    So use without fear,
    It's been tested a year
On a profligate, satyrite spastic.

1949.

2187

A romantic old maid in Pomona
Makes an odd nightly use of bologna.
    With a simpering grin
    She slips it way in,
While her old phonograph plays " Ramona! "

1965.

2188. WHO'S COMPLAINING?

A neurotic young chopcock, Portnoy,
Said, " I never screw Jews, just the goy.
    And a slice of raw liver
    Makes my weenie just quiver—
What a fabulous, best-selling joy! "

1970A.

2189

A round-heeled young girl of Pratt Falls
Loves to tickle the men's hairy balls.
    This she does to her cousins,
    And cocksmen in dozens—
You should just *see* her sperm-spattered walls.

1966.

2190

An elderly playboy whose prick
Was bent double from coming too quick
    Still could fuck unabashed—
    No one knew it was smashed—
A custom-made dildoe did the trick.

1970A.

2191

A two-timing welcher named Prideaux
Would never pay tarts what he did owe.
  And thus it is, latterly,
  He reads *Lady Chatterley*,
And sleeps with the five-fingered widow.

1968A.

2192

The black hair that covers Kay's pubes
Excites us susceptible boobs,
  And we shuck out good money
  To fuck her do-funny—
She prefers to use greased mailing tubes.

1966.

2193

There was a young man of Racine
Who invented a fucking machine.
  'Twas a mine of gold,
  The stock being sold
By Merrill, Lynch, Fenner & Beane.

1952A.

2194

An inventor who lives in Red Oak
Built a gadget girls find is no joke.
  With it plugged in his rear
  He can bang a whole year,
And never miss once on a stroke.

1965.

2195. TECHNOLOGICAL FALLOUT

My friends, if from sex *you're* refraining,
The vibrators and dildos are gaining.
  Though computers we master,
  The machines can fuck faster,
And we spend our whole lives in retraining.

1967A-1975.

2196

Said Scrunch : " Well, I simply refuse
To pay whores good money for screws.
I go more for knotholes
Than twenty-buck twatholes,
And spend what I save on bad booze! "

1965.

2197

That super-hot satyr named Rex
Is an absolute Master of Sex,
With his hot, hairy hands
Massaging girls' glands,
Causing all the expected effects.

1966.

2198

An itchy-crotched dolly of Ryde
Finds it terribly hard to decide
Between using a candle,
An old bicycle handle,
Or a man with a twenty-inch clyde.

1966.

2199

There's really a lot to be said
For hearing Sinatra in bed.
If you can't stand the tune
It's so easy to swoon,
Or to *umptity-umpti* instead.

1946*

2200

There was a young man from St. Paul
Who went to a fancy-dress ball.
In the midst of the dance
He fucked two potted plants,
And they smuggled him home in a shawl.

1970A.

2201

A young German lady named Schickel
Would lay on her back for a nickel.
And when she was through,
For something to do,
She would fuck with a kosher dill pickle.

1975.

2202

A Scotsman once made self-abuse
Pay off by collecting the juice,
And selling the slop
To a bakery shop
As the filling for *charlotte russe*.

1958.

2203

There was a young man from Shalott
Who always was talking of twat.
The chambermaid said
As she made up his bed:
"My God! was he dreaming—or what?"

1950.

2204. THE KNACK, BOYS!

A passionate girl on the Shannon
Said, "Here's why I spend my time mannin':
If you twiddle my clit
While you're slipping me *it*,
I go off like a twenty-ton cannon!"

1974A.

2205

Another young lady, named Shirring,
She started a-trembling and purring.
Said the man, "Are you ready?"
She replied, "Not yet, Freddie.
I believe I still need some more stirring."

1975.

2206

A sweet little deb named Miss Shore
Was fucking the boys more and more.
She knew digital pleasure
Was a far safer measure,
"But hell!" she said. "What's a cunt *for*?"

1948.

2207. THE SIX-MILLION-DOLLAR PRICK

A sexual cripple and spastic
Had a prosthetic penis of plastic.
He could twirl it and spin it,
And reload in one minute—
It performed in a manner fantastic!

1975.

2208

A chumpy old duffer named Sprague
In his penis had unending ague.
With *a* dirty book he
Got plenty of nookie,
But the juice always ran down his lague.

1948.

2209

There's a hopeless young man of Starflecks
Who never can get enough sex.
When he isn't just diddling,
He's twiddling or fiddling—
He claims it's unconscious reflex.

1971*ff*.

2210

Said a nympho, "I find that each suitor,
For my needs is no better than neuter.
Now my passion's fulfilled—
Though I just may get killed—
By a large, well-equipped Roto-Rooter."

1972.

2211

A lonely golf widow named Sutter
Used to diddle herself with a putter,
First washing it clean
To protect her machine,
Then oiling with real country butter.

1965.

2212

A hard-peddling hooker named Syke
Always peddled her cunt on a bike.
She sniggered, " The seat
Keeps my pussy in heat,
Which of course is an item I like. "

1966.

2213

A silly old maid of Tarzana
Remarked as she ate a banana :
" Shoving fruit up my bun
Is such glorious fun,
It's a shame eating it up in this manna! "

1966.

2214

A dear little urchin named Ted
Fell asleep in his grandfather's bed.
Oh, what could be sweeter?
One hand on his Peter
Pan book and one hand on his head.

1969A.

2215

Cried an Indian maid in her teepee :
" What you're diddling is making me weepy.
Either give this here sookie
Some boiling-hot nookie,
Or I'll tear out of this teepee and peepee! "

1968-1976A.

2216

An acey-deuce switch-hitter from Texas
Has the sexual parts of both sexes.
When he tries self-abuse
Think what *he* has to use,
And think of *her* Freudian complexes!

1965.

2217

Said an old lama high in Tibet,
As he viewed his dead whang with regret :
" Though I no longer jape,
I shan't drape it in crêpe,
For it's rare fun to fondle it yet. "

1965.

2218. PERMISSIVE PARENTHOOD

To her grandson said inquisitive Miz' Todd :
" Do you spend your nights rubbing your rod?
Your old man, as a kid,
Most undoubtedly did—
If you *don't* do it too, you're quite odd. "

1965.

2219

Cried a slender young lady named Toni,
With a bottom exceedingly bony :
" I'll say this for my rump,
Though it may not be plump,
It's my own, not a cotton-stuffed phoney! "

1959A.

2220

Said a prudish young lady of Trinity :
" Thank heavens I've got my virginity—
At least as to men!—
I admit, now and then,
I've stuffed objects about the vicinity. "

1966.

2221

There was a young lad who, in truth,
Was a most seminiferous youth.
When he went out with whores,
Spunk would ooze from his pores,
Leaving odors that needed no sleuth.

1955J.

2222

There was an inventor named Tucker
Who built a vagina of yucca.
But his words were obscene
When the fractious machine
Got a grip and refused to unpucker.

1945.

2223

A candid young lady named Tudor
Remarked to the chap who'd just scrudor:
"After dildos, vibrators,
And cunt exhilarators,
The *real* thing feels like an intruder."

1966.

2224. NEVER SAY DIE!

Well, I laid there and twiddled her twat,
And gave the job all that I've got.
Yet my trusty repeater
Somehow couldn't heat her,
Though I worked on that hole quite a lot.

1965.

[2225]

Since transplants have proved to be viable,
And my dong is less plied now than pliable,
Why not graft, as a ringer,
My trusty third finger,
Which, these days, is far more reliable?

1970A.

2226

Said the bride, just before she undressed,
" There's something I should have confessed :
To get to the altar,
I padded my halter—
There are falsies where *you* think there's chest. "

[2227]

" Quite a joke, " said the groom, " but don't cry, love.
I'll give you a laugh you may die of.
Your deception will seem
Less important, I ween,
When I tell you what trinkets I'm shy of! "

1972.

2228

Said a Bryn Mawr professor, quite vicious :
" These short skirts bring visions lubricious.
When I look down my class
At those acres of ass,
I come in my pants. It's delicious. "

1970A.

2229

A frustrated fellow was Vince,
His girl took too long to convince.
When at last she agreed,
They could only proceed
With a roll of Scotch tape and some splints.

1975.

2230

In grandmother's day, in the waltz,
You could tell if girls' bosoms were false.
Nowadays top and bottom
Are padded with cotton,
With foam-rubber falsies for faults.

1966.

2231

With her maidenhead gone with the wind,
Cried a happy ex-virgin named Lynd :
"It makes me just sick
To have missed all that prick—
That thing has a darn candle skinned! "

1966.

2232

Said a newlywed lady named Wright :
"This gross self-abuse is a fright.
I must really repeat
That you can't beat your meat,
And cohabit with *me* the same night. "

1965.

2233. A MODERN HERO

"I'm sure I am hearing it wrong, "
I wailed to that little Miss Strong.
"Did I hear you say
You won't lay me today?—
When I brought my whole sex kit along! "

1965.

2234

For sex our man Joe's always yelling ;
At the sight of a breast's slightest swelling,
He whanks in his hanky
To prove he's a Yankee,
And what he'll do next there's no telling.

1953-1966.

2235

At the table, a young man named Zobblett
Liked to take out his wienie and wobble it.
His mother said, "Urk!!
Use the bathroom, you jerk ;
I *don't* want that cream in my goblet. "

1954J.

XVI

ASSORTED ECCENTRICITIES

2236

To barbarity man said adieu
As brilliant inventions accrue.
    To create wheel and lever
    Was remarkably clever,
But divinely inspired was the screw.

1967A-1975.

2237

Though at lying my aunt is adroit,
I can't see what she hopes to exploit.
    She claims she was zood
    In Kalamascrood,
And I know it took place in Detroit.

1970A.

2238

In the mountains of eastern Albania
The warlords developed a mania
    For padding their lairs
    With the curly snatch hairs
Of raped virgins from western Rumania.

1965.

2239

Said a middle-aged man, " God Almighty!
I'm dying of *tedium vitæ,*
    And the only thing sure
    To accomplish my cure,
Is a girl in a Philippine nightie. "

1953.

2240

There was an old maid named Alvina
Who crouched on the bedroom's best china.
But the Cranes and the Kohlers
Improved on one-holers,
And now she bidets her vagina.

1953.

2241

A repellent old whore of Amarillo,
Sick of finding strange heads on her pillow,
Decided one day
To keep men away,
And stuffed up her crevice with Brillo.

1966A.

2242

Narcissus achieved his ambition :
He was taught by a mathematician
To perform with great ease
A Möbius-strip tease,
With an auto-erotic emission.

1967.

2243

A Connecticut maiden named Annie
Developed an oversized fanny.
When asked, " Why not diet? "
She answered, " I'd try it,
But I'm sure it would make me *uncanny.* "

1960A.

2244. THE LIMERICK

The Limerick packs laughs anatomical
In a space that is not astronomical.
The clean ones we've heard
Are not worth a turd—
It's the "dirties" that stiffen your barnacle!

1973A.

[2245]

The limerick is callous and crude,
Its morals distressingly lewd.
It's not worth the reading
By persons of breeding ;
It's designed for us vulgar and rude.

1975.

[2246]

The limerick form is so easy
It's no trick at all to be breezy.
But its lines and its wit
Are oft flavored with shit,
Arousing the qualms of the queasy.

1967A.

[2247]

The limerick's easy to chart,
It's more of a craft than an art.
The trick's to be cautious
And not use those nauseous
Words : *shit, peter, piss, fuck,* and *fart.*

ff. 1969A.

2248

There was an old man of Australia
Who painted his arse like an azalea.
A penny a smell
Was all very well,
But sixpence a lick was a failure.

1948.

2249. DAD-NABBIT!

The biologists Hanson and Babbitt
Crossed a camel one time with a rabbit.
The offspring was jumpy
And frightfully lumpy,
With a very lascivious habit.

1953.

2250

A Roman who hailed from Barundum
Used a dried hedgehog's hide for a condom.
His mistress did shout,
As he pulled the thing out :
De gustibus non disputandum!

1959A.

2251. A WORD FROM THE BARTENDER

A word of advice, you dumb bastard :
Never drive, shoot, or screw when you're plastered.
For you tend to forget,
When your pecker is wet,
The mechanical tricks that you've mastered.

1976A.

2252

An astute obstetrician named Baugh
Shaved the crotch of his mother-in-law.
Since it wasn't as firm as
His own epidermis,
He asked her to make it go " Nyawww! "

1948.

2253

A fakir on his spikey old bed
Wants his sex desires all to be dead,
While a satyr in Ardmore
Wishes he could stay hardmore,
And fuck all the virgins unbred.

1965.

2254

A repellent young fellow named Bellow
Was kicked out of a Paris bordello :
He sawed his bow fiddle
Across a whore's middle,
Insisting that she was a cello.

1966.

2255

Though your cock isn't broken or bent,
She will lick but not suck, till you're spent.
And when questioned, she'll say :
" Sorry, dear. Agent's way—
I get that marvelous top ten percent! "

1967.

2256

There was a young maiden named Biddle,
Who was charitable with her middle.
In an airplane, one day,
She let a youth play,
And enjoyed a high diddle-diddle!

1950.

2257

A young man, whose wife couldn't be bigger,
Says dirty words help him to frig 'er.
So he says, " Tits! " and " Suck! "
" Asshole! Cock! Prick! " and " Fuck! "
But he's never yet used the word " Nigger! "

1967.

2258

Old Richbucks, the shame of Biloxi,
In matters of sex is quite foxy.
His equipment's expired,
But he's got a kid hired
To fuck his old girlfriends by proxy.

1965.

2259. THE PASSIONATE UNDERTAKER

" Ah'm prayin' fuh *guidance!* " says Blab,
Who fucks corpses laid out on the slab.
And he searches the Bible
In case he'd be liable
To get his ass lost in the flab.

1976A.

2260

A moral young fellow was Bliss,
So pure he would not even kiss.
He took care not to touch
Any ass, cunt, or such,
And used tongs when he went out to piss.

1975.

2261

Though I walked around town endless blocks,
And searched haberdashery stocks,
I couldn't find any stuff
To make a ball muff,
And nothing like sweaters for cocks.

1966.

2262. A WOMB WITH A VIEW

There was a neurotic named Bloom
Who wished to return to the womb.
Having plenty of scratch,
He rented a snatch,
And had it fixed up as a room.

1953.

2263. ART PILGRIMAGE

Bleary-eyed, blithering, and blotto,
Having paid his homage to Giotto,
He painted a nude,
Dreamed he got screwed,
And called himself Dear Uncle Otto.

1967K.

2264

While the Danube may look nice and blue
To a myopic moron like you,
To me it looks red
From menstrual blood shed
By ten million females and two!

1966.

2265. A TALE OF TWO CITIES

Elgar's opera, *At the Boar's Head,*
As a title makes no one's face red,
  Save for Jessica Snood's—
  That prude of all prudes—
Who thinks of what Spooner would have said!

1974.

2266

A Brooklyn boy ready to boist,
Shacked up wit' a French goil, his foist.
  When she said, "*Ah, mon cher*!"
  He replied, "Stop right dere!
Would ya radder we fucked or convoist?"

1948.

2267

We feel that exotic young Bodd
Should give far more thought to his God.
  He lolls in the garden
  With the world's finest hardon,
And drips *crème de menthe* on his prod.

[2268]

Yes, the morals of horrid young Bodd
Are a frightful affront and a fraud:
  His particular joy
  Is to catch a small boy,
And poke angleworms in his pod!

1966.

2269

Grandma Johnson, while bombed on bad booze,
Painted "Pecker Attacking Large Cooze."
  Said she, "It ain't quaint,
  But I just had to paint
One the greeting-card people can't use."

1967.

2270

There once were two whores from the Bosphorus
Who declared : " The men are all after us.
    And the light is so dim
    They can't see to get in. "
So they painted their privates with phosphorus.

1953.

2271

A prostitute named Miss Bowers
Was stopped by juridical powers
    From smoking in bed
    When the sign clearly read :
" *Do not smoke during orifice hours.* "

1967.

2272

There was a young lady named Brenda
Who appeared on the U.N. agenda.
    The decision went forth :
    The U.S. got the north,
And the Russians obtained the pudenda.

1963B.

2273

A prudish young lady named Brock
On sex had a bad mental block :
    When the mating of flies
    Passed in front of her eyes,
She practically fainted from shock.

1965.

2274. HOT BUTTERED RUMP

When Arthur was homeless and broke,
He would suck off his friends for a coke.
    The suckees would mutter :
    " Please bring some drawn butter—
We're going to have Artie choke. "

1967.

2275. A SESSION OF THE POETS

There was a young poet named Browning
Who rescued a virgin from drowning.
    Next day they got married,
    Next month she miscarried—
His philosophy kept him from frowning.

[2276]

There was a young poet called Keats
Who shagged every day in the streets.
    He did it because
    The alternative was
To shit every night in his sheets.

[2277]

There was a young poet named Shelley
Who much preferred bottom to belly.
    He argued the former
    Was tighter and warmer,
Though it does make the shooting-stick smelly.*

[2278]

An old poet named Coventry Patmore
Would say he thought no man had shat more,
    Or wetter or worse,
    Or a niftier verse,
And added : " I piss and I cat more. "

[2279]

There was a young poet named Swinburne
Who swore : " May my soul and my skin burn!
    The prospect appalls
    Not a person whose balls
To bugger a Siamese twin burn. "

1920C.

2280

" Good God! " cried the Duke of Buccleugh,
" I've been struck out of this year's *Who's Who*!
    All because of that day
    I rolled nude in the hay
With my grandmother—very nice too! "

1958A.

2281. ONE BORN EVERY MINUTE

Said an old occult faker named Bukhi :
" America for me has been lucky.
    I've got pots full of gold
    From the fools in my fold,
And fat boys if perchance I feel fucky! "

1976A.

2282

We envy our neighbor, young Burke,
That beady-eyed, potbellied jerk!
    To his wife, life's so boring
    She spends her time whoring,
So *he* can stay drunk and not work.

1966.

2283

Gwen Crotch and her boyfriend get calls
To screw for the public in halls.
    Folks scream, " Let us sing, Gwen,
    ' The Song of the Inguin' ;
We'll follow the two bouncing balls. "

1967.

2284

A young man on the banks of the Cam
Thought that sex was a snare and a sham.
    So he writhed in the fetters
    Of menstrual wetters,
And said, " What a good boy I am! "

1954A.

2285

A Dirty Old Man from the Cape
Kept his mattress in excellent shape
    With pubic hairs plucked
    From the women he'd fucked
In the course of a lifetime of rape.

1945.

2286. GENESIS I : 28

Said a wise old padre from Cape Cod :
" That the function laid on us by God
    To ensure human birth
    Should be subject for mirth,
Is surely exceedingly odd. "

1973.

2287

To the prissy bitch fucked in his car,
Joe said : " You're too stuffy by far.
    There is *no* polite term
    For cunt juice and sperm,
So why not just say what they are? "

1966.

2288

A steamy young slut in Carmel
Told her boyfriend : " We can't very well
    Do it here, for my folks
    Don't care for slow pokes.
Let's yance in a modern motel! "

1955M.

2289

We were shocked that the cunt of old Carrie
Was all bare, where it once had been hairy.
    She'd been screwed by a barber,
    Just east of Bar Harbor—
Now of barbers old Carrie is wary.

1965.

2290

A young lady cashier named Cass
Could handle the money with class :
She could pick up each coin
With a twist of her groin,
And zip off the bills with her ass!

1954A.

2291

A spinster in Chasuble Chasm
Is gifted with double orgasm.
She comes once on your gland,
Then again in your hand,
Which (in grammar) is called pleonasm.

1967.

2292

Two duo-pianists from Cheam
Would even make love as a team.
One aft and one frontal,
With strokes contrapuntal,
They developed a fucking good theme.

1960.

2293

There was a young couple named Chisholm
Whose wedded life ended in schism.
When she pulled on her glove
She found that her love
Had playfully filled it with gism.

1945.

2294. THAT CERTAIN PERFUME

" What have I done! " said Christine ;
" I've ruined the party machine.
To lie in the nude
Is not very rude,
But to lie in the House is obscene. "

1963A.

2295

There was a young fellow from Clare
Who just loved to run around bare.
He'd dangle his screwer
Through the gate of a sewer—
The poor thing's begun to show wear.

1948.

2296

Her ass, claimed a lady named Claribel,
To the greatest of queens was compárable.
But a fellow named Bower
Fucked her only an hour,
And stated the stench was unbearable.

1975.

2297

There was an old rake of Cohoes
Who loved to sniff cunts up his nose.
He said, quoting Shelley :
" A violet is smelly,
But a cunt is the polecat's pink hose! "

1950.

2298. BUSTER CHERRY SPEAKS

I teach nubile cuties coition :
I charge not a dime for tuition :
I teach 'em the ways
In which a prick plays,
And I fuck 'em in any position!

1966.

2299

Miss Gryce, the coloratura,
Sings her high C's *con molto bravura.*
Her attack's never blunt
'Cause she sprinkles her cunt
With cayenne moistened with Angostura.

1967.

2300

Once a sexy conundrum composer
Asked a Sunday school teacher a poser:
"Did Nero or Pharaoh
Have a narrow bone-arrow?"
After class she allowed him to hose her.

1956J.

2301

A voyeur when hailed into court
Came out with this shameless retort:
"When I see couples screwing,
It's interesting viewing—
It's a *wonderful* spectator sport!"

1966.

2302

A party called [Aleister Crank]
Was respected in ev-er-y bank.
Why *must* we assume
That they put on his tomb:
"He lived—and he died—and he stank."

1942C.

2303. SECOND THOUGHTS

This stuff is a nightmare of crap.
I'm sorry I'd ever the hap
To work it and ferk it—
I wish I could shirk it,
But now I am caught in the trap.

[2304]

It's grubby doings, pricks and cunts,
Fucking, sucking, dirty stunts;
Screwing, spewing,
Bad-rhyme hewing,
Bitter with smiles and tears at once.

1974A.

2305

There's a lady who dotes on pop culture ;
She has sex with a lesbian vulture.
She likes pancakes and crabs,
Pop music and scabs—
She's devoted to vivisepulture.

1967.

2306

At an orgy John Venn once said, " Damn!
I hate math! I'd much rather ram!
Let's forget aliquots! "
(Overlapping three twats)
And invennted the Venn diaphragm.

1967.

2307

There once was a monarch called Darius
Whose habits were rather nefarious.
He'd lie in the grass
With his crown on his ass,
Saying : " Alas, how my kingdom's precarious! "

1956U.

2308

There was a young girl of Darjeeling
Who used to stand up on the ceiling,
So her long evening gown
From her waistline hung down—
We all thought it most sex appealing.

1954.

2309. CARE FOR A DRINK?

A phantasmagorical darky
Was enthralled by the Ghoul Hierarchy.
She arranged a spectacular
Just for Count Dracula,
Celebrating her menarche.

1967.

2310

At Harvard a randy old dean
Said : " The funniest jokes are obscene.
    To bowdlerize wit
    Kicks the shit out of it—
Who wants a limerick that's clean? "

1965.

2311

In the Zambezi jungle old Deazy
Makes weak-stomached bystanders queasy :
    With soft words and smiles
    He castrates crocodiles,
Which on the Zambezi is easy!

1966.

2312

While the Prof wrote a Latin declension,
The pupils did things one can't mention,
    Like balling, and blowing
    Each other, and showing
A singular lack of attention.

1967.

2313. I LIKE IT

Fucking is a filthy deed.—I like it.
It satisfies a normal need.—I like it.
    It makes you sick, it makes you well,
    It turns your spine to fucking jell,
It damns your soul to Eternal Hell!— I like it.

1957A.

2314

A haughty young wench of Del Norte
Would fuck only men over forty.
    Said she, " It's too quick
    With a young fellow's prick ;
I like it to last, and be warty. "

1948.

2315

A classical student named Dewey,
Whose Latin and habits were screwy,
Addressed to his bag
This Thrasonical brag :
Ego multas puellas futui.

1948.

2316

Prickautious young Frogsnipper Dilke
Keeps his pecker encased in green silk.
As to why, we won't quibble,
It's well known for its dribble,
And that drop on the end isn't milk.

1966.

2317. PRACTICE MAKES PREGNANT

There was a young girl from the docks
Who could pick up small coins with her box.
She practiced these tricks
Till she'd pick up gold bricks ;
Then she rifled the vaults at Fort Knox.

1948.

2318

There was a teenager named Donna
Who never said, " No, I don't wanna. "
Two days out of three
She would shoot LSD,
And on weekends she smoked marijuana.

1965.

2319

There was a young lady named Dot
Who would diddle more often than not.
She was held in the Bozenkill
Up to her nose, until
Nothing was left but her twat.

1950.

2320

A hot-blooded swordsman named Doyle
Didn't fence quite according to Hoyle.
When challenged to duel,
He would whip out his tool,
And brandish it 'round like a foil.

1945.

2321

The buzzard you never must dread,
By your wife's standards he's ahead.
His sensitive vein
Makes him refrain
From chewing your ass 'til you're dead.

1953.

2322

There was, on a time, a blind Druid
Who persistently women eschewèd.
He said, " Fucking's all right
When a man's got his sight,
And can watch for that menstrual fluid. "

1948.

2323

Cleopatra to Antony : " Duck,
If you'll just shift a bit, I will suck. "
But that's nuttin' : the glutton
Gave her (up the butt) an
Anachronismatical fuck.

1967.

2324

Michelangelo Horsepecker Dwight
Is a chip off the old block, all right.
He sculpts *putti* and Venuses,
And shy lads whose penises
He tucks under leaves, out of sight.

1973.

2325

A modern young girl from Eau Claire
Remarked as she sprawled in a chair :
“ I can tell by your glance
I forgot to wear pants,
So *stare* at my crotch—I don’t care! ”

1965.

2326

A turd dropped by Sister Ecclesia
Reached from Key West to Southern Rhodesia.
The cause of this dump
Was a three-foot-square lump
Of Ex-lax laced with milk of magnesia.

1967.

2327. DOWN WITH MEN!

A nasty old biddy, Eclampsya,
Sobbed : “ Slap a guy down if he vampsya!
He knows what he’s doing—
All he wants is some screwing—
But the baby! my gawd how it crampsya! ”

1966.

2328

A queer in the depths of Eurasia
With a talent for paronomasia,
Said : “ Be Pericles’ consort,
The fuck-on-and-on sort ;
You’ll get rich—you will find you’re Aspasia. ”

1967.

2329

There are *some* things we mustn’t expose,
So we hide them away in our clothes.
Oh, it’s shocking to stare
At what’s certainly there—
But why this is so, heaven knows.

1973.

D
nd

cious
sur-
f dis-
ohols,
es se-
h or
way;
ally
hip-
li-

n-
g

Danny

HA

1
ba
Ch
in
M
S

our 1992 Bar of the Year and Pub of the Year —
don. For weeks our judges have been trawling the
drinking and, of course, working very hard. Here
L names the winners and, on Page 42, we explain
reached their verdicts

zing a New Age trail

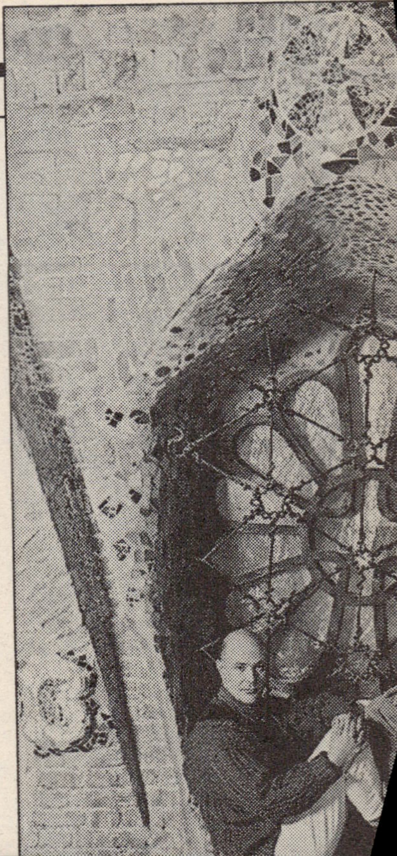

2330

For the poop in the sex-changing field,
See the Blessed St. Lizzie Bathilde.
By assiduous skipping
She altered her flipping;
Vagina now pecker doth wield.

1969.

2331

Some bird watchers through their field glasses
See flashes of heaving bare asses.
So do you see why,
Though bloodshot of eye,
Bird watching appeals to the masses?

1971 *ff.*

2332

A fiendish old fossil named Fife
Stuffed old razorblades up his wife.
He leered: "She's quite cut up,
And it *does* rust her butt up,
But it certainly simplifies life!"

1966.

2333. A THOUGHT FOR TODAY

The lewd thoughts and complexes one finds
In even the higher-type minds
Are a thing for dismay—
Can it be that today
All we think of are tits and behinds?

1965.

2334

3 cheers for Aloysius Fitzgerald
Who, being nine-eighths unappareld,
Went strolling the Strand
With his prick in his hand,
Proclaiming the End of The Werald.

1954E.

2335

A professional WASP named Fitzgerald
Was spotted last week by the *Herald*
In a Village café
Sucking off an old gay:
Do you think his career is imperilled?

1967.

2336

Concerning them bees and the flowers
In the fields and the gardens and bowers,
You will note at a glance
That their sexless romance
Has little resemblance to ours.

1966A.

2337

A flautist who fucked his own flute
Got the instrument stuck on his root.
When he enters erection
His woodwind section
Now comes with a terrible toot!

1958.

2338

In the beauty salon at Fort Flavier
One observes some eccentric behavior:
Said one girl, "I don't care
For my straight pussy hair.
I came in to have it made wavier."

1965.

2339

A cautious young lady named Fox
Gives her would-be seducers wild shocks:
On checking, they fail
To find any tail—
It's home, safely locked in a box!

1966.

2340. FROM " A FRIEND "

A fetishist living in France
Sniffed his bin full of slurpy girls' pants.
And their heady aroma
Sent him into a coma,
As he fondled his fetid *free-lance.*

1965A.

2341

A spunky young schoolboy named Fred
Used to toss off each night while in bed.
Said his mother, " Dear lad,
That's exceedingly bad—
Jump in here with your mamma instead. "

1968A.

2342

An old Anglo-German named Fred,
So repressed that he nearly was dead,
Scouted weeks till he found
A girl who was sound,
But even so would not take her to bed.

1970A.

2343

Ah Vienna! the fortress of Freud,
Where surgeons are never employed.
Where boys with soft hands
Are provided with glands,
And two-fisted girls are de-boyed.

1968A.

2344. TOTAL CONSUMERSHIP

There was a young fellow from Frisco
Who greased up his organ with Crisco.
But such was the heat
When he wielded his meat,
That his children were made of Nabisco.

1954A.

2345

A sadistic young fellow named Fritz
Was fond of biting girls' tits.
    With a snap and a growl
    He would make them all howl—
The younger ones sometimes had fits.

1955A.

2346

For diversion my foolish friend Frott
Tattooed all around his wife's twat.
    It'd give many pleasure
    To view her art treasure,
But only us *two* view the spot!

1966.

2347

A transvestite gal for a gag
Was matched with a pansy in drag.
    A silly seduction
    Confirmed the deduction
That heterosex was their bag.

1971 *ff.*

2348. THE REVIEW OF KOOKS

The Marquis de Sade and Genêt
Are most highly thought of today.
    But torture and treachery
    Are not my sort of lechery,
So I've given my copies away.

1966*

[2349]

In limericks I am not a trafficker,
For my nature is really seraphicker.
    My stomach is queasy,
    I blush far too easy,
And I *do* not collect pornographicker.

1970A.

2350

There was a young fellow named Gene
Who first picked his asshole quite clean.
He next picked his toes,
And lastly his nose,
And he never did wash in between.

1975.

2351

A drunken Scot fresh from Glasgow
Was asked if he wore aught below
With a tilt to his kilt
He replied, " If tha wilt,
Tha may'st feel for thysel' ; then thou'llt know! "

1973.

2352

As he gazed through high-powered glasses
At the nudist camp laddies and lasses,
He said, " It's a romp,
But if that were a swamp,
Just think! we should have some morasses. "

1967.

2353

There was an old Spanish grandee
Who affected a forkèd goatee.
He grew it so long
It curled 'round his dong,
And gave girls he fuckèd great glee.

1971 *ff*.

2354

From Bangor in Maine to Grant's Pass,
Purists bad-mouth the feminine ass.
Well, on monkeys and such
I agree overmuch,
But thank God for a *lush little lass!*

1966.

2355

There was a young lady from Grasse
Who loved showing folks her bare ass.
    With skirts up, and bent over,
    She'd waddle through clover,
Which *some* people thought rather crass.

1968.

2356

It is said, with appropriate gravity,
Thomas Hood lived a life of depravity.
    (Though he had just one ball,
    And his cock was so small
It could *just* fill a small molar cavity.)

1967.

2357

There's a mixed-up young fellow named Gray
Whose prowess is hard to relay.
    He feeds intravenous
    His oversize penis,
But washes with Cashmere Bouquet.

1956A.

2358

Said the captain of the Green Bay Packers :
"Youse guys are a bunch of coke-sackers.
    In case you don't knows
    How de story goes,
It goes : Sock-tucker, cork-soaker, lip-smackers! "

1968.

2359

A madam named Kay, of Green Turds,
Threw old cundrums out for the birds.
    When ten thousand collected
    Her neighbors objected
In a torrent of four-letter words.

1966.

2360. SEPARATE BUT EQUAL

Big cities are reeking with grief,
A haven for rapist and thief,
And designed in a way
So that half of us pay
To maintain all the rest on Relief.

1975.

2361

There was an old lecher named Gus
Who wore a prostatic truss.
It would pinch, sweat, and itch
When the son of a bitch
Got too close to young girls on the bus.

1958A.

2362

A young lady lawyer named Hawte
Was undoubtedly guilty of tort:
She'd peed in the tea
Of defendant's Q.C.
And dropped her briefs in full view of the court.

1968A.

2363

There was a young fellow named Hector
Who said to his girl as he necked her:
"Do you very much care
If I pull out some hair?
You see, I'm a box-top collector."

1973A.

2364

On moving away from Hell Gate,
A man nailed his cock in a crate.
He murmured, "I guess
It can go by express,
At the Household Appliances rate."

1939-1966A.

2365

Herr Siegfried, the handsome young Hessian,
Represents a new height in repression.
He gets off his rocks
Just by screaming, "A pox
On the whole Apostolic Succession!"

1967.

2366. B.A.R.F.

An unfortunate maiden named Hester,
A peculiar repugnance possessed her.
Her reaction compulsive
Made fucking repulsive,
Which was tough on the men who caressed her.

1966A.

2367

There once was a poet from Hexameter
Whose mistress kept calling him amateur.
She said, "Your technique
Is too rough and antique,
And your rhythm's a jerky pentameter."

1959R.

2368

"I'm a hardware store clerk," said Miss Hughes,
"But some kinds of work I refuse.
I'll handle their nuts,
Their bolts and crosscuts,
But I refuse to hand out the screws!"

1966.

2369

That queen of burlesque, Pussy Hunt,
Could whistle hymn tunes with her cunt.
But close investigation
Proved Pussy's vocation
To be just a ventriloquist's stunt.

1960.

[2370]

Another young lady named Hunt
Could smoke a cigar with her cunt.
"Smoking stunts growth!"
She exclaimed with an oath,
Giving birth one fine day to a runt.

1960.

2371

A virgin who lived in Iago
Was fucked by a bum from Chicago.
When he wouldn't get wed,
She audibly said
Several rude things beginning with "Ah, go —"

1967.

2372 ! ! !

Ever since time immemorial
Math has made sex appear incorporeal.
When a lady screams "FUCK!"
Mathematicians are struck
By the elegance of FUCK factorial.

1967.

2373

Dora's groom, a small, bald intellectual,
As a lover proved quite ineffectual.
Now she rubs him with grease
Derived from fat geese,
To increase his low sexual potentual.

1973.

2374. KITSCH-KLATSCH

A sculptor of Pop, known as Jacques,
Intends each new statue to shock.
Outsize genitalia
Gave the critics heart-failia,
But the public said: "Pure poppy-cock."

1970A.

2375

A lissome psychotic named Jane
Once fucked every man on a train.
  Said she, " Please don't panic ;
  I'm a bit nymphomanic—
It wouldn't be fun were I sane. "

1960A.

2376

There was a young man from Japan
Who lived on this excellent plan :
  Whene'er he saw women
  He stuck his fifth limb in
Her mouth or her cunt or her can.

1950.

2377

The poet named Robinson Jeffers
Wrote quatrains as light as the zephyrs.
  He was fragile and lean
  And a bit epicene
(Except when hucking the feifers).

1967.

2378. DAMN COMPUTERS !

A mathematician named Jones
Was fonder of cunts than of cones.
  Said he on his rambles,
  " Ah whoors an' Ah gambles—
Gonna roll them Napierian bones! "

1970.

2379

A Venus—a bit Junoesque—
Stripped down at the local burlesque.
  Her tits were tremendous,
  Her bottom stupendous,
But her cunt was a trifle grotesque.

1958A.

2380

A scribbler from Kalamazoo
Wrote stroke-books on sex for the zoo.
  But his constant erection,
  Caused so much ejection,
His pages were spattered with goo.

1971 *ff.*

2381

There once was a poet named Keats
Who enjoyed smelling bicycle seats.
  For those used by men
  He had no great yen,
But those squiffed by girls he thought treats.

1945R.

2382

There was a young woman of Kent
Whose cervix got frightfully bent,
  'Cause she reached in too far
  With a five-cent cigar,
Which was *not* worth the money she spent.

1948.

2383

There was a young lady from Kew
Whom the men all delighted to screw.
  She had stuffed up her scrotch
  The works of a watch—
When they fucked her, my God! how time flew!

1948.

2384

The crown jewels of Fuckingham Kew
He's painted a hideous blue.
  When the curious ask why, he winks a wise eye,
  Saying, " That's my reply to the dumb gal or guy
Who invariably asks, ' Well, what's new?' "

1966.

2385

When the gal saw an eye at the keyhole,
She cried, " Come on in! Plug my pee hole! "
Said the pansy voyeur,
" Oh, go comb your fur!
If *I'd* only been born with that she-hole! "

1965.

2386

There was a young fellow of Kiel
Who enjoyed slyly copping a feel.
On trying this ploy
On a girl who was coy,
She knackered his balls with her heel.

1968A.

2387

A frigid young girl of Kilkenny
Is troubled by suitors so many,
That this frantic young bitch
Plans to raffle her twitch,
And the tickets *ain't* two for a penny!

1968A.

2388

There was a young man of Killiecrankie
Who gathered his sperm in a hanky,
Which he left on the seat
Female buttocks to meet—
I guess you'd call *that* hanky-panky?

ff.1955A.

2389. PERILS OF PAULINE

When the heroine was fucking King Kong,
And found lubricant for his great dong,
She thought that it *was* spittle,
She's now in the hospital—
It seems she was horribly wrong.

1967.

2390

I'm terribly sorry I kissed Ed—
His mind is, I fear, a bit twisted.
    I like, *quelque peu*
    Masturbating *à deux,*
But it hurts me to find he's tightfisted.

1967.

2391

A cautious young lady named Knopp
Put a cork in her cunt for a stop.
    But it caused undue strain
    When she opened champagne :
She got fucked when a man heard it pop.

1975.

2392

There was a young girl from Korea
Who liked sticking flutes up her rear.
    After eating escargots
    She could fart Handel's " Largo, "
And encore with " Ave Maria. "

1968A.

2393

There was a young man named LaFarge
Whose tool was exceedingly large.
    His razor he'd hone
    On the edge of his bone,
And lather his face with the charge.

1945R-1953.

2394. JUST JEALOUSY

A sex-crazy prof in La Jolla
Has a habit that's sure to annoy ya.
    His amusable beds
    Are chockfull of coeds—
He's a sexual tank and destroyer!

1965A.

2395

A chippie who whored in Lake Nash
Crocheted the cunt hair on her gash.
Said she, " Ain't it silly
To make my cunt frilly?
But it brings in lots more fuckin' cash. "

1966.

2396

A prudish old person named Lear,
On seeing a cow from the rear,
Said, " Its milk is delightful,
But that figure is frightful—
I shall knit the poor beast a brassiere. "

1966.

2397

There once was a lecher of Leeds
Who did up his privates in tweeds,
With a zipper installed
To keep them close-hauled,
Or unfurled for his amorous needs.

1970A.

2398

A curvaceous young lady named Leeman
Refused naval dates with much screamin'.
It was not that the army
Was any more charmy,
But the gal was allergic to semen.

1953.

2399. AUTOBIOGRAPHY OF ALICE

There once was a naughty old Lesbian
Who went into a bookstore for cat food.
But the ceiling fell down
And she died of a stroke,
And nobody came to the funeral except the
immediate family. 1967.

2400

A bird fancier of Leverstock Green
In his flat kept the first peacock seen
Trained to warm its behind
At the stove when inclined,
With its tail spread to form a fire screen.

1973.

2401. ABOVE SUSPICION

Calpurnia lived quite a life :
She would masturbate with a sharp knife,
Or have sex with a bear
While her husband would stare,
Mumbling something about Caesar's wife.

1967.

2402

Composing a lewd limerick
Is hardly a difficult trick.
Once you've mastered the stunt
Of ramming a cunt,
There's nothing to rhyming a dick.

1958.

2403

An effeminate fellow named Lincoln
One night did some serious drinkin' ;
Met a gal—now his wife—
Learned the real facts of life,
And now blesses the day he got stinkin'.

1958A.

2404

A Latin professor from London
Feared women so much that he shunned 'em.
When his prick urged, " Let's go!! "
He shuddered, " No! No! No!
Illegitimi non carborundum! "

1968A.

2405

Jack performs mental rape, the lewd lout,
On each sweet little lassie about.
All day long he's pursuing
His vicarious screwing—
No wonder at night he's worn out!

1966.

2406

A Lancashire nympho named Lunt
Has a clever promotional stunt :
When the fog is so thick
That she's lacking for prick,
She burns a red flare in her cunt.

1970A.

2407

The rapist began to luxuriate
In the trial, though it seemed to infuriate
Both the lawyer and judge,
But his prick was pure fudge,
Can you guess, little girl, what the jury ate?

1967.

2408

There was an old miser of Lyme
Who saved every nickel and dime.
He would save anything,
Even pieces of string,
And thought sexual spending a crime.

1975.

2409. ENQUIRY INTO OBSCENITY

" I am *no* prude! " cried Viscount McAudrey,
" But these novels are really quite tawdry.
The new movies are smut,
And slavering rut—
I'll go to Denmark and study their bawdry. "

1971A.

2410

An unhappy young bride named McBryce
Had a husband who came in a trice.
  But she managed to cool
  His impetuous tool
By stuffing her cunt with dry ice.

1960.

2411

There's a very prim gal named McDrood :
What a combo—both nympho and prude!
  She wears her dark glasses
  When fellows make passes,
And keeps her eyes shut when she's screwed.

1965.

2412

That flatulent farter McGee
Was as gassy as humans can be.
  He delighted his friends
  With duets from both ends,
But he goofed on " Oh Promise Me! "

1958A.

2413

A lazy young girl named McGlore
Trimmed her pussy fur often, belower.
  For she got up quite late,
  And her hair was so straight
That putting in curlers was a bore.

1965.

2414. MEDIA BLOW-HOW

That jazzy professor, McLuhan,
Tells the public that sex will be soon
  " More erotic than now, "
  Through media know-how,
So prepare for a terrible screwin'.

1970A.

2415

An entrancing young girl named McWhiston
Thought her bum an odd place to be kissed on.
So she turned on her back,
Showed her lover her crack,
And demanded: " Now work like a piston! "

1968A.

2416

A much-admired rabbi from Macon
Found the faith of his followers shaken
When they learned he'd a taint
(See *Portnoy's Complaint*)
Of fucking both ham-hocks and bacon.

1969A.

2417

An unfortunate lad from Madrid
Had both Superego and Id.
So whether he screwed,
Or completely eschewed,
He felt guilty whatever he did.

1970A.

2418. MALMAISON

A crumbling Edwardian manse hid
A crime both repugnant and rancid,
Involving a twat
That was virgin, and what
The Episcopal minister fancied.

1967.

2419

There was a strange creature named Marks
Whose idea of diversion and larks
Was murdering tramps,
Disturbing boys' camps,
And buggering statues in parks.

1960A.

2420

There was a young butcher named Marvin,
And expert on choppin' and carvin':
He'd cut the sex parts
Off young pansies and tarts,
And send them to folks who were starvin'.

1948.

2421

A binary mathematician
Had the curious erotic ambition
To know what to do
With the powers of *two,*
When the two are in proper position.

1954.

2422. LAPSES LINGUÆ

A hungry cunnilinguist named Mays
Fucked a Nesselrode pudding for days.
He cried, "Who wants a cherry?
I seek a red berry—
If I'm permitted to coign a *fraise*!"

1948-1970A.

2423

A wigmaker working in Maze
Shocks girls with his unpleasant ways.
He traps 'em, and snatches
Their sex fuzz in batches,
Which he uses for making toupées.

1966.

2424

There was a young dumbbell in Mensa
Whose girls found his blunders intense-a.
Instead of hard swinking,
In bed he'd be thinking
Of square roots and suchlike nonsense-a.

1976A.

2425

A playboy whose name we won't mention
Had a transplant to lower his tension.
He'd bathe in a Jacuzzi
While served by black pussy,
And hoped his penis would snap to attention.

1970A.

2426

There was a young fellow from Merton
Who went out with only his shirt on,
From which did peep shyly
His *membrum virile,*
For people to animadvert on.

1948.

2427. THE INVISIBLE GOVERNMENT

The sex books of Doctor Methusalem
Are the Word, from Key West to Jerusalem.
But alas, you poor suckers,
And would-be art fuckers—
He's C.I.A., picked to confoozle 'em!

1974A.

2428

There was a young man from Metuchen,
Had a terrible blot on his escutcheon:
He forcibly laid
A crippled old maid,
And ended by shoving her crutch in.

1963B.

2429

Said a lustful old man from Montclair,
As he leered at a girl's *derrière*:
"Though touching's unlawful,
And the mental strain awful,
Can they put me in jail if I stare?"

1965.

2430

An eccentric from old Monticello
Was really a horrible fellow.
    In the midst of caresses
    He'd fill ladies' dresses
With garter snakes, ice cubes, and jello.

1958P.

2431

There was a lewd fellow named Mott
Who remarked, as he fingered a twat:
    "Some guys, so I'm told,
    Like to lay a girl cold,
But they're more fun to fuck when they're *hot*!"

1966.

2432

There once was a couple named Mound
Whose sexual control was renowned.
    While engaged in coition
    They had the volition
To study the *Cantos* by Pound.

1960.

2433

A horny young girl of Mount Lassen
Said, "I sure wish my cunt would unfasten.
    For I'd leave it with you
    A whole month—maybe two—
Till you were fucked out, you ass-assin!"

1966.

2434

A hog-eyed abortion named Mudd
Was like a one-eyed rotten spud.
    His one chance to clean
    His person obscene
Is to wash himself out in his blood.

1924C.

2435. THE CLASSICS REVISITED

The *Iliad*'s really no mystery,
Though highly confusing and blistery.
  It's a long story tellin'
  Of the search for Queen Helen
By the prize horse's ass of all history.

[2436]

That play about *Oedipus Rex*
Has a plot that is very complex :
  He clobbered his pa,
  Then screwed his mamá,
While the chorus sang dirges on sex.

[2437]

Parsifal was a faggotty knight
Who knew how to shoot swans in flight.
  But when Kundry gave in,
  And turned up her quim,
He turned down her offer outright.

[2438]

Taras Bulba was an ugly old fart
Who blasted his son clean apart,
  When the boy tried to dick
  Some cute Polish chick
Who had captured his wild Russian heart.

[2439]

Count Tolstoi, a thinker of note,
When young was a raunchy old goat.
  But as he grew older
  His ballocks grew colder,
And of sinners repentant he wrote.

[2440]

Seven Pillars of Wisdom, they say,
Is a volume exceedingly gay.
To put it quite blunt,
Lawrence hated a cunt :
He preferred it the pederast's way.

[2441]

Henry Miller of literary fame
Thought the words in most novels too tame.
So he ran quite amuck
Writing *cunt, shit,* and *fuck,*
And others too nasty to name.

[2442]

H. Spencer Ashbee, oil-seller,
Was a rather cunt-crazy old feller.
He hated his wife,
Led a wild *Secret Life,*
Which today has become a best-seller.

1970A-1971.

2443

A vicious old codger in Natchez
Demonically lights pads of matches,
Which he pokes in the drawers
Of defenseless young whores,
Where it singes their sex fur in patches.

1966.

2444

There was a young man from New York
Whose morals were lighter than cork.
" Young chickens, " said he,
" Have no terrors for me—
The bird that I fear is the stork. "

1959*

2445

There was a young lady from Norway
Who crawled on all fours through a doorway.
    The door slammed shut
    And pinched her butt,
And she shit all over the floorway.

1958P.

2446

There was a young girl named O'Farrell
Who went 'round without any apparel,
    And when she detected
    A penis erected
She took it—lock, stock, & barrel.

1953.

2447. AMERICA, AMERICA!

There once was a cuntry of, oh
Such lofty ideals that no
    Man could ever mention
    (Imagine the tension)
What might have offended Jane Dough.

1948E.

2448

A lady who hailed from Oklahoma
Would come when she heard " La Paloma. "
    In Mexico City—
    Ah, more is the pity—
The lady is still in a coma.

1948.

2449

There was a young fellow named Ollie
Whose dong slithered strong in a dolly.
    In the midst of his thrust
    It expanded with lust,
Which was jolly for Dolly, by golly!

1976A.

2450. THE BLUE OX

A cowgirl who calls the guys " Pardner "
Can fix limber pricks : she's a hard'ner.
    But she got a rude shock
    When she sat on the cock
Of that Bunyanesque fellow named Gardner.

1967.

2451

There once was a passionate pastor
Whose feelings he never could master.
    His ejaculations
    Baptized congregations,
And hung from the ceiling like plaster.

1953A.

2452

There once was a Frenchman from Pau
Who went for a slide in the snow.
    He traveled so fast
    Down the old Simplon Pass
That his asshole developed a glow.

1949.

2453

A cannibal cook yclept Paul
Was eating an arm in the hall.
    As he spit out the pit
    He looked up and said, " Shit!
In the fall we will all have a ball. "

1976*

2454. KEEP TRUCKING

There was a young girl of Penzance
Who went to a Birth Control dance,
    Complete with accessories,
    French letters and pessaries,
And then had to dance with a nance.

1968A.

2455

A necrophile fellow named Perce
Once kissed an old corpse in a hearse.
He drew back with a shiver
Which threw chills down his liver ;
Then he tried something more and fared worse.

1975.

2456

There was a young bugger named Percy
Who let a most poisonous fart ;
He collected the spend
Of an intimate friend
From the cunt of a twopenny tart.

1904C.

2457

A peculiar young lady named Piltz
Delights to be diddled on stilts.
Men are all wild to try,
But she's up so damned high
That before you can reach her—it wilts!

1965.

2458. A VALENTINE

In my heart you've a permanent place ;
I'm enthralled by your charm and your grace.
You give my heart ease,
And now, if you please,
Get your big grimy ass off my face.

1967.

2459

A musical harlot was Polly ;
Her students found sex classes jolly.
She taught the legato,
And rapid vibrato—
The crescendo was saved for finale.

1975.

2460. AIMEZ-VOUS BRAHMS?

An English conductor named Poole
Conducted Brahms' *First* with his tool.
Such ambidexterity!
Grace and celerity!
(Critical comment was cool.)

1945.

2461

There was a young lady named Prim
Who kept a dead cat up her quim.
The meat of her pussy
Was constantly juicy,
But no one could push past the rim.

1948.

2462

New Mexico, college of prudes,
Has forever banned artists' nudes.
No more buttocks and tits,
To delight the nitwits :
The female form turns off the rubes.

1971.

2463

These verses about the pudenda
Have neither beginning nor end : a
Few more I submit
Just to tickle your shit,
And fill out the list of Addenda.

1954J.

2464

There was a young girl from Purdue
Who covered her pussy with glue.
She was minus one tit,
And stunk like shit—
I wouldn't fuck her : would you?

1975A.

2465

The canny young bride of friend Pyte
Furred the hem of her nightie—that's right.
Her reason you've guessed,
And she plainly confessed,
'Twas to keep her neck warm through the night.

1966.

2466

There once was a very small Quaker
Who (though short) was a true Sabbath breaker.
Sundays, he'd screw a dame
And then shout, as he came:
"It is true! I am God's little acher."

1967.

2467

In a high-fashion journal for queers
A drawing by Dali appears
It depicts a June bride
With three breasts on each side,
Caressing a penis with ears.

1970A.

2468

A device more ancient than recent
For cutting out something indecent,
Is to break off the story
When it gets slightly whorey,
And mark the gap: [*Cetera desunt.*]

1954J.

2469

Said Oedipus Rex, growing red:
"I wish all head-shrinkers were dead!
They make such a bother
Because I hate father—
I shall go and fuck mother instead."

1962A.

2470. LATENT QUEER

Said a prudish young person named Reed:
"The gross way that we humans breed,
Viewed coldly, looks frightful,
Though I'm told it's delightful,
So if you don't mind, let's proceed."

1965.

2471

There was a young girl from Regina
Who loved to paint her vagina.
She said, rather blunt:
"Yes, it gets in my cunt,
But I don't do this for money, anyway."

1959A.

2472

He swears that the girls can't resist him,
Keeps a list of the ones who have kissed him.
The amount's not too hot
But it *looks* like a lot,
Since it's kept in the binary system.

1967.

2473

A lascivious fellow named Rex
Needed physico-mental effects.
But even after he'd laid
Every wife and old maid,
He was *still* somewhat hung up on sex.

1970A.

2474. SYMBOL-MINDED

That inspiring cathedral at Rheims
Has figured in many wet dreams.
It looks like a phallus,
But bear it no malice:
'Twas the builder's intention, it seems.

1954A.

2475

There was a young fellow named Riffer,
In matters of sex he did differ.
    Though girls seldom object
    To the method direct,
He was more of a smeller and sniffer.

1967A-1975.

2476

There was a old fellow from Rome
Who diddled a girl with his dome.
    The results were most horrid :
    The girl grew quite torrid,
And he could not withdraw to go home.

1960.

2477

A girl who appeared in *La Ronde*
Once confessed, as she drank a *bière blonde* :
    " My life's quiet, " she wept,
    " I do nothing. Except—
Well, I fuck a group called *tout le monde.* "

1967.

2478. MATTER IN THE BATTER

Like a glittering gem on a rose,
A dewdrop hung from father's nose—
    Unwiped and suspended
    Until (puncture mended)
We cried, " Good old Dad! Off she blows! "

1973.

2479

A peculiar old fellow named Rutter
Once pickled his bollocks in butter,
    Which changed his orgasm
    From a thunderous spasm
To an oleomargarine mutter.

1976A.

2480. SIGNS OF THE ZODIAC

The men of the sign Sagittarius
Have customs obscene and barbarious.
They sow their wild oats
With girls, boys, and goats,
In postures ingenious and various.

[2481]

A fellow with stars Capricorn
Only wished he had never been born.
And he wouldn't have been
If the druggist had seen
That the end of the rubber was torn.

[2482]

A girl who was born an Aquarius
Engaged in a custom nefarious.
She practiced fellation
With highest elation,
Till her teeth became yellow and carious.

[2483]

A Lesbian born under Pisces
Has dildoes of various sizes.
The big one with warts
Squirts several quarts,
And gives all her girlfriends surprises.

[2484]

A young lady born under Aries
Consults the stars each time she marries.
Although she gets hope
From each horoscope,
Her husbands turn out to be fairies.

[2485]

A man of the natal sign Taurus
Joined up with a folksinging chorus.
    But he didn't last long
    For in every song
He pooped like an old brontosaurus.

[2486]

A lady skin-diver, a Gemini,
Encountered a monstrous anemone.
    Far under the sea
    It seized her with glee,
And ate up her *pudenda feminæ*.

[2487]

A zoophile born under Cancer
Joined up as a cavalry lancer.
    But he died of despair
    When his favorite mare
Was replaced by a motorized panzer.

[2488]

A cowboy, by birthright a Leo,
Once met a young lady in Rio.
    They engaged in coition
    In every position,
And now our poor Leo can't pee-o!

[2489]

A girl who was born under Virgo
Denied that the stars could make *her* go.
    Again and again
    She proved this with men,
Till the friction made all of her fur go.

[2490]

A lady philologist (Libra)
Was raped by an oversexed zebra.
She cried out her anguish
In every known languish,
Including Swahili and Hebra.

[2491]

A poet, by birthright a Scorpio,
Was trying to rhyme the word " Scorpio. "
He fretted and fried,
Till in torment he died—
There IS *no rhyme for Scorpio!*

1969B.

2492. SEX BREAK

A much-worried mother once said :
" Daughter dear, you've been fucking with Fred,
All over the walls,
The kitchen and halls—
For God's sake, *please* go up to bed! "

1960A.

2493

A heifer from up by Sainte-Sault
When approached by the bull, answered " Moo. "
Then, on quite the wrong tack,
She lay down on her back—
(But the bull figured out what to do.)

1970A.

2494. WRITE YOUR OWN

—— —— is colored, they say.
—— —— is a terrible lay.
—— —— is a kike,
—— —— is a dyke,
And President —— is gay.

1967.

2495

A hunchbacked old prophet named Samuel
Had the habit of humping his camu-el.
    The congregation was furious—
  " Miscegenation! Injurious! "—
And expelled him from Temple Emmanuel.

1976A.

2496

There was an old couple from Sayville
Whose habits were quite medieval.
    They would strip to the skin,
    Then each take a pin
And pick lint from the other one's navel.

1956A.

2497

A bashful young fellow named Schick,
The sight of young girls made him sick.
    Whenever they found him
    They gathered around him,
But he beat them all off with his prick.

1975.

2498

There was a young bridegroom of Schledding
Who grew so aroused at his wedding,
    And the sight of his bride
    When he got her inside,
That he creamed all over the bedding.

1945.

2499

There was an old sailor named Schlitz
Who landed on an island of tits.
    When the nipples would function,
    Without any compunction
He'd avidly gum them to bits.

1954A.

2500

An old man who lived in Seattle
Engaged a tired whore in—well, battle.
He shot off three times,
And then shouted : " The crimes
Of the fathers are— " (*Offstage death rattle.*)

1967.

2501

There was a young man in our section
Who began an immoral collection.
He had great Caesar's balls
Which he hung on his walls,
And the tool of Don Juan in cross-section.

1950R.

2502. RECIPE FOR A BESTSELLER

Take a naked girl, eaten by sharks,
Add another, shot dead by the narcs,
A mad killer or two,
A perverted fag screw,
And peddle for millions of marks.

1976A.

2503

There was a young man of Siam
Who went to a ball dressed as Spam.
Utterly whimsical
He tried to be quimsical,
And wore frills 'round his tool like a ham.

1974A.

2504

Said a Mensa snob with a sigh :
" Although my I.Q. is quite high,
When it comes to real wit
I'm just not worth a shit,
And I cannot determine the ' why '. "

1971.

2505

A Greek—let us call him Silvanus—
Is strange : he has one extra anus.
    The one up in front
    Can be used as a cunt,
Which makes him a queer sort of Janus.

1967.

2506

There was a young plumber named Simms
Who acted on impulse and whims.
    When he dated Miss Bruce
    Who was said to be loose,
He brought plenty of caulking and shims.

1975.

2507

A quixotic old Spaniard of Sitges
Kept all the girl tourists in stitches
    By parading around
    The main square of the town
With his tool hanging out of his britches.

1974A.

2508

There once was a gangster called Slug,
A most reprehensible mug.
    He called his moll's dress
    A shitten-arsed mess,
And referred to her teat as a dug.

1948.

2509. SOUND YOUR "F"

A flatulent fellow named Snite
At farting was terribly bright.
    He blended with art
    His belch with his fart,
But the *timing* was never quite right.

1958A.

2510

Confession is good for the soul.
I dream day and night of a hole :
    It's lined with red silk,
    And the doorknobs squirt milk—
Do you think Doctor Freud should be tole?

1970A.

2511. KEEP ME HIGH !

A coed at old South Dakota
Collected a clutch of male scrota.
    The hairy brown hide
    She opened and dried,
And the contents she smoked with peyote.

1970A.

2512

A pernicious old wino from Spain
Has whims even *he* can't explain.
    He sends his friends parcels
    Of homogenized arseholes,
And REPEATS when they write to complain.

1965.

2513

A Roman whose name is Spartillicus
Had sex with his girlfriend's umbilicus.
    In spite of strong doubts, he
    Deflowered her out-sy,
And made it an in-sy, the silly cuss!

1967.

2514

There was a philosopher, Spencer,
Who never knew pleasure intenser
    Than once, when he saw
    Mr. George Bernard Shaw
Attempting to bugger the Censor.

1921C.

2515

The whimsies of dirty old Spink
Are lower by far than you think,
    For the genital zone
    Of a girl from Athlone
He's filled with indelible ink.

1966.

2516

A malicious young maiden from Spitz
Scared a parson half out of his wits.
    When he dropped in to call
    She appeared in the hall
With eyes painted on both her big tits.

1966.

2517

The furry, wet twat on Miss Sprott
Fellows find is continuously hot.
    Gallon jugs of thick semen
    She's saved from her reamin',
And to fill one of *those* takes a lot!

1965.

2518

The yen of a young man of Spruntz
For girls with four tits and two cunts
    Is both childish and silly
    When you think, willy-nilly,
He can only fuck *one* cunt, just *once*!

1966.

2519

There was a young man from Stamboul
Who thus spake unto his tool :
  " Last night you declined
    A bloody good grind,
And now you can't piss. You damn fool! "

1962*

2520. KISMET

There was a pure lady of Stame
Who resolved to live quite free of blame.
    She wore four pairs of drawers,
    And of petticoats scores,
But was fucked in the end just the same.

1968A.

2521

A sausage-lipped songster of Steyning
Was solemnly bent on attaining.
    But he broke all the rules
    About managing tools,
And so he broke down in the training.

1930C.

2522

There was a young lady of Stockholm
Who went through the park for a walk home.
    And she's still talking yet
    Of a man that she met,
Who knew how to drive the old cock home.

1975.

2523

A young man on the bus line at Stoke
Unzippered his fly for a joke.
    Two girls gave a shout,
    An old lady passed out,
And the homo right next had a stroke.

1974A.

2524

There was a young fellow from Stroud
Who could fart unbelievably loud.
    When he let go a big 'un,
    Dogs were deafened in Wigan,
And the windowpanes splintered in Oudh.

1967A.

2525

A lecherous whore from Swoboda
Amused all the men who bestrode her.
She had put in her cunny
Some turds from a bunny,
And she foamed like a chocolate soda.

1948.

2526

When you think of " A-Tisket, A-Tasket, "
Remember the lady named Haskett.
She contrived a good stunt,
Stuck her feet in her cunt,
And carried her teats in a basket.

1945.

2527

There were once two young people of taste
Who were eunuchs right down to the waist.
So they limited love
To the regions above,
And so remained perfectly chaste.

1959A.

2528

A mixed-up young person from Texas
Was full of syndromes and complexes.
So they sent him to college
In search of pure knowledge,
And to locate himself in the sexes.

1955A.

2529

They've a fine school at Texas State Teachers :
Fucking classes are one of the features.
Go to lab, if you're lonely,
And learn—there's not only
No charge, but they've put up new bleachers.

1948.

2530. NAME-DROPPERS

There was a young man of Thames-Ditton
Who found Sartre and Freud unbefittin'.
While Marcuse and McLuhan
He felt were just doin'
What's commonly known as bull-shittin'.

1966A.

2531

There was a young lady from Thrace
Who had whiskers on half of her face.
As you may surmise,
She garnished first prize
At a six-day bisexual race.

1948R.

2532

Two profs were confused by a totem
About which an Eskimo wrote 'em :
It was forty feet high,
Had one gorgeous blue eye,
And the rest was all balls, prick, and scrotum.

1945R.

2533

A randy old Moose of Toulouse
Loved to give giddy girlies the goose.
Though of germs highly sceptic
He would use antiseptic
Before his thumb went into use.

1966.

2534

A learnèd old justice of Trent
Defined what obscenity meant :
He said, " *Duck* is not clean,
But three-quarters obscene ;
And *fudge* is foul forty percent. "

1975.

2535

The whimsy of Constable Trent
He follows with filthy intent :
    For he's stuffing a chair
    With the curly cunt hair
Of the unfaithful housewives of Kent.

1965.

2536

There was a young harlot named Trilling
Who went to the dentist for drilling.
    In a fit of depravity
    He filled the wrong cavity,
So each cancelled the other one's billing.

1975.

2537

There was a young lady from Tritt
Who on her front porch loved to sit.
    With her feet on the rail
    She'd exhibit her tail,
And also the place where she shit.

1948.

2538. BITCH ARITHMETIC

My dearest, I do love you truly,
But don't expect *me* to get drooly,
    Or fall into fits
    For a couple of tits
Like the lemniscate drawn by Bernoulli.

1967.

2539

The big, buxom bust on Miss Trust
Stirred our lust, so she said : " If you must,
    Take a whack at my crack, Jack,
    Though I'd rather play blackjack— "
To hell with her cunt! Let it rust!

1966.

2540

A neurotic young fellow named Tuttard
Would stutter each word that he uttered.
He had more of a block
In the use of his cock,
For instead of just coming he sputtered!

1960.

2541

Decrepit old Vice-Admiral Twynn
Took a Wren to his cabin for sin.
Though he boasted of screwing,
Three knots he was doing :
Not long, not hard, and not in!

1969A.

2542. OUT OF THIS WORLD

On the latest moon rocket unfurled,
A cat into orbit was hurled.
As it shot out of sight
They screamed with delight :
" That pussy is out of this world! "

1967A-1975.

2543

A spinster who lived in Vancouver
Claimed pornography never would move 'er.
But she got a hot twat
When she spotted a shot
Of the testes of J. Edgar Hoover.

1967.

2544

A young parson professing in Vynn
Said he thought fornication was sin.
But a girl said, " You fool! "—
Went and whipped out his tool,
Pulled her drawers off and shoved his thing in.

1967A.

2545

A nymphomaniacal Wac
Had a certain amorous knack:
    Her erotic resources
    So pleased the Armed Forces
That she fought the whole war on her back.

1945R.

2546

Perhaps I have mentioned Miss Wade?
A most reprehensible jade:
    It's stuck in her head
    She'll get knocked up in bed,
So she stands on her head to get laid.

1965.

2547

There was a young Moslem from Ware
Who had not one wife but a pair.
    The fact was, he said,
    That being in bed
He could tell them apart—to a hair!

1948.

2548. LIFE IN A PENTHOUSE

Our playboy this month is well-dressed,
His Jaguar just matches his vest.
    He has sexy conceits
    And a pantsful of pleats,
But his penis is *not* of the best.

1977A.

2549

There was an old duffer named West
Whose pecker came up to his chest.
    He said, "I declare!
    I have no pubic hair."
So he covered his nuts with his vest.

1955.

2550

A sexy young virgin said, " What
Shall I do with my elegant twat?
It's so wet and so hot,
And it's itching a lot—
Oh God! shall I wipe it or not? "

1968A.

2551

A Vassar professor named Whipple
Loved to suck on a girl student's nipple.
Though he did it with ardor,
His prick got no harder,
And he climaxed with hardly a ripple.

1970A.

2552

Quiff, quahog, and whiskey
Were the passions at Point Zabriskie.
Not to mention some boys,
A few lesbian joys—
Salubrious, silly, but risky.

1967K.

2553

When a young boy turns into a whore,
He should take lots of cold cream and pour
In some sweet sassafras,
Rub the stuff up his ass,
And it ain't necessarily sore.

1967.

2554

Said a naked young lady of Willow
While placing a polka dot pillow
Beneath her trim bum:
" Sex is sinful to some,
But to me it's a mere peckerdillo! "

1965.

2555. THE NIGHT OF THE DINOSAUR

A dinosaur pair were a wonder
When he was on top and she under.
Her whale of a tail
Knocked down trees like a gale,
And his pounding resounded like thunder.

[2556]

When a dinosaur got an erection
He did it slow, section by section.
Gibraltar'd look small
Beside either ball,
Or Niagara by his ejection.

[2557]

A dinosaur male found his bride
Could not give him the usual ride.
For the weight of his freight
And her tail were too great,
So they fucked lying each on a side.

[2558]

When a dinosaur entered the quim
Of his mate, they had both gone to swim,
For their weight on the land
Was unliftably grand,
Including his masculine limb.

[2559]

When a dinosaur wanted a male,
She must bury a seed without fail,
Then be patient, poor dear :
It took many a year
Till a tree was upbearing her tail.

1970.

2560

When fucking, a lady of Woking
Reacted so fast to the poking
That her gyratory motion
Caused heat and commotion,
And her arsehole and cunt started smoking.

1975.

2561. SPEAK FOR YOURSELF, JOHN

Lewis Carroll lived (some note with wrath)
Loving paronomasia and math.
And they swear that it's true
He was like me and you:
A pedophile *and* psychopath.

1967.

2562

There was a young juggler named Wruggling
Who attempted coitus while juggling.
And today in my dreams
I can still hear his screams,
And his tormented cries and his struggling.

1975.

2563. THE VOYEUR SPEAKS:

Through back alleys in Wuthering Heights
I sneak around peeping, of nights.
To most windows I creep
I find folks fast asleep,
But I sure see some fine pillow-fights.

[2564.] THE SPHERES REPLY:

When the sexes are found in conjunction,
Performing love's physical function,
That's no time for prying
And telescope spying—
So *beat* it, bub! Show some compunction!

1965.

XVII

SCIENCE FICTION

2565

Our ambassador to Venus, Mz. Abner,
Hoped the lesbian Veenies would be havin'er.
    But to her surprise
    They crossed all six thighs,
While the masculine Weenies were grabbin'er!

1976A.

2566

Most females, it seems, can't absorb it,
For the virile emission of Corbett
    Extrudes far too fast:
    The results of his blast
Are ten dollies today out in orbit.

1966.

2567

A gorgeous and shapely young alien,
Who was quite beyond question mammalian,
    Once slipped on a stair
    And fell through the air,
And her proof of it stuck in the railien.

1968G.

2568. VAGINA DENTATA

A man back from Alpha Centauri
Told a perfectly horrible story:
    Their women have teeth
    Both above and beneath,
And whatever goes in, comes out gory.

1963B.

2569

The lecherous men of Altair
Fuck sitting upright in a chair.
So when you are seated
And joyously greeted—
Beware, Earth woman, beware!

1952.

2570

An alien, anthropomorphic,
Quite handsome, but definitely dworphic,
Had not one wife, but three . . .
And 'twas rumored that he
As a lover was slightly terrorphic.

1968G.

2571

Of Burroughs, it's safe to assume
He wished that Freud lay in a tomb.
But Innes's ride
To the Earth's inner side :
What is that but Return to the Womb?

1963B.

2572

A creature once lived on an asteroid,
A strangely desexed little basteroid.
He might have been *Her*
But you couldn't be sher—
If *She* was a *He,* he'd been casteroid.

1968G.

2573

There was a young girl from Barsoom
Who took a Thark up to her room.
He was three times her size,
And proportioned likewise,
But in no time she lowered his boom.

1963B.

2574

There once was a physicist named Bohr
Who said on Pigalle to a whore:
 "I'm full of hv
 How about a good screw?
Why, that's what my Fulbright is for!"

1960.

2575

There was an old German named Brecht
Whose penis was seldom erect.
 When his wife heard him humming
 She knew he was coming—
An example of Döppler effect.

1974A.

2576

An innocent maiden from Brighton
Had a night that was rather excitin':
 She was raped by a slan,
 Three Martians, one man,
And a slimy green monster from Titan.

1963B.

2577

There was a young spaceman named Brimbles
Who mounted his girl while on gimbals.
 And he marked the conclusion
 Of their curious fusion
With a violent crash on brass cymbals!

1975.

2578

A maiden from distant Capella
Once married an Earthian fella.
 Their offspring were queers,
 With cunts in their ears,
And their pricks were striped purple and yella.

1963B.

2579

The mechanical natives of Cetus
Do not start out as a fetus.
    But nuts and the screw
    To them are not new,
So they must have some form of coitus.

1952.

2580

Under Venus's blanket of cloud
That hides it from Earth like a shroud,
    Winged people cavort
    In sexual sport
By methods of which they are proud.

1952.

2581. BEYOND JUPITER

When the race for the stars runs its course,
And we invade with a Female Task Force,
    Will our sterile embrace
    In cold outer space
Be called fucking, or just " outercourse "?

1970A.

2582

The love life of Jovian creatures
Has many curious features.
    If I just owned a ship
    I'd take me a trip,
And bring some to Earth as teachers.

1952.

2583. "SO SORRY"

The people in other dimensions
Have organs with hyperextensions.
    They can sneak up on you
    And give you a screw
Before you've divined their intentions.

1952-1970.

2584. SOLAR SYSTEM'S SEXUAL SURVEY

A Mercurian male, although elfin,
Is unable to thrust all himself in,
    Throughout the hot season
    For one private reason—
A cunt at 2000 degs. Kelvin.

[2585.] VENUS

On Venus, I'm bound to relate,
The females refuse to fellate.
    For the cocks of the guys
    Have got spines, spikes, and eyes
Tasting strongly of smegma sulphate.

[2586.] EARTH

The Venusians, out on a mission,
Found Earth in a puzzling condition.
    They could understand part
    Of our laws and our art,
But got stuck in the fifteenth position.

[2587.] THE MOON

Vita brevis, ars longa, is true,
As the better-read Lunatics knew.
    They looked much as we,
    But the light gravitee
Made head bigger and ars longa too.

[2588.] MARS

An upper-crust Martian said, "Yes,
We old families are snobs, I confess.
    It really is vital
    To get tits *and* title."
So he married a cute Martioness.

[2589.] THE ASTEROIDS

Though the music of love is Schubérty,
Love itself here is sordidly dirty.
    The men are all queer
    Till their ninety-ninth year,
While the menopause strikes at pubérty.

[2590.] CERES

On account of its orbital sloth,
A lover on Ceres is loath
    To propagate coldly
    Or fornicate boldly,
So sometimes he simply does both.

[2591.] JUPITER

Girls are something Jove's planet has not:
There is only one huge, flaming twot,
    Soaking up like a sponge
    All the men as they plunge—
On Terra, it's called the Red Spot.

[2592.] SATURN

On Saturn the sexes are three,
A nuisance, I think you'll agree.
    For performing *con brio*
    You must have a trio,
While it even takes two for a pee.

[2593.] URANUS

On Uranus, to shout " Up your anus! "
Is to get yourself rated insane, as
    The arse is no hole
    But a flexible pole
From which the piles grow like banánas.

[2594.] NEPTUNE

There's a season in Neptune's affairs
When the lovers get frozen in pairs.
    Though the sunshine's appealin'
    Towards perihelion,
It's for Winter they all say their prayers.

[2595.] PLUTO

The Plutonian male is so small
He lives in the vaginal wall.
    He dreams of seductions,
    Wild rapes and abductions—
Much like you and me, after all.

1974.

2596

Flash Gordon, when looking for fun,
Poked Dale with his little space gun.
    Murmured she, "I'm not shy,
    But quick, button your fly—
In comics that just isn't *done!*"

1970.

2597. A FIG FOR NEWTON

A spaceman and girl in free fall
Obeyed the progenitive call.
    But Newton's Third Rule
    Grabbed hold of his tool,
And shot him across to the wall.

1952.

2598

A robot named Gamma Thirteen
Once seduced a computing machine.
    But his bold intromission
    Caused nuclear fission—
Who knows what the kids might have been?

1963B.

2599

A space jockey now is old Hall,
With his famous octagonal ball.
And his bifocal penis
When weighed upon Venus
Still equals pi times fuck-all!

1971A.

2600

Poor Joe-Jim, with one extra head,
Could not have a woman in bed.
"Since I cannot abet you,
I never will let you,
For *I'm* no voyeur!" each head said.

1970.

2601

There once was a fellow named Hector
Whose tool had a sector-trajector,
To correct for the mass,
And the heat of the ass,
And the bore and the stroke and the vector.

1975.

2602

A girl who was raped by a humanoid
Soon felt life in her abdumanoid.
But the pregnancy was
Not quite average because
In darkness her belly was luminoid.

1968G.

2603

The legs of a lady named Ida
Were quite a potential divider,
But she thought it much cuter
To act as computer,
And have rigid digits inside her.

1954.

2604

An impotent robot called Jack
Had a brain like a cool Univac.
    But nothing handy for sex,
    Just this dandy cortex—
He hadn't been tooled for dual-sack.

1955A.

2605

There was a young spaceman named Joe
Who was making a spacegirl too slow.
    She said, "Don't be morbid;
    Eject into orbit,
Because all of my systems are '*Go!*'"

1959*

2606

The Flying Men coming from Jupiter
Have sexual habits far stupider
    Than ours when we're shady:
    Their way with a lady
Is nothing but looping-the-loopiter.

1970.

2607

There was a young man of Khartoum,
The strength of whose balls was his doom.
    So strong was his shootin',
    The third law of Newton
Propelled the poor chap to the Moon.

1954A.

2608

The choice of a Jovian king
Is determined by the size of his ding.
    Unscrupulous lechers
    Use pecker-stretchers,
And pumps to inflate their thing.

1952-1957A.

2609. STARSHIP "ENTERPRISE"

A starship commander named Kirk
Emerged from his cabin berserk.
He grabbed a girl yeoman
Beneath the abdomen,
And gave her a physical jerk.

[2610]

A girl of the *Enterprise* crew
Refused every offer to screw.
But a Vulcan named Spock
Crawled under her smock,
And now she is eating for two.

[2611]

There was a young spaceman named Gene
Who left Earth, never more to be seen.
At a point out in space
He essayed the embrace
Of a girl who was contra-terrene.

[2612]

The *Enterprise* girls, so one hears,
Have chased Spock for several years.
His look of disdain
Has spared them great pain,
For his prick is as sharp as his ears.

[2613]

The work of Mess Sergeant Potgieter
Is not merely reading a meter.
By orders of Kirk
A part of his work
Is dosing the food with saltpeter.

[2614]

Said crew girl Angelica Bauer:
"The captain's withdrawn, cold, and sour."
Uhúra said, "No,
At night that's not so—
He doesn't withdraw for an hour."

[2615]

McCoy's a seducer galore,
And of virgins he has quite a score.
He tells them, "My dear,
You're the Final Frontier,
Where man never has gone before."

[2616]

There once was a spaceman named Spock
Who had a huge Vulcanized cock.
A girl from Missouri
Whose name was Uhúra
Just fainted away from the shock.

[2617]

The *Enterprise* crew when off work
Will fuck like an Ottoman Turk.
Uhúra the Zulu
Is shacked up with Sulu,
And Spock shares a crew girl with Kirk.

[2618]

Each Friday his engines abort,
But Scotty is never caught short.
He fills his machines
With space-navy beans,
And farts the ship back into port.

[2619]

An *Enterprise* crewman named Amos
Became universally famous
When his penis one night
Went up out of sight,
And deflowered six virgins on Deimos.

[2620]

The prick of the engineer, Scott,
Fell off from Saturnian rot.
He went to the basement
And made a replacement
Of tungsten and plastic and snot.

[2621]

Though most of the crewmen are whites,
Uhúra has full equal rights.
Her crewmates, you see,
Love De-mo-cra-cy,
And the way that she fills out her tights.

1967B.

2001½. DEUS EX MACHINA

A film impresario named Kubrick
Made computers and space-jocks his rubric.
When they cried, " There's no sex! "
He tried Clockwork effects—
Rape, buggery, and foul blows sub-pubric.

1972A.

2623

When I read my first S.F. literature
I was struck by the front-cover piterature :
A beautiful girl
On some alien wirl
Being (*er*) wooed by an alien criterature.

1968G.

2624

An explorer from Earth named MacCrimmon
Found a planet of nothing but women.
When he asked how they bred
Without husbands, they said :
" There's an ocean of sperm that we swim in. "

1963B.

2625

A young astronaut named McGraw
Sailed his spaceship with never a flaw.
But when he tried to maneuver
His girlfriend's *hors d'œuvre,*
They went into a roll, pitch, and yaw.

1975.

2626

A nympho named Pussy McManus
Had a very good time on Uranus.
The native male's dong
Is exceedingly long,
So she took them by way of her anus.

1952-1957*

2627

Mercurians, female and male,
Whenever they rip off some tail,
Do all of their lovin'
Inside a hot oven,
And think of us Earthlings as frail.

1963B.

2628

The sex-maddened natives of Mars
Don't make out with women in cars.
Instead, it's their custom
To rush in and bust 'em
On the floors of cafés and in bars.

1970.

2629

There was a young fellow from Mars
Whose cock was all covered with scars.
He'd tell you, when candid,
That when it expanded
It frequently bumped into stars.

1963B.

2630. THE MYSTERY UNVEILED

Those little green boogers from Mars
Shit tobacco in neighborhood bars.
Right there in the crapper
They put on the wrapper—
And that's how we get cheap cigars!

1965.

2631

An aerodynamicist's mate
Was reviling the orderings of Fate,
For the configuration
Of their connubial relation
Was prismoidal instead of oblate.

1959*

2632

A rocketship captain named Mills
Was fond of uranium pills.
This powerful tonic
Made his farts supersonic,
And sent him far over the hills.

1952.

2633. BUG-EYED MONSTER

There once was a BEM from Neptune
Who had balls like a purple baboon.
So long was his thing
That, from Saturn's first ring,
He could bugger the Man in the Moon.

1963B.

2634. TESSERACT TESS

There was a young girl from North Carolina
Who had a tesseract for a vagina.
  She was raped one day
  In a 4-D way,
By a Möbius dick clear from China.

1952.

[2635]

The tesseract tale of Sweet Sue
Is a libel and grossly untrue.
  While the Chinamen stand
  With their . . . cash in their hand,
The Hindus, with ESP, jump the queue.

1954*

2636

A young man of Novorossisk
Had a mating procedure so brisk,
  With such superspeed action
  The Lorentz contraction
Foreshortened his prick to a disk.

1946-1951A.

2637

A charming French miss named Odette
Set a record for sex in a jet.
  At speeds supersonic
  Her vagina went clonic,
And her orgasms haven't stopped yet.

1960.

2638

The Venusians do not kiss or pet,
Nor work themselves up in a sweat.
  As to sex : they get wed,
  Then all feeling goes dead—
How like our Earth can you get?

1970A.

2639

The epicene natives of Pollux
Engage in the strangest of frollux :
  They get their sex kicks
  Sucking martini sticks,
Which makes them, of course, alcohollux.

1960A.

2640

A girl of Terrestrial race
Tamed a terrible monster of space.
  Though its kind lacked a dong
  She took it along,
For its tentacles served in that place.

1952.

2641

On the inmost Saturnian ring
I found me a very good thing :
  She had two good cunts,
  And knew many stunts—
For instance, with one she could sing.

1952.

2642. " 7/6THS OF THE TEXTS "

The quasi-statistical screw
Is physically something quite new :
  Differentially slow
  Its nature is so,
That it's still going on when you're through.

1960.

2643

A space marine taken in shame
On a new-subdued world with a dame,
  Confessed at his trial :
  " I know it was vile—
I conquered, I saw, and I came. "

ff. 1970.

2644

The natives of Sirius B
Excrete pure vitamin C.
    In symbiotic
    Relations exotic,
Terrestrials suck them with glee.

1952.

2645

If you honeymoon out in space
There's this that you'll have to face :
    In a state of free fall
    There is no weight at all,
And your pecker just won't stay in place.

1952.

2646

The meteor miners of space
Never lose their preëminent place.
    Their suits, I suppose,
    Can be joined by a hose
To a girl's to replenish the race.

1952.

2647. A MÖBIUS RIPOFF

Yes, he screwed her, but under great tension :
'Twas done with severe apprehension.
    She possessed (to be blunt)
    A true Klein-bottle cunt—
Now his prick's in another dimension.

1967.

2648

Two monsters who hailed from Uranus
Preferred to fuck each other's anus.
    They said, " Earth girls are cute,
    And they're willing, to boot,
But they're not deep enough to contain us. "

1963B.

2649

The handsome young natives of Venus
Have a three-foot retractable penis.
The women of Earth
All contend for a berth
To the world of this curious genus.

1952.

2650

There was a young spaceman from Venus
Who had a prodigious penis.
Cried his girlfriend, " Alas!
It just came out my ass,
And there's still fifteen inches between us. "

1963B.

2651

There was a young man from Woonsocket
Who flew to the Moon on a rocket.
The rocket went bang,
His balls went twang,
And they found his cock in his pocket.

1946-1973*

2652. THE HOBBITS

An Ent-wife of five thousand years
Was enthralled by a Hobbit named Piers.
This Halfling, 'tis said,
Would shove in his head,
And vomit while wiggling his ears.

1963B.

2653

A girl from the twin suns of Xentacles
Was attacked by a thing with six tentacles.
It was big as a moose
But she promptly got loose
By kicking it right in the gentacles.

1968G.

2654. THE MARTIAN CHRONICLES

Een rashondenkweker in Drongen
Die wilde een teefje doen jongen.
  Daarom nam hij een reu,
  Maar die werd het vlug beu,
En toen is hij er zelf op gesprongen.

[TRANSLATION]

A pedigreed dog breeder in Drongen
Wanted one of his bitches to pup.
  So he took a male dog
  Who got tired of it soon,
And so he jumped on her himself.

2655

Een kerel in Hoedekenskerken
Die wilde een hoertje bewerken.
  Maar in al zijn haast
  Schoot hij er naast—
Dat is aan de vloer nog te merken.

[TRANS.]

There once was a guy in Hoedekenskerken
Who wanted to do a young whore.
  But in his hurry
  He shot nearby—
You can still see it on the floor.

2656

Er was eens een maagd in Wuustwezel
Die doorging voor zuurzoete kwezel.
  Maar eens, na een bal,
  Hoorde iedereen " knal "—
En er WAS eens een maagd in Wuustwezel.

[TRANS.]

There was a young virgin in Wuustwezel
Whom everyone thought an old spinster.
But once after a ball
Everyone heard "ping"—
And there WAS a young virgin in Wuustwezel.

2657

Er was eens een man in Timboektoe
Die ging op een dag naar een hoer toe.
Hij kwam er buiten
Wel zonder zijn duiten,
Maar hij knoopte tevreden zijn broek toe.

[TRANS.]

There once was a man in Timbuktoo
Who went one day to a prostitute.
He came out of the house
Without his money, of course,
But buttoned up his pants satisfied.

2658

Er was eens een meisje uit Urk
Die st:' in haar gaatje een kurk.
Toen kwam de pastoor,
Die kon er niet door,
Maar hij stak ze van achter, de schurk.

[TRANS.]

There was a young girl from Urk
Who put in her cunt a cork.
Then came the pastor,
He couldn't get through it,
So he took her from behind, the skunk.

2659

Er was eens een meisje in Naarden
Die had een heel erg behaarde.
    Nieman kreeg het klaar,
    Behalve een Huzaar,
Die kende het nog van bij de paarden.

[TRANS.]

There once was a girl in Naarden
Who had a very hairy cunt.
    No one could handle it
    Except for a hussar,
Who knew all about it from the horses.

2660

Er was een sadiste in Landen
Die sloeg elke man op zijn handen.
    Ze krabte en beet,
    En was onnoemlijk wreed—
Want ze had nog een kutje met tanden.

[TRANS.]

There was a sadistic lady in Landen
Who beat all the men on their hands.
    She scratched and she bit,
    And was incredibly cruel—
She even had a little cunt with teeth.

2661

Een zaadhandelaartje uit Duiven
Ging heel de nacht fuiven.
    Maar bij dageraad
    Liet hij zijn zaad
In de voor van een hoerebeest schuiven.

[TRANS.]

A seed merchant in Duiven
Made whoopee the whole night.
But at sunrise
He sowed his seed
In the furrow of a whore.

2662

De burgemeester van Drachten
Die wilde zijn dochter verkrachten.
Maar die vent had een strop
Want zijn zoon zat er op,
En toen moest hij vijf minuten wachten.

[TRANS.]

The mayor of Drachten
Wanted to rape his daughter.
But he'd a bit of bad luck,
Because his son was on her,
So he had to wait nearly five minutes.

2663

Er was eens een meisje uit Lillo
Die leek sprekend op Venus van Milo.
Korte armpjes allicht,
Maar als tegengewicht
Had ze borsten van bij de tien kilo.

[TRANS.]

There once was a girl from Lillo
Who looked exactly like Venus de Milo.
Very short arms, of course,
But to balance things
She had breasts weighing ten kilo.

2664

Er was eens een meid uit de Lemmer
Die had een kut als een emmer.
    Iedere man die zijn worst
    In haar pruim steken dorst
Riep vertwijfeld : " O help, 'k ben geen zwemmer! "

[TRANS.]

There once was a girl from Lemmer
Who had a cunt like a bucket.
    Every man who dared
    To stick his sausage in her cherry
Cried desperately : " Help, I'm no swimmer! "

2665

Er was eens een meisje uit Petten
Die wilde graag koffie zetten.
    Ze dronk hem niet puur
    Maar de melk was te duur,
Daarom tapte ze maar van haar tetten.

[TRANS.]

There once was a girl from Petten
Who liked to make coffee.
    She didn't like it straight,
    But milk was too expensive
So she tapped it right from her tits.

2666

Er was eens een meisje uit Sussen
Die wilde haar vrijer slechts kussen.
    Zij gaf hem een pieper,
    Maar hij wilde dieper
En dat deed hij dan ook ondertussen.

[TRANS.]

There was a young girl from Sussen
Who only wanted to kiss her lover.
She gave him a smack
But he wanted her crack,
So that's what he did in-between.

2667

Er was eens een hoer uit Den Helder
Die kroop met een boer in de kelder.
Die vent stak zijn pik
In de vouw van haar mik :
Op haar kut groeit er nu een knolselder.

[TRANS.]

There once was a whore from The Helder
Who crept with a farmer in the cellar.
This man put his prick
In the fold of her crotch :
On her quim there's now growing a turnip.

2668

Er was eens een meisje in Londen,
Die had een kapotje gevonden.
Ze vroeg aan een knul :
" Zeg, wil jij hem om je lul?
Want weggooien is toch zo'n zonde. "

[TRANS.]

There was a young lady named Kitty,
Who found a safe in the city.
She asked a young fool :
" D'you want it 'round your tool?
'Cause to throw it away is a pity. "

1964.

XVIII

CHAMBER OF HORRORS

2669

There was a young girl whose acoustical
Acuity matched her statistical
    Ingenuity : from
    The faint squish of a come
She could tell the sperm-count of a testicle.

1957J.

2670

There was a weird fellow most adipose,
'Twas a rare day indeed if his pecker rose.
    He found that cunt sucking
    Was worse than no fucking—
The pussy juice made his beard crepitose.

1971 *ff*.

2671

A girl was frequently annoying
Her boyfriends by coyly employing
    Hawaiian guitars
    To cover her arse :
When fucked from the back, she went *boeing*!

1954.

2672. HIPSTER

I go for fads new and arcane :
Crippled girls, shooting shit—that's my name!
    I'm a sadist, a hustler,
    A reformed pussy-muzzler ;
Square head-shrinkers say I'm insane.

1977A.

2673

A large, colored dyke from Atlanta
Said, " If ya' mus' know dear, I plan tuh
Finger-fuck Mother Hayes
On Tahmes Squah fo' three days.
It's a project that's sponsored by ANTA. "

1967.

2674

Said the Duke to the Duchess of Avery :
" I trust I'm not disturbing your reverie?
You've been sitting on *Punch*
Since long before lunch—
May I have it? I find cunt unsavoury. "

1958A.

2675

The impotent Bishop of Bilbo
Used his walking stick as a dildo.
His gal, with a grunt,
Took it all up her cunt—
Her sex life was utterly killed though.

1958.

2676

Now, when you go out on a binge, Les,
I'm sure that the fellows would cringe less
If your Brooks Brothers suit
Were a little less cute—
You know, not so much lace, dear, and fringeless.

1967.

2677. NON CONSCIENTIUS

Out behind the barn Willie fucked Binnie,
Though she's bowlegged, crosseyed, and skinny.
He's been heard to declare :
" Out this way, cunts are rare,
And with a hardon, you'll fuck any! "

1966.

2678

A hoodlum took out a tough bit,
And by her surprisingly got hit.
He sneered, " What's da catch?
I just felt ya snatch. "
" You jerk, " she replied, " first the tit. "

ff. 1963A.

2679

A French woman *maquis* named Blérot
Who took Winston C. for her hero,
Said : " He told the *Entente*
'Twould be hard, tough, and long,
And the chance of withdrawal was zero. "

1969A.

2680

There was a young lady from Cincinnati
Who liked hearing the rain go pitti-patti.
Her lover did too,
And when they would scroo,
He'd tap a tattoo on her titti-tatti.

1968.

2681

If on self-abuse you'll concentrate,
You can understand odd young Miss Straight.
She will say, " A burst meat, "
Or she'll cry, " Ma rubs teat! "
(Anagrams for the word " masturbate. ")

1967.

2682. ABLE WAS I ERE I SAW MELBA

There was an incestuous Corsican
Whose only delight was to force kin.
He fucked his kid sister
Till he raised such a blister
That now he can't pull back his foreskin.

1955J.

2683

A voyeur was caught in the dark as
He spied on erotic car parkers ;
    But when told to desist
    Said, " I just can't resist
Couples who lark when they're starkers. "

1968A.

2684

There was a young fellow named Dave
Whose demeanor was icy and grave.
    He claimed such great effort
    To keep his cock inert
Was why this expression he gave.

1971*ff*.

2685

That orator Señor Demosthenes
Said, " Girls show too much when they cross
    their knees. "
    But all of the flappers
    Just out of di-apers
Cried, " Stupid men never shall boss the knees! "

1950.

2686. THE PASSIONATE ALBION

Said a forward young damsel of Dijon
To her timorous swain, " Why, you're shy, John.
    Since at billing & cooing
    There's not very much doing,
Do you mind if I undo your fly, John? "

1968A.

2687

There was a young steno from Dorset
Who let her boss see her new corset.
    He wrote her a check
    As she lay on her back,
And then took down his pants to endorse it.

1968A.

2688

A scrusading newspaper editor,
A studsman, beast, sex fiend, and prédator,
Got a madam dismayed
Saying, " Look for a raid,
If you don't promptly become my best creditor. "
1966.

2689. CHIRPS FROM A PURPLE TWERP

There was a young poet named Earp
Who was moved by his Maker to chirp.
Blithe Spirit! the lark
He would dare in the dark,
That the Nightingale used to use Earp.

[2690]

He moistened his gullet with turp-
entine, and he sang to the purp-
le night skies of velvet,
But when it struck twelve, it
Was bedtime for well-behaved Earp.

[2691]

He sang of the new moon and her p-
ale Beauty, till neighbours cried, " Sir p-
lease remember that what
You think touches the spot,
To us may appear a ple-hurp! "
1924C.

2692

A suspicious old husband from Funtua
To his wife said, " How bulky in front you are.
You have not been imprudent,
I should hope, with some student? "
She replied, " Really, dear, how blunt you are! "
1968A.

2693

A baby was born to Miss Gellicutt,
Delivered by means of a belly cut.
After sewing the patch
The doc tickled her snatch.
She awoke and exclaimed, " You're indelicate. "

1975.

2694

An ascetic parochial graduate
Made a vow that he never would masturbate.
But his glans grew so firm
And so loaded with sperm,
That a glance was enough to ejaculate.

1957J.

2695

Said a crafty old doctor named Hammon :
"Im*po*tence is getting too common.
Pills, oysters, and honey
Are sheer waste of money.
What works, is to bed a fresh woman. "

1969A.

2696

A sea cruising widow named Hassage
Declared that her quim needed massage.
The ship's masseur, vile,
Did the job with a file,
And gave her a very rough passage.

1968A.

2697

A gay young Lothario, Hazlitt,
Likes to feed every flame that he has lit.
Rare the cunt who denies
When that look in his eyes
Hints a fuck that is certain to frazzle it.

1954J.

2698

There once preached an old hierophant,
On the subject of sex most adamant.
Anything that deterred
From sex was absurd :
" Fuck thou " was his singular chant.

1971 *ff*.

2699

I *don't* think you want to fuck *him,* Rick.
For, though he is slender and trim, Rick,
When you say, " Let us lay, "
He will answer, " O.K.,
But first let me tell you this limerick! "

1967.

2700

There once was a heavy-hung Hindu
Who coaxed every maid, " Let me in-do! "
His drooping mustache
Would tickle her gash,
And the hair on his balls made her grin, too!

1971 *ff*.

2701

An agile young fräulein of Innsbruck,
It seems very lightly her sins took.
She stood ten men in line,
Screwed them one at a time,
And then two at a time she ten twins took.

1975.

2702. DELUSIONS OF GLANDEUR

A volcanic eruption in Java
Led the Baron of Fritzil Palaver,
In that moment sublime,
To bequeath for all time
The imprint of his balls in the lava.

1968A.

2703

An exotic young lady quite kooky,
Once danced in a troupe of Kabuki.
When asked for a fuck
She said, "Sorry, no luck;
I've got ants in my pants, but no nooky."

1960A.

2704

The holy Theosophist, Leadbeater,
At a *battue,* who said to the head beater:
"Your prick I am crazy
To suck, but I'm lazy—
Just fuck your five fingers instead, beater."

1920C.

2705

Said her brother, the host, "You must lemme, sis,
Proclaim that martini's your nemesis.
One or two, I have found,
Make your heels go quite round,
And I *won't* have you laid on my premises."

1972.

2706

"I think that my boyfriend from Limerick,
On the whole had a longer and slimmer wick.
But yours, dear, is thicker,
And slick past the knicker—
As a sticker far quicker and trimmer, Dick."

1973.

2707

There once was a fighter named London
Who gave and took blows with abandon.
But a boxer named Clay
Knocked him K.O. ¡*Olé*!
And they carried him off in a condom.

1966M.

2708

An innocent girl said : " Lumme, Mum!
I fear I shall soon be a mummy, Mum.
    Knobs yes! it was fun,
    When we did what we done,
But he lied when he called it a dummy run. "

1968A.

2709

A honeymoon couple from Lunn
Found the bedsprings were so overstrung
    That the rhythm soon harassed
    Their duet and embarrassed—
So they left the finale unsung.

1968A.

2710

There was an old maid named McComb
Who liked her men tall and handsóme.
    (She could also make do
    With a finger or two,
Or the tip of her calloused old thumb.)

1972*

2711. THERE'LL ALWAYS BE AN ENGLAND

A Britain-backing bawd name of Maud
All loyal Britons will applaud.
    For she went to the States,
    Where she charged double rates,
Thus earning many dollars abroad.

1968A.

2712

The son of a stingy old miser
Couldn't buy any tail, so he'd try, sir,
    To fulfill expectation
    By slow masturbation,
And now he's a real human geyser.

1945R.

2713. ELECTION BY ERECTION

" All right, you bastards! " cried Norton,
" Of the people's choice there'll be no thwartin'.
    My opponent may be
    A true statesman—not me!—
But his pecker is surely a short'un! "

1976A.

2714

There was a short-kilted North Briton
Who promiscuously sat on a kitten.
    But the kitten had claws—
    The immediate cause
Of that North Briton's abrupt circumcision.

1968A.

2715. BLACK BACKLASH

There once was a passel of Negroes
In the land where the coconut tree grows.
    Said one, " I must say,
    After fucking all day,
I find that my sense of fatigue grows. "

1968A.

2716

A contortionist, eager and nubile,
Interlocked with the Duchess of Argyll.
    At the climactic point
    He fractured his joint,
And the Duke had him buried in style.

1971 *ff*.

2717

For Jason, the one panacea
Was to fuck (up the ass) his Medea.
    But a germ in her box
    Gave the poor man the pox :
It's reported she had a dire rear.

1967.

2718

There was a young man from Panama
Who took a very strong enema.
It blew out his guts,
All over his nuts,
So he won't take an enema *any* more.

1953.

2719

A vulgar old fellow named Petri
Has canine habits excrétory.
Every night after dark
He visits the park,
And lifts up his leg at each pee-tree.

1954J.

2720

Bill Jones is a lad who will pluck some
Fast tail from the slim or the buxom.
But when he met Bunnie,
And tried out her cunny,
He swore that no whore was so fucksome.

1950.

2721. HIRSUTER (HER SUITOR)

When she met a man pogonotrophic,
She fixed on thoughts only erotic.
Till one day she was scratched
By one really tough-thatched—
Incidentally, turned out lycanthropic.

1971*ff*.

2722

There once was an old Gallup pollster
Whose ego much needed a bolster.
So he charmed little girls
And showed them his curls,
And acquired local fame as a molester.

1971A.

2723

A divorcée, as cold as popsicles,
Waived all her ex-husband's nickels.
She transplanted, instead,
To each side of her head
Two earrings carved from his testicles.

1970A.

2724

If Puqua is called Puckaway
As it is in Wis. a-lack-a-day,
What would you do
If it happened to you
To meet Miss Hope U. Fuqua?

1915*

2725

There was a young man from Purdue
Whose bride was both bold and untrue.
When his friends called him cuckold,
This young bridegroom chuckled :
" So what? I'd much rather yoo-hoo! "

1959*

2726

There was a young miss from the Pyrenees
Who was diddled so much she had weary knees,
A distended quim,
With no hair on the rim,
And gism from navel to smeary knees.

1950.

2727. MENÉ MENÉ TEKAL

A ballistical student named Rafferty
Went down to the gentlemen's lavat'ry.
When the walls met his sight,
He said, " Newton was right—
This must be the center of graffiti. "

1968A.

2728

There was a young shipwright named Roos
Who made all the toilets too loose.
With a clash and a clatter
They sprayed so much water,
One took either an enema or a douche.

1942M.

2729

A bell-ringing, Mid-eastern ruler
Caught his wife on the roof with Abdullah.
Said he to this shagger,
As he lunged with his dagger :
" My cupola is *not* a copúla! "

1967A.

2730. DEMOCRATIC FOOTNOTE

Our candidates vie in servility
While pretending to heights of humility.
They would jack off a goat
To garner that vote,
And end up as a public liability.

1973A.

2731

Sex^1 and Sex^2 and Sextera,
Of these some are the bettera.
But few of the many
Are worse than not any,
And sad are the ones who can't gettera.

1953.

2732. THE WORLD'S WORST LIMERICK

Da-da-da, da-da-da, da-da
Da-da-da, da-da-da, da-da
Da-da-da, da-da-da
Da-da-da, da-da-da
Da-da-da, da-da-da, da-*shit*!

1948.

2733

I'm terribly sorry you're sick, Nick,
And I'm glad that the poison's not strychnic.
It's that fat girl you ate—
What's her name? Oh, yes, Kate.
You just overate on the pyknic.

1967.

2734

There was a young lady of Spitz
Who wobbled her "thirty-eight" tits,
Whilst her boyfriend, a Pole,
Got that up her hole,
Till she was fucked, squirming, for "six."

1953U.

2735

An impressionable curate from Stamms
Said, "These mini-skirt girls are such lambs.
But my duties I'm lax in,
And my vows get such cracks in,
When from my knees I see all their young hams."

1968A.

2736

This book on erotical theme
Contains a poem, "*Doigts Obscène,*"
The which, who can doubt,
Is the author's bold shout
How he felt up some twats *bohème.*

1969.

2737

Into a bordello in Tiflis
Strode the latter-day image of Triphallus.
Three whores strove with might
To provide him delight,
But the outcome was tertiary syphilis.

1956J.

2738

Aging old queers are no treat :
Sucking cocks, raping kids, smelling feet.
They talk like a preacher,
Pervert every creature,
And worry about being indiscreet.

1970A.

2739

A man who could *not* find a twat hole
Attempted to diddle a knothole,
When a dog took a quick
Snap! and bit off his prick—
Where the man once had prong, now he's *got* hole.

1950.

2740

A misogynist stubborn and volatile
Was compelled to perform matters coital.
He'd once lost his head,
And by shotgun was wed,
Though he raged that he'd rather be stoical.

1971 *ff.*

2741

A sailor who sails o'er the wave'll
See a girl ; what the seaman will crave'll
Be more than a feel,
Love her up until she'll
Suck the semen 'neath his naval navel.

1950.

2742

I'm lascivious too, in my way,
Not straight and not beat and not gay.
But the sight of brass rowlocks
Makes me reach for my bollocks,
With the thought I'd best hide them away.

1970A.

2743

The fellows that live on West Nichols
Are forever scratching their testicles,
For a tailor at Wallachs
Likes to fit young men's bollocks
Into trousers so tight that the " dress " tickles.

1956J.

2744. CALLIPYGIAN

Fucking birds is, for old Mister Widgeon,
A comfort not unlike religion.
He fell madly in love
With a gay, big-assed dove
Whom he named (here's the pun) Cal E. Pigeon.

1967.

2745

A wanton young lady of Wimbley,
Reproached for not acting quite primly,
Replied : " Heavens above!
I know sex isn't love,
But it's *such* an attractive facsimile. "

1962A.

2746. MY AN-DRO-GYNE !

Three faggots got ploughed on May wine,
And, dressed in high drag screamed, " Divine! "
Amid giggles and shrieks
They behaved like the Greeks,
And harmonized " Sweet Androgyne. "

1967.

2747

My dear, I'm an absolute wreck!
Just had lunch with Madame Sky Trek.
With her snatch she could pick up
Chopsticks, chow mein, and teacup—
Everything she could find but the check.

1967.

2748

A misanthrope named Wyn N. Nims
Thought humans much lower than Houyhnhnms.
 Without mincing words
 He called them all turds,
And other unsavory synonyms.

1954J.

2749

A drunken old guy from Yankipoo
Drank a bottle of cologne shampoo.
 Said he, " It's perfection,
 And helps my erection,
And tastes better than joy-juice Kickapoo. "

1968.

2750. LAUS DEO

" I am the Bishop of Yardleigh,
And though you mightn't think it of me,
 I've a face like a lamb,
 A prick like a ram,
And a mind like a W.C. "

1968A.

BIBLIOGRAPHY

D'onde hai tu pigliato tante coglionerie?
— CARDINAL D'ESTE (to Cellini)

NOTE

The following 30 limerick-sequences, generally of three or more limericks each, are included:

BIBLIOGRAPHY

NOTE : *Sources already listed in the Bibliography to the First Series, I : pages 361-69, are not repeated here except as to new editions.*

Adam Bedside Reader. See COULTHARD.

ALDISS, Brian. *Solar System's Sexual Survey.* MS., Oxon. 1974.
See Limericks 2:2584-95. With 15 other original limericks on Terrestrial themes. The *S.S.S.S.* first published in variant form as "Is Uranus Bigger Than Mars?" in *Penthouse* (London, 1974) Vol. IX, No. 7, with amusing illustrations by Ray Campbell and Robin Boutell.

ANDERS, Greg. *17th Wild Weasel Songbook.* [U.S. Air Force, Vietnam, *c.* 1968.] (4) f. plus 115 songs, 4to, mimeo.
35 favorite limericks at No. 58, as "Sing Us Another One Do," with chorus. Compare STARR.

ANDERSON, C. V. J. *Forbidden Limericks.* [New York, 1960?]
"With sickening drawings by Pablo Kamastra." Reprinted, San Francisco : Logos Books [*c.* 1965], 16 p. 8vo.

— *same* : *Book 2.* New York : Beatitude Press, Inc., 1961.
"Edited and/or composed by C. V. J. Anderson & Jack Stamm." Four-letter words expurgated as *verb* or *noun.*

ANDERSON, Poul. *The Night of the Dinosaur.* MS., California, 1970.
See Limericks 2:2555-59. With 40 other limericks, mostly original, some on science-fiction themes. See also *Salacious Science Limericks.*

Anecdota Americana. Being, explicitly, an anthology of tales in the vernacular. Elucidatory Preface by J. Mortimer Hall [*pseud.*] Anecdotes collected and taken down by Mr. William Passemon [*pseud.* : Joseph FLIESLER]. 'Boston' [New York, 1927].

See further details in *The Limerick : First Series,* Bibliography, p. 361.

— *same* : Edited without expurgation by J. Mortimer Hall [*pseud.*] Second Series. 500 more. With 37 illustrations. 'Boston : Humphrey Adams' [New York : V. Smith] 1934. 224 p. 8vo.

Reprinted as *The Unexpurgated Anecdota Americana,* edited by J. Mortimer Hall, Ph.D. Introduction by Frank Hoffmann, Ph.D. North Hollywood, Calif.: Brandon House, 1968, 208 p. 16mo, offset from the original edition, omitting the illustrations. Not compiled by Joseph Fliesler, editor of the First Series. Contains limericks *passim,* especially at Nos. 438-46.

ARMSTRONG, John. *There Was a Young Lady Named Alice,* and other limericks. With drawings by Anatol Kovarsky. (New York : Dell Publishing Co. 1963.) 192 p. 16mo.

240 standard and expurgated examples, "laundered as literary tradition demands," and printed two to a page. Title was originally intended to be *Sweet Alice from Dallas,* referring to a censored version of the female-castratory Limerick 1:1234.

ASIMOV, Isaac. *Lecherous Limericks.* Illustrated by Julien Dedman. New York : Walker and Co., 1975.

100 original limericks, one-to-a-page, with autobiographical notes. (Reprinted, Greenwich, Conn.: Fawcett, 1976, 208 p. 16mo.) Further volumes : *More Lecherous Limericks,* 1976 ; *Still More Lecherous Limericks,* 1977 ; and *The Sensuous Dirty Old Man's Complete Book of Limericks* (in preparation). No science-fiction limericks are included.

The Bagman's Book of Limericks. 'Milan : Regalia Press' [Paris : Brentano's, 1962?] 100 p. 12mo.

250 examples from *The Limerick,* the title here being a satirical allusion to the name : G. Legman. Four erotic spoonerisms are added, p. 91, as "Some Riddles, by Dr. Spooner."

— *same.* Paris : Brentano's, Excel Books, 1963.

Baker House Super-Duper Extra Crude Song Book. (At head : *The* ONE *The* ONLY.) [Cambridge, Mass. : Baker House, Massachusetts Institute of Technology, *c.* 1963.] 4to.

Only title-page and first 17 pages present in hektographed copy seen. Contains 25 limericks, p. 14-16, as "In China They Never Eat Chili," with that opening chorus.

[BARING-GOULD, William S.] *Fifty Famous Limericks.* Minneapolis : Privately Printed, 1934. mimeographed.

"Limericks popular among the students and faculty of the University of Minnesota." [Co-edited with David DONOVAN.]

[—] *Fifty More Famous Limericks.* Minneapolis : Privately Printed, 1935. mimeographed.

— *The Lure of the Limerick* : An Uninhibited History. New York : Clarkson N. Potter, Inc. 1967. (ix), 246 p. obl.8vo.

Introduction and limericks heavily expurgated from *The Limerick,* with illustrations from Aubrey Beardsley, etc. Important as combining mildly bawdy and polite limericks for the first time in book form. But compare : *Eros.*

'BARR, George.' *Science Fiction and Fantasy Limericks Illuminated.* [Philadelphia, 1968.] 8 p. 4to.

9 science-fiction limericks, on punning rhymes, illustrated with full-page drawings.

The Bedroom Companion. [Edited by Philip WYLIE.] New York : Farrar & Rinehart, 1934.

With a section of off-color limericks. Reprinted, New York : Arden Book Co., 1941.

[BEILENSON, Peter.] *Little Limerick Book* : (*An Uncensored Collection.*) Mount Vernon, N.Y. : Peter Pauper Press, 1955.

Totally censored. Supplemented by the same compiler-publisher's more frankly titled *Laundered Limericks,* 1960.

Be Pure! [Perth, Western Australia : Engineering Students' Society, University of Perth, 1963.] (66) f. sm.4to, mimeo.
No title ; "Be Pure!" is the title of the first song (in the copy seen), noted as published "For all loyal adherents to the S.C.I.I.A.E.S." Final song, "Rhodians School." (*Note* : This collection is sometimes confused with another Australian mimeographed songbook of close date, *Snatches & Lays,* 1962.) Limericks, p. 14-19, entitled "Tell Us Anotherie."

[BISHOP, Morris R.] *The Widening Stain,* by 'W. Bolingbroke Johnson' [*pseud.*] New York : Alfred A. Knopf, 1942. 242 p. 12mo.
Murder-mystery, on a college-library background, including several "just-barely-printable" limericks by Professor Bishop. For his polite limericks see his *Spilt Milk* (New York, 1929), and "Limericks Long After Lear," in E. B. White, *Sub-Treasury of American Humor* (1941) ; and in particular Bishop's splendid "The Sonnet and the Limerick," in *The New Yorker* (3 Oct. 1937) p. 21, of which the limerick portion is reprinted in the First Series, Introduction, p. xi. See also Foreword here, p. xxix.

Blankety Blank Verse. Boston : Carol Press, 1910. 18 p. 32do.
Doggerel and limericks illustrating the typographical expurgation of profanity, principally by means of the dash —.

The Cathouse of Time. MS., U.S. 1965-66.
Outstanding group of 1130 original limericks by one author, almost none beginning with the inactive "There was . . ." Concentrates heavily on the subjects of Prostitution and (averted) Motherhood.

CERF, Bennett. *Out On a Limerick.* A Collection of over 300 of the World's Best Printable Limericks. Assembled, Revised, Dry-cleaned, and Annotated by Mister Cerf. With illustrations by Saxon. New York : Harper, 1960. 125 p. 8vo.

Standard weak-sisters and expurgated items, as the title-page announces. The title is a pun on the phrase "out on a limb," but there is not much danger really.

[CHAPLIN, Albin.] *The Limerick That Has the Appeal.* Over 2000 limericks by 'Fillmore P. Noble' [*pseud.*; Detroit : Limericks], 1976. iii, 334 p. 8vo, offset from typewriting.

2033 originals by one author, written over the decade 1966-76, and arranged in the chapter-order of *The Limerick.* Mostly erotic, except those over-modestly grouped as "Weak Sisters," Nos. 1593-1948, which are actually among the best. Cited in the present work to the Chaplin MS. (1975) containing over 200 items not in the printed form.

[—] *The Noble Five Hundred Limericks.* Being a Partial Compilation, Never Heretofore Published, of the Works of 'Fillmore P. Noble' [*pseud.*] New York : Vantage Press, 1967. ii, 126 p. ills. 12mo.

Lightly expurgated version of originals later appearing in their real form in Chaplin's *The Limerick That Has the Appeal,* and including a few not so reprinted, here cited as : 1967A-1975.

Close Harmony & Barbershop Chords. MS., Cincinnati, Ohio, 1968. — 20 originals, not published elsewhere.

Corn on the Cob. MS., New Jersey, 1971.

55 original bawdy limericks, by a woman, 8 of these printed in variant form as "Dirty Ditties," by 'C. Condon,' in *Screw* (New York, 10 May 1971), No. 114 : p.11/4, illustrated graphically.

[COULTHARD, John Thompson, 1903–1966.] *Grand Prix Limerix* : 1,001 New Limericks You Never Saw Before. 'Fort Worth, Texas : SRI Publishing Co., 1966' [Arlington, Texas : John Newbern Co., 1965]. ii, 65 p. ills. 4to.

Forms "Volume" 4 of the bawdy cartoon magazine, *Sex to Sexty,* edited by John Newbern. 1000 "semi-dirty" originals by Coulthard, without four-letter words, the cartoon illustrations also being by him (and including a caricature of G. Legman at No. 393). Note that the first printing refers to Coulthard, page 1, as "Mr. Limerix, the genius with the drepanoid peenius." In the second printing [1966] this is changed, by request, to "the once-in-a-lifetime genius," and many other changes were also made at Coulthard's demand, diminishing the amount of expurgation, and replacing certain limericks and cartoons. See also supplement :

[—] (caption-title :) *There Goes the Phone — Who's Gonna Answer It?* [San Francisco : The Author, 1966.] Single folding sheet, 22½ X 17½ inches, printed both sides. (100 copies.)

An erotic supplement to *Grand Prix Limerix,* with 40 unexpurgated originals by Coulthard, of the thousands he wrote, each one illustrated here by him ; with 10 further erotic cartoons. The title illustration shows a daisy-chain orgy, captioned as above. The author died a few months after issuing this, having circulated only about 20 copies. See also his "13th Sign of the Zodiac" in Note 2:2480.

— "Verses for a Swinging Lady," in *Adam Bedside Reader,* Los Angeles, 1965-66, No. 24 : p. 35.

The last of a series of one-page-per-issue of Coulthard's "erotic but not obscene" limerick originals, in issues No. 18, 21, and 24 of this periodical.

(CRAY, Edward B.) *The Erotic Muse.* New York : Oak Publications (1969). xxxvi, 272 p. lg.8vo.

The compiler's name does not appear on the title-page but only in the copyright notice, page iv. Reprinted, New York : Pyramid Publications, 1972. Includes 40 limericks under the chorus-title, "I-Yi-Yi-Yi," pp. 74-79 and 211-12, with the music (verses : "The Gay Caballero" ; choruses : "Cielito Lindo" and "Sweet Violets"). Preliminary edition as *The Dirty Songbook,* 'compiled by E. R. Linton' (Los Angeles, 1965).

CRI, LeDernier & SCHREY, D. Letzte [*pseuds.*] MS., Rome, 1954. (Untitled : original limericks.)

[CRIST, Clifford M.] *Crist College Collection.* MS., U.S. (various locations), 1937-1948.

Blank dummy volume in which 240 original limericks by faculty members of various colleges in western American states have been written by their authors. Transcribed by the collector in 1971 for the present work. This is the best such collection ever made in America. Some, but by no means all or even the best of the limericks contained, are given in lightly expurgated form in the following:

— *Playboy's Book of Limericks.* Edited by Clifford M. Crist. (Chicago: Playboy Press, 1972.) xxiv, 248 p. nar.8vo.

655 limericks, somewhat expurgated by the publisher, from printed and MS. sources. Overdone *kitsch* typography, with first word of each limerick printed in red; color of book-paper changing from white to yellow at p. 105; white binding with black-tinted edges, etc.

CROWLEY, Aleister. *Diaries.* [Transcript of 50 original limericks in Crowley's manuscript *Diaries,* to 1945, prepared by his literary executor, Gerald YORKE, London, 1954.]

[—] *Snowdrops from a Curate's Garden.* '1881 A.D. Cosmopoli: Imprimé sous le manteau, et ne se vend nulle part' [Paris or Amsterdam, *c.* 1904]. (3), xx, 167 p. sm.8vo.

100 copies printed, of which only three are now known to survive (Bibliothèque Nationale, Enfer 1355). Contains "The Nameless Novel," p. 1-77, a parody pornographicum with curious erotico-humorous neologisms in the style of *The Demi-Wang* [by Gene Fowler, New York, 1930?]; and "The Bromo Book," p. 101-167, including howlingly obscene parodies of Shakespeare and other verse; with 9 original limericks pp. 129-31 and 139.

CUMMINGS, E. E. [Original limericks sent to various correspondents, 1919-54.]

NOTE: Most but not all of Cummings's off-color limericks are collected in his *Poems: 1905-1962,* edited by George James FIRMAGE, London: The Marchim Press, 1973, pp. 607-9.

Death Rattlers. (Old American Ballads.) [Korea : Marine Air Squadron VMP-323, "Death Rattlers," 1951.] (1), 41 f., f°, mimeographed.

Page 11 not present in copy seen. Mostly songs, with 24 favorite limericks, f. 24-25, entitled "In China They Never Eat Chile," with that opening chorus.

'DE WITT, Hugh.' *There Was a Young Lady.* London : Tandem (1969). 160 p. 16mo.

413 limericks, letter-expurgated (and otherwise). The compiler's name given is believed to be a pun on "You Do It." See also his *Bawdy Barrack-room Ballads* (1970), pp. 127–37, "Tell Us Another One, Do."

— *There Was a Fair Maid.* London : Tandem (1969). 160 p. 16mo. 444 further limericks, as above.

Dirt : An Exegesis. (at head : *An Introductory Collection of Real Folk and Traditional Songs.*) [Los Angeles : U.C.L.A. Co-Op House, *c.* 1965.] (1), 22 p. 4to, mimeo.

Violent and aggressive song collection, ending with 67 limericks, p. 19-22, with the odd opening chorus (to the tune of "Home On the Range") :

Down by the river Pardee, Pardee,
Down by the river Pardee.
Where nothing is heard
But the slush of a turd,
Down by the river Pardee.

'DODGSON, Charles L.' MS., U.S. 1967.

A collection of 60 largely punning originals. Author's pseudonym taken from Limerick 2:2561.

The Dolphin Book of Limericks. Drawings by Robert Osborn. Garden City, New York : Doubleday & Co. (1963). (5), 110 p. 12mo.

350 standard items and "Weak Sisters," in part based on Peter Beilenson's *Peter Pauper's Limerick Book* (1940, ed. 1955), on which see Note 1:1597.

'DOTSON, Lee.' MS., New York, 1972.
50 original "Gay Liberation" limericks, wittier than most, and frankly bisexual.

DOUGLAS, Norman. *Some Limericks.* [Florence] 1928.
Other than the editions listed in Bibliography to *The Limerick,* pp. 362-64, a reprint appeared for the first time openly, in London, 1969; and a curious semi-public reprint [New York : J. R. Brussel], without place or publisher given, with imprint : Collection "Le Ballet des Muses," 1964, 95 p. sm.8vo. This is offset from the German-printed edition of 1929, but with all bawdy words blanked-out except for their first letters, and the entire pages 68 and 86 omitted, owing to their sacrilegious limericks (1:999, 265, and 510-12, "Siam"). Unexpurgated, pocket-reprint, N.Y. 1967.

Eros (New York : Ralph Ginzburg, editor, Winter 1962), Vol. I : No. 4, pp. 60-64 : "Bawdy Limericks : The Folklore of The Intellectual."
Brief unsigned textual introduction, and 34 examples also appearing in *The Limerick.* Of historical interest as the first open publication of actually bawdy limericks in America, as opposed to the namby-pamby expurgations in the "men's" magazines. *Eros* ceased publication after this issue, owing to legal prosecution for its advertising methods.

FIFE MS. *Some Limericks of the Pacific.* MS., Utah, 1956.
Group of 7 original limericks "composed during a night-watch in a foxhole at Morotai, Dutch East Indies, by members of the U.S. Army, November 1944."

Fifth Line Society : Transactions. [Chicago, 1953-54.] 10 p. 4to, hektographed.
96 limericks not appearing in *The Limerick,* arranged in the same chapter order, from the Transactions of the Society for the Preservation of the Fifth Line, in Chicago, to date 1953. See also the letter or manifesto concerning this limerick club, by one of its members, Merlin BOWEN, in *Evergreen Review* (New York : Grove Press, 1966), Vol. X : No. 42,

pp. 16 and 93-94, quoted in part in *The Limerick* (ed. 1970), Introduction, pp. lxvii-iii.

Later volumes as the Proceedings of the Fifth Line Society are all printed, in 8vo, (except 1958 : 4to), and in some years two volumes were issued : the "Annual Norman Douglas Memorial Lecture," and other material, these being the original limericks presented at the annual meeting — always in early May. General title to each volume (the volume numbers being fanciful and not in sequence) : *Proceedings of the* (199th) *Annual Meeting — Society of the Fifth Line.* The *Minutes* are humorous in intent, and always by the "Chairman *Pro Tem.*," who has never changed since the founding of the Society. Volumes also contain reproductions of various ancient prints of suitable nature. Titles as follows:

1957 : *Where the Scatological Is the Necessary* : A Prolegomena to a Poetics of the Limerick. 24 p. (This volume, only, notes : "All copyrights reserved by the Society. Publication, reproduction or circulation not authorized.")

1958 : *The Limerick of the Nuclear Age.* First Annual Award. A Study of Virtue among the Fauna of the Limerick. An *Ad hoc* Plea for More Functional Scholarship Annotation. 50 f. 4to. (Printed on recto of paper only.)

1960 : *Little Known Limericks of Ella Wheeler Wilcox.* 16 p.

1961 : *North Against South : A Centennial Reappraisal.* 20 p.

1962 : *The Gray Flannel Limerick,* or Friendly Persuasion Through the Ages. 12 p., bound in gray flannel.

1963 : *Venus Looks at Earth's Genitalia, or Cox and Box.* 32 p.

1964 (I) : *Ontogeny Recapitulates Phylogeny?* 12 p. — (II) : *Minutes* : Letter from the Top of the Ivory Tower. Limerick in Mexico. Society Work Project. 16 p.

1965 (I) : *The Curious Case of the Crypto-Limerick.* 29 p. — (II) : *Minutes* : A Scientific Commentary. 12 p.

1966 : *The Five Lines of Force of Gall & Spurzheim.* 20 p. (As *Quincunxes Snatched From the Veil of Time.*)

1967 (I) : *Miracle on Majorca.* 20 p. — (II) : *Minutes* : Two Q Project. Comments on Pollution. New Material. 16 p.

1968 (I) : *Transplants.* The Organ Transplant Panel. 12 p. — (II) : *Minutes* : Hand Across the Sea (A Letter). Limericks of the Transplant. 16 p.
1969 (Minutes) : *True Confessions and Dying Warnings in Colonial New England.* Thoughts on Confession. The Generation Gap. 28 p.
1970 (Minutes) : *When Knighthood Was Deflowered. Women's Liberation.* 24 p.
1971 (Minutes) : Report of Women's Lib Committee : *Groping in the Secret Drawers of Publishing.* Report of Fifth Line Chartered World Tour. Minorities. 24 p.
1972 (Minutes) : *Making It Hard for Pornographers.* Unlikely Candidates. Consumer Protection. 24 p.
1973 (Minutes) : *The Fifth Line & the Fifth Column* : Kenny Hissinger. Sex Education. Women's Lib. 24 p.
1974 (Minutes) : *I'd Rather Be Naked Than Dead, or The Monroe Doctrine,* by Mormon Nailer. Report of the Committee on Streaking. Exorcism. Inflation. Energy Crisis. 24 p.
1975 (Minutes) : *The Double Helix* : A Geneticist Looks at the Limerick. Spontaneous Limerick Exercise. Colonial & Revolutionary Poems. 24 p.

The Gardener's Tool (1944). See *To Solace the Blind.*

Glad to Obscene You. By Mr. Anon, Poet Emeritus and Merry Tous. MS., Old Lyme, Conn., *c.* 1966.
Cited by Baring-Gould, *The Lure of the Limerick,* p. 241, as in the possession of Carleton Holmes Davis. Not seen.

The Golden Convolvulus. Edited by Arthur MOYSE. Blackburn, Lancashire : Screeches Publications [1965]. 4to, mimeo.
Poetry of revolt, and folklore, including a music-hall song in the limerick metre, "Rose Ormesby-Gore" (Limericks 2:1846–47). Banned from the mails by the British postal authorities.

GORDON, George, & EISENBERG, Lawrence. *Limericks for the John.* New York : Kanrom, Inc. 1963.

42 godawful limericks. The volume is supplied with a chain for hanging by the toilet.

GOREY, Edward. *The Listing Attic.* New York : Duell, Sloan & Pearce. Boston : Little, Brown, 1954.

60 purposely nauseating "macabre" limericks (with illustrations by the author), in which sadism replaces sexuality. Reprinted in the author's collected *Amphigorey* (1974).

Grand Prix Limerix. See COULTHARD.

Gregory-Boomer-Fouff Collection. (No title. Opening index signed : 'George Gregory, Paul Boomer, François Fouff.') [Washington, D.C. : Navy Bureau of Aeronautics, 1945.] (2), 25 f. sm.4to, mimeographed. (150 copies.)

222 limericks : the best collection of the folk-transmitted favorites. According to the senior editor, this is the 3rd and final, enlarged edition. The first edition (of 75 copies) appeared under the same auspices in 1944. There is also a 9-page typescript supplement of 73 additional "Limericks Acquired After the Untitled Mimeographed Paper" to 1959 (Washington, D.C., 1966).

Hall, Donald. *The Gentleman's Alphabet Book.* Illustrated by Harvey Kornberg. (New York : E. P. Dutton, 1972). (61) p. obl. 4to.

Sick-sex limericks in the style of Edward Gorey.

Hall Collection. MS., U.S. *ca.* 1960?

Card index, repositoried in the Folklore Archive, Indiana University, Bloomington, Ind. The "Vintage" group of cards, covering the bawdy limericks, is largely composed of an incomplete transcript of the contents of *The Limerick.*

'HARDE, Dick.' See *Lusty Limericks.*

HARLEY-DAVIDSON MS. Virginia, 1969.

Includes the sequences : "Dumaricks," "Thurmericks," "Fog on Capitol Hill," and a *camp* chrestomathy in 22 limericks : "Homage to Ronald Firbank : Limericks on Themes from the Master's Works."

HART, Harold H. *The Complete Immortalia.* New York : Hart Publishing Co. 1971. (4), 475 p. ills.8vo.

Limericks, printed two-to-a-page, pp. 30-123. The illustrations by Lindi are charming. Reprinted, New York : Bell Publishing Co., *c.* 1975. The limerick section was first printed as *Immortalia : Volume One* (N.Y.: Hart, 1970), 192 p. 8vo, with the limericks only one-to-a-page.

HEDGPETH, Joel W. See TICHENOR, Jerome.

'HERWELL, Roger.' *Pillycock* #6. "Limerick Issue." [Brooklyn, N.Y.] (October 1963). Mimeographed single-sheet, 4to.

— *Pillyspock* #1. [Brooklyn, N.Y.] (Operation #349 ; November 1967). Mimeographed single-sheet, 4to.

A science-fiction fanzine, with caption title : "Ms. found in an empty oxygen tank . . . by Mr. Roger Herwell, a freelance poet of Intercourse, Pennsylvania," in the form of a limerick-sequence satirizing a television space-jock serial, "Starship *Enterprise.*" See Limericks 2:2609-21.

— *Pillyspock* #2. [Brooklyn, N.Y.] (Operation #403 ; June 1969).

Limerick-sequence, "Signs of the Zodiac." Plus further manuscript communications, 1971.

HOLLAND, Vyvyan. *An Explosion of Limericks.* New York & London, *c.* 1968.

"Weak Sisters" and expurgated items, edited by the son of Oscar Wilde.

Hurler avec les Loups. [U.S. : American Amateur Press Association? *c.* 1966?]

Cited by Baring-Gould, *The Lure of the Limerick,* p. 242, as a "privately printed edition of fifty-eight (mostly familiar) limericks . . . a choice example of the bookmaker's art." Not seen.

IBM Limericks. Compiled, collated, and programmed by Dr. Spurl S. VERSENKT [pseud.] MS., New York, 1960.

See also *Klimericks : An Orgy* (1973).

Immortalia. An Anthology of American ballads . . . By A Gentleman About Town [Thomas R. Smith. New York : Macy-Masius] 1927. (1), iii, 184 p. lg.4to.

See further details in the Bibliography to *The Limerick*, p. 365. NOTE : Harold H. Hart's *The Complete Immortalia* (1971), above, is not an edition or an enlargement of T. R. Smith's original *Immortalia.* See also *The "Wrecks"* [1933?]

— *same.* 'Edited by Arthur Mackay. The Karman Society' [Japan, *c.* 1959]. (1), iii, 184 p. 12mo.

Reset with certain errors and double-settings, *e.g.* the note on p. 40. Copy seen bound (by accident?) in a cover intended for a reprint of the pornographic flagellation novel, *Dolly Morton* [by Hugues Rebell], on which see G. Legman, *The Horn Book*, pp. 32-33.

— *same.* '250 copies reprinted by Another Gentleman About Town for his friends. None is for general sale. 1964' [San Francisco, 1966].

Offset from original edition.

— *same.* (Facsimile title-page. On verso : 'Presented to the public, 1969, by Parthena Press, Venice, California') [Arlington, Texas : John Newbern]. (3), iii, 183 p. 16mo.

Entirely reset. Announces a sequel in preparation for which contributions are to be sent to 'Betty Parthena'(!) Sequel did not appear.

JOHNSON MS. Arlington, Va., 1954-59.

Letters sent to the compiler containing 64 original and other limericks "to fill out your Addenda." The writer of these letters, who was the editor of *Index Limericus* (MS., 1947) noted in the Bibliography to *The Limerick*, p. 366, also prepared a remarkable lexicographical index of over a quarter of a million cards concerned with the human penis, based on dated quotations from the world's literature. (See Limerick 2:950.) This should be published.

'JOHNSON, W. Bolingbroke.' See BISHOP.

'KIMBO.' *Tropical Tales.* Nice, 1925 [1926].

Contains erotic jokes and facetiæ, with a few limericks, p. 90 *et passim.* Editor apparently Bradley GILMAN, author under his own name of *Clinic on the Comic* (Nice, 1926). There is also a second series, *More Tropical Tales* (1927).

Klimericks : An Orgy. Proceedings of the First Secret Meeting of the Triangular-Limerick Industrial Complex. By Our Special Bugging-Team. Editor : Dr. Spurl S. VERSENKT [*pseud.*]. London School of Sexual Economics : Triangular Bumwad, Ltd., 1973.

MS. typewritten on slips. A collection of 380 original British limericks arranged by subjects, all apparently written by one person (during trips on KLM airlines?), despite the subtitle. See also : *IBM Limericks* (1960).

LARSON, Kenneth. *Barnyard Folklore of Southeastern Idaho.* MS. Salt Lake City, Utah, 1952.

Repositoried in the Folklore Archive, Indiana University. Mostly folksongs and tales, with several limericks.

Laundered Limericks from Wicked Pens. [Edited by Peter BEILENSON.] Illustrations by Henry R. Martin. Mount Vernon, New York : Peter Pauper Press (1960). 60 p. 12mo.

140 expurgated examples, largely original : the best such collection. Beilenson notes that "on the old-fashioned theory that a book should not read like a public comfort station," he must "beg the indulgence" of his contributors "for having in so many cases altered or rewritten their contributions."

LAVENDER, Roy. See *Lost Limericks.*

[LEGMAN, Gershon.] *The Limerick* : 1700 Examples, with Notes, Variants and Index. Paris : Les Hautes Études, 1953. xv, 519 p. sq.8vo. (Limited edition.)

The First Series of the present work.

[—] *same.* With an introduction by L. T. Woodward, M.D. San Diego, Calif. : Greenleaf Classics, Inc. (1967). 1 vol. in 2 : xx, 522 p. 16mo.

— *same.* Edited by G. Legman. New York : Brandywine Press, 1970. lxxix, 517 p. 8vo.

With a long historical Introduction, pp. vii-lxxiii. Reprinted, New York : Bell Publishing Co. [1974] ; and London : Jupiter Books, 1974.

— *same.* London : Panther Books, 1976. 2 vols. 16mo.

Paperback reprint, in which the order of the chapters and numbering of the limericks are entirely changed without authorization.

— "The Limerick : A History in Brief," in G. Legman, *The Horn Book* : Studies in Erotic Folklore and Bibliography (New Hyde Park, N.Y. : University Books, Inc., 1964), pp. 427-53.

This essay is revised and much enlarged as the Introduction to *The Limerick* (ed. 1970), omitting Part IV, pp. 441-45, on "Toasts."

— *Limerick Addenda.* MS., U.S. and France, 1942-1977.

The basic collection of the present Second Series, supplementing *The Limerick.*

— *Rationale of the Dirty Joke : An Analysis of Sexual Humor. First Series.* New York : [Basic Books &] Grove Press (1968). 811 p. 8vo.

With unexpurgated limericks *passim.*

— *same. Second Series.* (*No Laughing Matter.*) New York : Breaking Point, Inc. (1975). 992 p. 8vo.

LETTS, John. *A Little Treasury of Limericks Fair and Foul.* Illustrations by Ralph Steadman. London : André Deutsch (1973). 94 p. 12mo.

An interesting British collection, reasonably unexpurgated, but spoiled by purposely hideous line-drawings.

Limerix. (Phonograph recording.) U.S. : Cook Co., *c.* 1962.

Expurgated limericks recorded as the purported transactions of a mock limerick society.

LOGUE, Christopher. See 'VICARION.'

Lost Limericks & Bar Room Ballads. [Edited by Roy LAVENDER, for World Science Fiction Convention, Cincinnati, 1949. *Third edition.* Reynoldsburg, Ohio, 1957.] (3), 69 p., ills. 4to, mimeographed. (150 copies.)

Rare and valuable collection of folk-verse, "mimeographed from stencils cut by many persons." Reprints the 15 science-fiction limericks from *Salacious Science Limericks* (1952), with others.

Lusty Limericks & Bawdy Ballads. Compiled and edited by Dick Harde [*pseud.*; New York? 1956]. (1), 49 f. 4to, mimeographed. [Copy : Kinsey-ISR.]

238 limericks, mostly taken from *The Limerick* and 'Vicarion,' followed by ballads, ff. 35-49.

Lyra Ebriosa. Being certain narrative ballads of a vulgar or popular character and illustrative of the manners of the times. With An Appendix. [Edited by Littleton M. WICKHAM. Norfolk, Virginia,] 1930. 31 p. 8vo.

Limerick-sequence "Siam," in 7 stanzas, p.14 (see Limericks 2:1045-68). In the unique repository copy known, at the University of Virginia, 8 further stanzas have been inserted marginally by an unknown hand. NOTE : The "Appendix," pp. 26-31, is Mark Twain's "*1601,*" in the old-style spelling.

MCCOSH, Sandra. *A Joke for Every Occasion* : A Study of Children's Humour, British & American. With an Introduction by G. Legman. London & New York : Hanau Publications, Ltd. 1977. xlix, 332 p. sm.8vo. (Forthcoming.)

Unexpurgated jokes and poems, collected among children in England and America. Limericks, pp. 162-64.

MACINTYRE, Carlyle Ferren. MS. additions to *That Immoral Garland* (MS., 1942 : see Bibliography to *The Limerick*), Mexico and France, 1955-66.

The Martian Chronicles. MS., Stabroek, Belgium, 1964.

15 Flemish-Dutch limericks, with literal translations into English. (See Limericks 2:2654-68.) Despite the title, not on science-fiction themes.

(MORGAN, Harry.) *More Rugby Songs.* London : Sphere Books, 1968. 158 p. 16mo.

30 letter-expurgated limericks, with chorus, as "Sing Us Another One, Do," p. 151-58. Compiler's name appears in copyright notice only.

MOYSE, Arthur. See *The Golden Convolvulus.*

A New Book of Nonsense. London, 1868. 12 p.(?)

No copy known to exist. Erotic limericks edited and written by Capt. Edward SELLON, G. A. SALA, and especially by a barrister, Frederick Popham PIKE ; probably reissued as the last 12 pages of *Cythera's Hymnal* (1870) by the same editors. Not to be confused with the polite volume of Civil War limericks, *The New Book of Nonsense* (Philadelphia : The Sanitary Commission, 1864).

New Statesman (London, 5 July 1974), p. 27. "Weekend Competition No. 2312, " set by J. F. Sinclair.

15 limericks in fractured French on sexual subjects, mostly by Britons. "Competitors were invited to daze a Frenchman with limericks written in French, a form apparently alien to the *génie latin.*" (See Limerick 2:1733.)

New York Magazine (1971). Competition No. 102, "for limericks incorporating clichés apposite to women's rôle as second-class citizens," and their liberation therefrom. (See Limerick 2:31.)

'NOBLE, Fillmore P.' See CHAPLIN.

North Atlantic Squadron. [Gander Bay, Newfoundland : Eastern Air Command, 1944]. 24 p. f°, mimeographed.

Reissued [Ottawa, 1950] for an Eastern Air Command reunion, without title (caption-title : "*Tune — My Bonny*"), 11 f., f°, mimeographed ; and in this form giving 16 favorite limericks (in long couplet form), f. 7, with title and chorus, "Sing Us Another One."

'NOSTI.' *A Collection of Limericks.* With commentaries explanatory and critical, as well as geographical notes. [Berne?] Privately Printed in Switzerland, 1944. (3)-111 p. 16mo. (1000 copies.)

Noted by Jacques Pley, *Bibliothèque "La Léonina," III : Curiosa* (Monte Carlo, 1955), p. 32, as at that time in the library of Arpad Plesch, of Beaulieu-sur-Mer. Essentially a plagiarism of Norman Douglas's *Some Limericks,* somewhat revamped, abridged, and reworded by a person imperfectly acquainted with the English language, with additional would-be humorous notes. Fortunately very rare.

Ohio State Sailing Club. [Song book, 4to, mimeographed (?) ; collected on typewritten sheets by Xenia Blom, *c.* 1962, and preserved in the Folklore Archive, Indiana University, the sheets being scattered. Contains limericks.]

Old American Ballads (1951). See *Death Rattlers.*

'PEPYS, J. Beauregard.' See WEST.

Playboy. (Chicago). Various pages of expurgated limericks in issues of Dec. 1954, Nov. 1955, and others. In the batch appearing in Sept. 1963, the wood-engraved humorous illustrations by Arnold Roth are excellent.

Playboy's Book of Limericks. See CRIST.

The Poets. Edited by Ward BYRON. New York, *c.* 1966.

According to Baring-Gould, *The Lure of the Limerick,* p. 110 : "an earnest effort to create and publish new and original limericks (not all of them *risqué,* by any means) is now [1966] being made by The Poets' Club of New York City in their (more or less) monthly newsletter, *The Poets,* edited by Ward Byron." Compare : *Fifth Line Society.*

Purple Plums Picked from the "Pink 'Un." A Carefully culled collection of clippings from the famous London weekly – *Sporting Times.* Privately Printed. [London : The Sporting Times, 1931?] 150 p. 12mo.

53 mildly offcolor limericks selected from issues of the "*Pink 'Un*" from 1914 to 1924. Printed on pink paper. See

the history of this theatre-&-racing newspaper of the 'Nineties, by J. B. Booth (London : Laurie, 1938).

PYNCHON, Thomas. *Gravity's Rainbow.* New York : Viking Press, 1973.

Götterdämmerung novel, in the style of William Gaddis, Joseph Heller, John Barth, Kurt Vonnegut (and a few others), concerning the launching of the Ultimate Bomb. Book 3, "In the Zone" includes a series of proto-Nazi science fiction limericks, entitled "Rocket Limericks" (Bantam Book reprint, pp. 355-62), with mock chorus, "*Ja, ja, ja, ja, In Prussia they never eat pussy!*" In Book 4, "The Counterforce" (Bantam ed., pp. 832-36), a food-dirtying "Menu" of folkloristic type is shown in the process of being created by presumed "communal improvisation" at a German banquet *de grand apparat,* featuring "scab sandwiches with mucus mayonnaise," etc. See Chap. IX, "Gourmands," here, especially Note 2:1511, and *No Laughing Matter* (Rationale II) pp. 376-77.

RANDOLPH, Vance. *Vulgar Rhymes from the Ozarks.* MS., Eureka Springs, Arkansas, 1954.

Ends with 15 limericks, Nos. 102-16, including one *clerihew* dated 1952. (A clerihew is just a 2-line limerick gone wrong):

Said Hone on the Kinsey Report,
" I have not read it, in short,
For I prefer screwing
To reading and viewing ;
I'm not just a spectator sport. "

The Raunchy Reader. 'Fort Worth, Texas : SRI Publishing Co.' [Arlington, Texas : John Newbern Co.] 1965.

Includes off-color limericks reprinted from the same publisher's humor magazine, *Sex to Sexty.*

REUSS, Richard A. *An Annotated Field Collection of Songs from the American College Student Oral Tradition.* (Master of Arts thesis, Dept. of Folklore, Indiana University. Bloomington,

Indiana : The Author, 1965.) vii, 355 f. 4to, offset from typewriting.

An important collection of college songs, mostly bawdy. 28 limericks at No. 39, ff. 216-24, given in song form, with 5 variants of the connective chorus, and music.

Ribald Limericks. San Francisco : Discovery Bookshop [1961]. (Not seen.)

[RUBINGTON, Norman.] 'Bernhardt Von Soda' [pseud.] *The Beaten and the Hungry.* Paris : Olympia Press, 1962. (Othello Books, No. 111 [*i.e.* No. 1?]) 223 p. 16mo.

In Chaps. ix-x, "Les Mandarins," a porno satire on the then foreign colony on the Left Bank in Paris, gives a scattered group of rather contrived bawdy limericks, *intra* pp. 98-131, on the inspiration of the volume of same by 'Count Palmiro Vicarion' (*q.v.*), referred to p. 129, as "Cunt Puby's Lipsticks."

Rugby Jokes. See YATES.

Salacious Science Limericks. 31 February 1952. [By Poul ANDERSON & Oliver SAARI. California? 1952.] 26 p. 16mo, hektographed.

An erotic parody of a typical issue of *Astounding Science Fiction* magazine, with 15 science-fiction limericks. See also : Poul ANDERSON, and Roy LAVENDER.

Satan. ("Devilish Entertainment for Men." New York, April 1957) Vol. I : No. 2, pp. 3, 39-41.

A dozen cleaned-up limericks under title "Satan and Swinburne."

Screw. (New York : Milky Way Pub. Co., July 31, 1969) No. 22.

A page of bawdy limericks are given in this main "pornzine" (pornographic newspaper) of the period. See also : *Corn on the Cob,* 1971.

'SEDLEY, Sir Maurice' [pseud.] *Between Piety and Playfulness* : Limericks for Discretionary Use in Higher Education. MS., Las Vegas, Nevada, 1971. (5), 65 f., 4to.

The author's pseudonym, as originally given on the typewritten manuscript, is 'Kilroy TROUT, Bart.' Contains 68 original limericks, none using "There was" openings, with satirical and socio-critical commentary much superior to the limericks.

[—] *Caveat Emptor* : Precedent-Setting Limericks for the Legal Profession, by Viscount Harold BOHUN [pseud.] MS., Las Vegas, Nevada, 1973. 19 f. 4to.

A supplement to the preceding, with 48 further limericks and commentary.

Sex to Sexty. (*Super Sex to Sexty,* No. 7 : "296 Snix Pix Limerix".) 'Fort Worth, Texas : SRI Publishing Co' [Arlington, Texas : John Newbern Co.] 1969. (2), 49 p. ills. f°.

296 bawdy limericks, without "four-letter" words. All the limericks are illustrated with cartoons (by various artists), six-to-a-page! Edited and in part written by a woman, 'Goose Reardon' [*pseud.*] See also COULTHARD.

SHOOLBRAID, Murray. "Burns and Bawdry," in *Come All Ye* : The Vancouver Folk Song Society Journal (Jan. 1974) Vol. III : No. 1, pp. 6-13.

On limericks, pp. 9-13, with the music to the usual "Gay Caballero" tune and "Cielito Lindo" chorus.

Smile and the World Smiles With You. Guam, 1948 (reprinted 1952), mimeographed.

A folio of jokes, poems, etc. including limericks.

Snatches & Lays. Songs Miss Lilywhite Should never have taught us. Edited by Sebastian Hogbotel & Simon ffuckes [*pseuds.* : K. D. GOTT & Stephen MURRAY-SMITH. Melbourne, Australia :] Boozy Company, 1962. 4to, mimeo.

Only the cover, titlepage, and pages 28, 38, 41 of this original edition are now unique, these including the following items omitted from the printed edition (below) as sacrilegious : "My Heart Belongs to Daddy" (Jesus Christ and Mary Magdalene, noted as from *The First Boke of Fowle Ayres,*

Sydney, 1944), "All the Saints in Kingdom Come," and "Sydney Orr" (a parody of "Samuel Hall"). Not to be confused with the similar Australian mimeo publication of close date, *Be Pure!* (Note : Ian Turner, to whom the editing of *Snatches & Lays* is ascribed in *Southern Folklore Quarterly,* 1976, vol. 40 : pp. 73 *ff.,* did not edit, but only contributed to this collection.)

— *same* : *Snatches & Lays.* Hogbotel & ffuckes. Melbourne : Sun Books, 1973. 112 p. sm.4to.

Reprint of 1962 edition with omissions as noted above. 41 limericks, pp. 96–106, divided into "Ecclesiastical," "Geographical," and "Cognominal."

— *same* : (facsimile title of 1962 edition). Hong Kong : Boozy Company, P. O. Box 20561, Causeway Bay, 1975. (3), xii, 147 p. 12mo.

The best edition, re-edited by K. D. Gott, with additions. Limericks, pp. 131-39. This edition was reviewed by Nick Quinn in a Far East journalists' magazine, *The Correspondent* (Hong Kong, Feb. 1976), clarifying the senior editor's name and marvellously captioned : "GOTT IN HYMNAL!"

Snowdrops from a Curate's Garden. See CROWLEY.

The Stag Party. (This Book contains : . . . The Chestnut Club Yarns . . . and thousands of other stories, full of pith and point.) [Boston? The Papyrus Club? 1888.] (296)p. unnumbered, 12mo.

Rare and important source-work on American bawdy folk-humor, with limericks *passim,* and containing most of the erotic poems of Eugene FIELD. Only two repository copies are known : Kinsey-ISR, and Yale (lacking 2 pages).

STARR, William J. *The Fighter Pilots Hymn Book.* [Cannon Air Force Base, Cannon, New Mexico, 1958.] (1), v, 121 f. 4to, hektographed ; with f. 9*a,* and *Smegmafax Addenda* (1959) f. 122-52, not present in most copies.

The best and most extensive of the American Air Force

bawdy song collections of World War II and the Korean War, and one of the few giving the compiler's name. (Compare ANDERS.) Based in part on a similar collection, *Stovepipe Serenade,* by a woman, Logan BENTLY. Includes 35 favorite limericks as a song, "Sing Us Another One Do," f. 69-72 ; with 83 less common limericks in the *Smegmafax Addenda,* f. 139–48.

Super Sex to Sexty. See *Sex to Sexty.*

The Tenth Muse Lately Hung Up in America. Being Lewd Lines and Vulgar Verses Newly Inscribed, By a Gentleman. MS., New York, 1958.

Brief group of original limericks, some on religious themes.

THOMPSON, Dana. (Original limericks) in *Hall Collection, c.* 1960 (*q.v.*)

This author's limericks are the only valuable contribution of the *Hall Collection.*

THOMPSON, Robert S. *Limericks for the Literate.* Wilkinsburg, Pa. : International Ham Press, 1967. (6), 63 p. sm.8vo.

120 rather charming "salty" limericks by a 75-year-old author, published by a group of friends to whom they had been sent over the years.

THORNELY, Thomas. *Provocative Verse, and Libellous Limericks.* Cambridge : W. Heffer, 1936. ix, 62 p. sm.8vo.

"Libellous Limericks," pp. 51-62, largely anti-intellectual.

'TICHENOR, Jerome.' *Poems in Contempt of Progress.* Edited by Joel W. HEDGPETH. Pacific Grove, Calif. : The Boxwood Press, 1974. viii, 70 p. 8vo.

Limericks *passim,* with a version of "Screwy Dick with the Spiral Prick," p. 60.

To Solace the Blind. Including *The Gardener's Tool.* Revised and enlarged edition. Universitäts-Buchhandlung, Frankfurt-am-Main, 1945. (Limited edition.) 64 p. 24to.

142 limericks, including many originals on musical themes. (Copy : Dr. Clifford Crist, Dallas, Texas.) First published as *The Gardener's Tool — A Reader for Rakes* (Napoli, 1944).

Union Jack. MS., Chelmsford, Essex, England, 1948-57.
A collection of British erotic folk-poems and jokes, including many limericks.

UNTERMEYER, Louis. *Lots of Limericks : Light, Lusty and Lasting.* Illustrations by R. Taylor. Garden City, N.Y. : Doubleday & Co., 1961.
Reprinted London : W. H. Allen, 1962 ; and as *The Pan Book of Limericks* (London : Pan Books, 1963). Mr. Untermeyer wrote to the present editor about this work, 20 Jan. 1965, as follows : "The last two sections had to be camouflaged in one way or another to get the book through the mails . . . ten or twelve of my favorites had to be omitted."

VAUGHAN, Stanton. *700 Limerick Lyrics* : A Collection of Choice Humorous Versifications. New York : T. J. Carey, 1904.
The largest polite collection of the 1900's, and venturing several semi-bawdy specimens.

'VERSENKT, Dr. Spurl S.' See *IBM Limericks,* and *Klimericks : An Orgy.*

'VICARION, Count Palmiro' [Christopher LOGUE]. *Count Palmiro Vicarion's Book of Limericks.* Paris : Olympia Press, 1955. (128) p. sm.8vo, printed on various colors of paper.
207 limericks, printed two-to-a-page, largely paralleling *The Limerick* (1953) pieced out with originals by Logue. His Foreword is a masterpiece of non-humor. See RUBINGTON.

[WEST, Roy W.] *Limericks For the Main Line,* or The Art of Social Descending Made Easy. Vol. I, No. 1, November 1973. J. Beauregard PEPYS [*pseud.* Philadelphia : The Author, 1973]. (64)p. sq.16mo.

In black & orange wrappers imitating the American *Social Register.* 60 mildly bawdy limericks about Philadelphia "Main Line" society families. The author is identified in the *Evening Bulletin* (Philadelphia, 26 Oct. 1973, p. 1) as the proprietor of a haberdashery establishment, who states he wrote the whole book while "crocked on Scotch," on wet paper cocktail-napkins. In the *Philadelphia Inquirer* of same date he promises two further collections : *Limericks for the Whoresy Set,* and *The Young Lad from Penn Charter,* an enlargement of "The Farter from Sparta" (Limericks 1:740-51).

WESTERMEIER, Clifford P. "The Cowboy and Sex," in Charles W. Harris & Buck Rainey, eds., *The Cowboy : Six-Shooters, Songs, and Sex* (Norman, Oklahoma : University of Oklahoma Press, 1976) pp. 85-105.

An excellent, no-nonsense article, giving 4 presumable "cowboy limericks," at p. 93, specially contributed, of which one (in monorhyme) on *Dallas/phallus* suggests a rather different vocabulary for the modernized cowboy than one might expect.

WILLIAMS, Oscar. *The Silver Treasury of Light Verse,* from Geoffrey Chaucer to Ogden Nash. New York : New American Library, 1957.

Gives several excellent erotic limericks by modern poets.

WILSTACH, Frank J. *Anecdota Erotica, or Stable Stories.* MS., New York, 1924. 44 p. 4to.

Typewritten on stationery of the New York Lambs' Club, and repositoried in the New York Public Library (3*). Limericks, pp. 24-28 *et passim.*

WOOD, Clement. *Around the Horn — in Limericks.* MS., Delanson, New York, *c.* 1950. 50 f. 4to.

A collection of about 300 limericks, one-third apparently originals by Wood, intended as a supplement to his *The Facts of Life — in Limericks* (1943 : see *The Limerick,* Bibliography, p. 369). Folio 46, "Venereal Disease and Disability (page 1)" missing in copy examined.

The "Wrecks" : An Anthology of Ribald Verse, Collected at Reno. Privately Printed for Subscribers Only. [Reno, Nevada? *c.* 1933.] 192 p. sm.4to. (450 copies.)

Only known repository copy : University of Nevada. Bawdy songs and poems, issued by the Reno "Wrecks," a sporting-life club. Largely derived from *Immortalia,* with pages of limericks *passim.*

[YATES, John A.] *Rugby Jokes.* London : Sphere Books (1968). 176 p. 16mo.

Each of the twelve sections ends with a page of limericks, in part original, created by the method described by the author in the Introduction here. So also : *Son of Rugby Jokes*, and *What Rugby Jokes Did Next* (both 1970).

NOTES & VARIANTS

NOTES & VARIANTS

NOT-QUITE LIMERICKS : Lent, 104 ; Doll Tearsheet's Song, 208 No Jews, 523 ; Fuck Freud! 559 ; Petrucci's Saloon, 692 ; Terrestrial Paradise, 719 ; Spitz, 762 ; The Muff, 925 ; Dan's Glans, 950 ; Old Mother Hubbard, 1220 ; The Cat's Ass, 1234 ; Beans, 1391 ; Around the Horn, 1432 ; Tooty-Toot-Toot, 1494 ; McNabs, 1502 ; The Dirtiest Dozens, 1520 Drawers and Gloves, 1769 ; Piccadilly, 1851 ; Abelina, 1938 Jobbing Gardener, 2029 ; So Far In, You're Out, 2133 ; I Like It, 2313 ; Autobiography of Alice, 2399 ; Poisonous Percy, 2456 ; Regina, 2471 ; The World's Worst Limerick, 2732 ; Japan, Note 104*.

I. LITTLE ROMANCES

2. ABERYSTWYTH. A pendant to the classic on the same rhymes (*The Limerick*, 1:1) attributed to Swinburne. A recent variant :

There was a young chap from Aberystwyth
Who said to the girl he'd just kissed with :
  " That hole in your crutch
  Is for fucking and such.
It's *not* just a gadget to piss with. " [1967A.

' Nosti ' (1944) p. 17, gives another :

There was a young man of Aberystwyth
Who took his best girl to play whist with.
  When she trumped his first trick
  He took out his prick,
And they connected the things that they pissed with.

20. There was a strange poet named Seán
Who cared not *who* he laid upon.

But she gnashed a tooth loose
When he called her abstruse :
A gal so far out she was gone. [*ff.* 1971A.

26\. Variant couplet & conclusion :

He says, " They're the kind
It takes sniffing to find,
But when found, man, they're put to good use." [1965.

30\. LIFE. By the compiler, being a limerick reduction of a British folk-poem (printed slip, London, 1965) entitled " Is It Worth It? " in 22 tersely graphic couplets, ending :

That silky hole with hair around,
He's dug his grave in stony ground.
As he draws his dying breath
He knows he's shagged himself to death ;
And on his tombstone, plainly laquered,
His epitaph — JUST FUCKING KNACKERED.

Another version, not identical except for the man's death, in *The Stag Party* [Boston? 1888] unnumb. p. 86, beginning : " Shady tree, babbling brook, Girl in hammock reading book. "

31\. By Jack Labow, submitted to *New York Magazine* (1971) Competition No. 102, for " limericks incorporating clichés apposite to women's rôle as second-class citizens, " and their Liberation therefrom.

37\. Given by ' Nosti ' with the purposeful non-rhymes *fish* and *shoulder* in 2nd and 4th lines, forming an inferior version of Limerick 1:1154 ; and compare 2:2058.

50\. By the late John Newbern, humor-magazine publisher, on the challenge of my remark in the Introduction to *The Limerick,* p. viii, that there are no rhymes for *swollen, spoilt, silver,* and *sylph.* He made a gallant try at the others too :

They're craven and spoilt, ye
Oversexed royalty!

with a punch line on " SERF-riding. " Say what you will, " gotch-eyed " is great.

51. A FOLKTALE RETOLD. Compare the similar capsule biographies of Limericks 2 : 140-49 and 2435-42.

54. A children's riddle : " What's the difference between a sin and a shame? " (For answer, see Note 1:896.) On the rhymes here compare Limerick 2:2668A, and the folk-poem (Yale, 1939) :

Isn't it a pity, a young girl from the city,
Young and very pretty, and her name was Meg.
One of the committee, thinking to be witty,
Hit her on the titty with a *hard-boiled egg!*

58. On Mrs. Simpson and this famous abdication — the milk-&-water *Mayerling* of the 1930's — see Limerick 1:339 and its Note. On the scandalous sexual folklore concerning the original Mayerling, we read in Lajos Zilahy's historical novel, *The Dukays* (New York, 1949) p. 317-18 that : " thrill-hungry men and women feasted their salacious imaginations on that erotic history . . . [that] the crown prince had committed suicide because, in the course of a drunken Black Mass on that memorable night, Baroness Vetsera had cut off the archduke's genitals with her scissors. "

59. Hall Collection (" Vintage " group) No. 2528.

62. There was a young fellow named Bryce
Whose life was devoted to vice.
He shattered the morals
Of thousands of gorrels,
And never fucked any ONE twice. [1969A.

71. A honeymoon pair from Nantucket
Went to bed, and by god they did fuck it!
Next morning, said he :
" Do you feel like some tea? "—
" No! I feel like a billposter's bucket! " [1968A.

75. Hall Collection, No. 4709*a*, with a variant at No. 4576 :

There is a young lady named Frances,
And I'd love to get into her pantses.
But since she's a nice girl
And I'm not a rough churl,
I don't get *too* many chances. [1959.

82. NIGHTPIECE. A splendid example of the acceptable pun, on *the lion and the lamb* (actually the *wolf* and the lamb, in *Isaiah,* 65:25, where the lion only " shall eat straw like the bullock "). Oscar Williams' *Silver Treasury of Light Verse* (1957) credits this to the late Conrad Aiken, novelist and imitator of Joyce, most of whose original limericks were terrible. (See the Introduction to *The Limerick* : First Series, p. lii.) Reprinted with ignorant improvements in line 2 — padding it out to the finger-counted metre — under the title " Speak To Me of Love, " in *Super Sex to Sexty* (1969) No. 7 : limerick 67, illustrated with two moonlit lovers in a bush.

83. One of the few examples of the omnipresent Learic " *They* " in bawdy limericks. But compare Limerick 2:2622 (Kubrick : 2001½).

90. A REAL LOVER. By Waldo Lee McAtee (in his Library of Congress manuscripts, D.364, envelope 3) with two further stanzas in the same hyper-romantic style. A note indicates that the entire piece is built around the striking final line here, dropped in conversation by an outdoorsman, George R. Winnie, of Traverse City, Michigan.

92. By the light of the silvery moon
I danced with my sweetheart too soon.
When I reached down to tickle
I felt a warm trickle,
And the band played an old *ragtime* tune. [1969A.

Definition of *whorehouse piano* : " Three weeks of jazztime, and one week of ragtime. " (N.Y. 1946.)

99. Robert S. Thompson, *Limericks for the Literate* (1967) p. 45.

100. The French erotic poet and novelist Pierre Louÿs has observed, concerning his bestseller in the 1890's, *Aphrodite,* that most of the fan-mail he received on this sensuous novel of a prostitute's life in ancient Greece came from lady-readers intrigued by his tongue-in-(*er*)-cheek reference to the variously numbered places one can caress a woman.

101. " Fucked by the Fickle Finger of Fate ," and " Diddled by the Dirty Digit of Destiny " : alliterative phrases in folk-currency in America. So also : " a Pimple on the Prong (or

Pecker) of Progress. " An entire alphabet in imitation of these — very contrived and in part anti-godlin — was composed about 1945 in New York by N. R. de México (Robert Bragg), including lines like " Reamed by the Rotten Rancor of Revenge! " As usual, none of these imitations have entered into circulation. Folk-poets are born, not made.

104. Also in the " run-on " style, both dated 1967A (and compare Limericks 2:2133 and 2399) :

There was a young man of Japan
Who couldn't resist a nice fan.
    When asked for his reason
    He said, " When in season,
I always try to get into just as many nice-looking,
long-legged, sexy, immoral young girls as I possibly can! "

Another young fellow, from China,
Has a method essentially finer.
    His amours always tend
    To come to an end
Suddenly.

106. Variant, by another limerick poet :

    To a lecher like Willie
    Such fucking seems silly,
But he's the last one to yell " Stop! " [1966.

127. Said she, " Let's try sucking,
    There won't be much fucking—
That prick is too limp to slip in." [1966.

130. Deeply sensual, in her life as in her poetry, Edna St.Vincent Millay, whose book *Wine from These Grapes* (1934) is alluded to here, had her own way of saying the same thing, in " The Poet and his Book " :

Boys and girls that lie
    Whispering in the hedges,
Do not let me die,
    Mix me in your pledges.

140. HISTORY WITHOUT MYSTERY. See also Limerick 2:2401, " Above Suspicion, " and 2:542. Another missing stanza :

Said that luscious blonde lady of joy
Known in legend as Helen of Troy :
" Having sex with Achilles
Just gives me the willies—
That Greek butters me like a boy! " [1966.

150. When he came to a stop
He said, " That's the last drop. " [1965.

160. Compare Limerick 2:32, and another version printed in ' Hugh De Witt, ' *There Was a Young Lady* (1969) No. 195.

162. Based on a folk-spoonerism : " *What's the difference between a whore coming out of a Salvation Army meeting, and a girl getting out of a bathtub? — One has her soul full of hope, and the other has her hole full of soap.* " (Pa. 1934.) Under the name of *contrepéterie* (cross-farting), this is a form of verbal humor as old as Rabelais ' *Gargantua & Pantagruel* in 1533, Bk. II, chap. 21. A recent British spoonerism forms the couplet of Limerick 2:176 on " Cupid's stunts *vs.* stupid cunts. " The cunt is apparently thought to be stupid because " *it has a mouth but never speaks* " (though " it can hold water upside-down "). The word *cunt* (in French : *con,* with feminine back-formation, *conne!*) has thus become a common slang term for a fool, in both France and Britain since World War I. See Joseph & Georgette Marks' and Charles B. Johnson's extraordinarily frank *French/English Dictionary of Slang* (London : Harrap, 1970-75) in 2 volumes.

165. PAGING LYDIA PINKHAM. Some mistake here : It is not vitamin E but vitamin B2 (riboflavin) that colors the urine bright yellow within a few hours after ingesting it. Of the mildly bawdy satirical song on the original Lydia Pinkham's Vegetable Compound " for female weakness, " and the wildly exaggerated claims made for it in the song, two good texts are given in Ed Cray's *The Erotic Muse* (1968) pp. 57 and 217-18. Compare also Limerick 2:525.

167. Reliably attributed to the Welsh poet, Dylan Thomas, who died of alcoholism in 1953, in Oscar Williams ' *Silver Treasury of Light Verse* (1957). " *Ich dien* " — I serve — is the armorial motto of the Prince of Wales.

168. HINC ILLÆ LACRIMÆ. Compare Limerick 2:203, " Famous Last Words. "

To Susie the touch of the male meant
An emotional cardiac ailment,
    And acute loss of breath
    Caused her untimely death
In the course of erotic impalement. [1968A.

178. HISSES FROM THE MRS. See Part I at Limerick 2:96, and a further word at 2:182.

180. There once was a lady of Sodom,
For women she cared not a goddam.
    But a virgin she died,
    For each male she espied
Was pursuing some other guy's bodom. [1972.

183. Credited to Dana Thompson in the Hall Collection, No. 2651. The touch of King Solomon talking Yiddish is pure genius. (Compare Napoleon's comedy-Italian dialect in Limerick 2:194.) On this millennially famous encounter-in-riddles between King Solomon and Balkis, Queen of Sheba, recorded briefly in *1 Kings,* 10:1-13, see further G. Legman, *Rationale of the Dirty Joke* : Second Series (" *No Laughing Matter,* " 1975) 15.V.2, " The *Escoumerda,* " p. 953.

192. FOOTPRINTS ON THE DASHBOARD. These " high-heel holes ," punched through the canvas top of the convertible car by young ladies in their passion, are the modern equivalent of the equally passionate young swains ' " footprints on the dashboard upside-down " of horse-&-buggy days, as recollected in " A Letter from the Postmaster " (sung to the tune of Dvorák's " Humoresque "). A text is given in *Immortalia* (1927) p. 100 ; another from Australia, as " Penfriends, " in *Snatches & Lays* (ed. Melbourne, 1973) p. 49 ; and still another, from British India, by G. Legman, " Bawdy Monologues and Rhymed Recitations, " in *Southern Folklore Quarterly* (University of Florida, 1976) vol. 40 : pp. 59-122, at p. 104.

206. Maud FitzGerald and Gerald FitzMaud.

208. DOLL TEARSHEET'S SONG. Evidently the song Falstaff calls for in *1 Henry IV,* III.iii.14 : " Come, sing me a bawdy song — Make me merry! " with more than a touch of " Eat, drink, and be merry " (see : *Ecclesiastes,* viii : 15, passage beginning : " Then I commended mirth . . . ") The refrain here is from Thomas Jordan's 17th-century drinking song, " Let us drinke and be merry " (*Oxford Book of English Verse,* No. 335) ; the marvellous opening line being that of the old Scottish folksong, " Barm " (in Herd's Collection, 1775). Altogether a fake, but not bad.

215. Superior version of Limerick 1:1700, dated 1952.

225. BEDIQUETTE FOR BEGINNERS. Metaphorical songs and poems of this kind are very old, using the phraseology of various professions in an erotic sense, such as the " ordnance metaphors " of soldiers and sailors, for the pleasure of thus erotizing the work of the listening men. See G. Legman, *The Horn Book* (1964) pp. 189-91. One such song still current in Australia is " My Husband's a Jockey " : text in *Snatches & Lays* (ed. Melbourne, 1973) p. 16, " Marriage à la Mode. " This is hardly more than a translation of a well-known South German erotic *Schnaderhüpferl* entitled " Mei Schatz ist a Reiter, " given in Hans Ostwald's *Erotische Volkslieder aus Deutschland* (Berlin, 1910) p. 118.

A young fellow about to be wed
Took a course of six lessons on " Bed. "
When shown how to do it,
He said : " Nothing to it!
I could do that all night on my head. " [1968A.

228. To the duffer's delight
For once he'll aim right [1966.

230. On the final " twatter a-twitter, " see the charming story told as true in John Aubrey's *Brief Lives* (before 1690) concerning Sir Walter Raleigh and the girl he is making love to, up against a tree, who cries out at her paroxysm : " Nay, sweet Sir Walter! . . . sweet Sir Walter . . . swisser-swatter! . . . " This anecdote was later set to music as a catch, and is one of the earliest references in European literature to the female orgasm.

234. The couplet here is a modern American rhyming proverb as to why *old women are best to make love to.* Both the proverb and this limerick draw ultimately from Benjamin Franklin's famous paradox, " A Letter on the Choice of a Mistress, " which comes to the same mock-serious conclusion, with various proofs. Two centuries earlier than Franklin, however, this same Oedipal choice is taken very seriously in Brantôme's *Lives of Fair and Gallant Ladies* (MS. 1584), the Fourth Discourse : " On the Love of Old Women, and how some love them as much as young ones, " which takes the same simplistic " practical " point of view as here. Consider also, more recently, Mistinguett, Mae West, and other " Last of the Red Hot Mamas. "

II. ORGANS

235. " *Aggies* " : inmates of the widely disliked Texas A. & M. (Agricultural & Mechanical) college, essentially a military training-school, with a bad reputation for sadistic public hazing of undergraduates in imitation of the notorious Parris Island training camp of the U.S. Marines.

251. Lavrenty Beria, Russian secret police chief, disgraced and executed at the death of Russian dictator Stalin in 1953.

263. Chaplin, *The Limerick That Has the Appeal* (1976) No. 2028, gives independently another original on these identical main rhymes.

265. There was a young girl named O'Dare
Whose body was covered with hair.
    It was really great fun
    To probe in her bun,
For her pussy might be anywhere. [1968A.

266. THE HIGHER LEARNING. See Part I at Limerick 2:40.

275. Apparently drawn from a printed novelty card (U.S. 1945?) showing a pregnant " Ozark " farmwife holding her naked husband wheelbarrow-fashion in the field, and thus using his prick as plough.

282. OLD CLASSIC. Intruded in a pornographic story in *The Pearl: Christmas Annual* [London: Lazenby] 1881, p. 30 (reprint, Atlanta, Georgia: Pendulum Books, 1967, p. 62), and given by the host, the Hon. Priapus Bigcock, as the "new Aesthetic Nursery Rhyme," in mockery of the pre-Raphaelite school of art. Revised by Lazenby the following year in *The Cremorne* ("March 1851" [1882]) No. 3: p. 87, the source of the present text. A defective monorhyme version in oral circulation is given as Limerick 1:1600, dated 1943, under "Chamber of Horrors." Compare also 2:2379, certainly inspired by the couplet here.

285. Widespread folk idea, that sexual and intellectual potency cannot be combined: "*Big prick and no brains.*" (Politely: "Strong back and a weak mind," as in the mining song that became a pop best-seller during the 1950's, "Sixteen Tons.") The line is improved, as quoted in Archie Green's *Only A Miner* (Urbana, Ill., 1972) p. 309: "During my apprenticeship I was told constantly that a 'woodbutcher' needed only a strong back and his brains knocked out." In its sexual form this is a basic tenet of Eastern religious asceticism, at least as ancient in the West as Falstaff's insulting remark on "a weak mind and an able body," in 2 *Henry IV,* II.iv.275. ("Body," pronounced *bawdy,* seems to have been a common Elizabethan pun alluding to the genitals, as in the description of Mercutio by Romeo.) Reviewing *Midnight Cowboy* in its usual, well-expurgated prose, *Time* magazine (3 Sept. 1965, p. 86, "Joe's Journey") cops-out in the obvious pantywaist metonymy of *pants* for *penis*: "Joe Buck is . . . strong in the trousers [!] and weak in the head." See also Limerick 2:292, on the fool's "bauble" (which is to be "hidden in a hole" in *Romeo & Juliet,* II.iv.98); and Note 2:370 below.

Further, that sexual excitement drives out conscience and intelligence (*Penis erectus non conscientius*; also given as a Yiddish proverb in Philip Roth's *Portnoy's Complaint,* 1968, p. 128: "*Ven der putz shteht, ligt der séchel in d'rerd,*" When the prick stands up, the brains get buried in the ground). Ultimately, that excessive sexual activity "sucks out the brains" of the male (or "melts the fat off his bones," in the Trinidadian Negro expression); or that the semen is produced and replaced only at the cost of the spinal marrow or of " sixty drops of blood " for one drop of semen, and that masturbation therefore " causes insanity. "

303. There was a young lady named Greene
Who grew so abdominally lean,
    And so flat and compressed
    That her ass touched her chest,
And sideways she couldn't be seen. [1962A.

307. Variant conclusion, and compare Limerick 2:2044, " The Kidneycracker " :

    She wailed, " It's a shock,
    So much meat on a cock –
Are you *sure* it won't prove a cuntwrecker? " [1966.

309. She would take on a mate
    At a very low rate,
Like a dime or still smaller coins. [1948.

311. Improving the old classic, Limerick 1:155-156* (and compare 2:241), as does:

There was a young man of Devizes
Whose bollocks were two different sizes.
    One weighed a pound
    And dragged on the ground;
The other was small as a fly's is. [1967A.

317. First printed in Yates' *Rugby Jokes* (1968) p. 152, with " knocked the top off her womb " and " kidney-disturber. "

332. Uses the opening lines of Limerick 1:144. For the final line, in archaic form " And never spent less than a quartern, " see 1:205, dating from 1879.

335. VARIATIONS ON A THEME. For the theme announced, " Screwy Dick with the Spiral Prick " (clearly inspired by the corkscrew penis of a pig), see Limericks 1:1155 and 2:590-91. Limerick 2:336 is given without any opening stanza in *Poems in Contempt of Progress* (1974) p. 60, by 'Jerome Tichenor,' his editor Joel W. Hedgpeth observing that it is " strange that . . . this theme should be treated so ineptly as to require two lame limericks to accomplish what one sprightly erect one

should do." He adds an interesting description in French of the fish, the *Anableps,* in which the sexual organs of the two sexes can be either at the right or left side, and the fish can therefore copulate only with matching mates. (But of which of us couldn't *that* be said?)

350. THE UNSCREWTABLE ORIENT. On the myth of the oblique Oriental vagina (matching the eyes, of course; and compare the preceding Note 335), see also Limericks 2:295 and 2:459.

There was a young fellow named Viner
Who failed to get in a vagina.
    When visualized frontally
    It ran horizontally –
He forgot he was visiting China. [1968A.

354. Almost identical with Limerick 1:263* (Zerubbabel).

355.   So she practiced coition
    With a mathematician
Supplied with a square root to match. [1953.

356. SONATA APPASSIONATA. One notes with pleasure the illustrated phonograph record album of "Flute and Harpsichord Sonatas" by Telemann and the sons of Bach, played by Rampal and Veyron-Lacroix (Westminster Gold WGS-8115: Los Angeles, ABC/Dunhill Records, 1970), the cover being illustrated with a heavily symbolic gag-photograph showing a marvellously raunchy, bearded young bassoon player ogling a passionately intense young woman cellist (wearing glasses, and clutching her instrument between her knees) who is ogling him right back! Another record-sleeve in the same series (Beethoven's Piano Concerto No. 3, and "Choral Fantasy": soloist, Barenboim) shows a bare-shouldered girl holding against her chest two plaster busts of Beethoven in such a way that they seem to be her bare breasts cupped in her hands. Amusing and whimsical advertising series like these are rare. Compare Limerick 2:305.

358. When she hove into sight
All the men would take fright [1945.

364. Revising the old favorite Limerick 1:502 (on Peru, ending : " And found it was perfectly true! ") to include a reference to the American anti-Negro, anti-Northerner, and anti-Semitic secret terrorist society, the Ku Klux Klan.

365. Intruded, without notice of the missing 2nd line, as though a quatrain, in the opening story, " The Secret Life of Linda Brent, " in the erotic magazine, *The Cremorne* (London, '1851' [edited and published by Lazenby, 1882]). Compare Limerick 1:866 (Grimsby), also clearly of the same period, though first printed completely in Yates' *Rugby Jokes,* p. 18, ending : " But what could those hair-covered rims be? "

370. Article of folk-belief, perhaps based on Greek statuary (but compare Note 2:285 above) that athletes have very small genitals, and that all such narcissistic " muscle-builders " are really homosexuals — or homosexual prostitutes.

379. Dressmakers' joke : *How do you hug a fat girl? — Hug as far as you can ; then make a mark and go around and hug the rest.* (Told by a middle-aged Rumanian woman, Scranton, Pa. 1932.) Compare the folk-phrase, " *If I had a wife that ugly, I'd rope her off and sell tickets.* " (U.S. 1976.)

392. Compare the bawdy folksong, " The Landlady's Daughter, " sung to the fine Welsh tune, " The Ash Grove, " and ending with exulting emphasis :

> I've seen it, I've seen it,
> I've been in be-*tweeeen* it! —
> The hair on her dicky-dido
> Hangs down to her knee!

Limericks somehow never strike a note like that, even though on the identical subject-matter :

> There is a young girl named MacNeeze
> Whose cunt-hairs hang down past her knees.
> Great for polishing brass,
> Or for wiping her ass,
> But the crabs use it for a trapeze. [1965A.

398. Variant in *Playboy* (December 1954) p. 11.

404. By the late Howard Parke, of Los Angeles. On Henry Miller, see further Limerick 2:2441, The Classics Revisited. This series also to be compared with Limericks 2:803-09, " The Romantic Agony. "

408. Variant conclusion (and compare Limerick 2:1426) :

" I'll not wait till I marry
To get rid of my cherry –
I'm going to get fucked in a hurry! " [1966.

409. On the clichés of beginners' French lessons.

418. Written in Formosa by a member of the American air force (the " Winger ").

422. Thus earning him taunts
From his well-meaning aunts [1945.

424. When you got in her pants
She would moan in a trance [1950.

439. Larson MS. (1952) " Vulgar Stanzas, " No. 36, from a boy in Eden, Idaho, 1932. So also 2:450 below.

443. On the same main rhyme, parodying the faith-healer of Deal (Limerick 1:691) :

Said a godly young novice in Deal :
" Though sexual sin isn't real,
When Sister Sabina
Dilates my vagina,
I quite like what I *fancy* I feel. " [1968A.

467. REMEMBRANCE OF THINGS PAST. " But that was in another country, and the wench is dead. " – Marlowe.

474. One of the last of the Golden Period limericks. Credited to Dana Thompson in the Hall Collection (" Vintage " group) No. 2647*a*, with variant :

His balls hung much lower
And dragged on the floor,
And sometimes rolled under the bureau. [1959.

496. Rhode Island roosters are *red.* Compare the popular folk-stanza or toast sharing the couplet rhyme here, a stanza that can be traced to a polite original dated 1614 :

When a man grows old
And his balls grow cold,
And the head of his pecker turns blue,
And he goes to diddle,
And it bends in the middle –
Did that ever happen to *you*?
(*or* : You're through, old sport, you're through!)

III. STRANGE INTERCOURSE

500. Rather close to a clerihew. The taboo on incest has been much overdone since ancient Egypt, when it was a privilege reserved only to kings and their sisters. (This may explain the taboo.) Millennia of inbreeding do not seem to have done the slightest genetic damage to cats – those motherfuckers.

502. Upon meeting some satyrs,
To whom only sex matters [1966.

522. This identical evil dream is roughly the plot of the Canadian horror movie, David Cronenberg's *The Parasite Murders* (1976), which – even for neurotic Montréal – hits rock bottom in cinematic sexo-sadism.

526. There once was a fellow from Beverley
Who went in for fucking quite heavily.
He fucked night and day
Till his bollocks gave way,
But the doctors replaced them quite cleverly. [1967A.

536. In *Dirt : An Exegesis* (1965) p. 21. Compare :

A fellow from Nassau, Bahamas,
Was an actor in sexual dramas.
He'd grab at a skirt
And jab till it hurt,
After poking it through her pajamas. [1953.

548. See Limerick 1:282, " The Amorous Phantasm, " on the same theme and matching rhymes.

559. FUCK FREUD! " The Hermit of the Mohave " (Limerick 1:463) revised *again* for a pre-psychotic generation. See the even worse 1:1736.

561. Variant printed in *This Week* (U.S. newspaper magazine section, 22 Nov. 1959) attributed to a woman.

568. SAN QUENTIN QUAIL (S.Q.Q.) : young girls below the legal " age of consent " — usually 18 years. The term refers to San Quentin prison, in California. *Lolita* (Paris : Girodias, 1955), a best-selling novel when reprinted in America, on pædophilic relations with an underage girl of that name, by Prof. Vladimir Nabokov, satirizing yet continuing the inspiration of the similar pornographic novel of the 1890's, *Flossie A Venus of Fifteen,* " By One Who Has Worshipped at Her Shrine, " falsely attributed to Swinburne. Compare Limerick 2:1341, " Precious Bane. "

574. AD ASSTRA PER ASPERA. Compare Ogden Nash's " Home, 99 44/100% Sweet Home, " with its courageous line at that date (and still) : " *Home is heaven and orgies are vile, But I like an orgy, once in a while.* " As is not commonly recognized, it might be mentioned that the source of Ogden Nash's post-Whitmaniacal poetic style is a bitterly serious prose-poem by a man who died the year Nash was born : Samuel " Erewhon " Butler's " O Critics, Cultured Critics, " reprinted in John Bartlett's *Familiar Quotations* (13th ed. 1955) p. 672, where it is well worth turning up.

577. " *maisie* " — as in " Sadie-Maisie " (sado-masochist) — from the Dutch, *meisje,* a young girl. On sex and the Dutch, see urgently Limericks 2:2654-68, " The Martian Chronicles, " and Note 2:2537.

583. An epitaph unknown to fame
Puts the slogan of Caesar to shame.
    The tomb of a rake,
    Who spent life on the make,
Reads : " *I saw, I conquered, I came.* " [1954].

Limerick 2:2643 gives still another independent re-invention of the same punning reversal, on a science-fiction background.

600. On this matter of the phallic superiority of the Negro over the white, see also Limericks 2:302, 323, 498, 556, 600, and 1695, and my strictly impartial discussion in *Rationale II : No Laughing Matter* (1975) 13.II.1, " Negroes and Jews, " pp. 474-83. The uneasy folk-certainty among whites, at all cultural levels, that the Negro is the sexual superior of the white (both male & female) is certainly based on unconscious *guilt* over the enslavement and sexual exploitation of the Negroes for centuries, and the fear of sexual and other retaliation as the Black population rises in numbers and militancy. See the bitter prefiguration of the eventual anti-Black genocide really intended (as with the Indians) as the " Final Solution, " in John A. Williams' *The Man Who Cried I Am* (Boston : Little, Brown, 1967) – it is the whole plot of the book – and *Trick Baby* by 'Iceberg Slim' (Robert Beck ; Los Angeles : Holloway House, 1967) chap. 18, " The Haters, " pp. 245-53, which has the affluent WASP spokesman lay it right on the line.

Ice-skating on the crust of the volcano, the liberal comedy-waltz continues, and the American Secretary of Agriculture, Mr. Earl Butz, was immediately " allowed to resign " in October 1976, when a rock-music magazine, *Rolling Stone,* published an interview in which he was quoted as saying, off the record – during a presidential campaign in which it was realized that the Black vote would now become crucial – that the Republican party cannot attract Negroes " *because coloreds* [i.e. *niggers*] *only want three things: a tight cunt, a pair of loose shoes, and a warm place to shit.* " Actually, Butz could have run for president on a ticket like that, as was underlined by a private New Year's card for 1977 (from Canada) which used his line in rebus form as its good wishes for the year. Compare Sir William Osler, *Science and Immortality* (1904) chap. 2 : " The natural man has only two primal passions : to get and to beget. "

601. Essentially a limerick version of a rodeo joke in which : *The cowboy's bride has St. Vitus dance on their wedding night, and he cannot climb aboard. He calls in four of his cowboy friends at the wedding* (*or bellboys at the honeymoon hotel*), *has each of them hold one of the bride's arms or legs, positions himself over her, and shouts, " All right, let 'er* RIP! " (L.A. 1968.)

617. AMERICAN CULTURE. John Updike's remarkable poem, " Cunts, " in the style of Whitman and E. E. Cummings, published in his *Six Poems* (New York : Frank Hallman, 1976) is reprinted in his *Tossing & Turning* (New York : Knopf, 1977) pp. 71-75, as the dominating piece in this slender volume, followed by " Pussy : A Preliminary Epithalamium. " He notes his inspiration in the subtitle : Upon Receiving The Swingers Life Club Membership Solicitation — which he apparently refused, quoting five typical swingers' classifed advertising lines — and wrote these splendid poems instead, which announce: " *We must assimilate cunts to our creed of beauty,* " and goes on from there.

In fact, the beauty of women's bodies, and specifically of their genitals, breasts, and buttocks — recently even of their faces — has long exercised male humanity, at least since the time of the Judgment of Paris : the first recorded beauty contest, which is supposed to have started the Trojan War, about 1184 B.C. (And compare *The Book of Esther,* 1 : 10-12, seven hundred years later.) Pierre de Bourdeille, Seigneur de Brantôme, in his priceless collection of 16th-century anecdotes and scandals, *Les Vies des Dames Galantes* (MS. 1584 : English translation published by Carrington about 1900), spends the latter half of his Second Discourse on this subject, with exact anatomical details — " *pour venir encore plus bas* " — as to the genital beauty, pubic hair, etc., of the famous women he discusses. (Brantôme, *Les Dames Galantes,* ed. Maurice Rat ; Paris : Garnier, 1947, pp. 164-90.) He then continues with a brief Third Discourse on the subject — still something of a mystery — " Of the Beauty of a Fine Leg. "

619. A passionate lady named Popper
In heat goes completely improper.
  She gets hotter and hotter
  Till brawny men totter ;
The job's not to start but to stopp'er. [1966.

The current American folk-comparison for female heat is " *as hot as a half-fucked* (or *fresh-fucked*) *female fox in a forest fire,* " collected in Tennessee, Colorado, and elsewhere, with variations. See the remarkably frank and full contribution,

" Folk Comparisons from Colorado, " by Cathy M. Orr, in *Western Folklore* (1976) Vol. 35 : pp. 175-208, at No. I-286.

624. Robert S. Thompson, *Limericks for the Literate* (1967) p. 40.

625. As most men vaguely know but are not conscious of the facts (note the pitiful under-estimation of Limerick 2:771), and are overawed by male actors bragging in the men's magazines that they have had intercourse with several thousand women in a lifetime – nothing being said as to erotic *quality* – some simple arithmetic as to the life of an ordinary prostitute is appropriate here. If a woman services sexually only three men per day, a minimum for high-style call girls, while whores in cribs may turn as many " tricks " as fifty in a working night! – in a year that is 3 X 330 days=1000 men. In an average prostitutory career of ten years, that means a minimum of TEN THOUSAND MEN. (And damn few orgasms for the woman, in all that.) The common male-masochistic fantasy of finding a whore " with a heart of gold " and " marrying her to reform her, " therefore means believing that you have the *Golden Penis* that can succeed where all the other men failed, and wipe out the trauma of *ten thousand unloved pricks.* More power to you, sucker!

Of course you've heard of Casanova :
His wife, too, had passions that drove her.
    She tried ten thousand men,
    And then started again –
Don Juan! Casanova! Move over! [1977A.

630. Pedication of the adulterer while he is still in the woman's body, by the aggrieved male, is the classical punishment, though completely overlooking or repressing the homosexual tone and the possibility that homosexual triolism of this kind may be precisely what the " cuckolded " husband may have been trying to set up. See the " *Prompt* Husband, " the final sort cited in the prose typology, "Characters of Husbands" quoted completely from *The Pearl* (Dec. 1879) in *Rationale of the Dirty Joke : First Series* (1968) 9.II.5, " Punishing the Adulterer, " pp. 726-27. Chaplin's *The Limerick That Has the*

Appeal (1976) reworks this entire series into a limerick-sequence, Nos. 1546-64, entitled " What Kind of Husband Are You? " ending of course with the *Prompt* husband, who represents the punchline. Compare the more ancient, lethal form of the same riposte in the Biblical story of Cozbi and Zimri, in *Numbers,* 25: 7-8.

631. TOUJOURS GALANT! On a theatre joke (N.Y. 1952) on the famously lesbian actress, *Tallulah Bankhead replying to an attempted seduction by a young playwright at a party, by saying to him : " Of coss, dahling, I'm dying to! But I've got to get rid of all these people first. Go up to my bedroom, and undress and get in bed and wait for me. If I'm not there in fifteen minutes* — START WITHOUT ME! "

638. A variant of Limerick 1:1446, in the sequence " Back from Bohemia. "

639. Next door old Miss Klopps
Phoned up for the cops [1965.

649. From *Be Pure!* (Australia, 1963) p. 19.

A much-diddled dolly named Mabel
Always gets hers bent over a table.
" Fucking's fun, " the gal said,
" But it's *more* fun in bed,
And best on the hay in a stable. " [1966.

705. This is the famous 16th-century " Whirling Basket Trick, " first mentioned — without any whirling — in Pietro Aretino's *Ragionamenti* (1534), and later shown, with a Negro couple, as one of the illustrations in a late 17th-century edition of the early European prose work on sex posture and technique, *La Puttana Errante* (The Arrant Whore) by Aretino's sometime secretary, Niccolò Franco. See further, G. Legman, *The Horn Book* (1964) pp. 63 and 79-80 ; and David Foxon, *Libertine Literature in England* (1965) p. 24, note 12. In an astonishing survival at the folk-level, the illustration of the " whirling basket " position still continues to circulate (redrawn strictly from oral tradition) in a xeroxlore drawing showing an " Ozark " girl in a twisted tree-swing having intercourse with her supine, drunken father (Noah/Lot), in

Cathy M. Orr *et al.* : *Urban Folklore from Colorado : Photocopy Cartoons* (Ann Arbor : Xerox University Microfilms, 1976 ; Research Abstracts LD69-79) vol. II : p. 156.

709. Dysphemistic version of Limerick 1:34 (Flynn/gin). The couplet is derived from the 1930's mock-Pacific island song, " Mama Don' Wan' No Peas, No Rice, No Coconut Oil, " cited in Nathanael West's *The Day of the Locust* :

An' Mama don' wan' no whiskey,
' Cause whiskey makes her frisky,
An' keeps her *hot & bothered* all the day!

716. A pendant, of course, to Limerick 1:337 on Persian perversions. The " Yanks " in the couplet here are doubtless only for the rhyme, yet consider the remarkable photograph of acrobatic fellation — while the woman hangs by her hands from the man standing before a circle of admiring, cowboy-booted co-" swingers " — in Earl Kemp's *The Illustrated Presidential Report of the Commission on Obscenity and Pornography* (San Diego, 1970). As the publisher of this provocative reprint was indicted for literary " pandering, " and the edition presumably quashed, citation here is to the reprint in English made in Germany (Darmstadt : Melzer Verlag, 1972?) Vol. I : p. 157.

731. Supplied by the poetess with the understandable remark that her husband " hates this one. "

733. SMOG ON CAPITOL HILL. From a sequence of 17 limericks based on some American congressional sex-scandal. ' Jack S.[Ass] Phogbound ' is the loud-mouthed Southern senator in Al Capp's comic-strip, " Li'l Abner. " Compare *Time* magazine (7 June 1976) " The United States : Congress : Indecent Exposure on Capitol Hill, " followed by " Romances, " concerning less recent Washington sex-scandals, including those concerning Presidents Franklin D. Roosevelt and John F. Kennedy, but overlooking the more notorious case of President Warren Gamaliel Harding (who is also alleged to have been a Negro " passer "), alluded to in the final limerick here. Compare also Limerick 2:1741, " Legislative Perquisite, " and 2:2494, " Write Your Own "; also Cathy M. Orr & Michael Preston, *Urban Folklore from Type-*

script Broadsides (Ann Arbor, Michigan : Xerox University Microfilms International, 1976 ; Research Abstracts LD69-79) Vol. I : p. 106, " Job Description : *Sue Deau Sexretary,* " whose penultimate duty is " Rreepprroodduuccttiioonn Specialist. " Why it is perfectly all right for French and even British kings to have had endless concubines and mistresses, but scandalous in the case of American presidents and lesser fry, is difficult to explain : the leftover Puritan moral climate, no doubt.

738. WIFE-TRADING FROM A TO Z. Ugly and impossibly bad originals by Clement Wood, following up the orgiastics and Negrophobia of Limericks 1:346-47 by the same poet. His final limerick here (2:746, O'Bangeller) is at least runner-up for the title of " The World's Worst Limerick " in the final chapter, " Chamber of Horrors. "

750. MACHINOMANIA. Another example of the attempt of impotent modern man to *become* The Machine he fears :

A brazen hi-fi fan named Walter
Lured a girl to his audio altar.
  As she studied his tweeter
  He plugged in his peter :
'Twas coaxial bliss to assault 'er. [1960.

763. TALES OF MY LANDLORD. A travesty somewhere between Robert W. Service's " Shooting of Dan McGrew " and Thomas Hood's " The Bridge of Sighs " (" *One more Unfortunate, etc.* "), of which latter the dactylic couplets here parody and reprise some of the more god-awful rhymes.

768. Pendant to Limerick 1:348, and playing on its " Again and again " conclusion.

772.   With intentions to fuck
  He was shit out of luck,
For the gal uses only a carrot. [1966.

776. THE OLDEST JOKE. Limerick treatment of the favorite modern joke on incest, sometimes called "Happy Families," traced several centuries back in *Rationale II : No Laughing Matter* (1975) 14.1.4, " Anti-Family, " pp. 740-41. Nu-

merous tellers refer to this proudly as the " dirtiest " joke they know. Compare Limericks 2:598 and 778, Sibling Revelry. Trying to *clean it up,* as only a way of saving money (as with " The Hermit of the Mohave, " Limerick 1:463) :

There was an old fellow from Brest
Who openly practiced incest.
  " My sisters and nieces
  Are all dandy pieces,
And they don't cost a cent, " he confessed. [1968A.

782. Said a luscious young lady named Wade,
On a beach with her charms all displayed :
  " It's so hot in the sun,
  Perhaps rape would be fun . . .
At least that would give me some shade! " [1966.

783. RAPE!! Intended to be provocatively cynical, this (also the preceding, 2:782 and its Note) seem somehow less so than two clearly insincere American movies distributed in 1976, visually exploiting the rape of women and their violent revenge therefor. These are obviously really in favor of, and enjoying the idea, and the erotic spectacle of rape, not exposing it ; and are just another form of the new end-of-a-civilization fad for gruesomely sadistic " catastrophe "-exploiting films, on which see Limerick 2:2502, " Recipe for a Bestseller. " Unfortunately, the neo-Feminist literature concerning itself with rape, since Ruth Herschberger's *Adam's Rib* (New York, 1948), also somehow always ends up in the bathetic vengefulness of " Can Women Rape Men? " Not to mention more direct castratory revenges.

787. " As long as it *stinks!* " A folk-phrase (also existing in French) accepting the essential Woman, under the pose of crudity, and the naso-oral imperatives of sexual selection by means of *smell* — not sight, as the advertisers try to convince us — in all mammalian males. Compare Limerick 2:1849.

793. LO! THE WELL-HUNG INDIAN. Actually, owing to their Oriental origin, American Indians and Eskimos are believed to have penises shorter than those of whites (on the average), as well as sparse facial and pubic hair.

IV. ORAL IRREGULARITY

824. Definition of " a French lover, " or " the Perfect Lover " : *A man with a 9-inch tongue, who can breathe through his ears.* (Arlington, Texas, 1967.)

826. The author of this learned limerick notes in his covering letter — citing Martial's Latin *Epigrams* (1st century A.D.), and Forberg's *Manual of Classical Erotology* (1824) — that his limerick " alludes to the inability of the fellator to *whistle* (or talk for that matter) *while he works.* " On the challenge of this statement, a young Dutch-Sumatran woman in Paris, in 1955, responded without even a moment's thought by *humming* the opening bars of Johann Strauss' " Beautiful Blue Danube, " *in medias res,* as I note further in *Oragenitalism : Oral Techniques in Genital Excitation* (New York : Julian Press, 1969) pp. 240 and 266. This is now known jocularly as a " hum-job, " presumably an improvement on the standard " blow-job. "

829. " *Piece of trade* " : homosexual slang for a fellator.

830. NO SMOKING, PLEASE. Mormons frown upon smoking & drinking, except where these bring in money for the State of Utah through licensing taxes. Actually, this is the same in all states (and countries), and has been, at least since the time of the Opium War in the 1830's. In France, as a further cynical jab, *part* of the money earned by the government through its massive tobacco sales is allotted to the minuscule anti-tobacco health campaign. See *Matthew,* vi. 3 : " Let not thy left hand know what thy right hand doeth "; and compare Limerick 2:878.

831. On this matter of homosexual prostitution by guardsmen — not solely a British industry — the ultimate statement is the posthumous autobiography, *My Father & Myself,* by J. R. Ackerley (London, 1968), in which it is the author's *father* who turns out to be the homosexual prostitute, on the style of Limerick 2:1851, " Piccadilly " (which see). On Ackerley's hate-testament, see further *Rationale II : No Laughing Matter,* chap. 10.I, " On the Cause of Homosexuality, " p. 63.

832. " *If you can't lick 'em,* JOIN *'em!* " Rule No. 1 of the traitor's art, now the American national motto, expressive of the weak submissiveness of our century. This is expected soon to replace " *Business is Business* " (meaning the same thing) on the verso of the Great Seal of the United States.

840. CHRISTMAS PARTY. On cunnilinctus during menstruation, see *Rationale of the Dirty Joke : First Series,* 8.V.4, " Cunnilinctus and Masochism, " pp. 567-84, which includes my own favorite joke. John Updike's erotic poem, " Cunts, " in his *Tossing & Turning* (New York : Knopf, 1977) p. 74, notes boldly : " I pulled a Tampax with my teeth and found it, darling, not so bloody. "

841. RUSTY NAIL. Alcoholism being the principal drug addiction among Western men (and women), much pother and mystique is expended on mixing alcoholic drinks artfully, and calling them names like " cocktails " (once presumably used as a swizzle for mixing the drink) to hide the drug reality and addiction. The name " Rusty Nail " is a forgotten allusion to a folktale concerning *a trickster hobo cozening a housewife* (child-and-mother situation) *into " helping " him make a nourishing soup out of a rusty nail, or a magical stone* (in decayed versions frankly *out of a ball of horse-dung*). According to *Gourmet* Magazine (New York, Oct. 1976) p. 127, here is the correct recipe for the alcoholic drink, in which note the absurdly exact details of glass, ice, etc. : " Put 3 or 4 ice cubes in a chilled 6-oz. Old Fashioned glass, and pour ¼ cup Scotch whisky and 2 tablespoons Drambuie [whisky liqueur] over the ice. Makes 1 drink. " Other erotic or virilely symbolic " tool " names for mixed drinks include the " Screw Driver " — with aphrodisiacal overtones, of course — and the frankly menstrual " Bloody Mary " (tomato juice and vodka, with Tabasco sauce), on which see further Note 2:840 preceding. It should be noted that cunnilinctus (" a hair of the dog that bit you "?) is believed by men in America to be an unfailing *hangover remedy* after drunkenness, overdetermining the underlying orality.

856. On the slang phrase (originally British) for cunnilinctus, " *eating hearthrug pie,* " also " *munching the bearded clam* , " " *cleaning up the kitchen,* " and " *sneezing in the (shrimp) basket.* "

857. Deep Throat. Highly appropriate title of the first publicly-shown " hard-core " pornographic movie in the United States in the early 1970's, essentially a fellation-training film, directed by Gerard Damiano and starring the indeed deep-throated young woman known as Linda Lovelace. The title is the plot, and the star's autobiography, *Inside Linda Lovelace* (1972) tells all the rest, though it does not explain in a practical way how she trained herself to overcome the usual gag-reflex on deep penetration of the throat. On the relatively minor profits of this film, see Note 2:2502, " Recipe for a Bestseller, " concerning the competing horror-movie, *Jaws.* Based just on these figures, *five times as many* modern Americans would rather see spectacle sadism than exotic sex.

860. Intended as a thumbnail review of *Oragenitalism* (1969) by G. Legman, on which see Note 2:826 above.

865. *Be Pure!* (Perth, Australia, 1963) p. 19.

868. A flat-chested lady named Keyes
Had titties resembling two peas.
    But her oral technique
    Could stiffen the weak,
And left all the strong on their knees. [1968A.

870. *Super Sex to Sexty* (1971) No. 14 : p. 18.

872. On the original " twelve-year-old nymphet, Lolita, " see Note 2:568 above.

Said Ida naïvely to Pete :
" Though one's genital zone is raw meat,
    It seems quite incredible
    The stuff can be edible,
But they claim it's delightful to eat. " [1966.

881. Based, as also Limerick 2:884 below, on a 1930's tag-line said to a woman : " *Uncross your legs — You're breaking my glasses!* " Also (to a man) : " *Leggo my ears — I know my business!* "

893. Math for the Millions. " Thirty-four-and-a-half, " as half of the *sixty-nine* (*69*), is explained in Robert Anton Wilson's popularization of sexual linguistics, *Playboy's Book of*

Forbidden Words (Chicago, 1972) s.v. *Numbers game* : " A session of *balling* in which the emphasis is on variety and endurance. The implication is that the participants pass through the ' 69 ' (mutual oragenitalism), the ' 34½ ' (fellatio or cunnilingus — a witticism created by dividing 69 in half), the ' 79 ' (the ' 69 ' with all ten fingers in her rump), and the ' 99 ' (anal intercourse). " Apparently unknown to *Playboy* — or perhaps not forbidden — there are also the ' 71 ' (a 69 with another couple watching), the ' 73,' which is identical but with " two off-duty cops peeking through the window-blind " ; and the ' 68, ' which means that : " *You can six, but I won't nine!* " See also the ' 138 ' in Limerick 2:911, which doubles the sixty-nine instead.

903. So many girls tried her
That the diddler inside 'er
Was almost worn out by the traffic. [1967A.

The priests at the Temple of Isis
Used to offer us amber and spices.
Then back of the shrine
We would play sixty-nine,
And other unmentionable vices. [1968A.

913. Discussions of the flavor of semen are really pointless, since the enjoying of this flavor, and the willingness to swallow the semen at ejaculation, depend largely on the *passion* the oral participant feels.

A broad-minded virgin named Netty
Was sucking a cock on the jetty.
Said she, " It tastes nice,
Like pudding and rice,
But not quite as good as spaghetti." [1960A.

920. When properly handled,
And diddled and dandled,
It played Beethoven's Seventh Symphonica. [1958.

922. Auto-fellatory version of the auto-pedicational Limerick 1:1559 (and less difficult to achieve).

923. Owing to the early French population in the American South, oragenitalism has been much more openly accepted

there, throughout the 19th century, than in the rest of the country until the exposure of the American troops to " French culture " during World Wars I & II, and especially in recent decades. Although fellation was long thought of as a specialty of " nigger wenches, " both during and after Slavery, and in the form of prostitution, male Negroes still generally refuse to perform cunnilinctus (even or especially for their own women), as being too submissive to the woman's sexual needs and dominance. See the Negro " toasts " (narrative rhymed recitations) pointedly on this matter, printed in *The Life : The Lore and Folk Poetry of the Black Hustler,* by Dennis Wepman, *et al.* (University of Pennsylvania Press, 1976), and especially in Bruce Jackson's *Get Your Ass in the Water and Swim Like Me* (Harvard University Press, 1974), with Prof. Jackson's discussion of this matter, pp. 19-20.

She savors the flavor
But will, as a favor,
Go family-style now and then. [1965.

924. *Be Pure!* (1963) p. 17 ; " *fork*, " crotch.

V. BUGGERY

927. THE BEY OF ALGIERS. For Part I, actually a later development, see Limericks 2:503-6.

935. In the rottenest dive in Cawnpore
I asked a boy, " When do you whore? "
He replied, " Sir, at seven,
And suck cocks till eleven ;
Then we bugger from midnight till four! " [1968A.

This should be compared with the Earl of Rochester's 17th-century " The Debauchee, " beginning : " I rise at eleven, I dine about two, " also ending in the rectum.

937. Pendant or parody of Limerick 1:1186, on the couple named Kelly who became pasted together during inter-

course, and " had to live belly to belly. " See other frank examples of this fear of the mythical *vagina dentata* in *Rationale II : No Laughing Matter,* 13.I, " Vagina Dentata, " pp. 427-67. A curious, orally-displaced version of this ancient bogey was collected (as true) from a 17-year-old highschool girl from Redlands, California, in 1964 ; and ten years later from a 10-year-old American boy by Dr. Brian Sutton-Smith. *A boy and girl are kissing surreptitiously in the boys' toilet (in the basement) in school. They are caught by the school principal, and as they try to pull apart, their dental braces (which both are wearing) become tangled, locking them together!*

940. WUFF TRADE. On the homosexual pose of an ultra-tough ("butch") virility, see *Rationale II : No Laughing Matter,* 10. II.I, " The Tough Faggot, " pp. 81-84 ; and the extraordinary illustrated essay by Clifford P. Westermeier, " The Cowboy and Sex, " in Charles W. Harris & Buck Rainey, eds., *The Cowboy : Six-Shooters, Songs, and Sex* (University of Oklahoma Press, 1976) pp. 98-105.

Said a sodomous sissy from Siddon :
" I prefer my perversion well-hidden.
    Though a young man may suit
    The desire of my root,
I'm aware that such fruit is forbidden. " [1972.

949. " asshole *petite* " : Now that the defunct *Hustler* magazine and other " gynecological gazettes " in full color have apprised the *Playboy* public that *not all cunts look alike* (not even the pubic hair), the anus is also beginning to attract critical attention, as in John Updike's elegantly modern erotic poem, " Cunts, " in his *Tossing & Turning* (New York : Knopf, 1977) p. 71, noting that in a spread-leggèd age, " the snowflakes that burst forth are no two alike . . . [with] assholes a-stare like monocles tiny as dimes. "

962. Peter Doyle was the young streetcar conductor loved by the great American poet, Walt Whitman. They are seen in a famous photograph, dressed to the nines and doting on each other in a loveseat. Actually, Doyle is not thought to have been a transvestite, but appears to have been standard rough-

trade. " *Change one's oil* " : to induce a homosexual to become heterosexual (reversed in this limerick), as is popularly believed to be possible. See also Limerick 2:1077, " Leaves of Gr-ass. "

966. " Steatopygious " is good.

968. Thumbnail review of Mark Twain's bawdy lecture and poem, *The Mammoth Cod,* first published complete, with a long introduction—to be sure—by G. Legman (Milwaukee : Maledicta Press, 1976).

971. From a repetitive set of six " Dumaricks, " all on (homosexual) incest, and on the identical rhymes.

979. TALES FROM BOCCACCIO. Author of the oldest work of fiction still being read in the West — other than the Bible — Giovanni Boccaccio lives on in memory for the famous sexuality of a handful of the stories in his *Decameron* (written in 1353). Compare Limerick 1:386.

Girls! Beware of Boccaccio,
His favorite dish is fellatio.
    All the young girls in Florence
    Drink his semen in torrents,
So be sure *you* stay off his patio! [1975A.

995. Evelyn Waugh, *Private Diaries* (London, 1972), as reprinted in *The Observer,* with asterism expurgation of the name B*****, in diary entry of 14 Nov. 1920, during Waugh's college years : " Yesterday was rather pleasant. I cut chapel, spent the morning eating meringues and drinking tea and talking filth. Lux came to tea. We walked all the evening and made up filthy limericks. Perhaps the best was : [*as in text*]. " Typically unconscious self-parody. As to the priceless combination of " meringues and filth, " obviously not very brilliant, but " *like many a British student, likely to get it right in the end — notwithstanding.* " (Essex, Conn. 1976.)

997. The last line is a masterpiece.

999. Three-letter word : F-A-G. Four-letter word : F-U-C-K. Five-letter word : W-H-O-R-E (or B-I-T-C-H). In college-slang, a " four-letter man " is a S-H-I-T. Note in the caption of limerick 2:2366 that other American four-letter word, B-A-R-F,

meaning " to vomit " (from the German, *werfen,* to throw). California and other states which use combinations of three letters followed or preceded by numbers, on automobile license plates, such as THX 1138 — as in the depressingly real anticipations movie by George Lucas (1970) so entitled, in which that is the " name " of a unisex, robotized human individual, and not the license plate of a car — generally have official but uncirculated lists of three-letter combinations to be avoided as obscene or sacrilegious such as PEE, POO, FUK, TIT, ASS, GOD, and so forth. These lists would be worth hijacking and publishing for their lexicographical and future sociological interest. I have been told such lists are made up by inspection of the 17,576 possible combinations of three letters (26 X 26 X 26) extruded by computer methods. That must be an interesting job for somebody with a dirty mind. There would also have to be different lists for every language, particularly French : to avoid CON, CUL, VIT, and so forth. Thus, Canada would have to have *two* lists. See the 186 "Wiggy Words Forbidden on California License Plates" in the Los Angeles *Free Press* (Feb. 24, 1967), p. 9.

1019. Topper for the famous Limerick 1:417, on the " young man of Nantucket, whose prick was so long he could suck it. " And the equally famous 1:459 (Calcutta) likewise on autopedication, often collected as a folk-poem.

1022. Almost the only example in the present collection of the purposely inept limerick style affected by Edward Lear (see *The Limerick : First Series,* Introduction, pp. xii-xiii), in which the last line merely repeats and varies the first. But compare Limericks 2:1474 and 1696.

1025. Homosexual parody of Limerick 1:935, ending " Than ever went in through your mouth. "

1027. Ethnic-insult roundup : " *What are the four most dangerous things in the world? — An Irishman with a quart of whiskey, a Jew with a law-degree, a Polack with a hardon, and a Greek with a pair of tennis shoes.* " (N.Y. 1976.)

1030. *The Excursion* (1814), one of Wordsworth's worst. See Note 1:1139.

When girls on him palled
For a young man he called [1972.

1038. A simple young fellow named Spear
Had tricks both amusing and queer :
He tickled the asses
And cunts of the lasses,
And stuck in his cock from the rear. [1948.

1041. " *Change one's luck* " : a common superstition, that sexual intercourse with a person of other skin-color, such as Negro or Chinese, will change one's luck (especially bad luck at gambling), or will " unhex " any other type of evil magic operated against one by unknown enemies, and thus *in particular* cure psychic impotence in the male. All purported aphrodisiacs are basically similar " unhexings. " But see further, on the deeper psychological determinants (flight-of-Oedipus) in the search for " low " or " dirty " women, called by Freud " The Most Prevalent Form of Degradation in the Erotic Life, " in a famous essay, *Rationale II : No Laughing Matter* (1975) 11.III.4, " Prostitution : Impossibilities, " pp. 290–99.

1042. Said the groom to his blushing young bride,
" There is something I have to confide :
At the height of my passion
I prefer it dog-fashion,
So bend over and pooch out your back-side! " [1969A.

1043. A handsome whore-hopper named Shumate
Acquired him a masculine screw-mate.
As they feathered the bird
There came up a third,
Who said, " Let me in on that too, mate. " [1948.

The prison slang term " *feather the bird,* " referring to anal intercourse, will not be found in the extensive glossary by G. Legman, " The Language of Homosexuality, " in George W. Henry's *Sex Variants* (New York : Harper-Hoeber, 1941) vol. II, *ad fin.,* which is totally omitted from the one-volume reprint ; nor in the dictionary of homosexual *camp* issued as *The Queens' Vernacular : A Gay Lexicon,* by Bruce Rodgers (San Francisco : Straight Arrow Books, 1972) ; but the associated term, *bird-taker,* for a homosexual, will be found in the deeply authentic but unfinished manuscript glossary of prison slang by Frank Prewitt & Francis K. Schaeffer, *Vacaville Vocabulary,* of which the section of homosexual slang was issued in hektograph form [San Francisco, 1964] 28f.4to.

1044. Telling in five lines the same story on which Eugene Field spends 34 long-line couplets in his " Socratic Love, " first printed in *The Stag Party* [Boston? 1888] unnumbered pp. 241-43, and reprinted in T. R. Smith's *Immortalia* (1927) pp. 11-13. Smith notes that it was " Written for and recited before the Papyrus Club of Boston in September, 1888, " by Field, who would have enjoyed the *Alcibiades/Fri-a-days* rhyme here, though it will not compare with Field's :

The victim of his lust cried out :
  " Ehue! that all in vain I
Should to this hour have kept intact
  My rosy sphincter ani! "

1045. SIAM. Intended as an improved version of Limerick-sequence 1:510, " Royal Spasm in Five Fits, " this will be found (partly in manuscript) in the rare printed work, *Lyra Ebriosa* (1930), on which see the Bibliography here. Compare also Limericks 2:503, " The Bey of Algiers, " and 2:1895. The equally rare work, *The " Wrecks "* (Reno, 1933?) p. 117, gives a single stanza with refrain repetitions, ending :

  Cunt is all very well,
  But it hasn't the smell,
Nor the grip of the ass of a man, a MAN!

1066. A naïve young fellow named Sears
Once spent the week-end with two queers.
  Although we've inquired,
  He won't say what transpired,
But he hasn't sat down for two years! [1966.

1073. A completion of the 2-line " challenge " limerick, set in Note 1:1357 on *Hoover/Vancouver.*

1074. A BISEXUAL BUILT FOR TWO. Compare the actual use of this phrase in Limerick 2:991, on the tremendously popular musical-comedy song, " A Bicycle Built for Two, " in Harry Dacre's *Daisy Bell* (1892).

1076. Credited to 'E.W.' in Oscar Williams' *Silver Treasury of Light Verse* (1957), but actually only a softened version, from the Transactions of the Fifth Line Society, of Limericks 1:443 and 1:569. The culminating joke on "bottom" dates from the 18th century, when it was told as a true anecdote concerning Dr. Samuel Johnson.

1078. A ghoulish grave-robber named Fred
Would never fuck women in bed.
When he felt like a little
He'd cut out the middle,
And hang up the rest in the shed. [1969A.

VI. ABUSES OF THE CLERGY

1092. Based on the folk-proverbs: "*Christmas is a long time coming,*" and "*Tomorrow never comes.*" To observe that the modern standard English term, "*to come,*" meaning to experience an orgasm, is derived from or parallel to the same term referring to the "coming" of butter when cream is churned. See, beautifully on this point, Note 1:1350.

1095. AC/DC, slang for "bisexual"; literally, operating on either Alternating Current or Direct. Also "*acey-deucey.*"

1096. Glossing a passage from the faddish homosexual *precioso,* Ronald Firbank, *The Princess Zoubaroff,* Act I, Scene 11: "REGGIE: Claud's such an extremist, you know . . . They say when he kissed the Pope's slipper . . . he went on to do considerably *more* . . ." ("Homage to Ronald Firbank: Limericks on Themes from the Master's Works," *Harley-Davidson* MS. 1969.) Compare:

A divinity student named Bass
Soon rose to the head of the class
By reciting quite bright
And sleeping at night
With his tongue up the minister's ass. [1956.

1101. Fairly close translation of Norman Douglas' famous sacrilegious limerick in fractured French, "*Il y avait un jeune homme de Dijon,*" Note 1:265.

1108. While he goes out working
She stays at home ferking,
And teaching the repressed about life. [1966A.

1110. Variant conclusion (and compare Note 1:546 and Limerick 2:1857):

With a fashionable preacher named Sheen. [1954A.

1113. This story is also told of Mozart, backstage, trying to liven up the *scream* the soprano is supposed to give, on seeing the statue of the Stone Guest arriving for dinner on invitation, in *Don Giovanni.*

1123. THE BISHOP OF KEW. Sequel and parody of the well-known "Bishop of Birmingham" Limericks 1:534 *ff.* See also 2:1090.

1129. Variant of Limerick 1:1090 (and compare its original at 2:1905), with couplet:

He said, "*Pax vobiscum,*
I can't make my piss come —" [1928.

1131. A pendant to Limerick 1:530 (Alice/malice).

1132. THE OPHITE HERESY. Confuses the Virgin Mary with Mother Eve, in allusion to the Midrashic and folk-tradition that Satan, in the form of the phallic Serpent of *Genesis,* iii, taught Eve how to perform sexual intercourse, while his diabolical consort Lilith taught Adam: the earliest *swinger* or "mate-swapping" story on record.

1138. THE CHORISTER SPEAKS. To be compared with the folk-poem of similar libretto, "The Rehearsal," very probably by Eugene Field, first printed in *The Stag Party* [1888] unnumb. pp. 36-37, in ten stanzas; reprinted in *Immortalia* (1927) pp. 47-48, omitting stanzas 1, 3, and 10; and again reprinted, this time omitting stanza 8 only, in *Rowdy Rhymes* (ed. Peter Beilenson; Mount Vernon, N.Y.: Peter Pauper Press, 1952) pp. 13-16.

1170. *t'fillin*: phylacteries attached over the forehead and the left arm at the level of the heart, by means of leather thongs, by religious Jews during prayer. The Knights Templars were accused — among other things — of using similar devotional thongs in their mock-Islamic worship : see G. Legman, *The Guilt of the Templars* (New York, 1966).

1173. A MUSICAL PEAL OF TEN BELLS. A pendant by Aleister Crowley to a sequence of eleven polite limericks with the same refrain, written in 1924 by the musician Constant Lambert, and inspired by W. S. Gilbert's patter-song in the limerick metre, " My Name Is John Wellington Wells, " in *The Sorcerer* (1877). The " *Tintinnabula omnia* " refrain is of course a genuflection to the inspiration of Edgar Allan Poe's " The Bells " (1849).

1177. Ypsi : Ypsilanti, Michigan. Note the independent use of the same rhymes and idea in :

A conservative priest from Poughkeepsie
Made the error of becoming quite tipsy.
He was fired from his post
For defaming the Host,
While involved with three nuns and a gypsy. [1972.

VII. ZOOPHILY

1187. BIRDS : A FOUL BROOD. Strikingly unfunny, as are all of Aleister Crowley's limericks — his special delight — with the exception of 2:1201 (mandarin/philandering) and 2:1463 (*Vox, et præterea nihil*), which have already entered folk-transmission as Limericks 1:619 and 1:678. The " Birds " sequence was intended to include at least one further limerick, of which only an opening fragment has been recovered :

The youth declared, " Never love's bond or
[. . . *cetera desunt* . . .] a condor. "

Crowley also adds the following Sherlock Holmesian note on the " Birds " : " Above all written straight off under the influence of cocaine in the early hours of the morning on 11 Oct. 1920, at the Villa Santa Barbara, Cefalú, Sicily. "

1205. A Spaniard from old Albacete
Once fucked fifteen goats on a bet-a.
When asked how he felt,
He hitched up his belt
And said, "I can't tell just as yet-a."
Sing yippee-I-atty-I-ay! (bis)

From a veteran of the Spanish Revolution in 1937, with the atypical refrain line. The unusual tune used – which is not the usual "Spanish Nobilio" – will be found sung to this limerick (politely: "Took on fifteen goats," in line 2) on a phonograph recording, *Songs of the Lincoln Brigade* (1959?).

1211. Compare "The Good Ship *Venus,*" Limerick 1:527, also 2:1295 below.

1222. Further on birdwatchers, see Limerick 2:81.

1228. The animal scraunched her,
Then mouzled and munched her,
With sage and rosemary for spicin'. [1974A.

1236. Variant given in John Coulthard's private folio, *There Goes the Phone* (1966). In his accompanying drawing, Miss Fitch also speaks. With buttocks arched high in the air, she says "Oh oh oh oh oh!" (*Voice should flutter.*)

1265. The following variant conclusion apparently was inspired by Charles Edward Carryl's "*Walloping Window-Blind,*" as included in his marvellous children's book, *Davy and the Goblin* (1885), but often erroneously ascribed to his son, Guy Wetmore Carryl – for whom it was written. This from the stanza on the mad gunner who "FIRED salutes with the captain's boots, In the teeth of the booming gale!"

He leapt from his bed
With his arse painted red,
And pissed in the howling monsoon. [1970A.

1268. A fairytale princess from Sprogg
Had a passionate affair with a frog,
But try as she might
She just couldn't quite
Get her jollies while perched on a log. [1969A.

1283. MY SWEETHEART'S A MULE IN THE MINES. An American coal-miners' song, with its own tune. See Archie Green, *Only a Miner* (University of Illinois Press, 1972) pp. 20 and 30, note 19; with photo of a mine-mule and driver, p. 228, captioned "Darling on the Line." A polite version of the song is better known, in which sex-hatred takes the place of sex, in the ending:

On the coal-cart I sit
And tobacco I spit
All over my sweetheart's behind!

1286. Donald Duck is a virtuous bird
Whose lust is forever deferred.
His sex life is dry
For Walt Disney would cry:
"Hey, *love* is a four-letter word!" [1966A.

1296. That "All roads lead to Rome!" is his motto. [1966.

1311. A HERO REMEMBERS. The author supplied this with "a *clean* ending too," rhyming cynically on *triggers/niggers,* and ending: "*Till Freedom was heard through the land!*" This is in the line of sardonic self-recognition and mockery common in many air force songs during the various American wars since that against Korea in the 1950's, when saturation bombing and other forms of genocide were commanded and executed against civilian populations. Compare the following bitter burlesque collected by Dr. Roger Abrahams among adolescents in Philadelphia, 1959:

Oh we'll take a rugged rope
And we'll hang the fucking Pope,
And we'll burn the Sistine Chapel to the ground.
Then we'll turn around the guns
And we'll shoot down all the nuns,
Until Freedom's voice will be the only sound!

1316. *Ohio State Sailing Club* folio (1961?) Derived from Limerick 1:646, but with more than a nod to "The Highland Tinker," who rides to London "*with sword and pistol in his hand, his bollix by his side.*" Not to mention the "*half a yard of foreskin swinging well below his knee!*" (and other equivalents) in the chorus. See G. Legman, *The Horn Book* (1964) pp. 226-27 ; and good texts in Edward B. Cray, *The Erotic Muse* (1969) pp. 9-11, and 248-50. There is a text of another strain of this song in V. de S. Pinto & A. E. Rodway, *The Common Muse* (London, 1957) p. 438.

1317. In fact, orgasm behavior is only rarely observed in female animals other than anthropoids (women, apes, etc.) and in *cats,* which made this animal sacred in the Ancient Egyptian matriarchy.

1332. There was an old spinster named Rice
Who was frightened of little grey mice,
Till one crept up her cunt,
And she cried with a grunt :
" Oh Gawd!! what a thrill beyond price! " [1968A.

The symbolic reference to the mouse, presumably so feared by women for the reason the limericks note, as meaning the male penis, is very obvious here. A folksong on this subject — in which it becomes an excuse for cuckoldry — appears in all the early chapbook editions of Burns' *Merry Muses of Caledonia* from about 1830 onward (see my facsimile of the first edition, New Hyde Park : University Books, 1965, Bibliography, pp. 273 *ff.*) as " The Mouse's Tail. " This song is badly mangled and faked in the edition dated '1827' [really 1872] and its many reprints, but the real folksong has continued to exist until recent date as " Jackie and Master. " A text was collected in the Ozarks by Vance Randolph in 1942, recollected from 1898 : *Unprintable Songs from the Ozarks* (MS. 1954) No. 78, " Jackie and Mossy. "

1335. Compare Note 1:1183 and Limerick 1:1737. All of these food-dirtying exotica, on the style of *quails' fingernails and peacocks' pukings,* also *toasted humingbirds' foreskins,* are considered the worthless but expensive delicacies of the rich. See Note 2:1511, " Theobroma Papao. "

There was a young sailor from Yarrow
Who tried to bung-scuttle a sparrow.
But he failed to succeed
In this dastardly deed,
For the bones of its ass were too narrow. [1948.

There was a young fellow, a Kurd,
Who attempted to bugger a bird.
He picked up a sparrow
Whose ass was too narrow –
The whole bloody thing was absurd! [1951A.

1340. From an original in *The Pearl* (1870), given in Note 1:1125.

1341. PRECIOUS BANE. See Note 2:568. Attributed to the American literary critic, Edmund Wilson, and collected by Dr. Clifford Crist with the note : " Much too brittle for my tastes, but consider the source. "

VIII. EXCREMENT

1350. Also exists crossed with Limerick 2:1353, as :

I enjoy rectal violence
In moments of siolence,
And snigger when bystanders start! [1966.

1362. Aleister Crowley notes on this, his own creation : " The idea of this limerick is to imitate the stupidity, grossness and vulgarity of this refined and fart-mouthed cow-hippo. " It will be observed that the note is superior to the limerick : compare 'SEDLEY' in the Bibliography here.

1363. THE FARTING CONTEST. A reduction of a long folk-poem of the same title and subject (text in Harry Morgan's *More Rugby Songs,* London, 1968, pp. 14-16), on which see the anterior history and a prose " Contest " similar, in *Rationale II : No Laughing Matter* (1975) 15.III.3, "Ghost Voices," pp. 873-74.

1376. Note the revision of Descartes' famous line, as COITO ERGO SUM, in Limerick 2:232.

1377. Reversing the action of the ballad of " Kafoozalem, " in which it is the Philistine giant who is propelled by the force of the flatulent floozie's fart o'er the walls of old Jerusalem.

See the conflated text, made up of two others, in Edward B. Cray's *The Erotic Muse* (1969) pp. 72-73 and 212-13, which notes cheerfully that: "Stanzas 2, 4, 7 and 11, and the tune are from . . . an aerospace engineer who had learned it while attending CCNY, circa 1950. The balance is . . . as the song was sung at Carnegie Tech in 1959." The purpose of editorial *mischtexting* like this seems to be the notion that the public cannot endure to see two variant texts of the same folksong printed one after another, and to pick the one they prefer. We thus end up with volumes of presumed folksongs, as edited by Cray and the Lomaxes and other popularizers, "*stuffed with songs that no one ever sang.*"

1378. There was a young man who said, "Who
Will show me the way to the loo?
For I must 'ave a piss;
In addition to this,
I'm just itching to masturbate too." [1968A.

"*Loo,*" a British vulgarism, from the French "*les lieux,*" the place; for a public toilet.

1387. "Murdered in France," obviously a reference to World War I or II, from an American military academy. On these social-psychopaths not in ("mental") institutions, who seem to be increasing around us all the time, see Dr. Harvey Cleckley's excellent *The Mask of Sanity.*

1390. A favorite rhyme-scheme, on a children's chant (Pa. 1930): "San Francisco, watch my piss go!"

1391. Often recited with "poot" (from the French *péter*) lightly expurgated to "toot."

1407. Her stool was no fun,
And she feared, when she'd done,
That the ring of her arse'ole was split. [1973.

1408. Rodin's statue of "The Thinker," sitting with hand on chin in a notably defecatory "*Il Penseroso*" pose.

1414. Attributed to Harlan Logan by Baring-Gould, *The Lure of the Limerick*, p. 186, noting that it did not win a prize in the Salada Tea contest.

1416. Inevitable rhymes ; see Limericks 1:318 and 1294.

1419. Anti-rhyming reply to Note 1:350, ending " But he had a good time of it, didn' he? "

1428. FAREWELL, CRUEL WORLD. Also with variant line 2 : "Was careless as hell on the pissa. " (1969A.)

1429. As to this home-grown *goober industry,* children refer to hardened lumps of snot extracted from the nose as *boogers*, a forgotten allusion to demons causing them (compare *bugaboo*), as with the notion that the tangles that come in one's hair during sleep are caused by bad fairies, or that if a child throws an extracted milk-tooth down the cellar stairs, the tooth-fairy or " mice " will give him a strong new tooth. The *locus classicus* on these supernatural " sleep " superstitions is Shakespeare's *Romeo & Juliet* (1597) I.iv.53-95, Mercutio's " Queen Mab " speech, as extended in the Second Quarto of 1599 with other enlargements, to regain the pirated copyright.

1431. Variant conclusion of Limerick 1:725, dated 1870. A more modern version :

There once was a man from Newcastle
Who had a collapsible arsehole.
    It was handy, you see,
    When he farted at tea,
He could bend down and make up a parcel. [1967A.

1441. L'HOMME PÉTOPHONE. On this authentic individual of extraordinary talent, M. Joseph Pujol of Marseilles, who kept them in stitches with his artistic farting at the Moulin Rouge in Paris throughout the 1890's, see Limericks 1:740-51, supplemented by 2:1459, " The Farter from Sparta, " and more fully *Rationale II: No Laughing Matter* (1975) 15.III.3, "Ghost Voices," pp. 870-72 and 880. Musical entertainments of this type are very ancient, being mentioned in St. Augustine's *The City of God* (circa 430 A.D.). John Aubrey's *Remaines* (MS. 1687 ; ed. 1881, pp. 44-45) also notes a 17th-century game among young girls of attempting *to fart out a burning candle.* This is still current : see Note 2:2370.

Mark Twain's *Adventures of Huckleberry Finn* (1st edition : London, 1884) was intended to include another farce of this type, as "The Burning Shame," in the comedy theatrical performance in chaps. 22-23, in which a naked man prances about with a lighted candle stuck in his anus, but lost his nerve on the eve of publication and omitted all description, calling the scene instead The Royal Nonesuch. Francis Grose's *Classical Dictionary of the Vulgar Tongue* (1785) notes this as an 18th-century whorehouse entertainment, clearly a development of the farting game mentioned by Aubrey a century before. See further Wallace Graves, "Mark Twain's 'Burning Shame,'" in *Nineteenth-Century Fiction* (1968) vol. 23 : pp. 93-98 ; also and especially John Seelye's *tour-de-force* rewriting of Twain (!) as *The True Adventures of Huckleberry Finn* (Evanston, Ill. : Northwestern University Press, 1970), chap. 22, pp. 237-44, which attempts to restore the originally-intended scene. In an earlier chapter, "The Child of Calamity," pp. 122-29, rewritten from the fight on the raft scene in Twain's *Life on the Mississippi* (1883), Prof. Seelye also attempts courageously to reconstruct — but far too modernly — what Mark Twain really said when he famously swore.

1448. Many men who are partly impotent with, or not sexually interested in their no-longer-young wives, make use of the morning urinary erection, or "piss-hardon," to *perform their marital duty.* The fantasy, as in this limerick, or even the fact of urinating into the woman afterward, when the inhibiting erection has subsided, is an expression of the man's sometimes unconscious hostility.

1451. WOMEN'S LIB(ERATION). Urination standing upright, by a woman, is assessed by men as a usurping of male prerogative, and is often resented, as here. There is a parody of Leigh Hunt's "Abou ben Adhem," as "School-Day Recollections," in *The Stag Party* (1888) unnumb. pp. 235-36, immediately following Eugene Field's "A French Crisis," in which the school tomboy, Sal Adams, pisses higher than all the boys on the clapboard school-house door, by turning her back and aiming retromingently, like a lioness or mare. Freud also makes the curiously jealous remark, in *Civilization and Its Discontents,* that woman originally became the keeper of the hearth & home, because she is anatomically unable to piss out the fire! (This is not a challenge.)

1459. The Farter from Sparta. Continuing the famous Limerick-sequence 1:740-51, and see also Limericks 2:1441, "L'Homme Pétophone" (and its Note), 2392, 2412, and 2524, for further contenders. A definitive enlargement of this epic is promised by Roy W. West (see Bibliography), as "The Lad from Penn Charter," but has not yet appeared. Variant:

He could fart any tune,
Such as "Moonlight in June,"
And run the whole gamut from slow to staccato. [1948A.

1463. *Vox et præterea nihil.* — See the improved folk-transmitted version, Limerick 1:678, with couplet:

The abbot asked, "Was it
A goodly deposit?"

Questions of this type are more important than might be imagined. The headline-of-the-century, in the *International Herald Tribune* (Paris, 18 Feb. 1977) p. 3, announces in letters half an inch high: "U.S. SPEEDS EFFORT TO EXTINGUISH SLOW FIRE IN CAVE OF SLOTH DUNG." This refers to a cave in Arizona found earlier to contain a deposit of prehistoric sloth dung, *five feet thick,* which had meanwhile been set afire by naughty picnickers — or perhaps by freezing Indians, who have been burning the stuff for centuries. The article continues: "The Shasta sloth — about the size of a black bear, nothing huge — was not very notable except for producing a large and durable stool in the same place for about 25,000 years." It was also, as can be understood, extremely *slothful,* or that deposit could never have gotten to be five feet thick. Actually, the Chilean bat-guano of the South American caves is of much higher quality, though the quantity is perhaps less.

1464. There was a young moron named Bobby
Who gathered up turds for a hobby.
He'd drop 'em in wells,
And in fashionable hotels
He'd hide 'em in chairs in the lobby. [1966.

1465. Vance Randolph in his *Ozark Mountain Folks* (1932) pp. 189 and 278-79, describes a folk-charm or ritual he saw done by "an aged hillman whose wife had died . . . Before he drank, Bill poured a little whiskey on the ground, and drew a circle about it with his forefinger. He muttered something to himself, but I heard it. 'Just an old sayin',' he said gently, 'for them that's gone.' It is not a saying to be written down in a book. " The text suppressed here is given in Randolph's *Unprintable Ozark Folk-Beliefs* (MS. 1954) p. iii, adding: " I do not know just what this means. But I've heard it three times, from old men in widely separated parts of the Ozark country " :

> All you've et, turns to shit,
> And never comes no more.

Compare also the similar but more covert *lèse majesté* of Hamlet's speech to the King, just after killing Polonius behind the arras (*Hamlet,* IV.iii.25-33) : " Your fat king and your lean beggar is but variable service, two dishes, but to one table : that's the end . . . A man may fish with the worm that hath eat of a king, and eat of the fish that hath fed of that worm. KING : What dost thou mean by this? HAMLET : Nothing but to show you how a king may go a progress through the guts of a beggar. " (Meaning that the king, too, will finally " turn to shit. ") Also in *Hamlet,* V.i.222-35, just after the apostrophe, " Alas, poor Yorick! " on the jester's skull : " Why may not imagination trace the noble dust of Alexander, till he find it stopping a bunghole? "

1468. Compare the classic Old Lady from Wheeling, 1:762.

There was an old lady, God bless her,
Who tried to jump over a dresser.
    She caught her tail
    On an eightpenny nail,
And ripped her p, double-esser. [1971A.

1473. A HERO'S LIFE. On Richard Strauss' striking sado-masochism (the sadism being reserved for the listeners to his music, and the masochism for his insanely domineering wife, Pauline de Ahna), see the incredible passage translated from first-hand accounts in the historian Barbara W. Tuchman's *The Proud Tower* (New York, 1966) chap. 6, pp. 309-11. Dr. Tuchman notes the classic alternation of sado-masochism in the wife as well (*alternating the sexes involved,* as is usual) :

" Enthusiastically submitting to, as well as inflicting, punishment, Frau Strauss engaged the daily services of a masseuse of the violent school, during whose visits Strauss was obliged to go for a walk to avoid hearing the tortured screams of his wife. " *Sinfonia Domestica* . . .

1474. *The Stag Party* (1888), at unnumb. p. 156, captioned " Poetry and Beer, " solves the same monorhyme problem in another way by inventing the two-line (" throwaway ") limerick :

A young lady that lived in Toledo
Stood right over a big torpedo.
— How foolish.

1478. MY SECRET LIFE. Taking-off the mild undinism of the author of the Victorian sexual autobiography, *My Secret Life,* which I have argued, in the introduction to the modern reprint (New York, 1966), is very probably the work of the great erotica collector, of strikingly parallel interests and antipathies, H. Spencer Ashbee, here disguising himself as " Walter. " Note also Limerick 2:2442.

1480. Somehow reminiscent of Carolyn Wells' deathless Flea & Fly : " *So they flew through a flaw in the flue!* "

IX. GOURMANDS

1488. The meaning of the final line is that " Texans are full of shit! " a cardinal point in American *blason populaire,* and the subject of numerous jokes, in which lions (not cannibals) eat the Texans and are dissatisfied for this reason. See *Rationale II: No Laughing Matter* (1975) 15.VI.1, " Anal Sadism : Texans and Others, " pp. 959-64, ending with the joke that is probably the source of this limerick.

1489. " *Greasy kid-stuff* " : punning on an American advertising shibboleth of the 1960's, concerning hair lotion for males. So also Limerick 2:1824.

1498. " Down the hatch! " a common drinking-toast.

1502. *Be Pure!* (Australia, 1963) p. 19.

1506. Cannibalistic limerick shown in the process of being composed, in James Joyce's *Ulysses* (1918-22 ; ed. Hamburg : Odyssey Press, pp. 176-77, following the " Cavern of the Winds " section, all in NEWSPAPER HEADLINES), in " The Lestrygonians " chapter, where everything is food, food, food! The final line refers to the basic superstition in cannibalism : that one draws into one's own body the special strength of that part of the enemy's body which is eaten, generally the heart, liver, or penis.

1508. J.G. (" jaygee ") : Naval lieutenant, *j*unior *g*rade.

1511. THEOBROMA PAPAO. On " narsty-narsty " recipes and menus, see *Rationale II*: *No Laughing Matter* (1975) 12.IV. 4, "Sexual Smörgåsbord, " pp. 376-78 ; and a very full and frank transcript of a modern American folk " menu " of this type, in Mac E. Barrick's " The Typescript Broadside, " in *Keystone Folklore Quarterly* (Spring, 1972) vol. 17 : pp. 30 and 36-37 ; also a mock-folkloristic such menu, shown being created in " audience participation " style, in Thomas Pynchon's *Gravity's Rainbow* (1973) as noted in the Bibliography here ; as well as the totality of the purposely disgusting dishes served, beginning with " fried shit choplets, " in the Negro toast recitation, " The Ball of the Freaks, " in *The Life,* ed. Dennis Wepman, *et al.* (University of Pennsylvania Press, 1976) p. 112. Of extraordinary interest and significance is the long, spontaneous fantasy of a seven-year-old American boy, " Nixon's Favorite Menu : UnAppetizers, " beginning with Cross-eyed Goose egg broiled in butter made with mustard, given in full by Dr. Brian Sutton-Smith and David M. Abrams, *Psychosexual Material in the Stories Told by Children: The Fucker,* presented at the First International Congress on Sexology (Montreal, 1976) 31 f. 4to, at ff. 25-27.

There is also perhaps some historical or extrojective reality behind these strange " food-dirtying " folk imaginings. In Lajos Zilahy's historical novel, *The Dukays* (English translation, 1949) — the noble Hungarian family of the Esterházy's is apparently meant — at the wedding of the youngest daughter in 1930, as described in chap. 8, pp. 442 and 458-59, everything is to be done in imitation of the wedding of an ancestress, Katalin Dukay in 1632, of which "the entire record . . . even to the smallest expenditure, was intact in the Dukay archives." The wedding banquet features "roast peacock basted with raisins and almonds. And there was something else. The footmen held the platters so that the groomsmen were constrained to select the potato fritters especially prepared for them. These fritters contained shoestrings, lumps of pig bristles and large nails. Such practical jokes had been played on the gentlemen groomsmen at the wedding of Katalin Dukay too." (Of course, simply calling it a "practical joke" does not explain either the origin or the inner meaning of the usage.) Note, at this same presumed period, the similar but heavily erotized food-dirtying menu in the French mock marriage-contract *Grand-Jean-Ventru* (ca. 1627) quoted in *No Laughing Matter,* p. 377, as above.

1512. A revision of Limerick 1:792 (Rheims). This form first in *Be Pure!* (1963) p. 15.

1513. Standard undinist fantasy, of which this example appears only in Clement Wood's *Around the Horn — in Limericks* (MS. 1950), with auto-fellatory variant: "Who learned how to piss in his mouth."

1514. There was a young fellow named Sweeney
Who spilled some gin on his weenie.
  Being very uncouth
  He added vermouth,
And offered his girl a martini. [1959A.

1520. THE DIRTIEST DOZENS. Send-up of Limericks 1:785-86 (Shalott) and 2:1504, presumably the *crème de la crème* of the "narsty-narsty" variety.

X. VIRGINITY

1524. There was a young girl whose propriety
Caused all of her swains great anxiety.
  In spite of their urgin'
  She remained a pure virgin
(Which at least gives these verses variety!) [1968A.

1525. B.O. : " Body Odor, " the main American advertising shibboleth and bugaboo of the 1930's and since, actually referring to the odor of armpit and pubic sweat and, by implication, of the female genitals. The same anti-body and anti-sexual prejudice also requires that the armpit hair be shaved in women, but not in men — which gives away the show — though fortunately not the pubic hair, which is really what is meant. There is much of value on this " rejection of the body, " as expressed in polite (and impolite) speech, in Prof. Pierre Guiraud's study of insults and obscenity, *Les Gros Mots* (Presses Universitaires de France, 1975 : " Que Sais-Je? " No. 1597).

Various human races likewise purport to find each other's " essential odor " unendurable : whites often assimilate their prejudice against Negroes to this, and sometimes similarly as to Jews (at least since the time of Martin Luther and Sir Thomas Browne's *Pseudodoxia Epidemica,* in 1646, which devotes a whole appendix to the subject). A Japanese prince, writing on the presumable subject of " Japan " in the great 11th edition of the *Encyclopædia Britannica* in 1910, goes to elaborate trouble to obtrude an explanation of why the special odor of whites is objectionable to the Japanese, adding gratuitously that " most " of this odor rises from the armpits. He also *explains* similarly that the Japanese are just as tall, or taller than whites — from the waist up. They just have shorter legs.

1538. MAKE WAR, THEN LOVE. A U.S. Marines reversal of the slogan coöpted by the hippie movement in the 1960's, " *Make Love, Not War,* " on which see Note 2:1753.

1548. An inquisitive maid from Peru
Used to wonder what young couples do.
So she spied through a keyhole,
Where she saw a girl's pee-hole
Being rammed, and said : " I'd like some too. " [1967A.

1551. For the rest of the story, see Limericks 2:1006-7, " The Midnight Intruder. "

1554. THE HARD-BOILED VIRGIN. Attributed to novelist James Branch Cabell, about 1930, as a review of a sex-novel of this title, by a female author.

1556. To compare with Albin Chaplin's superior use of the same rhymes and idea in Limerick 2:1576.

1557. There is a more polite version in the Hall Collection, No. 375. Compare the French catch-phrase, when anyone acts ignorant or obtuse about some (usually sexual) matter : " *You want me to draw you a picture*? "

1558. She thought it lewd
The way men screwed [1956J.

1575. GERSHON'S GIRLS. Slipped anonymously into my office mail at the University of California at La Jolla, at the same time that a *graffito* appeared on the campus bulletin board, amidst much other WASP-backlash and xeroxlore, answering a request for a suggested title for the forthcoming student magazine, with the caption-title here.

1578. *Gone With the Wind.* – See Note 1:714.

1586. ORIGINAL SIN. Polite version, with " Original Sin " rather than " sexual sin " (if there's a difference?) in Elizabeth Manners' *The Vulnerable Generation* (London, 1971) p. 122.

1598. There once was a fellow from Reading
Who always was wetting the bedding.
His poor wife would say :
" I don't mind the spray.
It's the stench in the morning I'm dreading. " [1967A.

1604. Punning on the title of a best-selling Welsh novel of the period, *How Green Was My Valley.* Couplet expurgated in *Playboy's Book of Limericks* p. 173, to :

There was naught she could do ;
He was too young to screw.

1606. " *bun* " : the buttocks. The girl is presumably freezing up in nervous fear.

1622. YOU NEVER KNOW. Printed in a college humor magazine, the *Utah Humbug,* before 1959 ; and reprinted in *College Humor,* Vol. V : No. 3. Buck-fever and impotence, especially on the part of young (college) men, is a classic problem in brothels.

There was a young man from Mobile
Who went around a great deal.
He hadn't the pluck
For a good solid fuck,
But he used to be great on the feel. [1933.

XI. MOTHERHOOD

1632. But oh, how you paid ten days after! [1953.

1636. A flustered young floozie from Fiji
Discovered, alas, she was P.G.
Said she, " Now let's see,
Just *who* could it be?
I've run quite a few through my squeegee. " [1969A.

Apparently by a woman ; " P.G. " is women's slang for pregnant. Compare the same idea of the " indeterminability of putative paternity " in Limericks 2:1710 and 1719. A modern Greek proverb or riddle has *the girl who is asked who is the father of her child answer* : " *When you put your ass in a wasp's nest, which one bites you?* "

1639. THE CALL OF THE WILD. Attributed to Prof. Morris Bishop (see the Bibliography).

1642. WEAR YOUR BUTTON, BOYS! Sterilization of males by vasectomy, which was begun in the 1920's as a legal punishment (replacing castration : for rape, insanity, etc.), had become so popular as a self-castratory birth control measure by the 1970's that many of the 8,000,000 American men already sterilized now sometimes wear a special lapel-button insignia (showing a pair of scissors?) as a " go-ahead " signal to women : a complete misunderstanding of feminine psychology. This club should have quite a future, as the population panic increases. See much further on this subject, *Rationale II* : *No Laughing Matter* (1975) chap. 13, " Castration, " *ad fin.,* pp. 666-71.

According to Reuter's, 17 Oct. 1976, and *Time* magazine, 4 Apr. 1977, 1,300,000 men were " voluntarily " sterilized in India in the month of September 1976, bringing the total to 7,800,000 by January 1977. To achieve this, all pretense of democratic and elective government in India had to be dropped, under Mme. Indira Gandhi, which will of course be the case in all other countries too. There is still a surface air of voluntary acceptance about this ; male sterilization in India being required only after the second child, but write it on your calendar : *Tomorrow it will be compulsory everywhere.* Women who will be " permitted " to get pregnant will be able to request insemination only with the frozen, cubed sperm of our finest (non-sterilized) citizens, such as the then counterparts of President Richard Nixon and Vice-President Agnew. This is a higher form of obscenity than any limerick can aspire to, but see the brainwashed " people pollution " mutterings of Limericks 2:1643 and 1712 ; and Notes 2:1661 and 2056.

1647. " Peyton Place " : see Limerick 2:2003.

1648. There was an old person of Delhi
Who awoke with a pain in his belly.
  And to cure it, 'tis said,
  He shit in the bed,
For the sheets were uncommonly smelly. [1968A.

1649. Mark Twain wrote a well-known skit, flirting with the idea of incest with the mother in this same way, in which a father and son (the narrator) marry a mother and her daughter. But, as it happens, the father marries the daughter and the son marries the — though not his own — mother ; with the final result, when the daughter has a child, that: " I AM MY OWN GRANDFATHER! " A similar paradox had been published in a British jestbook of the 1790's, and must be traditional. Compare Limerick 2:1703, " Oedipus Redivivus, " with the further punchline that the young man " must now be called ' Dad ' by his aunts. "

1658. On some minor public scandal in the western United States concerning a satirical poster showing a Pregnant Girl Scout. That the attempt is often made to seduce adolescent Girl Scouts (two at a time), selling their " Brownie cookies " for charity from door to door, seems to be unknown to all members of the public, except the men — and the Lesbians

— who try it. The seduction of Boy Scouts by their scoutmasters is now too common even to attract much public attention.

1659. The furbearing hole of Suzanne
Has been poked at by many a man.
    But the wads of hot semen
    Shot in her by he-men
Are one and all flushed down the can. [1966.

1661. PEOPLE POLLUTION. Essentially, the " population explosion " scare of recent years, the movement for Z.P.G. (Zero Population Growth), use of abortive (Intra-Uterine Devices: see Note 2:2056) and castratory (sterilization) techniques of birth control, etc., are all just state-administered brainwashing for the genocides unquestionably to come — probably to begin with the " colored " populations, as has been charged. (See Note 2:600.) None of this was perhaps the intention of Dr. Paul R. Ehrlich when pulling the alarm-switch in his book, *The Population Bomb* (1968), but that is where matters certainly stand now. Compare also notes 2:1642 and 2056 ; and Limericks 2:1643 and especially 2:1712, " Bad Day Coming, " which cynically lays it right on the line : " *Give no help to poor bastards who roam, Seeking food in the trash-cans they comb* . . . " Next can only come the shotguns at the darkened windows, to protect one's hoard of groceries, when the food runs short : the part of the whole scare that is true.

The *Guinness Book of World Records* (1974) by Norris & Ross McWhirter, the standard barroom-betting authority on all " biggest & bests " in the world (except penis-length), adds its crumb of fantasy-figures to this propaganda hard-sell, p. 371, observing that : " The present population ' explosion ' is of such a magnitude that it has been fancifully calculated [*n.b.*] that, if it were to continue unabated, there would be one person to each square yard by 2600 A.D. and humanity would weigh more than Earth itself by 3700 A.D." " Fanciful " or not, a remark like that simply shows the naïveté of the McWhirters, who may be assumed to have been writing in simple liberal good-faith, perhaps with the unspoken intention of helping to liberalize the official Catholic objection to " unnatural " birth control methods. In a century notable already only for its genocides, one wonders what *else* the Atom Bomb was invented to do? Limerick 2:1643 tells the real and bitter truth — to Catholics and every one else—in seven words : "*It's either The Bomb or The Pill!* " The struggle of the century : Albert Einstein, discoverer of The Bomb, *versus* Gregory Pincus, inventor of The Pill!

1667. " Dianetics " : a psychology-*cum*-science-fiction religion, promulgated since 1950 by a pulp-writer, L. Ron Hubbard, as satirized by G. Legman in " Epizootics, " in *Neurotica* (1950) No. 7 : pp. 11-18, with illustrations. Renamed " Scientology, " to give Mary Baker Eddy's " Christian Science " (against which even Mark Twain fulminated in vain) a run for the money, Mr. Hubbard's " religion " is still operating very profitably — see *Time* magazine (5 April 1976) under " Religion: A Science-Fiction Faith " — and has now a new " self-help " mock-psychology competitor, *est,* of which the adherents are locked in at the sadistically-toned " training " lectures, until they piss on the floor. These are only two items in the squirming snakepit of new cults in America, as the New Irrationalism moves in : the death-watch for the end of a civilization. The never-to-be-equalled " Vomit Therapy " of Mr. I. F. Regardie, once a follower of Aleister Crowley (see Martin Gardner's *In the Name of Science,* 1952, pp. 290-91 ; and *Rationale II: No Laughing Matter,* 12.IV.5, " Sputum and Vomit, " p. 390), should be due for a comeback any day now.

1668. A plain-speaking lady named Myrt
Remarked as she hoisted her skirt :
" It ain't your long cock
That gives me a shock,
It's that potent emission you squirt. " [1966.

For a different poetic assessment of the male semen, compare the homosexual-narcissistic pæan, Walt Whitman's " I Sing the Body Electric, " Pt. V, in his *Leaves of Grass* (1855) : " Limitless limpid jets of love hot and enormous, quivering jelly of love, white-blow and delirious juice. "

1678. P.T. : Prick-Teaser ; also C.T., cock-teaser (compare Limerick 1:1707) : a *demi-vierge,* or girl who refuses sexual intercourse after having led the man on, or who will allow everything *but* vaginal penetration.

1679. But regrets the effects
Caused by careless free sex [1966.

1690. " Athlete's fœtus, " punning on " athlete's feet, " a minor fungal infection used as an advertising bogey in America, and really known to athletes as "jock-itch" or "crotch-itch" from its usual location, owing to the wearing of (sweaty) jockstraps to protect the testicles. Medication is calcium undecylenate ointment, also used for diaper rash in babies under the name of " Caldesene. "

1698. I *did* love the feeling,
And the view of his ceiling [1966.

1703. OEDIPUS REDIVIVUS. See Note 2:1649.

1705. There was a young housewife of Rhyll
Who decided to try out the Pill.
But she took the wrong one —
Yeastex — now the bun
In her oven is rising at will. [1967A.

1714. According to the literary diary of the brothers Goncourt, one of the greatest indiscreet memoirs of the 19th century, the Empress Eugénie, consort of Napoléon III of France, suffered from genital or venereal warts and made no particular secret of the matter from her courtiers. The implication (false) is of course that such warts, technically *condyloma acuminatum,* rise from promiscuous sexual intercourse. Compare Limerick 2:1950, " A Word to the Wise, " and a curious story, " Justice for M. Cornecon " in the McAtee MS printed in *Rationale of the Dirty Joke : First Series,* 9.II.6, " Conniving at Adultery, " p. 734.

1718. Bringing to mind A. E. Housman's " The Culprit, " in his *Last Poems* (1922) :

The night my father got me
His mind was not on me ;
He did not plague his fancy
To muse if I should be
The son you see.

1721. Jody Speaks. On " Jody, " mainly in Negro folklore, the-guy-who-comes-to-see-your-wife-when-you're-not-home, see *Rationale of the Dirty Joke : First Series,* 9.II.2, pp. 707-11, " Jody (Joe the Grinder). " A World War II character now replaced by the Mexican, " Speedy " González.

XII. PROSTITUTION

1732. Refers to the Ethiopian War, in the spring of 1936, in which General De Bono was the gallant Italian commander who ordered the use of dive-bombers and poison gas against the Ethiopians, armed with spears ; thus, with General Franco's attack on Spain, aided by Germany and Italy, in July of the same year, beginning and giving its profoundly genocidal aspect to World War II and its continuations since. It was in this heroic action against Ethiopia that Vittorio Mussolini, son of the Italian dictator, made his famous æsthetic remark that the bodies of the dead Ethiopians, exploding in the air when he dive-bombed them, looked " *like a beautiful rose unfolding.* " (We're up to mushrooms now.)

1733. By Peter Seward, one of the winners in Competition No. 2312, in the *New Statesman* (London, 5 July 1974), p. 27/3, for limericks in French that would " daze a Frenchman, " evidently for their non-colloquial French.

1737. Compare Limerick 1:989, obviously superior (on Jesus H. Christ and John Jacob Astor).

1741. Legislative Perquisite. Once-in-a-lifetime rhyme, on *Governor/shovenor.* On Senatorial sex scandals, see Limerick 2:733, " Smog on Capitol Hill, " and its Note.

1742. There was a young lady of Eccles
Whose cunt was all covered with freckles.
    But the boys didn't mind
    For she gave a good grind,
And she did it for love, not for shekels. [1968A.

1753. Make Love, Not War. (Compare Note 2:1538.) The slogan of the hippie movement, originated by the present writer (an opponent of the hippie movement: see *The Fake Revolt,* New York, 1967) during an address at the Ohio State University Library in autumn 1963, while discussing his book *Love & Death* (1949), and based on an old Jewish joke: *Grandmother* (*to children making noise in the attic*): " *What are you kids doing up there? Are you fighting?* " " *No, Grandma, we're fucking!* " " *Dot's nice — don't fight!* " Xaviera Hollander (de Vries), the young Dutch-American " madam, " co-author of the best-selling *The Happy Hooker* (New York, 1972), and the first lady of her profession to appear on American television; photographed naked — at the typewriter — in Earl Wilson's *Show Business Laid Bare* (1974), facing p. 168, with explanation, p. 183.

1756. W. L. McAtee, Library of Congress MS. D364, envelope 7. This (1913) seems to be the earliest use of the now cliché *Charlotte/harlot* rhyme.

1767. Somehow slipped by in Stanton Vaughn's *Limerick Lyrics* (New York, 1904), still the largest and most varied published collection of polite limericks. Compare the famous line concerning " the House with the little red light ": " Every man turns away his face, and every man goes in. " Although there is already a large literature of whorehouse reminiscences and memoirs of famous madams (see Note 2:1753, just above), by far the most informative works on American prostitution and the oldtime " red light districts " are *The Lively Commerce* (Chicago, 1971) by Charles Winick & Paul M. Kinsie; and *Sportin' House* (Los Angeles: Sherbourne Press, 1966) by Stephen Longstreet; with the older series by Herbert Asbury, *The Barbary Coast* (1933), also his *The French Quarter,* etc., on San Francisco, New Orleans, and other American towns till World War I. See also the interestingly illustrated *Brass Checks and Red Lights* (Denver, 1967) by Fred Mazzulla, and *Sailortown* (1967) by Stan Hugill.

1769. On the rare " tease-song " pattern of Great Expectations Deceived. See another example at Limerick 2:2058, which manages to maintain the rhyme anyhow by means of spoonerism; also Limerick 1:1154 and Note 2:37.

1773. "*tanner*" : a small British coin ; "*spanner,*" a monkey-wrench. The splendid couplet is taken from Limerick 1:208.

1778. "*gam*" : British slang for fellation, from the French *gamahucher,* meaning the same thing. The origin of the French word is obscure : the Japanese *gamaguchi,* purse, has been suggested.

1782. Punning in the last line on the assumed name of Josef V. Stalin (Djugashvili), dictator of Communist Russia and victor over Nazi Germany in World War II.

1783. The thinking man's sexpot named Fay [1965.

1785. FIFE'S WIFE. A later, darker note is struck :

An uxorious fellow named Fife
Found a stranger in bed with his wife.
He exclaimed, " Wanton creature,
Perhaps this will teach yer! "
And chopped off his balls with a knife. [1968A.

1826. To tour the town's cribs was his goal,
But a studsman from Sydney named Dole
Took a passionate fancy
To a harlot named Nancy,
And blew his whole wad on her hole! [1966.

1846. ROSE ORMESBY-GORE. Noted as a " London street song, to the tune of 'Frivolous Sal', " as collected by Arthur Moyse, and published in his *The Golden Convolvulus* (1965) p. 13.

1851. PICCADILLY. Actually the opening stanza of a scatological anti-family ballad, not in the limerick metre, called " Do You Ken My Sister Tillie, " and beginning : " If ye're ever doon in London, " and going on to : " There's a gentlemen's convenience a little south of Waterloo. " This is known in America (with a different opening) as "In Bohunkus, Tennessee" or as " Diamonds in the Dung. " See *Rationale II : No Laughing Matter,* p. 63 (a variant), and *The Horn Book,* pp. 421-22, giving a further stanza seldom collected. Still another is recorded in *Snatches & Lays* (ed. Melbourne, 1973) p. 66, as " The Finest Family " :

At the slightest provocation
We indulge in masturbation,
We all are ardent followers of Freud!
For the price of copulation
Is the risk of population,
And dependents are a thing we must avoid.

In fact, almost everything in the song except the present single stanza (given as a limerick) is being forgotten.

There was a young lady named Lily
With a craving to walk Piccadilly.
Said she, " Ain't it funny –
It's not for the money,
But if I don't take it, it's silly. " [1968A.

1859. She held up in the wash
Through nine teams of frosh [1975.

1876. EMPLOYEE RELATIONS. In an excruciatingly candid joke, collected in Arlington, Texas, 1967, the teller begins by explaining that : *The boss had taken his stenographer to a plush motel " for a day of swimming and sex* . . . NOT WANTING TO PAY THE GIRL OVERTIME, *he checked out at five and they went their separate ways.* " – 'Victor Dodson' [John Newbern], *The World's Dirtiest Jokes* (Los Angeles, 1969) p. 85, emphasis supplied here. When I asked the author of this joke collection whether he had meant the touch about overtime as humor, he answered in astonishment : " No, that's the way everybody does it. " (Well, maybe not *every*body.)

To her boss the stenographer said :
" Today we ain't hitting no bed.
You can ball the jack
When I'm back in the black,
But today my account's in the *red.* " [1965.

1879. Tucson : pronounced *Too-sawn.*

1883. On the "town widder " as the small-town prostitute in backwoods America, often a "grass-widow " (abandoned wife, especially during the Gold Rush period), see the remarkable novel on this background, John Sanford's *Seventy*

Times Seven (1939 : originally entitled *I Let Him Die*), a Great American Novel if ever there was one! Compare also Limerick 2:650, for the rhymes.

1887. THAT LITTLE PIECE OF WHANG. On the real folk-poem of this title, and underlying folktale, of which the present limerick is a very decayed reminiscence, see *Rationale II : No Laughing Matter,* 13.II.6, " The Doctor as Castrator, " p. 510, tracing its history in other languages.

1892. THE CATHOUSE OF TIME. Compare Eugene Field's (?) parody of " The Old Oaken Bucket " as " The Oldfashioned Harlot, " in *Immortalia* (1927) p. 14, reprinted in *The " Wrecks "* (1933?) pp. 144, 147. Further stanzas of " The Cathouse of Time, " or tryouts by the same poet :

Hail the big, meaty hooker of yore
With her fanny as wide as the door!
    She was probably smelly
    And wobbled like jelly,
But her two-dollar price ain't no more.

To the tart and the doxy of yore,
The frail *fille de joie* and the whore,
    The strumpet, the moll,
    The trollop and doll –
May their harlotry wave evermore! [1965.

XIII. DISEASES

1897. Variant conclusion, with the final line taken allusively from Thomas Carew's 17th-century poem, " A Rapture " :

    They talked of philosophy,
    Politics and theosophy,
While he moored his tall pine in her harbour. [1948.

1901. NIGHT THOUGHTS. Credited to Dana Thompson in the Hall Collection, No. 2649.

1905. *The Stag Party* [Boston? 1888] unnumb. p. 69, with two illustrations of a comedy-Chinaman, with pigtail, trying to piss against a barrel. Reprinted almost verbatim in *The Book of 1000 Laughs* by 'O. U. Schweinickle' (1928), as quoted in Note 1:1090, and collected among children in Idaho, 1920.

1906. ON ELEPHANTIASIS. The first line of the second stanza, on "The drawback to elephantiasis," is an allusion to the folk simile or Wellerism: "*Like an elephant's foreskin — it has large drawbacks.*"

1915. Mark Twain in his bawdy lecture, *The Mammoth Cod,* probably written in March 1902 (but first published, Milwaukee: Maledicta Press, 1976) p. 20, observes candidly as to the name of the club, "The Mammoth Cods":

"*2nd.* It is unfair for a set of men who are thus developed to arrogate to themselves, superiority. It is something they are not responsible for, except, indeed, they increase its size by means that no man should be proud of. In my green and salad days a lady whom I wickedly tried to overcome for months, finally yielded. In just eight days I had a penis, or as you term it, a 'Cod' of a size that would have entitled me to admission to your Order, were you all as well hung as jackasses. Was I to put on airs because injection of Nitrate of Silver swelled that organ? Heaven forbid! On the contrary I wore sack-cloth and ashes, as soon as I could get it out of its sling, and was ashamed."

1920. By the late John Newbern, humor magazine editor, on the challenge of finding a rhyme for "sylph." He noted marginally on his creation: "This ain't exactly clean, but the rhyme is in there, somewhere."

1925. ON THE DELTA. "*Triangle toupée*": usually called a *merkin* since the late 17th century in England. The word (now popularly *mugget*) is also used at present to refer to any artificial vagina for masturbatory purposes, matching the phallic *dildo,* as in G. Legman, *The Fake Revolt* (New York, 1967) p. 31: "In the end, the Sexual Revolution's idea of sex is either something flagellational or coprophagous, or otherwise nauseatingly gimmicked up; or else falls into the ultimate estrangements of the orgy ethic, which are really a sort of ice-cold dildo-and-merkin combination. One is tempted simply to leave the dildo and merkin discreetly alone, with their motors turned on, and go home." (See also Limerick 2:2182, "Guys and Dolls.") This is also the conclusion of Federico Fellini's sumptuously narcissistic and masturbatory motion-picture evocation, *Casanova* (1976), which ends with the human "fucking-machine," Casanova, affectionately known to himself as *Mr. Six-Times,* passing his "most beautiful night of love" with a mechanical doll.

1938. ABELINA (AND THE MAGGOTS). Collected as a song fragment from a college freshman from the U.S. southwest, at Ann Arbor, Michigan, 1935. The "maggots" are evidently a puzzled reference to tapeworm-section infestation. Compare Limerick 2:1451, "Women's Lib."

1943. Also heard chanted — the following two lines only — by children in North Las Vegas, Nevada, spring 1976; and later by a little girl 3½ years old (my youngest folksong source, so far!) who said she learned it from her brother, 6 years old: as opposed to pretenses, made by adults, that children do not really understand the bawdy songs they repeat, these two perfectly understood the meaning of their song.

> *Mama mia, papa pia,*
> Baby has the diarrhea!

1944. URBAN AMENITIES. Attributed to the American character-actor, Zero Mostel.

1946. Couplet taken (and not improved) from:

> But now he has *tabes*
> And sabre-shin babies,
> And thinks he's the Queen of May. [1928A.

This is from the "Luetic Lament" co-authored by Dr. William G. Barrett and another medical student at Harvard, and first published in the *Journal of the American Medical Association,* "Tonics and Sedatives" department, in 1928. An amplification to seven stanzas, also printed in *J.A.M.A.* (Jan. 31, 1942), is given in *The Limerick,* 1:1075 *ff.* Compare the following, on Capt. Roehm:

The head of the Nazi S.A.
Was commonly thought to be gay.
    He capered through Munich
    In sandals and tunic,
And sang, " I'm the Queen of the May! " [1963B.

1953. Punning on Sir Walter Scott's *The Lay of the Last Minstrel* (1805). In the catalogue, about 1950, of a New York book-auction house which shall remain nameless out of kindness, the opposite error or de-expurgation was immortalized, when Macaulay's *Lays of Ancient Rome* (1842) were politely printed as *Ladys* . . .

1956. Taking up where Limerick 1:789 leaves off :

We pity those two men of Perth
Who had crabs, clap and syphilis from birth.
    Said one to the other :
    " Alas, my poor brother,
We're the rottenest bastards on earth! " [1967A.

1959. That lovely young harlot, Miss Biddle,
Suffered vaginal pains when she'd diddle.
    Said the cynical doc, " I
    Suppose gonococci
Are making you burn when you piddle. " [1969A.

1966. SNOWDROPS FROM A CURATE'S GARDEN. " *The double event* " : syphilis and gonorrhea, contracted in the same act of intercourse ; also called " *a full house* " in America, a term which sometimes includes (in the case of a prostitute) becoming pregnant at the same time!

XIV. LOSSES

1969. On the legend and fantasy of the *vagina dentata* (displaced to the mouth in this case, as in many others) see *Rationale II : No Laughing Matter,* chap. 13.I. " Vagina Dentata, " pp. 427-67 ; and Limerick 2:2568, and Note 2:937 above. In various internationally exploited " New Freedom " movies, from Vilgot Sjöman's *I Am Curious* (*Yellow*) in 1967, to Nagisa Oshima's *The Empire of the Senses* (1976) and several others in recent years, intense close-up scenes of bloody castration of men, in particular by women, are made the central sick spectacle, all in the style of the woman's eye (really a pig's) slashed with a razor-blade to watch the vitreous humor spurt, in the original Surréalist goon-show of the 1920's, Luis Buñuel's *Un Chien Andalou.*

1973. He was hung like a horse,
And he fucked with such force [1975.

1976. WILDE PARTY. The story of Salomé and John (in Hebrew Iokanaan) the Baptist, is told in *Mark,* 6 : 16–28, and was used by Oscar Wilde — inspiring himself heavily from Flaubert's *Salammbô* and *Hérodiade* — for his bitch-heroine play, *Salomé,* apparently ghost-written in French for Wilde by Pierre Louÿs, then translated into English by Wilde (under the name of his pathic, Lord Alfred Douglas), and finally set to music by Richard Strauss in 1905. This became the greatest theatrical *succès de scandale* of the " Naughty-Naughts, " owing to Salomé's Dance of the Seven Veils, and in particular to her final scene, grovelling about with the Baptist's decapitated head onstage, screaming that she has kissed its mouth at last. See Barbara W. Tuchman's *The Proud Tower* (1966, pp. 323–25, and compare her superb pages, 328 *ff.*, on Strauss's even sicker, sado-masochistic *Elektra*), noting that the production of *Salomé* was withdrawn by the Metropolitan Opera in 1907, after its American première, but not mentioning the numerous popular productions immediately thereafter.

1977. An evil bridge-player named Sam
Once attempted to bugger a clam.
When it snapped shut its shell
He let out a yell —
This maneuver is called the Grand Slam. [1970.

2001. Intended, of course, as a topper to Limerick 1:1377, which uses the same typographical trick, though at a more drastic angle. " Shaped " typògraphy of this kind, nowadays occasionally erotic, is very ancient. See G. P. Philomneste [Gabriel Peignot], *Amusements Philologiques* (3rd ed., Dijon, 1842), pp. 163-68, a treasury of serendipity.

2002. " *Sausage & mash* ": British for frankfurter and mashed potatoes.

2003. *Peyton Place,* a sex-novel of the 1960's for the women's lending libraries, later a television soap-opera, also mentioned in Limerick 2:1647. On sado-masochistic affairs of the kind in the present limerick, see poet Karl Shapiro's excruciating novel, appropriately entitled *Edsel* (New York, 1971). This and similar recent novels about incredibly slobby and masochistic anti-heroes, such as Saul Bellow's *Herzog,* Philip Roth's *Portnoy's Complaint* and John Updike's *Bech : A Book* (all within one decade) carefully hew to a single line of what has been christened " insider anti-Semitism, " or self-hatred, worth further study.

2008. Compare Limericks 1:1162 and 2:1107, all on the same rhymes and castratory theme.

2017. INCIDENT IN RACINE. Probably the most frequently encountered American limerick (1:1325, on a young man of Racine), but not usually in the present " disaster " form, which should be compared with the almost equally popular castration ballad of " The Great Fucking Wheel " (see *The Horn Book,* p. 422, and *Rationale II : No Laughing Matter,* 13.I.7, " Decapitation, " *ad fin.,* pp. 473–74), in which the victim of the Fucking Machine is a woman. Pæonic metre version :

There once was a Swedish inventor named Dag
Who built a contraption that knew how to shag.
    In a manner obscene
    He was sucked into the machine,
And nothing was left but his balls and some cream!
(*or* :) but some hair and his bag. [1975A.

2019. Some mistake here. It is the Japanese (not the Chinese) who pronounce " *r* " for " *l*, " as in " *irregurar rabia* " and " *rots of ruck!* "

2020. By Ray Russell, novelist, poet (and singer) ; first printed in *Playboy* (Dec. 1954) p. 10, and picked up in the Transactions of the Fifth Line Society with last line : " As a promising lyric soprano. " Compare also the more old-fashioned Limericks 1:1171 and 2:1994.

2024. Aleister Crowley notes on this anti-Semitic item : " This was an impromptu, a challenge by Tom Driberg, C. K. Ogden, and McGregor Reid. Line 1 was given me. [N.B.] Idea is all right, but *Corton* is a bad rime. I don't know if the incident described is authentic. " Compare the activities of the British homosexual-*cum*-occult group, " The Golden Dawn," which was accused of being sympathetic to a plan, during World War II, involving the expected victory of Nazi Germany and the British Fascists.

2034. A visitor once to Loch Ness
Met the Monster, who left him a mess.
They returned his entrails
By the regular mails,
And his sexual parts by express. [1967A.

Alluding to the standard evasion of the U.S. Post Office's antisexual rulings of " unmailability, " owing to its Catholic Action domination for many decades, by sending purportedly " obscene " material by railway express. So also Limerick 2:2364.

2037. *North Atlantic Squadron* (" *Tune — My Bonny,* " 1950 : mimeo) f. 7. To observe that in all British contexts the condom was invariably considered as of French origin : " *French letter*," " *French safe* " (or " *safety* "), and in Australia " *Frenchie* " ; never as British. Dr. Condom, the presumed inventor, or adaptor of Gabriello Fallopius' invention of a century before, was probably a Frenchman at the Restoration court of Charles II, as *Condom* is actually the name of a small Cognac-producing town in Gers, in southwest France.

There was a young fellow of Grasse
Who constructed a cundrum of brass.
The first time he retired
The damn thing backfired,
And blew off both balls and his ass. [1967A.

2041. Gruesome vagina-dentata story on precisely this theme by Charles Bukowski, " Notes of a Dirty Old Man, " in a hippie " underground " newspaper, *Nola Express* (New Orleans,

Aug. 1973). The Love-Generation . . . Vaginas that eat men alive are also a not uncommon theme in the similar, but less literate, " underground comics " of the 1960's and '70's.

2054. Rural version of a pictorial obscœnum or " novelty " card (U.S. 1950), showing a mother-figure with one breast caught in a clothes-wringer, or, in animal-symbolic form, as a cow stepping on her own udder, caption : " *So You Think* YOU *Got Troubles!* " See Limerick 2:2067 for another version.

2056. As a nice example of modern socio-political brainwashing and the cozening of crowds, note that the now-popular I.U.D. (Intra-Uterine Device), used presumably for birth control, is actually a disguised method of inducing a *spontaneous monthly abortion* in the women wearing it. Formerly known as the " Gräfenberg Ring " (in all forms, including the " collar-button " cervical cap, etc.), this was condemned by all ethical gynecologists and obstetricians before 1945, and by the Hippocratic Oath of all physicians for over two thousand years. It has now been promoted cynically and silently, by the Z.P.G. (" Zero Population Growth ") propagandists, as a form of convenient sub-sterilizational handling of hundreds of thousands of women unconscious of what is being done to them, and who might well choose some less dangerous method of " birth control " if they knew.

Dropping all disguises, according to *Moneysworth* magazine, Dr. R. T. Ravenholt, a U.S. State Department population expert, revealed at a population conference in Tokyo, 1971, that the United States has already developed, and may soon market, a new pill that enables women to induce instant abortion at any time. The abortion-pill (based on prostoglandins, which are already used to induce labor in overdue pregnancies) is simply inserted into the vagina. We are close here to the " angel-makers " of the German concentration camps of World War II. See further, Notes 2:1642 and 1661, " People Pollution. "

2060. On sex and computers, compare Limericks 2:1021 and 2:2195, " Technological Fallout, " covering this same miscegenational marriage (already largely consummated) in which MACHINE FUCKS MAN. Old-style Wild West version:

The two-balled old sheriff of Broath
Gave vent to a horrible oath :
    When one ball chanced to ache,
    By a terrible mistake
The veterinary chopped them off both! [1968A.

2062. But I want to save *this* tit for Tet. [1972A.

2064. On the early 1950's newspaper sensation concerning George (" Christine ") Jorgensen " changing his sex " by means of castration and female hormone injections in Denmark : the first of these legal castrations or " transsexual " operations. That is to say, the first except for thousands of years of Levantine harem-eunuchs and the derivative male *soprani* of the Sistine Chapel choir — in despite of *Leviticus,* 21: 20, and *Deuteronomy,* 23: 1, which state unequivocally :

" He that is wounded in the stones, or hath his privy member cut off shall not enter into the congregation of the Lord. " For the further humor and joke-lore of the " Christine " case, see *Rationale II : No Laughing Matter,* 13.V, " Self-Castration, " p. 616.

2071. " *Mohel* " : Hebrew term for a ritual circumciser. The McAtee MS. (1937) D364, envelope 8, in the significant context of a story called " The Pleasures of Impotence " (!) and stated to have been " inspired by a dream, " gives the following early warning :

He loved to make his zipper zip
And see his fly-front gaily rip.
    But once his member tangled,
    Got hideously mangled,
And now the lad's no longer quite so flip.

XV. SEX SUBSTITUTES

2072. Actually, the antisexual superstition (centuries old) is that masturbation *will* cause insanity, a " *post hoc, propter hoc* " error probably based on observation of the open masturbation of the insane. See further Note 2:285, and Note 2:2424.

2078. Prosodic note: The first two lines here are not in the classic limerick metre, but in something close to the even catchier pæonic metre, on which see *The Limerick: First Series,* Introduction, p. lv; and other examples at Limerick 1:437 and Note 2:2017.

2080. Printed with "*tricks*" instead of "*pricks*" in line 4, headed: "NEVER TOO OLD ..." in *Super Sex to Sexty* (1971), No. 14: p. 24. Compare Limerick 2:2419.

2085. The man is evidently trying to prepare himself, and create an erection, despite his nervousness. Frank Harris's *My Life and Loves* (Nice, 1922-25) tells an excruciating story very similar to this, concerning the wedding night of the British art-critic and essayist, John Ruskin, presumably from statements later made by Mrs. Ruskin.

2086. "*Moxie*": a popular soft drink in the American South, its name taken from the slang word for (virile) strength.

2092. A hopeful young virgin, but frail,
Bought a Japanese dildo by mail.
Massaging and jerking
Couldn't get the thing working,
So it went to a church rummage sale. [1969A.

2094. Supplied by the erotic artist, Mahlon Blaine, New York, 1953, entitled "Christine" (Jorgensen), concerning whom see Note 2:2064.

2096. 'Nosti,' p. 73, observing that "Hallé's orchestra was one of the best in Victorian England . . . In some parts of England [and America] the boys' game of marbles is called 'alleys'." Note also that "twat" does *not* rhyme — as here — with "flat." This is the identical innocent howler made by Robert Browning in *Pippa Passes,* where he tried to rhyme it with "bat."

2103. Printed in the New Jersey Mensa newssheet, *Embrya* (Dec. 1971). Compare Limerick 2:2027, on the identical rhymes and standard *penis captivus* theme.

2106. Aleister Crowley's last known limerick, written (he explains) because: "I said I had seen Miss Clarke riding over the trees on her broomstick. She took umbrage! " With this summing-up of his output : " *Morale* : Don't take things too seriously! " For another summing-up, see Limerick 2:2302.

2108. A boarding-school lassie named Randle
Used to frig herself with a candle.
One day in the gym
It shot from her quim,
Which started a very grave scandal. [1968A.

2114. *Dirt : An Exegesis,* p. 22, the last item in this mimeographed college " underground " songbook. The reference to the left and right hands alludes to an old joke or catch-phrase (spelled out in Limerick 2:2177) and collected among high-school boys in Scranton, Pa., in 1933 : that what counts is not whether one can masturbate with either hand, but *" Can you change hands without missing a stroke?* "

2116. Collected in Boise, Idaho, 1939, from a young girl ; and often from college-boys since.

2118. MADE IN JAPAN. " *Spade* " : American slang for Negro or black. On vibrating dildoes, see especially the proposal made in my *The Fake Revolt* (1967), quoted above at Note 2:1925, and further Note 2:2092; and Limerick 2:2195, " Technological Fallout. " For details of the invention of the vibrating dildo in the late 1930's, and pilot construction then by the great Russian anatomical model-maker, Dr. Vladimir Fortunato, see my *Oragenitalism* (1969) pp. 98-101, with some important warnings as to their being habit-forming and other problems.

2124. Compare the erotic poem, " The Keyhole in the Door, " in *The Stag Party* (1888) unnumb. pp. 150-152, probably by Eugene Field, and now in folk circulation.

2128. RUGGED BUT RIGHT. To be paralleled with the lines in the college-girls' song, of Negro origin, "Rugged But Right" (also known as " Sexy Fuzzies "), quoted by Reuss (1965 : see Bibliography) pp. 315-18 :

We got a big electric fan to keep us cool
while we eat,
A great big handsome man to keep us warm
while we sleep . . .

Essentially, all these references to the anaphrodisiac electric-fan, to cool off sex-starved ladies, are unconscious specifications for the mechanical or vibrating dildo, on which see Note 2:2118, " Made in Japan. "

2131. Graffito collected at the Elephant & Castle, London (see Limerick 2:1851, " Piccadilly "), in May 1935, by Prof. Pelham Box. On graffiti in general, see Note 2:2727, " *Mené Mené Tekal.* "

2136. " *Knish* " : Yiddish term for a potato-fritter. On male masturbation with food objects — a deeply significant combination of the oral and genital levels — the *loci classici* are at present Henry Miller's *Tropic of Cancer* (Paris, 1934 : apple with core bored out, and lined with coldcream), and Philip Roth's *Portnoy's Complaint* (New York, 1968 : slice of raw liver). Folk-humor tops both of these with the more vivid and practical " can of hot buttered worms " (U.S. 1940).

2138. An illustrated obscœnum now in circulation as xeroxlore is reproduced in Alan Dundes & Carl R. Pagter's *Urban Folklore from the Paperwork Empire* (Austin, Texas : American Folklore Society, 1975) pp. 180-81, entitled " A Visit to the Butcher Shop, " giving three different versions of a folk-circulated drawing of a similar fantasy concerning the butcher offering his " sausage " to lady-customers.

2139. THE UNSCREWABLE BRIDE. Limerick reduction of a famous 19th-century joke or anecdote, first given in George W. Harris' *Sut Lovingood's Yarns* (1867), on which see fuller details in *Rationale II : No Laughing Matter,* 13.VI.3, " The Mechanical Man, " pp. 649-52. Chaplin's *The Noble 500 Limericks* (1967) p. 69, expurgates " cunt " to " denture" (!) in the last line, but the accompanying illustration purposely gives away the real point by showing a *pussy* smiling on the shelf.

2147. Anti-woman castratory combination of Limericks 1:1134 and 1234. (And compare 2:2651.)

They found her vagina
On a hilltop in China— [1962A.

Her navel perspired,
Her asshole backfired,
And her tits were picked up in Brazil. [1965A.

2151. *Ohio State Sailing Club,* mimeographed song folio (1961?) Compare Limerick 2:104.

2154. THE SLEEVE-JOB. A take-off on Limerick 1:1266, and itself parodied in 2:2136. " Goolies " (French *couilles*), a U.S. southernism for the testicles.

2167. On sex-training dummies, specifically an inflated condom (or a banana) for teaching the technique of fellation, see my *Oragenitalism : Oral Techniques in Genital Excitation* (1969) p. 221, quoting and translating a French manuscript of about 1915, *Traité de la Plume,* first published as by ' François Carabin' [Paris? *c.* 1965], 45 p. with 8 photo-ills., sq.12mo.

2172. The great metaphysician once said :
" Let's assume that I'm buggered in bed.
Is the thrill that I feel
In my rectum quite real?
Or is the whole thing in my head? " [1958R.

2178. " *Wimpus* " : a penile splint or prosthesis for attaining or maintaining erection. Other than the ancient Greek dildo (*olisbos*), it is perhaps the first of the sex-gadgets, centuries old in Japan (*yoroi-gata* : see Friedrich S. Krauss & Tamio Satow, *Japanisches Geschlechtsleben,* Leipzig, 1931 ; *Anthropophytéia* : Beiwerke, II. 162-72, illustrated), and has been sold in America by discreet ads as to "lost manhood" in the back of " men's " pulp adventure magazines since the 1920's. For fuller details on this and other modern erotic devices, see *Sex Gadgets* by 'Roger Blake, Ph.D.' (Cleveland : Century-K.D.S. 1968, cover-title : *The Stimulators*) chap. 12, " Penis Aids, " pp. 189-200 ; and a brief mimeographed work, *Erotic Appliances* (Chicago, *c.* 1915 : copy, Kinsey Library), compiled by a newspaper editor, Henry N. Cary, author also of an erotic slang dictionary.

2181. A pendant or reply to Limerick 1:909, in which it is a girl who " keeps her passions in check, " by " thinking of Jesus, venereal diseases, And the bother of having a child. "

2182. See Notes 2:1925, " On the Delta, " and 2107, on another mechanized merkin — more politely *The Mechanical Bride,* a title used in 1952 by Prof. Marshall McLuhan, on whom see further Limerick 2:2414, " Media Blow-How. "

He said, "To be blunt,
It don't beat a cunt, But— [1956J.

2187. "*Ramona*": a sentimental popular song of the 1920's, briefly revived in 1952, the "insider" joke being that *mona* is a principal Italian slang word meaning cunt, as in the Foreword here, Section III, "*I Sacri Misteri Gaudiosi,*" stanzas 4 and 11-15. Note also in particular the consciously symbolic womb-return procession of all men through the entrails of Mona the "Whale" — where they are shown magic-lantern pictures of the *vagina dentata* by Roland Topor, and are all laid low in body-wrestling with an impassive giantess — in the anti-erotic Italian motion picture, *Casanova,* by Fellini (1976).

2188. WHO'S COMPLAINING? Refers to Philip Roth's *Portnoy's Complaint* (New York : Random House, 1968), a purposely ugly sex-farce bestseller on which see Note 2:2136 above, and fuller details in *Rationale II : No Laughing Matter,* 12.IV.6, "The Defiling of the Mother," p. 393 : and 11.III.4, "Impossibilities," pp. 290-93.

2193. RACINE (Breen, Dean, McLean). A parody of the highly popular concavo-convex Limerick 1:1325, ending: "With attachments for those in between" (and several other endings at 1:1325A). To be distinguished from the "Losses" version, 1:1326 ("And ground both his knackers to cream"), with which should be compared Limerick 2:2017, "Incident in Racine," the ultimate disaster version.

There was a young girl named Irene
Whose ass was fit for a queen.
She was found in the nude
And successively screwed
By Merrill, Lynch, Fenner & Beane.
(—Pierce was out of town that day.) [1956A.

2195. TECHNOLOGICAL FALLOUT. Aside from vibrating dildoes, on which see Notes 2:1925, "On the Delta," and 2:2118, "Made in Japan"; see further, specifically on sex and computers, Limericks 2:1021 and 2060.

2199. From a science-fiction fan magazine, *The (Damned) Thing,* No. 2 (Tokyo, 1946) p. 24, edited by Burton Crane.

2200. In the midst of a dance
He went off in his pants,
And had to go home in a shawl. [1970A.

2213. Said Sonia of Staraya Russa :
" By Stalin! Why can't I seduce a
Young man to my bed?
I must keep there instead
The fruit of a species of *musa!* " [1942J.

Delivered by Dr. John Leighly before the American Limerick Society (Berkeley, Calif., 12 Nov. 1942), followed by the reading of a 6-page annotation by another member, concerning the erotic uses and terminology of the banana or *musa.* Compare *Fifth Line Society,* in the Bibliography here.

2214. By the late John Newbern, humor-magazine editor, in an unusual style : the *tease*-limerick, which is not " really " erotic at all, in the end.

2223. After carrots and candles
And bicycle-handles [1966.

2224. Though I tried half the night
She *never* got tight. [1965.

2230. Nowadays it's a treat
To view tits made of meat [1966.

2234. He'll pull out his cock
From the top of his sock [1953.

XVI. ASSORTED ECCENTRICITIES

2240. " Cranes and Kohlers " : manufacturers of " sanitary appliances " in the plumbing line. A later transcript of the *Fifth Line Society Transactions* gives the 2nd line as : " Who crocheted for the bedroom's best china, " assimilating this to the old-fashioned crocheted woollen covers for chamber-pot tops, to keep them from rattling on windy nights. *Eheu, fugaces!* Who remembers these today? Or the bellboys in the upstate resort hotels, like Saratoga Springs, called " *piss-cutters* " because one of their duties was to rush to chamber-pots from the guests' bedrooms on winter mornings, to chop free the frozen amber ice!

2241. " Brillo " : metallic woolshavings for scouring pots & pans.

2244. THE LIMERICK. Parodying a famous original :

The limerick packs laughs anatomical
In a space that is quite economical.
    But the good ones we've seen
    Are seldom quite clean,
And the clean ones quite seldom are comical.

2245. Other limericks-about-limericks will be found at 2:1, 2310, 2402, 2699, and 2732 ; while Chaplin's *The Limerick That Has the Appeal* (1976) opens with a section of eleven such, the present example being a variant of his No. 5.

We frankly hail just the obscene,
While prudes plump for limericks clean,
    Having loudly maligned
    Our rich, meaty kind—
Well, let's settle somewhere in between! [1966.

2247. By a woman-editor of sex humor magazines. Note the "nauseous" combination of sexual and scatological terms, and the absence of any for the female genital.

2248. Older British version of Limerick 1:1368. This was the first example collected for the present Second Series, and was encountered while correcting the page proofs of *The Limerick : First Series.* The Crist Collection (1948) has a variant conclusion, " But tuppence a fuck was a failure " ; and compare also the rather mannered revision, Limerick 2:1373.

2252. Based on a well-known joke, but in a deeper sense both involve the dangerous fetichistic urge to *cut or shave women's pubic hair* as a symbolic castration of the woman. See further, *Rationale* : First Series, 6.VII, " Pubic Hair and Shaving, " pp. 396-97 ; and Second Series, 13.II.7, " The Mad Barber, " pp. 521-25. Note 2285 below, and the limericks it lists, show this fetich in its merely charming " come-on " aspect, as the saving of seduced women's pubic tufts for love-tokens.

2257. On coprolalia, the use of obscene words, specifically during sexual intercourse, to excite one or both of the participants — but really to *replace* sexuality by insults and aggression, as in homosexual and other S. & M. activities — see Dr. Eric Berne's *Games People Play* (1964) especially the sado-masochistic *games* of " Uproar " and " Beat Me Daddy " ; also *Rationale II: No Laughing Matter,* 14.I.3, "Anti-Gallantry," pp. 718-19, citing in particular a short story by Norman Mailer, " The Time of her Time " (1959) in his *Advertisements for Myself,* also reprinted as " The Taming of Denise Gondelman. " Here the girl cannot have an orgasm in the unemotional one-night stand, and the male protagonist attempts to excite both of them by buggering the girl unexpectedly, and calling her " You dirty little Jew! " This is not guaranteed, and one would-be *macho* who tried it ended up with a magnificent kick in the balls. (Handsome is as handsome does.)

2261. " Prick-&-ball warmers " of red flannel (with drawstring) were sold as a humorous item in " slum " shops (magic and " novelty " stores) in the 1940's and since in America, and exist authentically in Holland in knitted form, as a joke. See further Note 1:1531. A commercial version of the " prick-sweater " or " Tool-Warmer " was offered in 1975 as a subscription premium by the never-to-be-forgotten ultimate men's magazine and " gynecological gazette, " *Hustler,* published in Columbus, Ohio, and famous for its full-color " split beaver " photos of female genitals. Like " French ticklers, " prick-sweaters are really a neurotic " unhexing " device.

2272. See Limerick 2:264, on the same rhymes. Also :

On the tits of a typist named Brenda
Were inscribed every kind of agenda ;
    And the first names of her bosses,
    Their profits and losses,
Were tattooed on her luscious pudenda. [1968A.

2273. What occurs in the marital bed,
And *any*thing sexual some dread.
    Poor prudish Miss Hocking
    Finds the word " gender " shocking,
And blushes bright red when it's said. [1965.

2275. A SESSION OF THE POETS. Written by Aleister Crowley, apparently at Cefalú, Sicily, 13 Nov. 1920, and headed: "Pity is the last insolence of pride." The asterisked 5th line of Limerick 2:2277 here (missing in the transcript supplied from his manuscript *Diaries*) is given from the recollection of a notable Crowley acolyte of that period.

2285. The most famous example of the castratory fetish of cutting, shaving, or saving tufts of women's pubic hair as erotic mementos was the ritual *wig* of the " Wig Club " in the 18th century in England. This was a whole merkin of such tufts, presumably made from the pubic hair of the mistresses of King Charles II, which was added to by all new members and worn on their heads during their initiation : a mock rebirth ceremony. See Louis C. Jones, *The Clubs of the Georgian Rakes* (New York, 1942) ; also my *Rationale of the Dirty Joke* : First Series, pp. 392-93, " Pubic Hair, " and Second Series, p. 523, " The Mad Barber, " with further literature there cited ; also Limericks 2:871, 1843, 2238, 2289, 2338, 2363, 2423, and especially 2535 here. The American Negro folk-poets of the pimping and narcotics world have improved on the notion, in *macho* style but still with evident ritual intention. In the Black narrative toast, " Good-Doin' Wheeler, " given in Seymour Fiddle's *Toasts : Images of a Victim Society* (New York : Exodus House, 1972, offset from typewriting) p. 60, the opening description of the big-time drug-peddler brags :

His shoes were thin, of baby's skin,
Lined from hair of ten-year-old girls' cunts.
It was so boss, imagine the cost,
And he only wore them once.

2288. " *Yance* " : anglicization of the Yiddish *yentz* as in Limerick 2:586, (*yensen*), to have sexual intercourse, and figuratively to cheat, as with most verbs for intercourse in both English and French (especially *baiser*).

2290. See Limericks 2:2317, " Practice Makes Pregnant, " and 2747.

She could count out each coin
With the cheeks [!] of her groin,
And shoot off the change with her ass. [1954A.

2291. " Orgasm " was once a polite word for any violent paroxysm, and was used as recently as the mid-19th century without sexual tone. It now refers solely to the climax of erotic sensation in both sexes during sexual intercourse, when (in men) the semen is ejaculated. The word is therefore now considered somehow improper, and I have been reprimanded (1965) by certain old women of both sexes for using the word in a jocular suggestion that erotic forms of the Japanese folk-art of paperfolding (*origami*) are possible, and might be called *orgasmi.*

2294. THAT CERTAIN PERFUME. Quoted in Charles Winick & Paul M. Kinsie, *The Lively Commerce : Prostitution in the United States* (Chicago, 1971) pp. 205-6, with various associated jokes and gloss on the Profumo political scandal in England in 1963, in which : " The relationships of prostitute Christine Keeler with some high officials in the British government attracted international attention . . . Minister Profumo's mistake was not in his consorting with Miss Keeler but in lying to the House of Commons about the liaison. " See further, Charles Franklin's *They Walked a Crooked Mile* (illustrated edition : New York, 1972) pp. 121-65, with almost-nude photo of Miss Keeler at p. 131.

2297. " The pole-cat's pink hose " : an elaborate equivalent of the 1920's slang superlative, " *the cat's pajamas,* " itself probably only an expurgation of " *the cat's ass.* "

2309. CARE FOR A DRINK? *Count Dracula* in the horror novel by Bram Stoker (1898?) is a Transylvanian vampire who sucks his female victims' blood — from the neck, in all the movie versions beginning with Murnau's *Nosferatu.*

2310. Said the thoughtful old Dean, looking haughty :
" The *real* funny things are all naughty.
Clean humor is boring —
No sex and no whoring —
Folks only laugh when it's bawdy! " [1968A.

2313. I LIKE IT. Parodying Graham Lee Hemminger's " Tobacco Is a Dirty Weed, " in the college humor magazine, *Penn State Froth* (Nov. 1915), reprinted in John Bartlett's *Familiar Quotations* (13th ed. 1955) p. 975.

2321. " *Chew one's ass* (*out* or *off*) " : to berate or scold, especially an underling by the boss.

2326. There once was a man from Rhodesia
Who drank too much milk of magnesia.
He suffered such pains
That he shat out his brains,
And contracted a case of amnesia. [1975A.

2331. On bird-watchers and their sex-life, or lack of it, see also Limericks 2:81 and 2352.

2335. " WASP " : White Anglo-Saxon Protestant American, the cultural cynosure class at present in America.

2338. Standard hair-fetich, rationalized in Limerick 2:2413, and see further Note 2:2285.

There once was a man from Belgravia,
Found guilty of indecent behavior.
He would grab little girls
And rub spunk in their curls,
Insisting that " Spunk makes 'em wavier! " [1967A.

2348. By the British poet, W. H. Auden, and first appearing in the *New York Review of Books* (12 May 1966), without this title. Limerick 2349 is a follow-up, doubtless original, graciously sent by Auden by way of apologizing for being unable to contribute further to the present collection. Compare also Limerick 2:2672, " Hipster. "

2350. Almost the classic progression of infection with Bilharzia and other parasitic worms, which enter skin-cracks between the toes of barefoot children in certain countries, and ultimately are transmitted through the respiratory system (by picking the toes, then the nose) to the intestine, when scratching the anus.

2357. The meaning is that the young man is thought to be homosexual because he uses scented soap. Catch-phrase, referring to a eunuch or a " heavy-hung " homosexual : " *All that meat, and* NO POTATOES! "

2358. Slaughtering a well-known, verbally oriented joke given in *Rationale II : No Laughing Matter,* 10.IV.1, " The Fellatory

Accusation," p. 127. The present limerick presumably satirizes the violent verbal whippings of his teams by the tough professional football coach Vince Lombardi (died 1970), with the Green Bay Packers team till 1967.

2364. "WIFE: An appliance you screw on the bed to get the housework done." (U.S. 1946, from a folk-circulated typewritten sheet giving a series of erotic mock-definitions of this kind.) Others include, "KISSING: Uptown shopping for a downtown bargain. – GOOSING: Hokus-pokus in the tokus. – KOTEX: Not the best thing in the world, but *next* to the best. – BABY: A loud noise at one end and bad news at the other. – ALIMONY: The screwing you get for the screwing you got. – PIMP: A nookie-bookie (A crack salesman). – BIKINI: Two postage-stamps and a cork."

2368. To be compared with a folk-poem, "The Troubles of a Tool-Crib Girl," circulated in America during World War II, on the identical male tool-metaphors.

2370. In the recent "soft-core" pornographic movie, *Emmanuelle* (from a pseudonymous novel actually by a man, Louis Jacques Rollet-Andrianne) — travelogue pornotopia in full color, for the readers of *Vogue* — a Siamese belly-dancer is shown puffing a cigarette with her vagina, as a nightclub entertainment. Most yogis can do this too, with their rectums, but disapprove of tobacco. Compare Mark Twain's "Burning Shame" in Note 2:1441, L'Homme Pétophone.

2372. "FUCK!" having entered officially into the English language in the 1960's (even the dictionaries have now discovered it), the word's protean expressiveness has been observed in a xeroxlore item printed in Robert Anton Wilson's *Playboy's Book of Forbidden Words* (Chicago, 1972) s.v. *fuck*, listing its use in phrases expressing Fraud, Dismay, Trouble, Aggression, Difficulty, Displeasure, and Incompetence. This is a weak piece. Compare the remarkable Colorado police scenario, "ELEVEN CODE," presumably for wireless phone messages, also retrieved from floating current xeroxlore, in Cathy M. Orr & Michael Preston, *Urban Folklore from Colorado: Typescript Broadsides* (Ann Arbor, Mich.: Xerox University Microfilms, 1976; Research Abstracts, LD69-79) ff. 79–80: "ELEVEN CODE"

11-1 How in the fuck am I supposed to know
11-2 You gotta be shittin me
11-3 Get off my fuckin back
11-4 Beats the shit out of me
11-5 What the fuck * Over
11-6 I hate this fuckin place
11-7 This place sucks
11-8 Fuck you very much
11-9 Beautiful just fuckin beautiful
11-10 Let me talk to that son of a bitch
11-11 Fuck it today is not my day
11-12 Fuck you and the horse you rode in on
11-13 You don't know do you
11-14 Just fuckin barely
11-15 Fuck it just fuck it
11-16 You must have me confused with someone else
11-17 Traffic Fuckup? Give it to someone that gives a shit
11-18 If you are so fuckin smart what are you doing here?
11-19 Go get fucked
11-20 Sheeit
11-21 Hang it in your ass
11-22 It is so fuckin bad I can't believe it
11-23 Fucking A
11-24 Father forgive them for they know not what they do
11-25 At the intersection of —— jacking off
11-26 Ask me if I give a shit
11-27 I didn't see anybody pull your cord
11-28 Anybody wanna buy this fuckin badge and gun?
11-29 I just trashed the fuckin patrol car
11-30 I just been fucked
11-31 Just thumped complainant – Send 10-52
11-32 Better find your jar of Vaseline by the time I get to the station
11-33 10-9 your ass
11-34 Fuck the Lt. get me some help
11-35 Wa-Dee-Doo-Da

2374. KITSCH-KLATSCH. Apparently refers to the sculptor Jacob Epstein's huge alabaster statue of *Adam* (1939) with a curiously misshapen wiggly dick (see Note 1:835), which was displayed as a peepshow in America about 1940.

Imagine a pile of pure shit,
With a dab of pink paint labelled " clit. "
Two cups for a bust,
And a guy with the crust
To peddle this junk-art as wit! [1977A.

2380. How grand that there's porn for the mob!
For the lonely sheepherder and gob,
For the impotent jerk
Whose penis won't perk,
For the pervert, the rapist, and slob. [1977A.

2381. Various mock folk-definitions on this style, since at least the 1910's when Aleister Crowley gives some examples in his pederastic leg-pull, *The Scented Garden, or Bagh-i-muattar* (c. 1910). Modern forms include the " *twerp* : a man who goes around sniffing girls' bicycle seats in summertime, " and other mythical critters such as Lewis Carroll's *snark,* of similar habits or worse. Crowley notes the *quirk* and *hufflah.* Some of these " top " or assist each other, on the style of the " *dibitzer* : the guy who gives advice to a kibbitzer. " As to girls' bicycle seats, the Italian movie director, Federico Fellini, makes this youthful fetich into a delightfully overdone visual orgy of women's bloomered enormous buttocks mounting on bicycle seats, in his autobiographical *Amarcord* (1974), which also shows a " circle-jerk " of the boys involved, in a parked car.

2384. On double-couplets of the type used here (from Shakespeare to Ambrose Bierce), see *The Limerick* : First Series, Introduction, pp. liv-lv.

2404. " *Illegitimi non carborundum!* " Dog-Latin for the defiant motto or proverb : Don't let the bastards wear you down!– usually given as : *Nil Illegitimi Carborundum*! (See *The Horn Book,* p. 248.)

2405. A frotteur whose morals were fetid
His associates deeply regretted,
Though they had to admit
He had ways with a tit –
Just see how much cunt the lout netted! [1966.

2409. ENQUIRY INTO OBSCENITY. On Lord Longford's private "Enquiry into Obscenity," on principles presumably similar to those satirized here.

2410. Compare the never-to-be-equalled (thank God!) "Ice-Spurred Special," consisting of jamming a bag of sub-flagellational icecubes up against a man's lower spine at his orgasm, on the pretext that this will make it nicer for him, proposed in Dr. John Eichenlaub's *The Marriage Art* (New York, 1961) chap. 6. As the saying goes, "With friends (and lovers) like that, *who needs an enemy?*" Or, "Give me that Old-Time Coition–it's good enough for me!"

2424. "*Mensa*": has been defined (by one of its members) as "an association of lonely Christians with high I.Q.'s." Presumably the man is trying to slow down his approaching orgasm so that the girl can come first, or even simultaneously with him: a rare moment. Many men silently use simple mathematics (cubes, etc.: see Note 2:2634 for one such exercise) to divert their minds and delay their impending orgasm in this way: "*Six times six are thirty-six*; *times six are* . ." Numbering compulsions of this kind are usually identified psychoanalytically with masturbation, as witness the plain statement of the little folk-rhyme of adolescent boys (Penna., 1934) given in Note 1:169.

2427. THE INVISIBLE GOVERNMENT. Supplied with the remark that these *44 syllables* refer to my pamphlet, *The Fake Revolt* (New York, 1967), as to fashionable fake-revolutionaries leading the kids into the dark of drugs and otherwise, during the hippie movement and since; whether or not they take the (Invisible) Government Dollar for doing so. See further, in the Bibliography: *Klimericks, an Orgy.*

2432. The *Cantos* (1925 *ff.*) by Ezra Pound, about whom and which the less said the better. But see the scathing chapter on Pound, as both poet and traitor, in Dr. Fredric Wertham's frightening *A Sign for Cain* (1966), the masterpiece of this social critic, and the only work yet to recognize the purpose of the New Pornography of Violence in all the mass-media, to soften up the population for the genocides to come.

2434. Limerick fatal to its recipient, Norman Mudd, Aleister Crowley's agent and acolyte, who killed himself upon receiving it, as the limerick recommends. Mudd's occult crime had been compounded by his abandoning to legal destruction by British Customs a shipment from Cefalú, Sicily (when Crowley was ejected from that island by the Italian authorities, for Black Masses and other occult horse-play), containing Crowley's erotic diaries and his manuscript obscene poem, " Léa Sublime, " painted on a screen. Of this latter, a copy has survived in Mudd's diary, now *pœnes* Crowley's literary executor, Gerald Yorke ; and the Los Angeles occultist, C. F. Russell, is also believed to possess a copy. Part of this poem is quoted in *Rationale II : No Laughing Matter,* 12.IV.1, "Cloacal Intercourse," pp. 345-47, the three least offensive stanzas being chosen.

2443. Frank statement of the dangerous pubic hair-burning fetich, discussed further (on the basis of an equally " nonsensical " joke) in *Rationale II* : chap. 11.III.1, " Prostitution : Specialties, " pp. 259-60. And compare Note 2252 here.

2444. Harris Collection, No. 3093. " *Young chickens* " : underage girls. " *The stork* " : the bird (in the nursery lie now going out of fashion) that " brings babies. " See note 2:2555.

2452. While spending the winter at Pau
Lady Pamela forgot to say No.
  The head porter laid her,
  The chief barman made her,
And the waiters were all hanging low. [1968A.

2453. By Mel Stover, in the " blue " magic magazine, *Chaos* (Winnipeg, 1976?) headed " Belches from the Ring. "

2454. KEEP TRUCKING. A twist on Limerick 1:931.

2455. Won't hold a candle to " maggot surprise " in Limericks 1:1736 and 2:1078, and to the ultimate necrophile story, " Butterballs, " of which the essential *matter* is given in *Rationale II : No Laughing Matter,* 12.IV.6, " The Defiling of the Mother, " pp. 412-14.

A wayout teenager from Poole
Necrophilia dug after school.

Oh Death, where's thy sting?
After doing his thing
He murmured, "She's cool, man, real cool." [1974.

2456. Crowley's *Snowdrops from a Curate's Garden* (1904) pp. 139-41, as the opening of a "Birthday Ode," which continues as six 8-line stanzas in two-couplet form (not limericks).

2462. A belly-dancer from far Samarkand
Tried to prance wholly nude in the Strand.
But the bobby on duty
Said, "No, me proud beauty!
Them foreign contortions is banned." [1968A.

2466. Purely a Christian anti-sexual idea, that intercourse should not take place on "God's day." In all pagan and pre-Christian religions, in particular Judaism, the opposite is the rule. Under paganism intercourse is considered the "dedicating" of oneself to special gods, in particular Venus. Although Judaism bitterly fought these matriarchal survivals (see under "groves" in Alexander Cruden's *Bible Concordance*), it is nevertheless considered by the Jews as a specially virtuous act — *oneg Shabbat,* "The joy of the Sabbath," on the basis of *Genesis,* i. 28: "Be fruitful, and multiply" — to have intercourse with one's spouse either on Friday night, which is the Sabbath eve, or on Saturday afternoon, when the complete *Song of Songs* is required to be read aloud by all religious Jews over thirteen years old, as a sort of sacred erotica. It should be added that the *Song of Songs,* a typical Levantine epithalamium or marriage-song politely attributed to King Solomon, was not considered entirely respectable in the early Judaism, and was given its present frank erotic prominence only by Rabbi Akiba in about 100 A.D. Implicated in the revolt of the Jews under Bar-Cochba against the Emperor Hadrian, Rabbi Akiba was crucified by the Romans and flayed alive in 132 A.D. (See also Limericks 2:2286 and 2698.)

2469. Polite original of this version (with homoerotic punchline) credited to J. A. Leventhal in Louis Untermeyer's *Lots of Limericks* (1961). Compare Limerick 2:2341.

2478. MATTER IN THE BATTER. Purportedly only an Oedipal mocking of the father's dripping *nose,* the symbolic sexual level here is very striking. There is a similar " clean " high-school song mostly sung by girls in America, in which the grandmother's nose drips into the cake she is mixing.

2479. Imitation of or pendant to Limerick 1:679.

2480. SIGNS OF THE ZODIAC. In a 19th-century bawdy music-hall song of the same title, printed in the very rare *Records of the Most Ancient and Puissant Order of the* BEGGARS BENISON *and Merryland* [London : Smithers, 1892] vol. II : pp. 68-70 (copies : British Museum, Private Case ; and National Library of Scotland), the poet successfully clears the hurdle which presumably kills the limerick poet here, and rhymes " Scorpio " with " be very slow. " Two of the Signs in the present horoscope, Capricorn and Leo, are rewritings of the better-known Limericks 1:917 and 2:1928.

The most prolific modern limerick poet, John Coulthard, just before his death won *Punch's* " Overseas Contest " (9 March 1966) for a *13th sign of the Zodiac,* with : " *Digitarius* . . . rules those born in the odd hours that give us Leap Year quadrennially. Digitarians are accident-prone. Crossing fingers and knocking on wood for good luck common habits. [*Graphic symbol of Digitarius* : *crossed-fingers and the ampersand* : &.] Black cats cross their paths. Spend lives getting traffic tickets, the itch, lost in big cities, being rushed to hospitals with virulent diseases having no known cures. Soup invariably splashes them, winds blow their hats away, loans to improvident friends are never repaid . . . Digitarians will be somewhere else when interesting things happen. " (And more in the same vein.) A complete bad-luck horoscope, " Astrological Signs, " circulated as xeroxlore, is given in Cathy M. Orr & Michael Preston, *Urban Folklore from Colorado* : *Typescript Broadsides* (Ann Arbor, 1976) f. 113, with such Signs as : " LIBRA : You are artistic . . . If you are a man, you are more than likely queer . . . Most Libra women are good prostitutes. All Libras die of venereal disease. " Altogether, a valentine for losers.

2495. A limerick reduction of Arthur Guiterman's great burlesque, " Samuel and his Cam-u-el. " Compare Limerick 2:1244, " Gossip, Gossip. "

2499. Strictly a variant of Limerick 1:775, where the hero has " planted an acre of tits, " and compare 2:2345. A science-fiction fake form also exists with " spaceman " for " sailor " in the present text, and as " planet " for " island, " on the simple-minded style of hack pulp-writers making " science-fiction odysseys " out of their rejected cowboy stories by replacing the cowboys and " bad Injuns " with the blue gloops and green bloops of Mars and Venus.

2501. Castratory male version of the Queen of Baroda, Limerick 1:1371, with which compare 2:246, on another such erotic collection. These collections of erotic objects, artifacts, scrimshaw and the like (in both folklore and art) have been made in our time particularly by the German sexologist, Magnus Hirschfeld — whose collection was sacked and " destroyed " by the Nazis, and later hijacked by the Allied " liberating " forces in the 1940's — and at the Lawrence Gichner Foundation in Washington, D.C., intended to be joined later to that of the Institute for Sex Research (Kinsey Foundation) at Indiana University, whose sexological library is already an important research tool. A number of private collections also exist, such as that of erotic art by the Drs. Kronhausen, in San Francisco, who have published several illustrated volumes on this subject ; and especially by rich collectors in Japan. A movie-short on the subject, *The Collector* (1973), was unfortunately composed in part of faked objects, produced for the baroque film-maker, Walerian Borowczyk, on whom see further *Rationale II: No Laughing Matter,* 15.IV. 7, " Shitten Luck, " *ad fin.,* p. 924.

Another young man in our section,
He had an eternal erection.
    In his gay, carefree way
    He bought doughnuts each day,
Which he wore on his tool for protection. [1950R.

2502. RECIPE FOR A BESTSELLER. Refers, of course, to the best-selling motion-picture of all time, *Jaws* (American, 1975), which opens with a naked woman being eaten alive before the audience's eyes by a killer-shark, and goes on from there. At the end of its first year of circulation, this pre-genocidal atrocity had grossed one hundred fifty million dollars at the box-office, far in advance of all competition from other horror-and-catastrophe films, such as *Earthquake, Rollerball, Taxi-Driver* and the like, and out-drawing FIVE-TO-ONE the fellation film, *Deep Throat* (on which see Note 2:857), which grossed only thirty million dollars. Gullet for gullet, would you rather risk your body politic to *Deep Throat* or to *Jaws*? The new Pornography of Violence reads the (million) dollar figures, and knows just what to do next. The audience-participation Roman circuses should be starting up again any day now, as the bestselling " death shows " become an international pre-genocidal cuisine. Paddy Chayevsky's *Network* (movie, 1976) spells this out as to the cynical exploitation and enjoyment of " media " violence in America. Folks, be sure your kids get *lots* of this : it's GOOD for them!

2516. In the parish of Douchewater Stench
Lives a highly unprincipled wench.
She bares her huge rear
When preachers are near,
And laughs when the Men of God blench! [1966.

2519. Based on an old joke, this is the first (and only original) item in *The Bagman's Book of Limericks* (Paris, 1962) p. 7.

2527. Attributed to Monica Curtis (with " beautiful " for " eunuchs " in line 2) in J. M. Cohen's splendid anthology, *Yet More Comic and Curious Verse* (Penguin Books, 1959) p. 324.

2533. On the ancient folkloric, buttock-directed aggression of " goosing, " as a ritual sexo-sadistic activity by men's club members, war veterans (with electrical animal-prods!) etc., since the time of the Roman Lupercalia, see *The Horn Book* pp. 248-49 and 388. Also Note 2:2364 above.

2536. A travesty of Limerick 1:102, with the identical couplet but with variant conclusion : " With a load of *gefüllte-fisch* filling. "

2537. The old-style whorehouse " cribs " still exist in Latin-American countries, as once in the American south and southwest, where the girls sat in scanty clothes and provocative poses in their tiny cubicles, with both legs (well-spread) up on the windowsill, as an advertisement ; also sometimes on outdoor staircases, as in Naples, Italy, and formerly in Marseille and Toulouse in France. In the well-regulated prostitution area of Amsterdam today, where women of indeterminate age sit fully dressed behind large glass windows waiting for their clodhopper customers — as in earlier centuries in the Japanese Yoshiwara, behind wooden cage-bars — more decorous poses are usual, and the women often sit working at their knitting or crocheting in their laps, like wives waiting up for their husbands. A faked photo of a Dutch whore at her picture-window is shown, *as an advertisement for Holland,* in a government tourist-industry magazine, *Holland Herald* (1974) Vol. 8 : No. 10 : pp. 9-11, the posed " window-girl " photo shooting right up into the panty-crotch, with text explaining that the girl students doing the posing " *did it for their country.* " (*Heil!*)

2538. BITCH ARITHMETIC. Continuing the " Valentine " of Limerick 2:2458, in the same coprolalic style, on which see Note 2:2257. As to great mathematicians and physicists, Albin Chaplin takes the cake(walk) with his miscegenational " jungle explorer named Biggar " (No. 28) :

> It was just like a tonic
> With her fanny harmonic,
> Which traced a fine Lissajous figure.

2541. THREE KNOTS. On a joke collected from a woman in Eureka Springs, Arkansas, 1953, for Vance Randolph's great unexpurgated collection, *Pissing in the Snow, and other Ozark Folktales* (University of Illinois Press, 1976) No. 28, in which *a drunken sailor asks a whore, " How am I doin', Babe? " The pretty girl just kind of yawned, and she says, " Oh, about three knots . . . it's not hard, and it's not in, and you're not going to get your two dollars back. "*

2542. Also with a cow rather than a cat " hurled into orbit, " to allow of the outrageously spoonerized punning final line—' *Twas the herd that was shot round the world!* (1975), on Ralph Waldo Emerson's " Hymn at the Concord Battle Monument, " July 4th, 1837, ending : " Their flag to April's breeze unfurled, Here once the embattled farmers stood, And fired the shot heard 'round the world."

2545. On Wacs and cracks left over from World War II, see also Limericks 1:1360 and 2:219.

2546. Your long-suffering editor's absolutely authentic experience with one of these head-standing (occult and surréalist) kooks, is recounted at length in his *Oragenitalism: Oral Techniques in Genital Excitation* (New York, 1969) pp. 302-3, with some practical notes on the "*69*" in that position.

2548. LIFE IN A PENTHOUSE. To be compared with Limericks 2:2425 and 2672, "Hipster."

2555. THE NIGHT OF THE DINOSAUR. A send-up of *The Day of the Dinosaur* by L. Sprague de Camp, which also elicited much correspondence in science-fiction fan magazines as to *where dinosaurs come from,* the most logical answer being: "The pterodactyls bring them."

2560. A curious young lady named Tite
Had movements much faster than light.
She drank water one day,
In a relative way,
That she'd passed on the previous night. [1947A.

Bowel-movements, that is. This probably belongs in the following chapter.

XVII. SCIENCE FICTION

2565. Aside from the Man in the Moon limericks (1:338 and 1:734), the following two on the Galactic Patrol — already printed as 1:358-59 — and that on the Lorentz contraction (1:1204, and see 2:2636) appear to be the first known science fiction limericks. All three are attributed to the late Anthony Boucher (A. P. White), murder-mystery writer, and are dated 1944-46 in *Index Limericus,* the transactions of Dr. MacIntyre's American Limerick Society in Berkeley, California, of which Boucher was a pillar.

A galactic patrolman from Venus
Had a hyper-extensible penis.
Of all forms of life
Which he'd taken to wife
He preferred a mere woman, from meanness.

The sex of the asteroid vermin
Is exceedingly hard to determine.
The galactic patrol
Simply fucks any hole
That will possibly let all the sperm in.

2568. VAGINA DENTATA. See Notes 2:937 and 2:1969, on this ancient legend and fantasy, as also Limerick 2:2660.

2571. On Edgar Rice Burroughs, writer of fantasy novels of escape from earth in all directions (to Mars, the center of the earth, etc.), including chronologically (back to the primitive world with *Tarzan* ; but also into the future with H. G. Wells). For a somewhat different interpretation of Burroughs' output than that in the present limerick — with which, in fact, it would be hard to disagree — see *The Horn Book* (1964) pp. 315-22, in a discussion of the prevailingly pessimistic science fiction as folk-literature (total message : " YES! *we have first-class tickets on the Titanic!* ") and Burroughs' simplistic cosmogony, of the planet Venus, which is green, wet, female, fertile, grappling, and marshy, and altogether evil ; as opposed to the proud, red, phallic, mountainous, sterile and scientific Mars.

2573. Barsoom is the name for Mars in the space-fantasy novels of Edgar Rice Burroughs. Its inhabitants include 15-foot green men (Tharks), and thoats (their giant steeds).

2576. In Burroughs' cosmogony, as above, Titan and Vulcan are newly-discovered planets. I forget what a *slan* is : some kind of extra-terrestrial critter.

2583. " SO SORRY. " Compare Limerick 2:2569. Likewise the sex prank, reported by a college freshman girl (La Jolla, Calif. 1965) of slowly milking the fingers of a girl's hand, on being introduced to her, then saying portentously : " *I am from Mars. I have just had sexual relations with you.* " In this tone of castratory rape as a helpless *fait accompli,* compare the faked Women's Lib novelty card (New York, 1976) reading YOU HAVE JUST INSULTED A WOMAN.–*This card has been chemically treated. In 3 minutes your prick will fall off.* A gross libel on Women's Liberation goals and methods (but compare the *SCUM Manifesto*), showing how men see liberation of women strictly as the castration of men.

2584. SOLAR SYSTEM'S SEXUAL SURVEY. Published in a variant text and different order, as *Is Uranus Bigger Than Mars?* (this is a British joke), by Brian Aldiss, in *Penthouse* (London, 1974) Vol. IX, No. 7, with excellent erotico-humorous science fiction illustrations. Here the conclusion of the Plutonian male is :

Though the climate is damp
And he daren't light a lamp,
He knows his is the best fate of all.

2596. Flash Gordon, and Gale (his scantily-dressed girl stooge, purely a non-sex object except for the readers : compare Note 2:2609), were the main cartoon characters in a popular interplanetary-cowboy " comic " strip in America since the 1930's. There was also a " Buck Rogers in the 25th Century," strictly a cowboy-&-Injuns spinoff.

2597. A FIG FOR NEWTON. This " Free Fall " limerick by Poul Anderson — with which compare Limerick 2:2607 — and his " Tesseract Tess " (2:2634), both first published in the parody science-fiction fan magazine, *Salacious Science Limericks* (1952), seem to have been the earliest of the modern crop in folk-circulation, but note Anthony Boucher's earlier examples, Note 2:2565. As first published, " A Fig for Newton " was accompanied by Limerick 2:2645 below. Recent variant by the same author :

A spaceman and girl in free fall
Found a new way of heeding Love's call.
" I've been tumbled, " she said,
" On floor, sofa, and bed,
But never halfway up a wall. " [1970.

2599. Pendant to the famous mathematical limerick 1:169 (and compare 2:355), where the ball is " hexahedronical " and other shapes, as noted,

> And the cube of its weight
> Times his pecker, plus eight,
> Was four-fifths of five-eighths of fuck-all.

2600. Obviously to be compared with Mark Twain's brilliant pre-Freudian story, " Those Wonderful Twins, " in which one of the two heads and bodies (on the same pair of legs) represents the violent, erotic and querulous *Id* – which has since been discovered in the hypothalamus gland – and the other the reserved and repressed *Ego* ; with the tragi-comic results of this standard human combination.

2601. Based on a current obscœnum, presented as a formula : " *The angle of the dangle is equal to the mass of the ass times the heat of the meat, divided by the sag of the bag.* " Also in various longer anti-woman versions (see Note 1:1415, collected as a blue-print in Brooklyn, 1951), with added line: *inverse to the droop of the poop,* meaning the female buttocks, which are here being blamed for male impotence. Chaplin (1976) Nos. 1582-88 builds this into a limerick sequence, ringing all possible variations. Compare the rebus of about the same date, on a novelty card : B 4 1 [screw] U – R U 18 ?

2605. Credited to Boris Mandrovsky, in the Hall Collection, No. 4766.

2609. STARSHIP " ENTERPRISE. " First appeared in a fan magazine, *Pillyspock* # 1 (Nov. 1967), headed : " MS. found in an empty oxygen tank . . . by Mr. Roger Herwell, a freelance poet of Intercourse, Pennsylvania, " as a takeoff on a science fiction television serial of the 1960's, " *Star Trek.* " Of the characters mentioned, Mr. Spock was " science officer " on the *Enterprise,* and was represented as half-human and half-" alien, " his father having come from the new planet, Vulcan ; while Uhúra was the integrated Zulu sex-job in the serial, replacing Flash Gordon's Gale (Note 2:2596).

2001½. Satirizing Stanley Kubrick's great interplanetary motion-picture and light-show, *2001 : A Space Odyssey,* and moving on with him to his lumpenproletarian anticipations film, *A Clockwork Orange,* which had a great deal more to say.

2624. In a 1950's Paris pornographicum, *Chariot of Flesh* (published in English), a woman takes a bath entirely in semen, supplied by a team of masturbating old hobos [!] and kept warm by electrodes in the bath. According to Jewish ritual practice, a woman who becomes pregnant when her husband has been absent more than ten lunar months may claim that when she went to the communal ritual bath (*mikveh*) at the time, she noticed a patch of floating sperm left behind by some man who had had a spontaneous orgasm in the bath. To keep this type of alibi possible, the men always bathe first: they are also terrified of the women's possible menstrual "uncleanness," and would not dream of going last. See the fabulous details of *Leviticus,* 15 : 18-30.

2626. No last line given as originally issued in *Salacious Science Limericks,* where it is instead marked: "To be concluded." Here as supplied in *Lost Limericks* (3rd ed. 1957) p. 42.

2631. A bit brittle, this is credited to Dana Thompson in the Hall Collection, No. 2650, possibly inspired by Limerick 2:2599 in earlier form.

2633. BUG-EYED MONSTER (B.E.M. in science fiction slang). A modernization of Limerick 1:338, in which it is the Man in the Moon who takes the active part.

2634. TESSERACT TESS. On tesseracts generally, compare "Legman's Law," the briefest (and most useless) of all mathematical formulæ : *To determine the number of plane surfaces of a cube* (tesseract) *of* n *dimensions.* The formula is : *n!* (*n* factorial). Thus a cube of the usual 3 dimensions has $3! = (1 \times 2 \times 3) = 6$ surfaces ; a "cube" or tesseract of 4 dimensions has $4! = 24$ surfaces ; of 5 dimensions, 120, etc. (See also Limerick 2:2372 and Note 2:2424 above.)

Limerick 2635, "Sweet Sue," is a reply by Paul Enever to "Tesseract Tess," printed in a science fiction fanzine, *Hyphen* (Belfast, March 1954), the original having been given with an erroneous attribution in the January 1954 issue.

E.S.P. is Extra-Sensory Perception (*it says here*). The original limerick has already been much corrupted and rationalized in folk-transmission, as in *Dirt : An Exegesis* (Los Angeles, *c.* 1965) p. 19 :

There was a young lady from Carolina
Who had a rheostat [!] for a vagina.
    She could lay all day
    With a man in Bombay,
While soliciting trade in Plina.

2636. Attributed to Anthony Boucher (A. P. White), and first printed in *The Limerick,* 1:1204, dated 1946. (See Note 2:2565, on Boucher's other early science fiction limericks.) A variant collected at Caltech (Pasadena, 1952) loses track of the Dutch physicist, Hendrik Lorentz, in the couplet here, and credits the effect instead to his Irish co-discoverer, George Fitzgerald :

    So quick was his action
    Fitzgerald's contraction
Had flattened his rod to a disk!

2638. Riddle : " *How do you keep a nice Jewish* (or *American*) *girl from screwing? – Marry her!* " (New Rochelle, N.Y. 1972.) This riddle was told by a married woman who, when I commented on its bitterness, added the following " woman's rhyme " (since men do not traditionally wet their pants when laughing uproariously ; thus a good joke is a " *one-pantser,* " a very good joke is a "*three-pantser,* " and so forth) :

    Laugh? I thought I'd die! –
    Thought my pants would never dry.

2639. A polite version is credited to a woman in J. M. Cohen's *Yet More Comic and Curious Verse* (Penguin Books, 1959) p. 327.

2651. A defective version, lacking the first (rhyming) line and with no mention of the Moon, as collected from a 13-year-old boy in Leeds, England, is given in Sandra McCosh's unexpurgated collection, *Children's Humour : A Joke for Every Occasion* (London : Hanau, 1977) No. 143, p. 164. (Compare the " disaster " Limericks 1:1134 and 1:1234.) 'Hugh De Witt,' in his *There Was a Young Lady* (London, 1969) No. 180, calls a version, similar to that below, " the limerick of the cruel — but our emotions are disengaged by the non-sense, as in *Three Blind Mice* and other nursery rhymes " : certainly an unprovable contention.

Have you heard about Jasper Lockett,
Who was blown down the street by a rocket?
  The force of the blast
  Blew his balls up his ass,
And his pecker was found in his pocket. [1968A.

2652. THE HOBBITS. Ents and Hobbits are dwarf creatures (halflings) of human character in J. R. R. Tolkien's modern fairy-tale series, *Lord of the Rings* ; intended as an inspirational adventure story for adolescents, this became one of the Bibles of the hippie movement in the 1960's in America, all the others being concerned with drugs, irresponsibility, etc.

2654. THE MARTIAN CHRONICLES. Science fiction enthusiasts will perhaps forgive the possibly misleading title here, which refers simply to the fact that these Dutch-Flemish limericks, with their literal translations, were supplied by a collector from Maarssen. (I mean, look fellas, I had to put them *somewhere*!) Another very graphic example in Dutch is given in *The Limerick* 1:1711, turning on the reputation of the town of Groningen for dirtiness, concerning a young woman who washed her cunt only once a year, and that was on Twelfth Night (" Driekoningen ").

XVIII. CHAMBER OF HORRORS

2672. HIPSTER. " Shooting shit " : injecting heroin.

2679. On Winston Churchill, British prime minister, still a hero to many, though others suspect he took to the grave with him the secret " sellout " that made possible the almost miraculous British withdrawal from Dunkerque in small boats during World War II, and delayed the opening of the Western Front in Europe for four further years.

2682. ABLE WAS I ERE I SAW MELBA. (Not quite the usual palindrome, admittedly.) Note the use of almost the same improbable rhymes as the present limerick in the superb Gallagher & Shean parody quoted by G. Legman, " Bawdy Monologues and Rhymed Recitations, " in *Southern Folklore Quarterly* (1976) vol. 40 : pp. 107-8.

2684. Apologizing for the poor rhyme in the couplet, the authoress notes that this was a *vers de circonstance* on being invited at a party to some mate-swapping by " a ' Swinger ' couple . . . I was appalled and repelled by the cold, calculating look that was the sole expression of this fellow, and wrote [the limerick as in the text]. He carries it in his wallet, and whips it out for all to read. "

2695. A pity that the impossible rhyme makes it necessary to relegate this to the " Chamber of Horrors. " Its point is well made.

2698. See Note 2:2466, concerning *Genesis,* i. 28.

2703. " *Nooky* " : American slang for the female genitals, or the sexual enjoyment thereof ; from the Dutch, *neuken,* to fuck. See the fabulous howler by Eric Partridge — almost worthy to rank with Browning's on " *twat* " (See Note 2:2096) — by which he attempts to folk-etymologize, or *klang*-associate " *nooky,* " meaning sexual intercourse : " *Ex* getting into nooks and corners to indulge in it. " Partridge's masterpiece in this line, by which he somehow demonstrates that the Yiddish word " *tochus* " (buttocks) means testicles instead, is quoted in full in my Introduction to John S. Farmer & William Ernest Henley, (*Dictionary of*) *Slang & Its Analogues* (New Hyde Park, N.Y. : University Books, 1966) *revised* vol. I : p. lxxxix. Partridge's *Shakespeare's Bawdy* (London, 1947) is similarly stuffed with imaginary erotica Shakespeare never intended, but manages to omit both his authentic uses of the word *cunt,* in Hamlet's twitting Ophelia as to lying in her lap or " country matters "; and in *Twelfth Night,* II. v.88 : " Her very *C*'s, her *U*'s, '*n*' her *T*'s. "

2708. In the style of Nat " Baron " Ireland's delicious " Ungrammatical Song to End All Ungrammatical Songs, " already in folk-transmission, beginning :

If we had of knew what we ought to of knew,
    We'd never of did what we done.
If we had of sawr we was breaking God's lawr,
    We'd never of ever begun . . .

2710. Clifford M. Crist, *Playboy's Book of Limericks* (1972) p. 128.

2718. Pluperfect example of anal-sadism. See the final section of *Rationale II: No Laughing Matter,* 15.VI.3, " All to Shit, " and note 2:1465 here.

2721. Title as supplied by the poetess. Another wish-fulfillment, also by a lady :

A sweet Southern belle named Magnolia
Will, with two lips and juleps cajoleya.
    Your drink the bitch baits
    With barbiturates ;
When you snore, then that cute whore'll roll ya.
[*ff.* 1969A.

2724. W. L. McAtee, MS. D364, envelope 6. (Puqua, pronounced Puckaway : a lake in Wisconsin.)

2725. Hall Collection, No. 442. " *Yoo-hoo!* " is presumably the mating-call of the male homosexual (" gay ").

2727. MENÉ MENÉ TEKAL. As the caption-title indicates, graffiti (on any public wall, but now particularly in toilet-rooms) are one of the oldest recorded forms of folklore, for we read in *The Book of Daniel,* chap. 5 :5-25, that at Belshazzar's Feast, on the night before the conquering of Babylon by Cyrus (Darius) the Great in 539 B.C. : " In the same hour came forth fingers of a man's hand, and wrote over against the candlestick upon the plaister of the wall of the king's palace . . . And this is the writing that was written : MENÉ, MENÉ, TEKAL, UPHARSIN. " The origin of advertising billboards, obviously. Large collections of toilet graffiti have been made in modern times, and published as listed in *Rationale II: No Laughing Matter,* only 15.I.4, " Ajax Revisited, " pp. 832-34, to which should be added Prof. Ian Turner's *Australian Graffiti* (with photographer Rennie Ellis, 1975). The most authentic and " unselected " collections — all as yet unpublished — such as those of Prof. Pelham Box (see Note 2:2131) now *pœnes* G. Legman ; of the Vance Randolph MS and of Thomas Painter & G. Legman's *Homosexual Prostitution in the United States* (MS. 1940 : Kinsey Library), all invariably show a large proportion of homosexual assignations and brags ; these are carefully omitted in the printed works.

2730. DEMOCRATIC FOOTNOTE. Alludes to an American presidential campaign joke told of every popular candidate since the 1960's. (And compare Limerick 2:2713, " Election by Erection. ") *Presidential candidate Bobby Kennedy has saved the Virgin Mary from being raped by seven Hell's Angels, and St. Peter comes down from Heaven to give him Three Wishes as his reward. Kennedy : " For my first wish, I want* TERRIFIC *television coverage!! " St. Peter : " Yes . . .? " Kennedy : " For my second wish, I want* MASSIVE *political clout!! " St. Peter " And for your third wish? " Kennedy (crosses his hands over his chest, and drops his eyes soulfully) : " For my third wish . . . deep humility. "*

2734. Failed version of Limerick 2:189. The same poet also constructed eight other (even worse) limericks, all on the same rhymes. Some of these British items are so slangy — complete with quotation marks to indicate the slang words, especially if in rhyming slang — as to be entirely beyond comprehension. " Holloway " puns on a women's prison; " bottle-&-glass, " arse; " Hampton Wick, " prick.

A lesbian just out of gaol
Was asked how she managed for tail.
    She said, " Up inside 'Holloway'
    Putting dildol away,
A miss is as good as a male! " [1968A.

There was a great swimmer named Hidges
Whose " bottle " was bitten by midges.
    To avoid this attack
    He swam on his back,
But his " Hampton " got bashed on the bridges. [1969A.

2736. DOIGTS OBSCÈNE. Certain modern writers have amused themselves with lightly-veiled erotic book titles, which most of the audience is expected not to understand, as an *in*-joke for the others. For example Maurice Dekobra's *Noeuds coulants* in the 1920's (" Running Knots, " in French, but also " Dripping Pricks ") ; also a British woman-author's *Sneezing in the Basket* (a reference to cunnilinctus), and most recently Elaine Shepard's *The Doom Pussy,* about the U.S. Air Force in Vietnam. The newer openly-bawdy book titles, containing worlds like *Ass* or *Piss* — but no sexual terms as yet, to match the permitted scatology — are mostly published only by American university presses, busting out in their New (verbal) Freedom.

2742. A reckless young sculler named Box
Forced the Oxford Eight onto the rocks.
The crew shouted, " Bollocks!
You've ripped off our rowlocks,
And horribly injured our cox. " [1969A.

2743. " *Dress* " : tailor's argot referring to the right- or left-hand pants-leg position in which the penis is carried. Compare Limerick 2:1020.

2745. Note the even worse rhymes on *facsimile* in Aleister Crowley's Limerick 2:1230.

2746. MY AN-DRO-GYNE! Punning, of course, on the barbershop-quartet favorite, " Sweet Adeline. "

2747. Men are always terribly intrigued by this vagina-dentata trick, among belly-dancers and similar, of using their vulvas to pick up folded bills (but not coins) placed on the table to pay them. Compare Limerick 2:2290, and Note 2:2370.

2748. " Houyhnhnms " are the superhuman horse-creatures in the last of Swift's *Gulliver's Travels* (1726) ; it is the subhuman " Yahoos " that are really meant here, but they would not rhyme.

2749. " *Kickapoo joy-juice* " : cheap, rotgut alcoholic liquor, that presumably only a Kickapoo Indian would drink.

INDEX

SUBJECTS

INDEX

[* *Asterisks refer to limericks in the Notes. A table of Subjects, by their inclusive numbers, faces this page.*]